The Real Odessa

The Real Odessa

Smuggling the Nazis to Perón's Argentina

UKI GOÑI

Granta Books

London · New York

To Santos and Vicky

Granta Publications, 2/3 Hanover Yard, Noel Road, London N1 8BE

First published in Great Britain by Granta Books 2002
This edition, with new Foreword, Conclusion and Afterword,
published in the USA by Granta Books 2002

A CIP catalogue record for this book
is available from the British Library.

1 3 5 7 9 10 8 6 4 2

ISBN 1 86207 581 6

Typeset by M Rules

Printed and bound in Great Britain
by Mackays of Chatham PLC

CONTENTS

ACKNOWLEDGEMENTS

Over six years of work have gone into this book, during which time I have been extremely fortunate to receive help and advice from a great many people. I would especially like to thank the academics Ronald Newton of Canada and Holger Meding of Germany; but above all Beatriz Gurevich, compiler of *Proyecto Testimonio*, the ground-breaking investigation into Argentina's dalliance with the Nazis published by the country's Delegation of Argentine-Israelite Associations (DAIA) in 1998. From the start, Gurevich pointed me to the primary documentary sources and was kind enough to share a large amount of previously unseen material. I also owe a truly special debt to Christel Converse, who was responsible for the documentary research at the National Archives in Maryland. In Belgium, I must thank Dirk Martin of CEGES (Centre d'Etudes et de Documentation Guerre et Sociétés Contemporaines), where the essential Pierre Daye papers are archived, for his kind assistance, and Jean-Pierre Lesigne for authorization to quote from Daye's letters and memoirs.

Although this book is based primarily on documentary sources, some 200 interviews were conducted during its research. I thank all of those who shared their memories with me. Many also refused to be interviewed, most notably the former head of Perón's Information Bureau, Rodolfo Freude. For help in translating documents from the

German I'd like to thank my father, Ambassador Santos Goñi, my dear friend Verena von Schoenfeldt, and especially Claudia Billourou, who kept the line continually open from Germany during the final haul. I also wish to thank the international news editors at the *Sunday Times* and the *Guardian* who made space in their pages for articles I wrote based on some of the early findings. I owe an extra special debt to George Russell, of *Time* magazine, who had faith in this book from the outset and published a cover story based on its Spanish-language predecessor, *Perón y los alemanes*, even though it meant an uncomfortable visit from Argentina's ambassador to the UN, bearing a letter of protest. My special gratitude as well to Sara Holloway of Granta, who has made the original manuscript readable, and to Lexy Bloom, who prepared the American edition of this book. And of course this book would never have seen the light had it not been for Colm Tóibín, who one summer midnight in Dublin pointed me in the direction of Neil Belton and Hanover Yard.

To all: *Gracias*.

ABBREVIATIONS

AGN   Argentine National Archives.

AGPJN   Archives of the Argentine Judicial Branch.

Casa Rosada   Argentina's 'Pink House', the equivalent of the US White House.

CEANA   Comisión de Esclarecimiento de Actividades Nazis en la Argentina, the historical commission set up by the Argentine government in 1997 to investigate wartime and postwar Nazi links in Argentina.

CEGES   Centre d'Etudes et de Documentation Guerre et Sociétés Contemporaines in Brussels; this archive houses Belgian-related wartime documents, including the papers of Pierre Daye.

DAIA   Delegation of Argentine-Israelite Associations.

DAIE   The Delegation for Argentine Immigration in Europe, opened by Perón's government in the postwar era, with offices in Rome and Genoa.

DNM   Dirección Nacional de Migraciones, the Argentine Immigration Office.

FPD   Fonds Pierre Daye, the collection of Daye papers at CEGES.

GOU   The secret lodge of colonels led by Perón that ruled Argentina between 1943 and 1946. The initials are thought to have stood for Group of Order and Unity.

ICE   The Swiss Independent Commission of Experts.

ICRC   International Committee of the Red Cross.

Information Bureau   The División Informaciones, the presidential secret service created by Perón in 1946, headed by Rodolfo Freude.

MI   Archives of the Argentine Ministry of the Interior.

ML   Musée de la Littérature in Brussels, which shares custody of Pierre Daye's papers with CEGES.

MRE   The archives of the Argentine Foreign Ministry.

NARA   National Archives and Records Administration of the United States.

PRO   The British Public Record Office.

RG   Record Group, grouping of records at NARA; RG 59, for example, corresponds to records of the US Department of State.

RSHA   Reichssicherheitshauptamt, Reich Security Main Office, the Interior Ministry of the Reich, a department of Heinrich Himmler's SS.

SD   The Sicherheitsdienst, the SS Foreign Intelligence Branch, Office VI of the RSHA's intelligence department, divided into Office III, the Inland-SD, home intelligence, headed by SS Brigadier Otto Ohlendorf, and Office VI, the Ausland-SD, foreign intelligence, headed by SS Brigadier Walter Schellenberg. The SD seen at work in this book is Schellenberg's Ausland-SD, operating outside Germany.

STP   Perón's Technical Secretariat, a record group of the Argentine National Archives.

KEY PLAYERS

Barrére, Agustín Argentine bishop. In 1946, Barrére travelled to the Vatican, where, with the French Cardinal Tisserant, he organized the smuggling of French-speaking war criminals to Argentina.

Benzon, Branko Wartime ambassador to Berlin from the Croatian Nazi puppet regime. At the end of the war, Benzon was sent on a special mission to Madrid by SS General Ernst Kaltenbrunner. He conducted a strict anti-Semitic policy at Perón's Immigration Office, forbidding the entry of Jews to Argentina while organizing the arrival of fellow Croatians. It was also rumoured that while in Argentina he became Evita's lover.

Caggiano, Antonio Argentine cardinal. Caggiano travelled with Bishop Barrére to the Vatican, where he met with Cardinal Tisserant and organized the smuggling of French-speaking war criminals to Argentina.

Daye, Pierre Belgian war criminal. In Buenos Aires, with the help of Perón, Daye was instrumental in setting up the SARE organization for the rescue of war criminals.

Diana, Pablo Argentine immigration chief during 1947/48. Diana cooperated with Perón's Nazi agents to arrange for the smuggling of Nazis, Rexists, Vichyites and Ustashi to Argentina.

Dömöter, Edoardo Hungarian priest who headed the Franciscan parish of San Antonio in Genoa. Dömöter worked with Bishop Hudal to aid the Nazi escape to Argentina. He was responsible for obtaining a Red Cross passport for SS criminal Adolf Eichmann.

Draganovic, Krunoslav Croatian war criminal. A priest, Draganovic was the Vatican's chief Nazi smuggler, operating out of the San Girolamo church in Rome. He was connected to both Vatican and American intelligence.

Durcansky, Ferdinand Slovak war criminal, responsible for the murder of tens of thousands of Jews. In Argentina, Durcansky became an informant for Perón's secret service and a founding member of the SARE Nazi rescue organization.

Durcansky, Jan Slovak war criminal who escaped to Argentina with his brother Ferdinand. Appointed by Perón to the Immigration Office, Durcansky helped fellow fugitives obtain Argentine IDs and citizenship.

Freude, Ludwig German millionaire in Argentina, connected to Nazi intelligence. A close friend of Perón, Freude coordinated contributions to Perón's 1946 presidential campaign from other Nazi-connected businessmen.

Freude, Rodolfo Son of Ludwig Freude. In 1946, Freude was named head of Perón's Information Bureau, the agency in charge of smuggling Nazis to Argentina.

Fuldner, Carlos Perón's chief Nazi smuggler and a former SS captain and special agent of the SS secret service. In 1945, Fuldner was sent on a special mission to Madrid and from there he proceeded to his native Buenos Aires. In 1948, he was back in Europe as a special agent for Perón, establishing Nazi rescue offices in Genoa and Berne, and liaising with Draganovic and Swiss officials to smuggle war criminals to Argentina.

Ghenea, Radu Romanian Nazi collaborator. Ghenea liaised with Fuldner and Daye in Madrid and then proceeded to Argentina, where he helped fellow fugitives to escape from Europe.

Goyeneche, Juan Carlos Argentine Catholic nationalist and a special agent of Perón, connected to Fuldner, Daye and Ghenea. During the war Goyeneche met in Berlin with Ribbentrop, Himmler, Goebbels and apparently Hitler himself, conveying news of Argentina's secret allegiance to the Reich.

Guilbaud, Georges French war criminal who hid assets abroad for French collaborationist president Pierre Laval. Guilbaud escaped to Argentina and became a financial adviser to Perón. He was also a leading member of the SARE Nazi rescue organization.

Heinrich, Ivo Croatian war criminal and financial adviser to Ante Pavelic, the Nazi puppet leader of Croatia. In Argentina, Heinrich sold part of Pavelic's looted gold.

Helfrich, Herbert Nazi scientist. Helfrich escaped to Argentina, where he was hired by Perón and then sent back to Europe to smuggle other Nazis out of Germany. He worked from Perón's Nazi rescue office in Berne.

Hudal, Alois Austrian bishop. One of the Vatican's chief Nazi smugglers, Hudal worked closely with Draganovic. He organized the escape of Treblinka commandant Franz Stangl, among others.

Kops, Reinhard Nazi spy. An aide to Bishop Hudal, Kops was employed by Perón's Nazi rescue office in Genoa.

Lagrou, René Belgian war criminal and founder of the Flemish SS. Lagrou escaped to Argentina, where he was hired by Perón's Information Bureau. He was a founding member of the SARE escape organization.

Lesca, Charles French war criminal. Born in Argentina, Lesca first met Perón in the 1930s. At the liberation of Paris, he escaped to Berlin and then to Madrid, where he organized the first 'ratline' to Argentina for agents of the SS secret service.

Luttor, Ferenc Hungarian prelate, posted to the Hungarian embassy at the Vatican during the war. After the war, Luttor organized false papers for Hungarian fugitives in Rome. Later he went to Argentina and became a founding member of the SARE escape organization.

Mandic, Dominic Croatian priest of the Franciscan order. Mandic acted as the link between Draganovic and Vatican intelligence. He also invested Pavelic's looted gold in Rome, in that way financing the escape of Ustasha fugitives to Argentina.

Monti de Valsassina, Gino Croatian Air Force officer who escaped to Argentina after the war. Hired by Perón, Monti de Valsassina was sent back to Europe to conscript Nazis for Argentina.

Peralta, Santiago Perón's Immigration Office chief from 1945 to mid-1947. An ardent anti-Semite, Peralta published books in which he claimed that the Jews were a detriment to society. He helped set up the first escape network to Argentina.

Petranovic, Carlo Croatian war criminal. A priest, Petranovic was Draganovic's main representative at the Italian port of Genoa, where he placed Nazi fugitives on ships to Argentina.

Pomeranz, Samuel Swiss member of Perón's Nazi rescue office in Berne. Pomeranz smuggled Nazis out of Germany into Switzerland and then accompanied them to Argentina.

Reuter, Carlos German-Argentine banker who worked for the SS secret service in Paris. Following his escape to Madrid, Reuter became the first member of Lesca's organization to travel to Buenos Aires on a test run for later arrivals.

Roover, Léonard de Belgian war criminal. Roover escaped to Argentina and was hired by Perón's Information Bureau. He fell out of favour when it was discovered that he also was arranging and charging for the illegal entry of Jews to Argentina.

Rothmund, Heinrich Swiss chief of police. During the war, Rothmund closed Switzerland's borders to the Jews. Afterwards, he allowed Perón's agents to smuggle Nazis through Switzerland on their way to Argentina.

Ruffinengo, Franz Italian officer during the war. At the war's end, Ruffinengo was employed by Perón's Nazi rescue office in Genoa. In Buenos Aires, he opened a travel agency that reportedly specialized in bringing Nazis to Argentina.

Schulz, Carlos German-Argentine who travelled to Scandinavia after the war to organize the first escape route out of Europe. Arrested in Sweden, Schulz later returned to Buenos Aires to work at CAPRI, the company set up by Fuldner to provide employment for SS criminals such as Adolf Eichmann.

Serna, Víctor de la Spanish journalist and member of the Spanish Blue Division, which fought alongside the Nazis in the campaign against Russia. In 1947, Serna was conscripted into Perón's Nazi rescue team.

Sinovcic, Marko Croatian press officer. Sinovcic headed Caritas Croata in Buenos Aires, where he obtained landing permits for Draganovic's fugitives.

Smolinski, Czeslaw Polish member of Perón's Nazi rescue team. In 1947, Smolinski travelled to Switzerland to gauge the level of Swiss official support for a passage through the neutral country for Nazis on their way to Argentina.

Tisserant, Eugène French cardinal at the Vatican. In 1946, Tisserant received the Argentine Cardinal Caggiano to organize the escape of French-speaking war criminals to Argentina.

Weiss, Georg Nazi rocket scientist. Conscripted by Perón to work for his Nazi rescue office in Berne, Weiss smuggled Nazis out of Germany to Switzerland en route to Argentina.

'Argentina was an important strong point and Germany tried to take advantage of it with every means at her disposal . . . the reason was that one could see a government based upon a similar world view as ours.'

SS Brigadier General Walter Schellenberg,
Head of Himmler's Ausland-SD,
the SS Foreign Intelligence service, 6 February 1946

'I see peace on the South American continent threatened by Fascism and by the lust for power of certain persons in Argentina . . . I have seen with my own eyes and myself experienced the unbounded and incalculable misery that invaded Europe and, especially, Germany during and after the war. It is for me an inner need to do everything to save my beloved Argentina from a like fate.'

Edvigia Weiglmayr,
Argentine expert at the SD's Berlin headquarters,
28 February 1946

'The special character of my secret missions could cause problems of conscience for some officials.'

SS Captain Carlos Horst Fuldner,
SD agent and post-war mastermind of Perón's Nazi rescue team,
12 September 1949

FOREWORD

They have cheered the invasion of Norway and of Greece, of the Soviet republics and of Holland: I do not know what merriment they have in store for the day when our cities and coasts are given up to the fire. It is childish to grow impatient: Hitler's mercy is ecumenical: in brief (if foreign lackeys and the Jews don't get in his way) we will enjoy the full benefits of torture, sodomy, rape and mass executions.

Jorge Luis Borges, *Sur* magazine,
Buenos Aires, December 1941

Ever since the end of World War Two, the existence of a shadowy organization dedicated to the rescue of Nazi war criminals has been the subject of countless media articles, documentaries, novels and movies. Some of these have claimed that leading members of the Third Reich escaped justice by crossing the Atlantic on submarines. Indeed in Argentina, where I live, there are many eyewitness accounts of nervous men in Nazi uniforms disembarking from rubber dinghies on the coast of Patagonia at the end of the war. Large crates packed with Nazi gold and secret archives of Hitler's Reich were reportedly collected at night from windy beaches and driven across the continent to secluded havens in the Andes mountains. According to these mostly fantastical accounts, Hitler lived out his final days in southern Argentina, where he still lies buried; his deputy Martin Bormann settled nearby as a rich landowner, first in Chile, then in Bolivia and lastly in Argentina.

Yet none of these far-fetched accounts has gripped the collective imagination as strongly as one novel, *The Odessa File*, by the best-selling British author Frederick Forsyth. The book portrays a group of

former SS men linked in a secret organization named Odessa
(Organisation der ehemaligen SS-Angehörigen), whose aim is not only
to rescue their comrades from postwar justice but also to establish a
Fourth Reich capable of fulfilling Hitler's unrealized dreams. Thanks
to extensive research and his own experience as a Reuters correspondent in the early 1960s, Forsyth wrote a novel that was not only
believable but also contained many elements of truth. Ever since its
publication 30 years ago, the existence of a 'real' Odessa has been
hotly contended by journalists, though frequently denied by serious
scholars.[1]

In the last ten years, however, the steady declassification of secret
documents in the United States and Europe has made it possible to
test those fictionalized tales of Hitler's survival, and Forsyth's more
plausible novel, against the hard stone of historical fact. The picture
that emerges is not necessarily one of an ageing Führer doddering
peacefully in the Andean foothills attended by faithful Nazi servants.
It does not even include an organization actually named Odessa, but
it is sinister nonetheless, and weighted in favour of an actual organized escape network. The documents reveal that the 'real' Odessa
was much more than a tight organization with only nostalgic Nazis for
members. It consisted instead of layered rings of non-Nazi factions:
Vatican institutions, Allied intelligence agencies and secret Argentine
organizations. It also overlapped at strategic points with French-
speaking war criminals, with Croatian Fascists and even with the SS
men of the fictional Odessa, all in order to smuggle Hitler's evil minions to safety.

But in Argentina the Odessa trail was growing faint, and was in
danger of being erased altogether. This trail led back to the presidential office of General Juan Perón; it could therefore conceivably tar
the figure of his beloved wife Evita, who remains an icon of almost
saintly devotion to her compatriots even today. In the wake of the
tardy revelations regarding Switzerland's role as a haven for Nazi gold,
it came as no surprise when Argentina attempted to blur the facts. In
a blaze of publicity in 1992, the Peronist government of then-presi-
dent Carlos Menem announced the opening of Argentina's 'Nazi files'

to researchers. The international press descended upon Buenos Aires, anxious to discover the truth behind the old rumours of Perón's secret dalliance with Hitler. But no such revelation was at hand.

Instead, reporters and researchers found a batch of dog-eared 'intelligence' dossiers containing mostly faded press clippings but precious little new information. The file on Bormann, who never really survived the fall of Berlin, included a press article claiming that he had been transported to Argentina via submarine. Conspicuously absent was the file on Adolf Eichmann, the architect of Hitler's 'Final Solution' and the most notorious Nazi criminal to have actually arrived in Argentina (under the auspices of both the Catholic Church and Perón's Nazi-smuggling team). The dossiers proved hugely disappointing to journalists, while the scholars inwardly cheered: the lack of evidence seemed to corroborate the growing consensus in academia that no Odessa had ever existed, and that the Nazis had arranged their escapes individually, finding their separate ways to Argentina without any organized assistance.

It was against this backdrop, unconvinced by the all-too-convenient lack of evidence, that in 1996 I began to dig for clues to Argentina's 'Nazi' past. I guessed, correctly as it later turned out, that there was a wealth of material out there just waiting to be uncovered. If a 'real' Odessa had ever existed, I was determined to find traces of it.

In Buenos Aires, much of the vital documentation had reportedly been destroyed back in 1955, during the last days of Perón's government, and again in 1996, when the burning of confidential immigration dossiers containing the landing papers of Nazi criminals seems to have been ordered. But tantalizing leads in other Argentine files that had miraculously survived these purges led me first to Belgium, where vital information on what I discovered to be Perón's long-denied Odessa-like organization had happily remained out of the reach of Argentina's document cleansers. Hundreds of pages of government documents were sent to me from Switzerland, detailing the cooperation of anti-Semitic Swiss officials in Perón's Nazi escape operation. In London, patient digging in British postwar papers finally paid off when these documents revealed direct Papal complicity in the protection of war criminals. Documents I requested from the United States under the Freedom of Information Act proved how Perón's top Nazi smuggler had actually been a secret agent of the SS, sent out of Berlin in 1945 on a mission slated to start after the end of the war. Declassified CIA documents also explained how gold looted from the Serb and Jewish victims of Croatia's Nazi puppet regime had found its way to Argentina in the early 1950s.

Incredibly, it sometimes proved easier to gain access to faraway archives in the US and Europe than to those at home. The progress I made in Argentina was maddeningly slow, hampered by the unresponsiveness of government officials and by the refusal of surviving participants in the Nazi rescue operation to be interviewed. One thing was clear, however: the cover-up had been so complete that only separate parts of the jigsaw puzzle survived in each country. I was forced to assemble and compare the varying information available in Brussels, Berne, London, Maryland and Buenos Aires. This was a gargantuan task that involved obtaining copies of thousands of pages of documents and indexing them all, while working simultaneously in four languages (French, German, English and Spanish) before the whole could be understood. And even that proved insufficient, for the assembled documentation left glaring gaps in the investigation which had to be filled in with some 200 personal interviews. It took six years of dedicated work. But finally, for the first time, the disparate pieces of the Nazi rescue puzzle slid into place, revealing the whole gruesome tableau.

I didn't know it when I started, but parts of that puzzle had been almost literally on my front doorstep all along. Looking out of my apartment window, for years I had unknowingly been seeing the grandson of Fritz Thyssen, the German industrial magnate who bankrolled Hitler's rise to power in the 1930s, take a stroll along the sidewalk. Four doors down, by the Swiss ambassador's residence, is the chalet once inhabited by SS Captain Carlos Fuldner, the Himmler agent who coordinated the main Nazi escape route and shielded Eichmann, among others. It sounds like Berlin, Munich or Vienna, but no, it is the sleepy Embassy Row of Buenos Aires. The street remains oblivious to its sinister past. I myself had been unaware of its notorious inhabitant when I cycled past Fuldner's house as a kid in the 1960s. What a missed chance for an interview!

The luxurious town houses and elegant curved streets of the Palermo Chico neighbourhood disprove the assumption that Hitler's helpers were somehow condemned to a life of squalor during their long postwar Argentine 'exile'. Most of them boasted select addresses in a city that rightly prided itself on being the 'Paris of South America'. Some, like Fritz Thyssen, who died in Buenos Aires in 1951, regretted aiding Nazism. The magnate had a falling out with the Führer and spent much of the latter part of the war in German concentration camps. Others, such as Fuldner, remained loyal to the cause long after Hitler's demise.

From my window, across the avenue, I can almost see the attractive red-brick townhouse where Thilo Martens lived not so long ago. He was a German millionaire who smuggled into Argentina the state-of-the-art radio sets used by Hitler's agents to communicate with Berlin. After the war Martens reportedly arranged money transfers for some of the more notorious Nazis who escaped to Buenos Aires with Fuldner's help. But his Nazi past did not spare the ageing collaborator from abduction by the generals of Argentina's genocidal 1976/83 dictatorship, who pocketed a substantial part of his fortune.[2]

A few blocks further along, in a comfortable modern apartment building, lived another SS captain *circa* 1943, Siegfried Becker. He was arguably Himmler's most cunning and successful agent in the western hemisphere. During the war he plotted the overthrow of the Allied-leaning government of neighbouring Bolivia with Perón. Afterwards he apparently helped channel Nazi funds to Argentina.

Finally, slightly up the hill from Becker lived the man who breathed life into the Nazi escape route, Colonel Perón himself. The Argentine strongman shared his bed there with a 14-year-old girl now remembered only by the pet name Perón gave her, 'Piranha'. In 1944, Evita arrived on the scene and threw the teenager out.

None of this was on my mind in mid-1996 when the *Sunday Times* of London called for a story. It had been a slow week in the rest of the world and the paper's editors needed some colourful copy for their international section. I offered up the usual Argentine fare – political scandals, new twists in the Falklands dispute, ageing generals from the 1970s and 1980s trudging through the courts on renewed charges of old human rights violations. The British voice coming down the line was not impressed. 'Well, and then there's the Bormann passport in Patagonia,' I offered, hoping the editor would decide there was nothing worth taking from my neck of the woods.

How wrong I was. That weekend the *Sunday Times* ran a big piece entitled 'Bormann File Reopened by Passport Find'. In it I reported that a Uruguayan passport had turned up in southern Chile made out in the name of Ricardo Bauer, one of the aliases allegedly used by Hitler's deputy during his flight to South America. It proved a shaky start for the investigation that resulted in this book, for two years later a DNA test conducted on a skull found in Berlin established that Bormann had died fleeing Hitler's bunker during the last days of the war. Nonetheless, tackling the Bormann mystery made one thing obvious to me – no well-documented research was available on the Argentine side of the postwar Nazi escape route.[3]

I had reasons of my own to start digging. For too long I had been aware of silence as a noisy presence in Argentina, a country that time and again has failed miserably the test of looking at itself in the mirror. Each Argentine carries around a fabricated version of the country's history, tailored to their own personal comfort. There is one version for the die-hard Peronist, another for the Catholic nationalist; one for the victim of the 1976/83 massacres, another for those who walked blindly through the horror. As I write this, in mid-2002, the country is going through another of its perennial crises, this time an economic collapse of unprecedented proportions. The current storm has plunged over half the population of an until recently fairly affluent middle-class country below the poverty line. Silence played its hand here as well, the collapse driven by tens of billions of dollars in ill-gotten assets funnelled out of the country by a hopelessly corrupt political class and its attendant financiers, with barely a single person ever convicted for corruption by Argentina's easily bought judges. But of all these silences, there is none so deafening as that surrounding Perón, the Catholic Church and the Nazis they helped to escape from justice. If this particular section of the wall could be cracked, I thought, then Argentines might feel encouraged to chip away at other parts of the edifice.

When I was born in 1953 in Washington, DC, where my father served at the Argentine embassy, the wife of Perón's vice-president suggested that since I had come into the world on 17 October – the anniversary of the popular uprising in 1945 that catapulted Perón to the presidency – I should be named Juan Domingo, in homage to *El Líder*. I was spared that particular ignominy, even though suggestions from Perón's presidential palace, the Casa Rosada, carried not a little weight back then. The awareness of that small jolt at the start switched me on to permanent alert mode during the strange years that followed.[4]

In 1955, Perón was ousted by a group of fanatically Catholic right-wing generals who gave cabinet posts to former collaborators of Himmler's espionage service. These generals were succeeded in turn by a series of oppressive military regimes that, apart from brief interludes, kept a firm boot against the Argentine throat until Perón's triumphal return to power in 1973. No better than Perón himself, these regimes forbade even the mention of Perón's or Evita's name in the press. Shockingly, Argentina's journalists obeyed the ban.

I grew up in the US, far from the centre of events that make up this tale, spending part of my childhood years in an old mansion called Downcrest that my parents had rented at the end of wooded Crest Lane in McLean, Virginia. The house, built in castle style with mock battlements, still overlooks the Potomac river today. Back in the late 1950s, one of its frequent visitors was Senator Eugene McCarthy, who, together with his wife and children, had become close friends of our family. The McCarthys and my parents, hailing from extreme ends of the same continent, had some life points in common: both couples had married in 1945 and both had four children. Although I was small, I can remember eavesdropping intently on the long conversations that my father – the South American diplomat – and McCarthy – the Democrat Congressman – had on the open veranda of Downcrest above the Potomac. I like to think that some wisdom filtered through despite my scant years. Afterwards, the lives of our two families took different directions, as my father proceeded to new diplomatic postings and McCarthy embarked on his failed but heroic bid for the US presidency in 1968, running a campaign against the Vietnam War that raised fundamental military, political and moral questions concerning America's role in the world.[5]

That same eventful 1968, after spending brief years in Argentina and Mexico, I was transplanted to Dublin, where my father headed the Argentine embassy. That was the year Ché Guevara was murdered in Bolivia. Each morning as I left the embassy residence in chauffeur-driven comfort for classes at St Conleth's College, I would see the scrawl of graffiti on our sidewalk: 'Guevara Lives', in white letters, painted during the night by Irish revolutionary sympathizers. Just as inexorably, each day the embassy staff would scrub the offending letters away. Driving over the reiterated scrawl, I shrank every time a little deeper into the red leather upholstery of our old Jaguar.

Erasing the evidence was a method that I grievously mistrusted even then. During the research for this book, some Argentine diplomats argued off the record that the country could best shake off its Nazi stigma by 'proving' once and for all that there had been no wartime collaboration by Perón and no organized assistance for fleeing Nazis; I disagreed. There was no shame in admitting old Nazi connections. It would be shameful only to be caught tampering with the evidence. Let the scrawl remain.

Between 1972 and 1975, I moved back and forth between Ireland and Argentina, unable to decide where I wanted to stay. While making the slow transition to Argentina, where I finally settled, I spent a lot of time walking around Buenos Aires, trying to adapt to a society that I barely knew. My arrival coincided with Perón's return after 18 years of exile in Spain. The country was spiralling into mindless violence, driven by armed confrontation between youthful Peronist terrorists who wanted to ride piggyback on Perón's return to power and the right-wing death squads that he used to shake the pesky youths off his ancient back.

During these long walks I came across a disturbing sign of the times that I should perhaps have heeded better. On the broad Nueve de Julio Avenue that divides Buenos Aires in half – 'the widest avenue in the world', according to some Argentines – stands a giant white obelisk that is the city's most conspicuous landmark. In 1974, the landmark lost its virginity in the strangest of ways. A revolving billboard was suspended around the *Obelisco*, snugly encircling the huge white phallus. Round and round the ring turned, inscribed with an Orwellian message in bold blue letters on a plain white background: 'Silence Is Health'.

I was stunned. With every turn, the ring reaffirmed its doctrine, schooling Argentines in the total silence they would practise in the years to follow. Anywhere else, people would have mocked loudly, but in Argentina nobody laughed at all. My attempts to discuss the ring with friends invariably foundered – met with blank stares. The ring's message, I soon learned, was self-fulfilling. A line had been drawn. Today, over a quarter of a century later, I still receive blank stares when I bring it up in conversation.[6]

After Perón's death and following the overthrow of his vice-president wife 'Isabelita' in 1976, a new military dictatorship set up Nazi-style death camps across Argentina. The generals were intent on defending what they considered to be the country's 'Western and Christian' lifestyle. Their instruments were electric torture prods and mass killings. Instead of gassing their victims, the generals slit their stomachs open and threw them alive from planes into the freezing South Atlantic. That way they sank faster.

Under the military the silence became asphyxiating and present everywhere, all the time. Only the *Buenos Aires Herald*, a small English-language newspaper read by Argentina's mostly conservative British community, dared report on the bloodbath. I gravitated to its offices in the port of Buenos Aires, first as a cub reporter, then as editor of national news.

Daily the mothers of the victims would come in to report their tragedies. Men in green uniforms had broken into their homes in the middle of the night and taken their children from their beds to an unknown destination. They were never to be seen again. The abductors returned to steal their TV sets and refrigerators, sometimes they even unbolted the doors and loaded those on their trucks too.

I asked the mothers why they didn't report their stories to the big Spanish-language dailies. Why bother coming to a tiny newspaper published in a foreign language? 'Don't be naïve,' the mothers almost laughed. 'We went and they wouldn't even let us in the door.' Just as Argentina's journalists had erased Perón's name from their vocabulary, now they erased part of a generation.[7]

Attempts to repeat outside the *Herald* what I had heard from these mothers came up against a brick wall, much in the way my previous attempts to discuss the ring around the obelisk had. Even friends, members of my generation who picked up guitars and sang 'Blowin' in the Wind' at the parties I went to, gave me the empty stare.

If I forgot the 'disappearances', life could hardly have been more glorious. The military obtained huge international loans and opened up imports, and for the upper layer of the population the economy boomed. Colour television finally arrived; the streets were suddenly full of new BMWs; flights to Europe and Miami were packed with Argentines, their pockets bulging with dollars. Rod Stewart came to Buenos Aires for the 1978 World Cup. After the matches he is said to have joined the dancers in the basement of Experiment, a trendy disco where I began spending much of my time outside the *Herald* in a haze of gin and tonics while the killing was at its bloodiest.

Hell managed to intrude even through the deafening disco beat pounding out of Experiment's loudspeakers. My then-girlfriend confided in a whisper that her aunt had been kidnapped by the dictatorship. She was placing great trust in me for she had been warned by her family not to tell anyone. I begged her to impress upon them that the only hope of saving her aunt's life lay in going to the international press immediately, before the military concluded their dirty work. The family stuck to their policy of silence until it was too late. Multiply that by thousands.

My scariest memories of those years are not of the middle-aged generals who ordered the killings but of the deep abyss that separated even the more enlightened members of my own generation from the rest of humanity. Some generals became obsessed with the 'Jewish question' during 1976/83, particularly the powerful chief of the Buenos Aires police, General Ramón Camps, who hoped to stage a trial against the country's most prominent Jews in order to prove the existence of what he imagined was a Zionist plot against 'Western and Christian' Argentina. To this end, he abducted Jacobo Timerman, editor and owner of the influential daily *La Opinión*. After confiscating his newspaper and torturing him for months, the 'doves' among the military finally caved in to international pressure, stripped Timerman of his Argentine citizenship and threw him out of the country.[8]

Enraged at being deprived of his prey, Camps called a press conference at the exclusive Alvear Hotel during which he played the tapes of Timerman's interrogation. The purpose of the exercise was to prove that Timerman was 'a Zionist' who sought Argentina's destruction.

'Do you admit you are a Jew?' Camps could be heard snarling on the first tape.

'Well . . . yes,' came back Timerman's frightened whisper.

'Then you are a Zionist!' hollered Camps.

'Well . . . I don't know, maybe,' said Timerman.

Camps ordered the tape stopped and beamed triumphantly at the gathered reporters: 'See, he admits he is a Zionist!'

The general's raving in the luxurious hotel in front of a gathering of foreign correspondents wasn't half as frightening as the composure of his civilian assistant, a finely educated young man who was the 'best friend' in Argentina of British writer Bruce Chatwin, someone Chatwin considered possessed of 'a culture and sensibility that has died out in Europe'. The assistant also happened to be a close friend of mine. He gave me Chatwin's address when I travelled to London in 1980.[9]

This young writer had a hard time making ends meet and had been set up with Camps by his father. The scene was unreal: here was an otherwise enlightened intellectual (together we used to pore over scholarly editions of T. S. Eliot's poetry) pressing the play button for the forced interrogation of Argentina's main Jewish journalist by a wildly anti-Semitic general.

I hung around after the press conference and nodded to my friend, inviting him for a cup of coffee at the hotel. He was smiling, thrilled that so many correspondents had turned up, completely oblivious to the dark significance of the role he had just played.

'You have to give up this job,' I said bluntly.

'What? Why?'

'Look, one day there's going to be a Nuremberg here and your name is going to be associated with this crazy general.'

'No! He's a friend of my father's. Do you think so? I really don't,' he said, stirring his coffee with a silver spoon. It proved impossible to press the point any further. Our friendship faded years later when I tried to bring up the memory of that bizarre press conference, the wall of silence intact even after all those years.

Argentines still lack a definitive understanding of the general moral blindness that allowed the 1976/83 dictatorship to carry out its gruesome exterminations. Almost equally, the country remains at a loss to comprehend how, even in 2002, the most egalitarian society in Latin America has lurched suddenly into a chaos of apocalyptic proportions, undone by widespread corruption and with the spectre of mass hunger haunting a land historically known as the 'breadbasket' and 'beef capital' of the world. It could take many more years before such an understanding is possible. Meanwhile, clues as to how that past horror of mass extermination and this present one of rampant corruption were generated may be found in Argentina's (still-denied) closure of its borders to the Jews at the beginning of the Holocaust and the warm welcome it extended to the Nazis afterwards.

Uki Goñi
Buenos Aires
2 July 2002

1

WAR GAMES

'I know that in many countries they don't or won't understand the Jewish problem, but we understand it well enough.' Thus Foreign Minister Joachim von Ribbentrop explained the dark core of the Nazi creed to a secret envoy from Argentina. Halfway through World War Two, and shortly before the military coup of 4 June 1943 that brought to power an Axis-leaning dictatorship of young colonels in Buenos Aires, an Argentine nationalist agent established personal contact with the leaders of the Third Reich, pledging his country's support for Hitler and requesting financial aid for 'resistance' against the US. As it turned out, the Allies were about to turn the tide against the once unbeatable Nazi war machine. With it would perish the dream of Argentina's colonels of forging a covert alliance with the German Reich. But the link cemented during these meetings in Berlin would allow the most notorious mass getaway in modern history.[10]

A complex political and religious mindset had allowed Argentina's leaders to fawn on the murderous Nazi regime. Since 1930 the country had been ruled by a succession of military dictators and fraudulently elected presidents, under whom a once forward-looking and fairly liberal society had taken a more destructive turn. These corrupt regimes sought to legitimize themselves by resurrecting a supposedly ancient Hispanic alliance of 'the Cross and the Sword'. The ties of race, faith and language with Spain and the dictatorship of General Franco were emphasized. Some of these fanatics even wished to undo the Argentine war of independence and import a Spanish regent to rule a reconstructed Viceroyalty of the River Plate. The country's powerful nationalist military officers and Church dignitaries dreamt of converting Argentina from a secular republic into a Hispanic 'Catholic Nation' that could act as a counterweight to its 'materialistic' northern cousin, the 'Anglo-Saxon' United States.[11]

By the 1940s the country's foreign policy was being determined by this group of Vatican-connected medievalists. They were convinced that Argentina, a country on the southernmost tip of South America, formed with Spain and the Vatican a transatlantic 'triangle of peace' in which the 'spiritual values of civilization' could be preserved until the war had ended in Europe. The 'values' to be conserved had little to do with democracy; these policy-makers longed instead for the restoration of a world in which the abhorrent consequences of the French Revolution could be erased from the pages of history.[12]

When World War Two began, Argentina was divided between pro-Allied and pro-Nazi camps. But while democratic-minded citizens were reduced to singing the 'Marseillaise' during the screening of war newsreels, German sympathizers in the country's nationalist movement held power, with the enthusiastic support of the Catholic Church. A weak civilian president, Ramón Castillo, maintained a façade of strict neutrality while his leading civilian and military advisers circumvented normal diplomatic channels and sought direct contact with Berlin.

The envoy who travelled to Germany for private conferences with Ribbentrop, Heinrich Himmler and apparently Adolf Hitler himself was Juan Carlos Goyeneche, an extremely well-connected Catholic nationalist whose grandfather had been president of neighbouring Uruguay and whose father had been mayor of Buenos Aires in the years just before the war. Goyeneche himself was on intimate terms with the Argentine foreign minister and served as the confidential agent of an army colonel whose presence would soon dominate the political stage, Juan Perón. Goyeneche collaborated closely with the Foreign Intelligence Branch of the SS, the Ausland-SD – SD for short. This political espionage network had agents all over the world, but in the case of Argentina it sought, in the words of one high-ranking German diplomat, 'to transplant the Nazi ideology to South American soil, in order thereby to injure the Allied war efforts'. To do so, this secret service had set up its main headquarters on the American continent in Argentina. A large roster of agents was connected to Berlin via an array of secret transmitters known as the 'Bolivar Network' that covered the length of the country.[13]

Goyeneche left for Europe in April 1942 carrying an Argentine diplomatic passport, officially in response to an invitation to Spain as a guest of General Franco's 'Hispanic Council', a cultural government institution, but actually on a secret mission for Argentina's foreign minister Enrique Ruiz Guiñazú and his trusted adviser Mario Amadeo. Until recently both these diplomats had been posted to Argentina's embassy at the Vatican, where Ruiz Guiñazú had been the ambassador. There they had developed close links with Monsignor Giovanni Montini, the future Pope Paul VI, as well as with Pope Pius XII. While in Rome they had met Perón, who was undergoing training in the Fascist army of Benito Mussolini and who had also been received by the Pope. These Vatican contacts proved vital to Goyeneche's secret mission, which stemmed partly from the foreign minister's fantasy of a 'triangle of peace' with Argentina at its southern apex. Goyeneche entertained similar delusions, even hoping that his country could play a mediatory role, although as he wrote in a letter to Ruiz Guiñazú on 25 January 1942, he feared that American pressure might endanger 'the possibility of a world peace being signed in Buenos Aires in the near future'.[14]

The foreign minister was so convinced Argentina could help bring about an accord that in late 1941 he had approached the Nazi ambassador in Buenos Aires, Baron Edmund von Thermann, with the idea. 'All of Europe is prepared for a New Order under German leadership,' he said. The possibility of a papal intervention hung over the proposal. Even though Thermann felt that Ruiz Guiñazú was angling for a Nobel peace prize he passed the initiative on to Ribbentrop. 'France had fallen and the moment seemed not unpropitious,' Thermann told American interrogators after the war. All the same, 'Ribbentrop declined the offer flatly.'[15]

But the fantasy kept being fed by Vatican envoys, Axis sympathizers, Italian Fascists, Portuguese emissaries and Spanish Falangists, who repeatedly approached Argentina's representatives in Europe with similar proposals. A clear picture of the role Argentina imagined for itself can be assembled from the incomplete records of the country's Foreign Ministry archives. In July 1941 the papal nuncio in Switzerland, who was 'in permanent contact with Fascist leaders', had informed Argentina's representative in Berne that following Hitler's expected military victory against Russia, the Führer would initiate peace proceedings through the neutral nations and that 'the good will of Argentina at the opportune moment' would be requested.

Around the same time Argentina's ambassador to Vichy was visited by Portuguese and Spanish messengers requesting Argentine backing for a German peace offer supported by the Vatican. Shortly afterwards the ambassador in Madrid reported similar rumours circulating in the upper echelons of Franco's government. In December 1941, Argentina's representative in Lisbon was approached by Spanish foreign minister Ramón Serrano Suñer and Portuguese dictator Antonio de Oliveira Salazar with a plan to form an Ibero-American bloc of nations that could serve as a basis for 'world reconstruction'.

In March 1942 an 'important Italian personage visiting Berlin' suggested that neutral Argentina and Chile could become mediators. In November 1942, only a few days before Goyeneche's meeting with Ribbentrop, an extremely telling note survives from the Turkish embassy in Buenos Aires acknowledging Argentina's offer to join a mediation effort. And in March 1943, the Romanian minister in Madrid approached the Argentine embassy with the news that Hitler was seeking a separate peace with Britain, giving rise to a newspaper report that 'a representative of an Axis country has initiated proceedings before the Argentine government to discuss the possibility of peace'.[16]

When Goyeneche arrived in Madrid in 1942 as 'cultural attaché' of the Argentine embassy he was warmly received by the Argentine diplomats there who were involved in extremely devious games with the Nazis. Both the ambassador, Adrián Escobar, and his consul, Aquilino López, were collaborating with Himmler's secret service, and the consul was crossing the border to France to provide reports on his conversations with Spanish officials and Allied diplomats. The ambassador, an important conservative politician who professed himself, in the words of one high-ranking SS officer, 'a great friend of Fascism in general and the Reich in particular', meanwhile travelled to Biarritz and Paris to seek SS financing for his likely candidacy in the upcoming Argentine presidential elections.[17]

Juan Perón was well known at the embassy; he had passed through Madrid on his way back from Rome in 1941 and enjoyed a long personal friendship with at least two diplomats posted there. The embassy also served as a transit point for Nazi arms purchased by Argentina. It had the secret support of Franco's regime, which provided cover for the overland transport of guns and munitions through occupied France to Spanish ports and their conveyance from there in Spanish ships to Argentina.[18]

In May 1942, Goyeneche got into a car with Escobar and López and headed into France to meet with Vichy President Pierre Laval. In occupied Paris, Goyeneche also met with the local SS boss (and later convicted war criminal) Herbert Knochen, who was in charge of the persecution of Jews, Resistance fighters and other 'enemies of the state'. A fourth Argentine went along, the former ambassador to Berlin and new ambassador to Vichy, Ricardo Olivera, a diplomat firmly convinced of Germany's eventual victory in the war. The Argentines told Knochen that they were 'for Germany'. Knochen began to arrange a secret trip to Berlin for Escobar, but the ambassador's political ambitions were frustrated when he was transferred to the Argentine embassy in Brazil; Goyeneche eventually accepted the invitation. But before that, both he and Escobar had an important meeting in Rome, one that attracted the special interest of SD chief Schellenberg in Berlin.[19]

In late July 1942 Escobar obtained authorization from Buenos Aires to go to France for two days, presumably to receive instructions from the SS secret service, and then to spend three days in Rome. Foreign Minister Ruiz Guiñazú cabled a circumspect note pointing out that given Argentina's 'position' in the Americas, the audience Escobar and Goyeneche had scheduled with Pope Pius XII would have to be labelled 'strictly private'.[20]

On 12 August, Goyeneche and Escobar boarded a flight to Italy. What did these two Argentine SS collaborators discuss with a Pope later challenged over his ambivalent attitude towards Nazism? Argentina's cherished role of mediator seems to have been the subject. 'Escobar had good connections with the Vatican and I intended above all to make use of him in this direction in putting out a feeler for a compromise peace,' Schellenberg told American interrogators after the war. 'Escobar was a man who was very strongly oriented towards Europe and he had a high estimation of Germany. I would like to contrast him with the military faction in Argentina – politically he was not as one-sided. He believed that under the influence of the Vatican, Latin America in conjunction with Spain and Portugal should create a new political sphere of influence. It was his idea to unite all the Roman Catholics. It was the *Hispanidad*.'[21]

Despite the participants' discretion, the conversations eventually filtered to the press. It claimed that Escobar had held a long meeting with the Pope, who had shown 'great interest in an eventual Argentine intervention'. Sources in Buenos Aires were pleased to proclaim that 'Argentina's influence as a power for peace has been recognized by other governments.'[22]

Following Escobar's visit, Buenos Aires ordered its ambassador to the Vatican to reaffirm Argentina's willingness to mediate 'for the conclusion of the war'. The talks were extensive and included the Vatican Secretary of State, Cardinal Luigi Maglione. They agreed that once peace had been established Argentina would 'apply its immigration laws generously, in order to encourage ... European Catholic emigrants to seek the necessary land and capital in our country'. Finally, on 10 October, the Argentine ambassador was received by the Pope, who welcomed the Argentine view that it was 'appropriate for the Vatican to participate in the search for peace'. Pius XII promised that 'when the time came' he would ask for 'the collaboration of the Argentine Republic'.[23]

No matter how comforting the Pope's words sounded, Argentina's fanciful notion that it could bring about a peace that included the perpetuation of the Nazi regime in Germany provoked hilarity even in South America. The international press, including that of Brazil, mistrusted the 'triangle of peace' proposed by Buenos Aires, considering it favourable to Hitler. It isn't hard to imagine how the idea must have been scoffed at in the halls of government in Washington and London. There Goyeneche's connections were well documented, and Ruiz Guiñazú was considered an Axis sympathizer; and anyway the Allies were demanding nothing short of Hitler's unconditional surrender.[24]

After his visit to the Vatican, Goyeneche travelled to Berlin in late October 1942. He was lodged at the Adlon Hotel, where 'special' visitors received free board from the Nazis and where Schellenberg's agents performed a brisk trade in jewellery and foreign exchange towards the end of the war. He left immediately to visit Franco's Blue Division on the Russian Front with his old friend Gottfried Sandstede, the former press attaché at the German embassy in Buenos Aires. Sandstede was a Schellenberg agent who had been forced to abandon Argentina when his spying activities became too evident. Upon their return to Berlin, Goyeneche was introduced to Otto Reinebeck, the head of the Latin American bureau at the German Foreign Ministry.[25]

'He called on me and requested a conference with von Ribbentrop and Adolf Hitler,' Reinebeck said in a postwar interrogation. 'He declared that he had already had similar interviews with General Franco in Spain and Benito Mussolini in Italy and that both these chiefs of state had assured him of extensive support for his proposals to train Argentine youth in accordance with Fascist and National Socialist principles.'[26]

On 30 November 1942, a few days after the start of the Soviet counteroffensive in Stalingrad, Goyeneche was admitted to Ribbentrop's Westphalia estate for an interview that lasted 'several hours'. Sandstede acted as interpreter. Goyeneche sought Nazi support for a nationalist candidate in the upcoming 1943 presidential elections in Argentina, or failing that, support for a coup that would maintain the 'neutral' President Castillo in office. 'The Argentine youth, the military and the Navy are putting up a life-and-death struggle against the US, which threatens the existence of the nation,' he told Ribbentrop.[27]

The minister, glad to hear that Argentina understood that this was 'a battle that would determine the fate of all civilization for centuries', launched into a long anti-Jewish diatribe. Stalin would never give up 'the fundamental ideas of Bolshevism, since the men behind it were and are Jews'. The same held true for President Roosevelt of the United States. 'We know that international Jewry, on the one hand behind the capitalistic mask and on the other behind the Bolshevist, pursues its end.'

Ribbentrop then proceeded to answer the three specific questions Goyeneche had regarding Argentina: first, would Germany acquire Argentine products after the war? 'If Argentina maintains its present stand, she will profit from it greatly over the countries which have not taken such a stand,' he answered. 'We could take everything that Argentina produced no matter how much it might be.'

Second, did Germany recognize Argentina's rights over the Falklands? 'England is our enemy ... Gibraltar is truly a grotesque example in this story, for certainly nobody can question that it lies on the Iberian Peninsula. Likewise, the Falklands are at least nearer Argentina than to England. Therefore, we have great sympathy for the justifiable Argentine interest. But I believe that, unless Argentina takes care, it may be that the United States will take over these islands.'

And third, did Hitler agree that Spain constituted the 'natural bridge' between Argentina and Europe? 'The establishment of her cultural and spiritual relationship with Europe is in the first rank of Argentine duties. We shall in any case constantly promote the existing unity between Spain and Argentina.'[28]

Goyeneche sat unperturbed through the long anti-Semitic diatribe that Ribbentrop delivered for his benefit. Such tirades were surely frequent during his stay in Berlin. It is unthinkable that Himmler failed to broach the subject. Before his departure from Buenos Aires, Goyeneche was well known for his racial views anyway, and some who knew him claim he maintained this posture in later life.[29]

Despite the attention lavished on him by Ribbentrop, who spent an unusually long time with the Argentine, Goyeneche was not impressed. He found the foreign minister simply obnoxious. 'As an individual he causes a bad impression, pedantic and closed-minded,' Goyeneche wrote to his close friend Amadeo in Buenos Aires. To the SS intelligence chief in Madrid, Karl Arnold, Goyeneche said that Ribbentrop 'had left a bad taste' in his mouth. Apparently Ribbentrop had done most of the talking, 'not allowing his guest to say more than a half-dozen sentences'. The truth of the matter was that Goyeneche's heart lay with Schellenberg's secret service, which had already supplied him with various 'gifts', including a Leica camera – plus a permit to use it in wartime Berlin![30]

The Argentine had come a long way from Sandstede, his first contact with the Nazi secret service in Buenos Aires. Now he entered the office of Walter Schellenberg himself, the 33-year-old SS brigadier with a duelling scar on his chin who headed Hitler's SD Foreign Intelligence Branch. This was Department VI of Himmler's Reich Security Main Office; Department IV was the dreaded Gestapo, and IV-B4 was Adolf Eichmann's department of 'Jewish Affairs'. Defined as 'pure Nordic' in his SS file, Schellenberg was an unusually smart, charming and boyish figure with the full support of Himmler, who tolerated his pursuit of secret peace initiatives with the Western powers. From very early on, Schellenberg realized from his intelligence sources that America's massive production of weaponry would decide the outcome of the war, an assessment that the top Nazi leaders refused to even consider. He therefore kept lines open with the West during the war, either acting personally or through special agents. His trusted aide Wilhelm Hoettl recalled decades later: 'Schellenberg repeatedly said that there is an international brotherhood of intelligence agencies, be they National Socialists or British or American, a strata of like-minded people, who were in fact pledged to intelligence agency work and who also have to be respected equally.'[31]

The most daring of these peace overtures took place in 1943 through Schellenberg's 'special sources' Max von Hohenlohe and Reinhard Spitzy, representatives in Madrid of the Skoda arms firm. They held a number of meetings in Berne with Allen Dulles, overseer of the American Office of Strategic Services (OSS) in Europe. In the lengthy report drawn up by Spitzy of these talks, the position taken by the American spy chief is spine-chilling: 'He [Dulles] was fed up with listening all the time to outdated politicians, émigrés and prejudiced Jews. In his view a peace had to be made in Europe . . . while he had scant sympathy for Soviet Russia, he did not reject National Socialism in its basic ideas and deeds . . . he added that it would be unbearable for any decent European to think that the Jews might return someday.' Interestingly enough, Spitzy was also one of Schellenberg's 'channels' for information about Argentina, one that bypassed the normal intelligence chain. Only a few months after the Dulles talks, Spitzy would be attempting to negotiate a secret arms deal with one of Perón's colonels in Madrid with Schellenberg's support.[32]

During his interrogations by US officers in 1946, Schellenberg proved himself extremely knowledgeable about Argentine affairs, even down to the names of Argentina's continually reshuffled cabinet ministers and presidents. His espionage service in Argentina had been resourceful and highly efficient. Its chief, SS Captain Siegfried Becker, was considered by American intelligence 'the most important German agent in the Western Hemisphere', and Schellenberg was especially proud of him.[33]

Goyeneche obtained clearance from 'Ribbentrop himself' to wire the results of his conferences to Argentina in the German diplomatic code. 'Argentina is the last German bridgehead in the Western Hemisphere, the maintenance and development of which are of greatest significance later on,' Ribbentrop repeatedly explained to Reinebeck. The use of the secret German cipher had been agreed upon because the Argentines did not trust their own diplomats in Berlin, who were kept in the dark about Goyeneche's mission. The chargé d'affaires, Luis Luti, was considered *persona non grata* by the SS as well, probably because of his efforts to protect the Argentine Jews who lived in Germany, which had angered Himmler.[34]

Luti was 'anti-Nazi, and for that reason undesirable publicity for these secret negotiations was to be feared,' Reinebeck later explained. 'The telegrams, which were designated "for Juan", were sent by me to the German chargé d'affaires in Buenos Aires.' The American intelligence officer interrogating Reinebeck must have been dozing off, for three days later Reinebeck was called back to explain who 'Juan' was. 'The name "Juan" was chosen as a covering address because the report was intended for Colonel Perón, whose first name is Juan,' said Reinebeck coolly. In Buenos Aires the wires were picked up at the German embassy by Goyeneche's friend, the diplomat Mario Amadeo, who took them to Foreign Minister Ruiz Guiñazú. Copies were also picked up there by Argentine military agents for delivery to Perón.[35]

Argentina's naval attaché in Berlin taught Goyeneche the procedure. First the message was ciphered employing the attaché's code. This coded message was then handed to Reinebeck, who re-coded it in the Nazi diplomatic cipher for transmission to the German embassy in Buenos Aires. There the message was deciphered, returning it to the attaché's original code, and handed to the Argentines for final decoding into plain Spanish. The complicated method was actually futile, for Allied intelligence had long ago deciphered both codes and was intercepting German messages. Unknown to Goyeneche his cables were being translated into English and included in the ultra-secret 'Magic' summaries of the US War Department, which kept a close track of the Argentine's movements through Europe.[36]

Did Goyeneche ever meet with Hitler? Conflicting versions exist. The first survives in postwar reports on Goyeneche by Wendell Blancké, an extremely sharp American diplomat who lived in Buenos Aires from 1932 until 1945, where Perón's secret police kept track of his movements while Blancké kept watch over Argentina's nationalists. At the end of the war he was called to Germany by General Eisenhower's command to become the leading interrogator of Argentine-related Nazis, including Schellenberg and Ribbentrop. According to Blancké, who was quoting from captured German records, Goyeneche met with Hitler on 7 December 1942, a week after meeting Ribbentrop. The Führer reaffirmed Germany's support for Argentina's claim over the Falklands and promised Goyeneche that 'Germany would not forget that Argentina had stood by her'.[37]

According to Reinebeck, however, who was interrogated extensively about Argentina's wartime relationship with Nazi Germany, Goyeneche had requested a meeting with Hitler to pose his three questions but the meeting finally never took place. Instead, Goyeneche 'had a second conference with Ribbentrop at which the latter handed him Hitler's written answer.' Goyeneche himself bragged years later that he kept 'Hitler's letters' among his papers in Buenos Aires, but denied he had ever met Hitler personally, supporting Reinebeck's version. The ageing nationalist died in 1982, saddened by Argentina's defeat in the Falklands war. Among his surviving friends the legend persists that he met secretly with Hitler in the Black Forest in 1944.[38]

Following his meeting with Ribbentrop, Goyeneche returned to Paris for Christmas to digest the significance of his meetings. Much of this time seems to have been spent writing reports for Argentina and drawing up proposals for the Germans. Among these, he penned one peculiar request: 'Argentina considers that at the conclusion of the war it would be of maximum interest to turn over the complete political and administrative control of the city of Jerusalem to the government of the Vatican, which would respect properties and religious creeds as they exist today. This measure would produce a definitive moral effect in the Western world and would achieve the total dissipation of the doubts that the Catholic-rooted Latin youth movements still have over full and passionate adherence to the norms of the New Order.'[39]

Towards the end of December Goyeneche was back in Berlin with a special gift for Schellenberg. 'Since I know you tend to disobey your doctor I am sending you some good English cigarettes that, like everything English, deserve to be consumed by fire,' Goyeneche wrote the SD chief.[40]

In early January 1943 Goyeneche was taken by Schellenberg to spend a day with Himmler at his headquarters on the Eastern front. Unfortunately, no written record of the meeting was made. What was said has survived only in Schellenberg's oral account and in Goyeneche's report to Amadeo. 'It was a general conversation,' Schellenberg told American interrogators after the war. 'Goyeneche was very cautious and Himmler, too, only showed his best side; in other words, he would only enter into discussions concerning political points. Goyeneche then went on to state very frankly that he was a Roman Catholic and he stated that you could not think of South America without thinking of Catholicism at the same time. He counselled Himmler to protect the Catholics in Europe because it was his opinion if Europe was to be lost to Bolshevism, then South America, too, would be lost.'

Himmler listened attentively, showing 'common sense and comprehension' and allowing the Argentine 'every opportunity to expound his ideas'. Unlike Ribbentrop, who Goyeneche had found impossibly pompous, Himmler turned out to be 'charming'. 'Himmler really gave very positive answers,' said Schellenberg, 'but then he very skilfully turned the discussion from Catholicism to common enmity towards Bolshevism.' According to Schellenberg, an Argentine 'link to the Vatican' was discussed. This is sustained in Goyeneche's account of the meeting for Amadeo. 'He was very interested to hear that I would be seeing the Pope and expressly asked me to inform the Pope that I had found him to be a very approachable person, especially in religious matters.'[41]

The level of Goyeneche's contacts in Europe was astounding. On his way to Rome after meeting with Himmler, the secret Argentine envoy lunched in Madrid with Spanish Foreign Minister Ramón Serrano Suñer, to discuss his upcoming encounters with Mussolini and Pope Pius XII. Goyeneche was organizing a conference of pro-Axis Catholic delegates from Vichy France, Hungary, Romania, Slovenia, Italy, Spain and Portugal, who would meet in Rome 'to integrate the Christian order in the New Order'. As the Nazi intelligence chief in Madrid told American interrogators after the war, the whole purpose of his trip to Europe was to 'reconcile Hitlerism with Catholicism'.[42]

Arriving in Rome in mid-March 1943, Goyeneche held various preparatory meetings with Monsignor Montini and then met twice with Pope Pius XII, presumably to pass on the secret details of his conversation with Himmler. 'You must preserve that treasure you possess,' said Pius XII to Goyeneche, referring to Argentina's neutrality. The Pope promised to draft a special message supporting Argentina in its 'battle for neutrality'. Afterwards Goyeneche wrote to Amadeo asking him to contact, 'very carefully', the Apostolic Nuncio in Buenos Aires to continue the work begun in Rome. 'I've opened the way for our letters to reach Monsignor Montini,' he mysteriously added.[43]

Despite rumours to the contrary, Goyeneche found Mussolini in vigorous health when they met in Rome. 'Today I have ridden a horse and a woman,' boasted Il Duce to the Argentine. Goyeneche spoke frankly about a delicate matter, obtaining Mussolini's support for a nationalist coup to prolong the 'neutral' government of Castillo in Argentina. 'It is painful for us that President Castillo fails to clearly see this solution,' he told Mussolini. Goyeneche hoped that a 'suggestion' from Mussolini would encourage the coup plotters or at least oblige Castillo's successor to maintain Argentina's neutrality. Mussolini for his part 'hurled furious words, accompanied with gestures, against the United States,' and acceded to Goyeneche's request. Between the two, a transcript of Il Duce's 'suggestion' to Castillo was drafted, to be delivered through the Italian embassy in Buenos Aires.[44]

Mussolini said he recognized Argentina's rights over the Falklands and promised to obtain a similar statement of support from Japan, the third member of Hitler's Axis. 'If the Axis nations . . . have not publicly acknowledged the magnificent resistance of Argentina . . . this has only been to spare the Argentine Republic understandable difficulties under the current circumstances,' said Mussolini. His message in favour of a coup was delivered by the Italian embassy in Buenos Aires to the Argentine Foreign Ministry on 4 June 1943, the same day that Perón's colonels finally grew tired of Castillo and ejected him from the presidential headquarters, the Casa Rosada, in Buenos Aires.[45]

2

PERÓN LEAPS TO POWER

With Castillo out of the way Perón's colonels launched themselves wholeheartedly into sealing a secret alliance with Hitler. A partnership with Argentina's military had already been formalized. As he told American interrogators after the war, SD chief Walter Schellenberg had approved 'an agreement for mutual collaboration' in May 1943. It included freedom from arrest for Nazi agents in Argentina, camouflage identification for them as members of the Argentine secret service, the use of the Argentine diplomatic pouch for transporting 'secret material' between Buenos Aires and Berlin, and even an early warning system in case of a 'cabinet crisis' that could endanger German agents. In return, Argentina's military were allowed access to the powerful radio communications network of the Nazi secret service, were provided with information culled from Nazi sources in Argentina's neighbouring countries and were promised collaboration in forming an Argentine-led South American bloc of nations. A month after this agreement had been implemented, a secret lodge of army colonels staged a coup, installing a military dictatorship headed by puppet generals who responded to Perón's directives. During this dictatorship of the mysteriously named GOU lodge (some say the acronym stood for 'Group of Order and Unity') Perón made full use of the agreement to increase his regime's power in South America.[46]

Schellenberg had been keeping an eye on Perón ever since the future president's sojourn in Italy between 1939 and 1941, when he had served as an adjutant to the Argentine military attaché in Rome. During these two years Perón apparently travelled to Germany, probably on an intelligence mission for the Argentine army. Schellenberg did not help elucidate this particular mystery for his American interrogators after the war. 'I recall dimly that the name of Perón appeared in reports, but I don't recall whether he was in Paris or in Germany,' he said.[47]

Schellenberg was certain, though, that once Perón had returned to Argentina he was contacted by Becker. The link was Perón's right-hand man, Colonel Enrique González, who had trained in the Panzer division of Hitler's 'Blitzkrieg General' Heinz Guderian right up to the start of the war.[48]

'Politically speaking, the reason was that one could see a government based upon a world view similar to ours,' said Schellenberg.

A 'hypothetical question' was put to the former Ausland SD chief at the end of a particularly gruelling interrogation on 6 February 1946. 'If you were still maintaining Department VI and Perón were head of the Argentine government, would you consider him a most favourable possibility from your point of view?'

'Yes.'

'Would you consider that he would double-cross you?'

'Not according to his original aims. Otherwise he would have had to undergo a change in the meantime.'[49]

A few days after the coup, Colonel González received two Nazi agents at his home, the middle-aged German businessman Hans Harnisch and the younger German-Argentine Osmar Hellmuth. Under discussion was an oil tanker built in Sweden for the Greek shipping magnate Aristotle Onassis. In his youth Onassis had lived in Buenos Aires, where he had obtained Argentine citizenship and begun to amass the fortune that would later make him a world celebrity. Since October 1942, through his agents in Argentina, he had been struggling to obtain delivery of the *Buenos Aires*, a 17,000-ton tanker flying an

Argentine flag that had been built by the Goetanerkem shipyard.
The Germans refused to grant a safe conduct for the ship, alleging
that once in the Western Hemisphere it could be conscripted into the
Allied war effort.[50]

For a long time Argentina had been seeking arms to strengthen its
position against its neighbour Brazil, and had even sent a special mission to Washington to seek American weaponry. The mission was not
successful. As a journalist at the English-language *Buenos Aires Herald*
remarked at the time: 'I don't think Washington will trust any planes,
guns and tanks to Argentine hands under present circumstances. It's
like slipping the baby a loaded revolver.'[51]

Sensing Argentina's frustration, Harnisch and Hellmuth offered to
enlist the might of the SS secret service to obtain German arms for the
GOU regime. The colonels took the bait and on 28 June Harnisch was
ushered into the presence of General Pedro Ramírez, the puppet
president installed by Perón's clique. The general stated that he had
just had a meeting with the American ambassador Norman Armour,
who had made his 'blood boil' by demanding that Argentina break off
diplomatic relations with the Reich.[52]

The atmosphere in the meeting with the German agent was in
contrast highly relaxed, and the president declared himself pleased to
be in the presence of an 'unofficial' Reich representative, which
allowed him to speak more freely. Ramírez explained how difficult it
was for Argentina to withstand Allied pressure and asked Harnisch to
explain to Berlin that any anti-German measures he was forced to
take should not be misunderstood. Argentina's situation would be
greatly eased if safe conduct were provided for Onassis's oil tanker,
and if Germany would also consider the delivery of anti-aircraft
artillery, pilots, aviation fuel, planes, munitions and licences for the
manufacture of war material. There existed the real possibility of war
with Brazil and Argentina's coastline was practically defenceless.
Could Germany and Japan spare submarines to protect the coasts of
Chile and Argentina? In return, Ramírez offered to stamp down on the
Allied spy rings in Argentine territory.

The meeting was the beginning of many the Nazi agents had with the GOU's leading officials. The secret transmitters of SS Captain Siegfried Becker hummed happily as the details of the talks were radioed to Schellenberg in Berlin. Whenever these cables arrived, the Argentine naval attaché, Captain Eduardo Ceballos, was called to SD headquarters to evaluate the progress of negotiations. The Nazis and the GOU had agreed to leave their respective embassies out of the picture. As before, during the Goyeneche talks, the Argentine chargé d'affaires Luis Luti was not trusted. Schellenberg had no time for the slow-moving German diplomats in Buenos Aires either.[53]

Finally, in September 1943, Harnisch and Hellmuth were called to the Casa Rosada. The colonels had decided to forget the various alternatives under consideration, which included transporting arms to Argentina via Nazi submarines or Spanish cargo ships. They had decided instead to send a special emissary to Berlin to discuss an alliance personally with Hitler. (For some reason Goyeneche was no longer considered a viable agent for these negotiations.) The Nazi agents were asked to draft a telegram for Himmler requesting such a meeting. Becker, Harnisch and Hellmuth spent a whole night drafting the momentous wire: 'The Argentine government requests . . . whether the sending of a special envoy with the purpose of meeting in a secret mission with members of the German government would be well received. Excluding normal means, that is, normal diplomatic channels, it is requested that the answer be conveyed through Captain Ceballos.'

But when Hellmuth arrived at the Casa Rosada the following day with the text of the proposed message a change of plan was announced. He was received by Perón. 'The idea of an initial consultation with the Reich government was brusquely rejected, and they decided instead to send Hellmuth directly,' Becker declared in the interrogations he was subjected to during his brief arrest in Argentina at the end of the war. Hellmuth was stunned. 'If your mission is successful,' Perón promised, 'you will become one of us.'[54]

Picking Hellmuth to meet with Hitler proved a particularly unhappy choice. A naval school dropout who had drifted into intelligence work on the strength of his passable German and a casual connection with Harnisch, the 35-year-old German-Argentine had little real experience in the spy world. During the war he sold insurance for Commercial Union, had an account at the Bank of London and had been taking lessons to improve his English. What free time he had he spent at the Argentine Yacht Club, having once sailed to Rio de Janeiro in a rally. His cover as a spy had been blown not long after the war started, and his name had appeared as early as 1942 in a book published in New York titled *The Nazi Underground in South America*. At first Becker threw his arms up in despair, but when he realized the GOU colonels were serious about sending Hellmuth he decided to make the best of a bad situation and set about instructing the yachtsman as best he could for the task.

At the German embassy in Buenos Aires, however, the news came as a bombshell. The Nazi diplomats, in conjunction with the powerful German businessman Ludwig Freude, had been grooming a GOU officer of their own choice, Colonel Carlos Vélez, to work out an arms deal with Hitler. A tough battle ensued over the rival plans. Finally, Perón settled the dispute, deciding to send both Vélez and Hellmuth on the same boat to Spain. Vélez would go as Argentina's new military attaché to Madrid, Hellmuth as consul to Barcelona. If the Hellmuth mission failed, Vélez was to serve as backup.

Perón called in Hellmuth and showed him a signed card stamped with the GOU's seal. He also showed him a 'military dossier' containing the shopping list for arms. Perón gave one half of the card to Hellmuth, and slipped the other into the dossier, which would be carried by an Argentine diplomat travelling on the same ship to Spain as a safety measure. The diplomat would deliver the dossier to Ceballos in Madrid, and he would hand it over to Hellmuth when he presented his half of the card. With control of the dossier, Hellmuth could embark on his mission. As arranged with Schellenberg, a plane provided by Himmler would be waiting in Madrid to whisk Hellmuth off to Berlin.

At least this is the best possible reconstruction of events available from the various interrogations Hellmuth, Becker and Schellenberg were subjected to after Perón's plan imploded. Unfortunately none of those interrogated was asked to confirm for posterity whose signature was on the card. The half carried by Hellmuth was probably confiscated by the British when they arrested him on his way to Berlin, in which case it is one of the documents still labelled 'Researchers Denied Access' at the Public Record Office in London. British intelligence has always been discreet. The signature almost certainly belonged to Perón.[55]

As the *Cabo de Hornos* left the port of Buenos Aires, Hellmuth already cut a ridiculous figure. The German diplomats in Argentina had done their best to discredit the envoy. First they sent an anonymous note to the Casa Rosada claiming that Hellmuth was actually a double agent for the British – not a far-fetched possibility. When this failed they wired a series of cables to Germany promoting their candidate Vélez instead. In retaliation, Becker instructed Hellmuth, once in Berlin, to demand from Schellenberg the removal of the Nazi diplomats in Buenos Aires. 'Hellmuth would learn something of the SD, its organization, functions and powers, from Schellenberg in Germany,' Becker comforted himself.[56]

Vélez and Hellmuth kept an icy distance from each other on the ship, but Vélez's young daughters were mesmerized by Hellmuth's comical behaviour at sea: 'He would spend the day on deck wearing a cap and scouring the horizon with a pair of binoculars,' recalled Zaira Vélez more than five decades later. 'He was so obviously playing the spy.'[57]

If Hellmuth had been fearing the worst then his fears were about to be confirmed, for, as we have seen, the Allies had been listening in on the German cable traffic with Argentina. The US War Department's 'Magic Summary' for 28 October 1943 gave a brief description of the communications between Becker and Schellenberg and ended by stating: 'The British have arranged to remove Hellmuth from the *Cabo de Hornos* when it reaches Trinidad tomorrow. He will be taken to England and questioned there on the basis of information from other sources.' A short time later Hellmuth was demanding diplomatic immunity from inside a police shack in Trinidad while British police ripped away the panelling of his cabin in the *Cabo de Hornos*.

Among the documentation they found there was apparently a highly embarrassing letter from President Ramírez to Hitler.

Hellmuth was flown to Bermuda and taken from there to Portsmouth on board the British warship *Ajax*. By 12 November he was undergoing questioning at a prisoner-of-war camp outside London.[58]

'I'm Argentine, not German,' he repeated over and again to his captors. It would take some years, but eventually he was able to joke about the unfortunate end to his ambitious mission. 'Before leaving he suffered from a stomach ulcer,' recalled a friend of the family for this book. 'But with the prison diet, which was porridge, morning, noon and night-time, the British cured him.'[59]

Hellmuth's arrest should have been enough of a warning against the Nazi–GOU machinations, but amazingly enough, they continued unabated. Schellenberg talked himself into believing that somehow Hellmuth would be set free by the British and that he would be able to continue his trip to Germany. In Buenos Aires, González blamed Hellmuth's arrest on Ludwig Freude and swore to take revenge on the German businessman as soon as the opportunity presented itself. For his part, Perón pushed forward undeterred. He continued to plot with Becker the overthrow of neighbouring governments to bring about an Argentine-led, pro-Nazi bloc of nations to offset Washington's influence over Brazil. 'Hitler's struggle in war and in peace will be our guide,' Perón had written in a secret GOU manifesto on 3 May 1943. 'Forming alliances will be the first step. We have Paraguay; we have Bolivia and Chile. With Argentina, Paraguay, Bolivia and Chile, it will be easy to pressure Uruguay. Then the five united nations will easily draw in Brazil because of its type of government and its large nucleus of Germans. With Brazil fallen, the American continent will be ours.'

On 20 December 1943 a military coup ousted the government of General Enrique Peñaranda in Bolivia and replaced him with General Gualberto Villarroel. This revolution had been jointly planned by Perón and Becker with various Bolivian collaborators in constant radio contact with Schellenberg's headquarters in Berlin. The conspirators had held their meetings at the Buenos Aires home of German-Bolivian tin magnate Gustav Eickenberg, a Perón contact who had known Becker since 1940. The American counterintelligence analysts at 'Magic' were aware of the cooperation between the GOU and the Nazis in Bolivia, as the summary written the day before the coup shows. 'The movement is partly supported by German agents and by certain members of the Argentine government,' it said.

Despite the effort invested, the Bolivian revolution turned out to be a letdown for the Germans. The primary interest had been 'to have one more state in South America enlisted against the US', as one of Schellenberg's agents monitoring the events from Berlin told American interrogators after the war. But the intrigue had been discovered and documented by the US, which now used the information to twist Argentina's arm, causing the loss of Germany's 'last bridge-head' on the American continent. Faced with an Allied threat to reveal its part in the Bolivian coup, as well as the threat to release the transcript of Hellmuth's interrogation in London, Argentina caved in to Allied pressure and became the last American nation to break off diplomatic relations with Germany in January 1944, though it remained neutral until the very end of the war. Villarroel, the president installed by the revolution in Bolivia, ended up the clear loser. Deposed in 1946, he was killed and his body hung from a pole by students during a bloody revolution in La Paz.[60]

Argentina broke off diplomatic relations with Hitler but it did not abandon its neutrality or declare war on Germany until a month before Hitler committed suicide in his Berlin bunker. According to Perón, the declaration was a ruse to distract Allied attention while the first escape routes to Argentina were opened for Nazi fugitives. 'Undoubtedly, towards the end of February 1945, Argentina's declaration of war had been decided upon,' Perón admitted in 1969. 'We had maintained neutrality but we couldn't maintain it any longer. I remember I got together some German friends and told them: "Look, we have no choice but to go to war" . . . but, of course, it was a mere formality.'[61]

In Cadiz, meanwhile, Goyeneche was experiencing 'true anguish' at the outcome of a war in which he had invested such high hopes. In March 1945, in a letter to his friend Amadeo, by now one of Perón's main foreign policy advisers, he wrote: 'Through secret channels I have addressed Himmler, whom I know well . . . Two days afterwards I was told that everything was satisfactorily arranged.' According to Goyeneche, Himmler's spirits remained high. 'Together with the reply I refer to above,' he added, 'I was told that the war would turn out right, although there will be much bad news to bear.' There is some evidence suggesting that Goyeneche's last-minute exchanges with Himmler were made in Perón's name. 'We let the Germans know that we would declare war against them to save thousands of lives,' Perón said in 1970. 'We exchanged messages with them through Switzerland and Spain. Franco understood our intention immediately and aided us. The Germans were also in agreement.'[62]

This false declaration of war had a clear purpose: 'We hadn't lost contact with Germany, despite the break in diplomatic relations,' Perón would say in 1967. 'Things being so we received an unusual request. Even though it may seem contradictory at first, Germany benefits from our declaration of war: if Argentina becomes a belligerent country, it has the right to enter Germany when the end arrives; this means that our planes and ships would be in a position to render a great service. At that point we had the commercial planes of the FAMA line [Argentine Merchant Air Fleet] and the ships we had bought from Italy during the war. That is how a great number of people were able to come to Argentina.' Perón was giving a clear nod to historians in these statements. 'We preferred to make the imperialist powers of the day believe we had finally given in to their belligerent requests. By then we were better off showing some good behaviour, especially to win time,' Perón said. 'There was, of course, a group of idiots who accused us of weakness. Those sorry souls who never understand anything of what's going on.'[63]

3

Undesirable Immigration

On 20 January 1942 the chieftains of the Nazi killing machine met at No. 56/58 Wannsee in Berlin to discuss the 'final solution of the Jewish question'. For the benefit of those present, Reich Security Main Office chief Reinhard Heydrich reviewed the progress so far. SS Lieutenant-Colonel Adolf Eichmann, head of the office for Jewish Affairs, took notes. Gestapo chief Heinrich Müller sat near by.

Heydrich said that he had been entrusted with the task of cleansing German territory of Jews. For this he had had to: a) make all necessary arrangements for an increased emigration of the Jews; b) direct the flow of emigration; c) speed the emigration procedure in each individual case.

Heydrich had been able to show some results. A total of '537,000 Jews were sent out of the country between the takeover of power and the deadline of 31 October 1941'. But emigration was 'not only a German problem, but also a problem with which the authorities of the countries to which the flow of emigrants was being directed would have to deal', and the Nazis had run up against a wall. The rest of the world was closing its borders to the Jews.

Prewar emigration as a 'solution' had been hampered by 'financial difficulties, such as the demand by various foreign governments for increasing sums of money'. The lack of cooperation from foreign countries, and the hefty bribes demanded from Jews by the diplomatic representatives of these countries, had been a real stumbling block. The 'restriction of entry permits, or the cancelling of such, increased extraordinarily the difficulties of emigration,' said Heydrich. After the start of the war there was therefore a shift away from emigration, and 'another possible solution' had taken its place. Heydrich now announced plans for 'the evacuation of the Jews to the East . . . Approximately 11 million Jews will be involved in the final solution of the European Jewish question.'[64]

There was probably no country which had taken such extraordinary measures to cancel its 'entry permits' for the Jews as Argentina did on the eve of Hitler's Holocaust.

This shameful policy is one of Argentina's best-kept war secrets. Fortunately, despite careful cleansing of Argentina's Foreign Ministry and Immigration Office archives, some of the relevant documentation has escaped destruction. And the families of diplomats who served in Europe during the late 1930s and early 1940s clearly remember the secret directives against Jews fleeing the Nazi horror.

At the time, Argentina's rulers saw themselves as standing at the helm of a predominantly white, Catholic, Hispanic nation unjustly forced to share borders with its mixed-race neighbours in South America. 'An Argentine is an Italian who speaks Spanish but thinks he's English,' is how many Argentines would define themselves, and the old saying was not far from the truth. The sparse native population of this vast territory on the southernmost tip of South America was decimated first by Spanish colonizers and later by the newly independent nation's voracious generals. Those still alive in the early twentieth century had virtually disappeared under a wave of Spanish and Italian immigrants, who, along with a fair smattering of French, English, Irish and German settlers, turned the nation's capital Buenos Aires into 'the Paris of South America'. The fact that the mix of 15 million inhabitants included Jewish settlers totalling half a million people was something the Argentine establishment first preferred to ignore, and later attempted to correct.[65]

A succession of medallioned sabre-rattling dictators and weak civil-ian presidents rode the back of fraudulent elections during the 1930s and early 1940s. They forged an alliance with the Catholic Church that reached its culmination in the colonels' revolution that catapulted Perón to power in 1943. The colonels, eager to legitimize their self-appointed role as 'saviours of the nation', heaped favours on the Church, allowing it to realize some of its oldest and dearest aspira-tions. Chief among these was the compulsory teaching of the Catholic faith in all the nation's schools, a concession to the country's prelates that ran contrary to Argentina's liberal constitution.

The Church hierarchy in Argentina, with encouragement from Pope Pius XII, began to harbour the illusion that a truly 'Catholic Nation' was in the making. Argentina's liberal tradition had slowly declined during the 1930s, and the reins of power passed to the hands of an anti-liberal amalgam of ardent nationalists steeped in Nazi mythology, young colonels outraged by government corruption and elderly bishops nostalgic for a reunion of Church and State. This blend led to the attempt to impose a 'New Christian Order' in Argentina. The colonels who took power in 1943 carried their Catholic devotion to extreme lengths, elevating the Virgin Mary to the rank of General in the Argentine army. In return, the bishops blessed their Nazi-style parades, ignored the excesses of Perón's military regime and supported the colonels' social policies.[66]

A particularly Argentine strain of anti-Semitism was part of the mix. To this mindset, Germany's Nazi regime was actually a tool of the Divine Will. 'Hitlerism, paradoxically enough, is the antechamber to Catholicism,' wrote Father Julio Meinvielle in 1940. This priest was the leading light of Catholic nationalism in Argentina. Spain, under General Franco, was becoming Christian, he declared, adding that 'the terrible German boot' assured the 'purification' of France. 'The anti-Christian structure must be destroyed. That is precisely the great service that unknowingly ... the Axis is providing the Church.'[67]

Again, the reconciliation of Nazism and Catholicism was the dri-ving spirit behind the Argentine elite's dalliance with Hitler. Even though the country's nationalist Catholics declared themselves opposed to the 'tremendous persecution' of the Jews in Germany, their disagreement was one of degree, not of substance. Father Meinvielle's 1936 bestseller *El judío* (*The Jew*) defined this attitude succinctly when it stated that 'we Christians must love the Jew in accordance with Christ's precept to love even our own enemy.' The book managed to systematize Argentine anti-Semitic thought while at the same time declaring itself against Nazi-style racism. 'We must love the lepers but this does not prevent them from being isolated to prevent contamination; we must love thieves but that does not keep them from being jailed so that they do not harm society,' the book held. Hitler's pogroms were wrong; what was needed were special laws that took into account the 'theological dangerousness of this race . . . They must not be exterminated from among the Christian peoples as the anti-Semitics pretend, nor must they be granted equal rights as Liberalism would wish.' Meinvielle's influence was long-lasting, and in the 1960s his book was reprinted without alterations.[68]

It was through such perverse reasoning that Argentina convinced itself it could obtain an undercover alliance with Hitler that took into account the country's Catholic and Hispanic roots while circumventing Hitler's overt racism. As the German embassy in Buenos Aires reported to Berlin in 1938, Argentina's Spanish ancestry had left the country too heavily 'brushed with the Semitic tar-brush' to expect any but the kind of 'religious' anti-Semitism espoused by Meinvielle.[69]

Against this backdrop, on 12 July 1938, Argentine Foreign Minister José María Cantilo bent over his desk and signed a secret directive that was the equivalent of a death warrant for thousands of European Jews. Wired that day to all Argentine diplomats around the world, Directive 11 was labelled 'strictly confidential' and its contents have never been revealed until now. The secret order came only a few months after Germany's annexation of Austria had placed 200,000 new Jews at Hitler's mercy. It was designed specifically to ensure that none of the German and Austrian Jews fleeing Hitler found their way to Argentina, and thus bears out Heydrich's justification at Wannsee that the cancellation of entry permits by foreign countries had proved emigration a non-viable solution to the Jewish question.

It instructed Argentine consuls around the world to 'deny visas, even tourist and transit visas, to all persons that could be considered to be abandoning or to have abandoned their country of origin as undesirables or having been expelled, whatever the motive for their expulsion'. In the dark climate of prewar Europe, Argentine diplomats knew the clumsily worded order defined one particular group of humanity over any other: the 'undesirable' Jews expelled from their homes by the German Nazis and Italian Fascists.

The order anticipated that Jewish refugees were unlikely to reveal their true status before hard-nosed Argentine diplomats and advised consuls to apply their own 'conscientiousness and sound criteria' when evaluating borderline cases. To ensure that they erred on the side of rigour, Directive 11 warned that the zeal applied to each evaluation would enable the Foreign Ministry to 'establish the functionary's aptitude for the post'. In other words, their jobs were on the line if any 'undesirables' slipped through the filter. 'These instructions are strictly confidential and must not for any reason be referred to before the public or before the authorities of the country of posting,' the order concluded.[70]

Directive 11 did not come alone. It was issued secretly to underpin new publicly announced restrictions to Argentina's hitherto fairly benevolent Immigration Law. This tightening of the cordon around the country's borders was decided on because Buenos Aires correctly feared that the persecution of the Jews in Europe would push them towards Argentina, where a sizeable Jewish community already existed. First of all, Decree 8972 lifted the quaint exemption from visas that first-class passengers had enjoyed until then, based on the belief that immigrants only travelled second- or third-class. Many Jews and even Communists had discovered the first-class loophole, the government realized, and it was time to plug it. Secondly, and more importantly, a new system was introduced, starting in October, whereby only the Immigration Office would have the authority to authorize landing permits. From now on Immigration officials in

Buenos Aires would judge applications on a case-by-case basis, relying on the personal information forwarded by the Argentine consulates in Europe. Consuls therefore lost their discretionary power to stamp visas based on their own judgement.

Pandemonium broke loose on 30 July when the decree was made public. Argentine consulates around the world were flooded with applications from Jews wishing to get in before the October deadline. In Buenos Aires the Immigration Office was also bombarded with applications for landing permits presented by Jews in Argentina for their persecuted relatives in Europe. Expecting this rush, Argentina had taken pre-emptive measures. As well as the secret Directive 11, on 12 July Argentine consulates were secretly instructed to apply the October changes as if they were already in force. The day the decree was issued the Immigration Office stopped issuing landing permits altogether, and by 25 August it took the more expedient course of simply closing its doors to the public.

There was some mild opposition to the decree in Argentina. In Congress a small group of legislators demanded explanations, particularly concerning instructions to consuls to ascertain the religion of applicants. Foreign Minister Cantilo defended the new restrictions, saying that refugees could not be considered immigrants and should therefore not be admitted. The restrictions were also defended by Conservative legislators, including future Peronist vice-president Vicente Solano Lima, who questioned the legitimacy of any Jewish presence in Argentina at all. 'We don't want the ghetto here,' he brayed. When a vote was taken in December over whether Congress should consider 'actively cooperating with other governments to further the arrival of Jewish emigrants and their settlement in this country', too few votes could be raised to bring the issue to the floor.

But there was no concerted effort by the large Jewish community in Argentina to oppose the new decree. No protest march was organized to match the week-long business strike that a Jewish umbrella group, the Delegation of Argentine-Israelite Associations, initiated at the end of November when news of the *Kristallnacht* atrocities in Germany reached Argentina. Alarmingly enough, on that occasion the Argentine authorities reacted by sending out the police to draw up a checklist of businesses that had closed in sympathy with the Jews. The Foreign Ministry in Berlin received a detailed report stating that 1,474 stores had shut their doors. Too much of the Argentine press was in 'Jewish hands', the German embassy in Buenos Aires concluded. For the local Jewish community, aware that it was under such ominous surveillance, immigration took a back seat to the more immediate threats of rising anti-Semitism and the growing Nazi presence in Argentina. Finally, the well-entrenched nationalist elements in the country won the day. 'The Semitic invasion must be opposed,' trumpeted the nationalist paper *La Fronda*. The combined effect of Directive 11 and Decree 8972 was calamitous. Immigration to Argentina fell by almost half. The number of legal Jewish immigrants plummeted from 4,919 in 1938 to 1,873 in 1939.

Safe refuge was not guaranteed even to those Jews who managed to slip through the net. On 25 February 1939 the SS *Conte Grand* docked at the port of Buenos Aires carrying 68 refugees. A few days later tearful relatives saw it pull away again carrying its precious load back to Europe. On the same day the SS *General San Martín* arrived with 27 refugees, of whom only two were allowed to stay. Identical scenes were repeated time and again during the war. Surviving records show that during 1939 alone some 200 Jews on 23 different ships were dispatched back to Europe. The actual number may have been far higher.[71]

Despite instructions never to refer to the existence of Directive 11, some consuls did mention it in their communications with the Foreign Ministry. Thus in August 1942 the consul in Barcelona informed Buenos Aires that a group of 27 Jewish refugees including children who had obtained visas from Paraguay and Chile were seeking 'transit' visas for Argentina, so that they could travel to their final destinations overland by train. The consul felt it his duty to make sure these visas were denied because of 'their race' and because of Directive 11. He also wished to warn Buenos Aires of the 'migratory movement of Hebrew families from Central Europe to our neighbouring countries'. Argentine consuls posted in those countries should be careful, the consul said. The Foreign Ministry responded with instructions not to issue visas to the group and to forward all such cases in future directly to Buenos Aires.[72]

Directive 11 was followed by other secret restrictions. In November 1939, for example, Foreign Minister Cantilo instructed consuls to refrain completely from forwarding any Jewish applications to Buenos Aires. Cantilo reminded the consuls that Jews should not even receive tourist visas. Some Jews were filling in application forms at various consulates simultaneously, the minister warned, fudging their data in different ways in the hope that one application might slip past the steely eye of officials in Buenos Aires. These new orders obviously reflect the zeal invested in preventing Jews from entering Argentina. But they also stand witness to the fact that many consuls were charging bribes for entry visas, and that Buenos Aires was aware and displeased.[73]

Selling visas to Jews became a kind of cottage industry for some Argentine diplomats. While this was many notches in the scale of infamy below the kind of ransom extracted by the Nazis, the Argentines based their extortion on providing loopholes to their own directives against the Jews. And while the ransom money extracted by the Nazis went partly to state coffers, Argentina's diplomats operated mostly on their own account, cashing in on the century's most sordid business opportunity.

The Argentine consulate in Milan attracted a great deal of trade, according to Eugenia Lustig, an Italian Jew from Turin who, with her Milanese husband, managed to obtain an entry visa there in 1939. The Lustigs were fortunately high-status professionals. Mrs Lustig was a doctor, her husband a Pirelli executive. 'We couldn't work because of Mussolini's race laws,' she told me. 'The Italians made us let go of the domestic help, two sisters, with us for 30 years, who couldn't understand why. The Italian police took our radio because they didn't want us listening to the BBC at night. The building superintendents were all Fascist spies. Then the Germans came. After that, you died.'

The Milan consulate became a rendezvous point for Jews of many nationalities on their way to the United States or South America. 'It was always full of people, Jews from Germany, Poland, passing through Italy,' said Lustig, who was in her late twenties at the time. 'There weren't many native Italian Jews but they were all trying to get to Argentina. A great number were fleeing Central Europe. It was a terrible moment. I arrived in Buenos Aires in August, just four days before the war started.'

Many were turned away at the consulate, either because they could not afford the bribe or because Directive 11 was being applied. 'Jews were clearly not wanted, it wasn't said expressly but it was talked about. So much so that many people went instead to Ecuador, Peru, Bolivia, Paraguay, countries that did issue visas, moving from there little by little to Argentina.'

Among the Jews in Milan word got around that bribes had to be paid. 'What price for an Argentine visa today?' was the standard question on the street outside the consulate. 'But the real and foremost problem was, they didn't want Jews,' recalled Lustig.

The refugee from Turin went on to become one of Argentina's leading cancer experts, but not before being subjected to additional humiliation: 'After the war Perón still didn't want to recognise my Italian medical degree.' Unable to open a private practice, Lustig applied herself to pure scientific research, at which she excelled. One day Perón's health minister, Ramón Carrillo, called her on the phone. 'He said he was sending a young man over who wished to look at the research I was doing.' The young man turned out to be a recent arrival from Germany. But he didn't stay long at Lustig's laboratory. He had to leave early to attend his private practice. 'I have a medical permit signed by the minister,' the smiling German explained.[74]

My grandfather Santos Goñi, who had served as Argentine consul in San Francisco, Vienna and Genoa during the 1920s and 1930s, was well aware of the existence of the secret directive and applied it rigorously during the early 1940s when he served at the Argentine consulate in Bolivia. The daughters of Eduardo Labougle, Argentina's ambassador to Berlin during the 1930s, also clearly recall the existence

of the secret order and the headaches it caused their father. Neither of
these two diplomats could have been considered pro-Nazi or anti-
Semitic, but they did combine a sincere dislike of the Nazis with a
marked absence of sensitivity towards the plight of the Jews. They
were both career diplomats imbued with an old-school sense of obe-
dience. And the orders they received were very clear.

My grandfather, posted to La Paz from 1939 to 1944, had to deal
with a large number of requests from Jews who wished to enter
Argentina from Bolivia. Dismayed by the difficulties in obtaining
visas for Argentina in Europe, many Jews travelled to neighbouring
countries and sought to enter surreptitiously from there. My grandfather was particularly struck by the case of a beautiful young woman
who emptied a purse of jewels on his desk and, failing to impress him
this way, stripped off her dress and offered her naked body in return
for admission.

Unable to get around my grandfather and Directive 11 in Bolivia,
Jews resorted to other means. Many died attempting to cross the
border with Argentina on foot, murdered for their belongings or abandoned to their fate by the guides they had paid to lead them over.
Others resorted to the safer method of bribing train inspectors and
border guards to allow them to ride hidden in the wagons crossing to
Argentina. One of Perón's closest friends and collaborators, the Nazi-
saluting General Juan Pistarini, got wind of the fact that Jews were
using the trains and moved to block their access. Another close associate, Colonel Juan Filomeno Velazco, who was chief of the Federal
Police, ordered an investigation into 'the gang leaders bringing Jews
into the country'.[75]

Ambassador Labougle in Berlin, posted in the eye of the storm, had
to deal with singularly painful problems produced by the secret order.
He found it difficult to get his consuls to apply Directive 11 at all. The
ambassador suffered venomous criticism, particularly from his consul
in Hamburg, Bartolomé Daneri, who felt he was a martyr to
Labougle's punctiliousness. Ambassadors in other European cities
were allowing their consuls to grow fat on money extorted from the
Jews, and Daneri was peeved at being excluded. 'Father knew the

consuls wanted to profit from the secret order and had forbidden them to charge the Jews for visas,' recalled his two daughters during an interview for this book almost 60 years later. Nonetheless, it was well known in Hamburg that the Argentine consulate sold visas to Jews at 5,000 Reichsmarks apiece.

The ambassador's insistence that the directive be obeyed did not stem from any Nazi sympathies. In fact, his career was cut short partly because of his failure to toe the covert pro-Axis line followed by successive Argentine governments. 'When father returned from official receptions in Berlin, he and mother, both still in their gala clothes, would send off ciphered cables to Buenos Aires warning of the Nazi threat,' his daughters recalled. 'But the cables ended up in the Foreign Ministry waste paper basket.'

Labougle resigned from his diplomatic career in 1942 precisely because he disagreed with Argentina's 'neutrality' in the war. While the Foreign Ministry archives still hold many of the cables in which he correctly warned of the growing Nazi threat and the effort by Berlin to indoctrinate German citizens in Argentina, others have 'disappeared' down some dark government channels. One cable in particular, dated 1940, warning Buenos Aires that a personal friend of Adolf Hitler was entering Argentina from neighbouring Chile, was removed from the Foreign Ministry files altogether and is now hidden in the restricted-access basement of the Ministry of the Interior.[76]

Other diplomats had their own peculiar proposals for slowing the growth of the Jewish community in Argentina. In August 1941 a plea by the British government for 20 Jewish German children residing in Britain to be allowed to join their relatives in Argentina failed miserably. Argentine ambassador Tomás Le Breton refused to issue them visas. An attempt at personal intervention by Lord Winterton, a personal friend of Le Breton's, failed to sway him. Jewish children 'were exactly the people whom the Argentine government did not want to have in the country as they would eventually grow up and would help to increase the Jewish population by propagation,' Le Breton argued – as Winterton informed the Foreign Office. 'In fact, he said emphatically that he would only grant visas to them if we were prepared to have them sterilised before they went there, a task which I told him was quite beyond our powers to effect.'[77]

The secret orders made it practically impossible for Jewish refugees to enter Argentina except through circuitous illegal routes. 'After 1941 hardly anybody else was able to get in,' recalls Marcelo Fuhrmann, a Jew from Vienna whose brother had been among the last to slip into Argentina in 1938; he himself had to wait until after the war to obtain a visa. Immigration Office statistics back Fuhrmann up. The number of second- and third-class transatlantic passengers who were willing to state their religion as Jewish upon arrival in Buenos Aires plunged from 2,006 in 1941 to a dismal 60 in 1942, falling further to only 26 in 1943 and to one solitary passenger by 1944.[78]

Both the US State Department and the British Foreign Office were aware of the widespread practice of selling visas to Jews. 'Among the consular officers in Europe such graft was the rule rather than the exception,' the American embassy in Buenos Aires reported in 1943. Although consuls took less than 1,000 pesos a case, officials at the Argentine Foreign Ministry received considerably larger amounts. Businessman Adolfo Hirsch, president of the Jewish Philanthropic Society in Buenos Aires, which aided Jewish refugees arriving from Europe, told the American embassy that Foreign Ministry officials received up to 30,000 or 40,000 pesos 'to arrange for the entry of a group of Jewish refugees'. The embassy had learned independently that the going rate was between 2,000 and 3,000 pesos for a single person and about 5,000 for a married couple. 'The immigration of the majority of refugees appears to be in violation of the strict Argentine immigration laws and regulations,' the embassy reported.[79]

The British ambassador to Buenos Aires reported to London that bribes of between 5,000 and 10,000 pesos were going to a long chain of officials. 'This traffic, which has enriched many with influence in Argentine political circles from the President's immediate entourage to lesser officials in the Ministry of Agriculture, the police and the port authorities, has helped only those whose relatives were ready and able to pay bribes,' Sir David Kelly wrote in April 1943.[80]

The Argentine consul in Barcelona, Miguel Alfredo Molina, seems to have run a particularly brisk business. The American military attaché in Spain, Colonel Wendell G. Johnson, drafted a Military Intelligence report about his activities in October 1945. Molina was the longest-serving consul in Spain, having been first posted in Seville in 1928. An obviously intrepid character, he had acquired the passports of some 70 Argentines looked upon as 'Reds' who had been detained at the Miranda POW and refugee camp, ostensibly to return them after checking their authenticity. But instead Molina put the passports up for sale to Nazis and Jews indiscriminately. Colonel Johnson reported that the passports were selling for 35,000 pesetas each. Johnson was obviously alarmed by Molina's activities. He suggested that 'there may be justification for an official protest to be made'. Moreover, he had on his desk files on Molina that confirmed he was a close collaborator of the Nazis. A 1944 report showed that Molina had formed part of an 'espionage and smuggling organization' involved in the transfer to Germany of vital war materials such as wolfram and platinum as well as gold.[81]

The diplomat rumoured to have raised the largest amount of money from the Jews was also one of the most distinguished Argentina ever had. Miguel Ángel Cárcano, while he was Argentina's ambassador to Paris from 1938 until the occupation by the Nazis, is said to have pocketed one million dollars selling visas to the rich Jews who sought refuge in France. His trade in visas was the talk of Argentina's diplomatic circles during the 1940s and 1950s. After Paris, Cárcano served as ambassador in London until 1946, where he enjoyed great standing.[82]

Who served the greater good, the diplomats who were willing to stamp the passports of Jews in exchange for a bribe or those who remained uncorrupted? The fact that Nazism gave rise to such unwholesome alternatives underlies the intrinsic evil of the system. In this case, those who took the bribes saved lives.[83]

Prior to the coup he led on 4 June 1943, Perón's writings reflected a fair degree of anti-Semitism. In May that year the colonel resorted with ease to a proto-Nazi vocabulary when he penned two 'strictly confidential' reports for his secret GOU lodge of colonels. In a report on 'the domestic situation' he subscribed to the notion of a vast Jewish–Communist–Capitalist plot against Argentina, and found 'hidden forces' and 'foreign agents of all types and with all kinds of purposes, in charge of sabotage against the State'. These agents were 'in league with . . . corrupt politicians, newspapers, Jews, foreign executives, etc.' In short, 'the whole country has been penetrated'.

Perón's analysis of the international situation claimed that the other South American nations who sided with the Allies had traded their independence for the hope of 'sharing in the spoils should the plutocracies manage to win the war', a victory he apparently deemed doubtful. In a train of thought which echoed Goyeneche's in the meetings he was holding in Europe, he considered Argentina 'a mediator in this conflict', believing that 'our neighbours are aware of the danger of an extraordinary growth in Argentina's influence should the Axis triumph.'

This anti-Semitism carried over in the first internal memos of the GOU after the coup, which attacked masonry as 'a Jewish creation' and the Rotary Club as 'a real network of Jewish international espionage and propaganda at the service of the United States'. According to the GOU it was necessary to 'destroy the atomizing anti-Argentine germ of the diverse groups and entities at the service of the Jews and the Communists'. A nationalist document appended to these memos recommended banning the appointment of 'liberals or masons or Rotarians' to government and demanded that 'the accountant Greffier – a Jew – who has recently been appointed by the overseer of the National Education Council, must also be immediately removed'.[84]

But for all his rhetoric in the secret GOU papers, Perón steered an even course when pressures from the more anti-Semitic members of his government later rocked the ship of state. Among these was the education minister, Gustavo Martínez Suviría, who had published a string of anti-Semitic bestsellers under the pen name Hugo Wast, including the hugely successful novel *666*. Some time in 1943 the rumour began to circulate that a concentration camp for 10,000 Jews was being built by the GOU regime in the suburb of Morón, while others spoke of a concentration camp in the outlying forests of Ezeiza. There may have been some truth behind the whispers. A British intelligence agent, Abraham 'Bob' Hamwee, had managed to secure the minutes of the GOU's cabinet meetings through bribery. He thus learned that certain ministers were pressuring for a 'solution to the Jewish problem' in Argentina. According to Hamwee's confidant, it was Perón who deflated their expectations. 'Why kill the goose that lays the golden eggs?' Perón had quipped.[85]

Nevertheless, the dictatorship proved even more adamantly opposed to aiding Jewish refugees than the previous civilian government. If Directive 11 was a difficult enough obstacle for Jews to surmount, the fence rose even higher after the 1943 coup. Although there was a succession of figurehead generals in the presidential seat, the colonels pulled the strings behind the scenes, and the puppet-master was, of course, Colonel Perón. 'The consensus of persons active in Jewish rescue and relief work is that so long as the present regime remains in power, no assistance whatsoever can be expected from the Argentine government in refugee matters,' the American embassy in Buenos Aires reported to President Roosevelt's newly created War Refugee Board on 21 April 1944.[86]

The colonels appointed the Nazi-trained, skull-measuring anthropologist Santiago Peralta to head Immigration. Born in the northern wine-producing province of Mendoza in 1887, Peralta moved with his family to Buenos Aires as a young boy, where he earned a degree in anthropology at the School of Philosophy. In 1922 he began applying his measuring tape to the bodies of army conscripts for an 'anthropological' study on 'military bearing'. Later he became a school inspector and travelled as far as the Jewish colonies in the northern province of Entre Ríos. By 1932 he was studying 'applied anthropology' in Germany.[87]

Many details of his life remain obscure, but one thing is clear enough: 'Peralta was a Nazi' is the succinct description provided by one of his successors at Immigration, Héctor Ciapuscio. According to this account, Peralta was connected to military intelligence. Even into the early 1960s, Ciapuscio, as head of Immigration, was badgered covertly on Peralta's behalf to try to block immigration from Japan and the Soviet Union.[88]

The virulently anti-Semitic book Peralta published in 1943, *The Action of the Jewish People in Argentina*, reveals a plodding, schematic, militaristic brain, and could almost serve on its own as sufficient proof that racism breeds from ignorance. It remains perhaps the most violent anti-Semitic tract ever published in Argentina, appearing at a moment when news of the Nazi concentration camps was becoming public knowledge worldwide. Deeply paranoid, Peralta feared a 'Jewish conspiracy' was planning to turn his beloved country into a new homeland for the displaced Jews of Europe. 'The Immigration Office has been in their hands for a long time,' wrote Perón's race expert. 'They are the ones who instated ignorant, barbaric leaders and brought about the cessation of European immigration so that they could remain the only settlers ... This strange turn of events coincided with the fall of the Jewish regime in Germany ... They needed a new homeland for the "persecuted" from Germany and that place was our country ... and the slow, silent tide of poor Jewish immigrants continues as the Argentines find excitement in Negro music, tropical dancing, and American cinema.' And so it goes on, and on, page upon page of quasi-scientific theory and a jumble of anti-Semitic stereotypes that clearly teemed inside Peralta's head.[89]

Peralta's career flourished, despite his anti-Semitism, and when Perón assumed office as democratically elected president on 4 June 1946 he confirmed Peralta in his post, raising a clamour of protest from liberal sectors and the Jewish community. Most mind-boggling of all, in 1946 Peralta returned to the charge with his second wildly anti-Semitic book. In *The Influence of the Arab People in Argentina* he contrasted the benefits of promoting Arab immigration against the disadvantages of admitting the Jews. The Jews 'lodge like a cyst in the people where they establish themselves, and the only relationship they require is the commercial contact to exploit them.' He subscribed to the notion that the Jews should be punished for the crucifixion of Jesus, 'who preached love, sweetness and paternity [*sic*] among men, against the religion of Jehovah, which was one of punishment, hatred and fear.' Peralta's pen oozed Nazi venom. The Jews were a 'parasitic plant' backed by 'great Empires of foreign money' and by 'deranged governments'. They 'exploit the whole Argentine people'. All this published by the head of Immigration while the Nuremberg trials were getting under way in Germany. 'We won't . . . make racist distinctions, but we will choose the best within the white race, to create the Argentine we all yearn for,' he said with a straight face to the press at the time.[90]

In mid-May 1946, on the eve of Perón's presidential inauguration, the SS *Jamaica* docked at the port of Buenos Aires with 70 Jews on board. Peralta refused to let them land. Jewish organizations were incensed, and a storm of public protest erupted a few days later when Perón assumed the presidency. Voices cried out demanding Peralta's resignation. The press carried daily notices reminding Perón that Peralta was still in office and asking how much longer he would remain. 'The permanence of an anti-Semite at the head of the Immigration Office is an insult to the country,' thundered the prestigious weekly *Gobernantes*. The *New York Times* carried an editorial on the *Jamaica* affair.[91]

During that crucial first year after the end of the war Peralta mounted guard at the gates of Argentina, refusing admittance to Jews. The *Jamaica* incident did not occur in a vacuum. Already in late 1945 Peralta's attitude had frustrated the leaders of international Jewish rescue groups who had visited Buenos Aires. When they pleaded with him to grant Jews already in Argentina permission to bring their children, spouses, siblings and parents over to join them, Peralta remained unmoved, and renewed pleas in 1946 were equally unsuccessful. The matter clearly had to be taken to 'The Leader' himself, President Perón. Towards the middle of November 1946, therefore, a group of ten Jewish community representatives entered the presidential office. The issues were laid out on the table: Jewish immigration was blocked, Peralta refused to make exceptions for the reunification of Jewish families even for next-of-kin. Perón was non-committal. He promised to investigate. As it turned out, he did nothing.[92]

What was on Perón's mind during such meetings with Jewish leaders? Fortunately we know, for he discussed the 'Jewish problem' with the fugitive Nazis he gave refuge to. 'I remember one of the Germans who came to Argentina after their defeat talking to me about the Jewish problem,' Perón recalled in memoirs he privately dictated into a cassette recorder during his exile in Madrid in the late 1960s. 'How do you figure I'm going to get involved in that mess of the Jewish problem when you know very well that Hitler, with his 100 million inhabitants, couldn't solve it; what am I going to do with 20 or 25 million Argentines?' Perón asked the German. 'If the Jews live here, we can't kill them, and we can't expel them either. There's no solution but putting them to work inside the community . . . preventing them from forming separate Zionist organizations.' The president shared Peralta's preference for the Arabs, as the tapes show. 'I was great friends with the Arab community, because it was a community that was Peronist at heart, the Jews were in it out of self-interest . . . I had Arab legislators, senators, governors . . . In my judgement, the Arabs have this superiority over the Jews: that they adapt more easily, they grow roots, they meld into the culture, while the Jew is always a stranger, he doesn't integrate. Maybe it's a question of race or religion. But that's how it is.'[93]

Perón never did dismantle the noxious bureaucracy acting against the Jews. Instead he made it work in his favour. Jews started being admitted on a case-by-case basis through the personal intercession of 'good guy' Perón, with Peralta playing the 'bad guy'. On 14 February 1947 the SS *Campana* docked at the port of Buenos Aires with 47 Holocaust survivors on board. Peralta again refused to allow the Jews to disembark. The president of the DAIA Jewish organization appealed directly to Perón, catching him off guard during a meeting with Jewish leaders interested in forming a Peronist organization. Perón listened to the plea put forward by Moisés Goldman and ordered the acceptance of the Holocaust survivors. The passengers were released in a blaze of media attention and taken to the presidential mansion to thank Perón personally. Perón wasn't in, but they were received by one of his ministers. The Jewish press was ecstatic, believing that a turning-point had been reached.

But Perón's move was not humanitarian, and time proved the *Campana* gesture to be an isolated political act. That same week Perón had managed to split the Jewish community in half, creating the loyal Argentine-Israelite Organization (OIA) that received favours from him and his wife Evita. Among the prizes OIA eventually gained for its Peronist loyalty were landing permits, which it could brandish as trophies before other members of the Jewish community. The older, more traditional and independent DAIA received only scraps from Perón's table from now on. 'When you include him in business the Jew enters into it; the Jew is, above everything else, a bargainer,' Perón confided to his tape recorder in Madrid.

An angry Peralta affixed a curt note to the passenger list of the *Campana*, making it clear that it was only 'in the name of the Most Excellent President of the Nation' that he was making an 'exception' this time and allowing the Jews to disembark. But the restrictions that made Peralta's 'exception' possible were held firmly in place by Perón.[94]

Nonetheless, demands for Peralta's resignation continued to grow. Goldman of the DAIA met with Perón twice in March and April 1947 to plead for 12 Jewish refugees with transit visas to Paraguay. Political turmoil in that country prevented their going any further, and Peralta had ordered their return to Europe. The following month 14 more refugees were held on board ship for three weeks, and it was only public opinion in the US that forced Peralta to relent. At the United Nations the interception of a secret memo instructing Argentine consuls to deny visas to Jews became an issue. Then a Jewish businessman who met with Peralta to plead for a landing permit for his brother was told to pack his bags and leave while he and the Jewish community still had time. An official protest was lodged by Jewish aid and rescue groups. Finally, in June 1947, Perón bowed to the pressure and Peralta was dismissed.[95]

Yet somehow, despite the closing of the gates, part of the wave of humanity expelled from occupied Europe managed to percolate to Argentina. Estimates vary, especially in a country with such deliberately patchy record-keeping, but between 20,000 and 30,000 Jews are believed to have found a new home in Argentina between 1933 and 1945. A final tally may ultimately prove impossible because the secret directives forced most Jews to enter illegally. For 1942 to 1945, for example, there exist only 240 documented cases of legal Jewish entries. Yet figures from some Jewish rescue groups place the total for that period as high as 4,460. The possibility that some of these groups may have inflated their figures to boost donations indicates how thorny the issue is and what pitfalls await the researcher.

Even this low number is higher than those for other countries in the Western Hemisphere, including the United States. This however reflects no merit on Argentina's part. The vast majority of Jews who arrived either managed to pass themselves off as Catholics or could afford to pay the heavy bribes demanded by Argentine diplomats and Immigration officials. Whatever the final number, it will still be abysmally low compared with how many could have been saved had Argentina not implemented its secret policy against the Jews with such rigour. How many thousands more could have been rescued if any measure of generosity and basic human decency had been applied by the bureaucrats of Buenos Aires?[96]

4

THE ABANDONMENT OF
ARGENTINA'S JEWS

As well as shutting out the European Jews who fled from Hitler, Argentina proved reluctant to rescue the estimated one hundred Argentine Jews marooned on German territory. To show its good will towards the only 'neutral' nation left in the Americas, the Nazi regime had decided to spare this small group of humanity. Over and over again during the war Berlin offered Argentina the opportunity to repatriate its Jewish citizens living in Germany, France, Belgium, Holland, Italy and Greece. Foreign Minister Joachim von Ribbentrop was especially concerned about them.

Ribbentrop, a notorious Jew-hater who became the first Nazi to hang after the postwar Nuremberg trials, went out of his way for the Argentine Jews. His battle was largely with SS leader Heinrich Himmler, who could not understand why Argentina's Jews should be exempted from the 'Final Solution'. Himmler also refused to rein in his secret agents in Argentina, who were involved in all kinds of dangerous liaisons with Perón's colonels – ties which, if discovered, could force a break in relations with the Axis. The head of the Latin American department at the German Foreign Ministry, Otto Reinebeck, recalled in postwar interrogations: 'The intimate relationship of the SD to Argentine representatives had for a long time been a thorn in the flesh of the Foreign Ministry, since we feared that sooner or later an international scandal would force Argentina to change the course of its policy in regard to Germany, if only for the purpose of saving face in its relations with the Allies.' Relations with Argentina were exceedingly good. German economic interests in the country were sizeable, and Argentina was providing discreet cover for the large Nazi spy network operating in its territory. Its financial system served as a pipeline for laundering American dollars; vital war materials such as platinum, industrial diamonds, insulin, liver extract, iron, steel and other products manufactured by German firms were being smuggled in a steady stream to Germany from Argentina.[97]

Yet the country's diplomats clearly had orders from Buenos Aires not to aid Argentine Jews in Nazi-occupied Europe. In January 1943 the ambassador to Vichy, Ricardo Olivera, was called in by the Germans to discuss the repatriation of some 15 Argentine Jews living in France. The Germans wanted to let them go, and gave the ambassador three months to arrange their evacuation. Six months later they were still puzzling over why the ambassador had not taken up their offer.[98]

The Germans were growing impatient. They began to press the Argentine embassy in Berlin for results. 'It is desirable that all Argentine citizens belonging to the Jewish race leave German territories . . . The Foreign Ministry would consider it as an act of special courtesy if the Argentine embassy would cause all Argentine Jews to return to their homeland,' states one surviving Nazi document. The Germans had compiled lists of Argentine Jews in Greece, Holland and elsewhere to speed up their evacuation. All they required was approval from Buenos Aires.[99]

In March the invitation to evacuate all Argentine Jews from Nazi-occupied territories was formally extended to Argentine embassy secretary Luis H. Irigoyen. The tall, handsome Argentine was extremely well-connected, a fluent German-speaker, a diplomat's diplomat, rumoured to be the natural son of Argentine former president Hipólito Irigoyen and a Viennese lover. Irigoyen's lack of enthusiasm was so disconcerting to the Germans that they mused afterwards that 'in Buenos Aires there was absolutely no understanding of this matter.' All the same, just to be on the safe side, the

Foreign Ministry sent Adolf Eichmann a reminder to spare Argentine Jews from the killing.[100]

Not much later, around 29 April, Irigoyen was again invited to the Foreign Ministry and asked whether Argentina could arrange the repatriation of six Argentine Jews in Salonika. Eberhardt von Thadden, the diplomat in charge of liaising with Eichmann's office for Jewish Affairs, stated it was 'inconceivable' that these Argentines should remain after Greece had been 'cleansed' of all its Jews. Seven Argentine Jews in Belgium and others in Holland were in the same situation. The Germans wanted Buenos Aires to arrange their swift departure. Irigoyen played for time, his mind surely recalling the secret instructions contained in Directive 11. 'For Argentine Jews it is difficult to be transported home,' he told von Thadden vaguely.[101]

In July 1943, when the Polish community in Krakow had been all but destroyed, 59 Jews from Argentina were still alive there. Eichmann's office forwarded the documents of 16 of them to the Foreign Ministry, and Irigoyen was again invited to von Thadden's office. The diplomat took a cursory look at the papers. 'They're forgeries,' he concluded, stating that 'the Argentine embassy has of course no interest in the bearers of these fake documents.'[102]

The Argentine embassy in Berlin was actually packed with Nazi sympathizers, some of them in the pocket of Himmler's secret service, such as Naval Attaché Eduardo Ceballos, who was a constant visitor to SD headquarters in Berlin. The attitude of these Argentines contrasted sharply with that of the Brazilian ambassador, who 'during the Allied air raids became delirious with joy, even running into his garden and flashing a lantern to help the bombers', as the Nazi secret service discovered. Perhaps the only exception was Chargé d'Affaires Luis Luti, who made some few attempts to at least ease the situation of Argentine Jews. Luti managed to obtain an exemption from 'Jewish rations' for Argentine Jews living 'in the Reich and in the Protectorates of Bohemia and Moravia'. In his report to Buenos Aires, he was exultant: 'Jewish citizens from the remaining neutral countries are subjected to the rationing for German Jews which implies the near total suppression of food.' Ribbentrop had acceded to Luti's demands even in the face of the 'almost unyielding opposition' of Himmler's office. 'This arrangement, which is a complete diversion from legal regulations, has been made only because of the desire to please the Argentine embassy,' said Ribbentrop's ministry. Even the little that Luti did got him into trouble. Agents of the Nazi secret service placed him under surveillance, opened his mail and spread harmful rumours about him. In Buenos Aires, his superiors didn't like him any better. Luti 'was not pro-Nazi and therefore trusted neither by the Argentines nor the SD', Reinebeck said in his postwar interrogations.[103]

In March 1943, apparently in response to Luti's appeals, Ribbentrop urged Himmler to exempt Argentine Jews from stringent anti-Semitic rules, in view of the country's neutrality. Besides, there were not that many Argentine Jews, he argued. Ribbentrop was actually going to a lot of trouble for nothing. In September 1943, Ambassador Olivera in Vichy wired Argentina to ask whether he should continue his efforts to arrange exit permits; he received a negative reply. Securing permission to leave was up to the Jews themselves, Buenos Aires responded.[104]

Around 21 January 1944 Ribbentrop moved again to protect Argentina's Jews from Himmler. This time he offered them exit visas. Argentina was on the verge of breaking off relations with Germany, and Ribbentrop had been alarmed by an order from Himmler for the arrest of all foreign Jews, including Argentines, in Holland. The Jews were to be taken to the concentration camp of Bergen-Belsen, where foreign nationals were held in transit. Von Thadden immediately phoned SS Major Rolf Günther, Eichmann's deputy, asking for the Argentine Jews to be spared.[105]

Clearly possession of Argentine citizenship was a life-saver for Jews in Nazi Germany, but it was not a permanent privilege. Shortly after Ribbentrop's new appeal it ran out. On 26 January 1944, under heavy pressure from the Allies over the connections between Himmler's secret service and Perón's colonels, precisely as Ribbentrop had feared, Argentina finally broke off diplomatic relations with the Reich. Hitler was furious, and the very next day cables from Eichmann and from RSHA chief Ernst Kaltenbrunner flew out of Berlin rescinding the exemptions for Argentine Jews. 'All Jews and Jewesses of Argentine citizenship are to be arrested at once. The assets of the arrested must be secured. These Jews must be taken immediately, under guard, to Bergen-Belsen internment camp,' read the cables.[106]

Ribbentrop flew into a rage when news of the diplomatic break was confirmed. He penned a letter to Himmler putting the blame 'squarely on the SD' for the loss of Argentina. 'The letter closed with the remark that the Foreign Minister could no longer bear the responsibility for foreign policy if the activity of the SD in foreign countries were not radically limited and with immediate effect,' recalled Reinebeck after the war.[107]

Even after the break Ribbentrop continued to appeal to Himmler and Eichmann to spare Argentina's Jews and to refrain from the 'Aryanization' of their property, fearing that Buenos Aires might take retaliatory measures against the 80,000 German citizens in Argentina. Ribbentrop's appeal was only moderately successful. The Argentines were taken to Bergen-Belsen anyhow, although for a time at least they were granted preferential treatment. After the war, Bergen-Belsen survivor Rudolph Levy, who arrived at the camp in January 1944, recalled having met 35 Eastern European Jews with Argentine citizenship there.[108]

In France the Nazi authorities began to get itchy about the 'Aryanization' of the property belonging to certain wealthy Jews that Ribbentrop had postponed. 'I am asking whether . . . the Aryanization of ETAM companies can now take place, since the relations between the Reich and Argentina have been fundamentally changed,' the Nazi representative for economic affairs in France cabled Berlin in February. Two weeks later Ribbentrop replied recommending caution, since Buenos Aires could take much worse measures against German property in Argentina.[109]

After the break, von Thadden drew up a final tally of how many Argentine Jews had been interned and how many remained free. Out of the estimated one hundred, a total of 51 had been identified by name. Of these, 34 had been arrested at Himmler's orders and were either on their way to or already at Bergen-Belsen. Their release 'cannot be counted on', Thadden regretted. The remaining 17 identified Argentines were apparently under arrest in Holland. Elsewhere, 'no response yet from Greece and Italy, meaning that it is possible that the number of interned Argentine Jews may rise above fifty-one.'

Von Thadden suggested making one last approach to the Argentine regime over the repatriation of its Jews. The Argentine diplomats were still in Germany and Argentine interests were now being represented by the Swedish embassy in Berlin, just as German interests were now represented by the Swiss embassy in Buenos Aires. The repatriation of Jews from all other countries had taken place already and had gone smoothly. Argentina remained 'the only state in the world' failing to repatriate, he reported.[110]

After that the records peter out, apart from brief typed and handwritten notes from von Thadden that indicate that the Argentine Jews may still have been alive in April 1944. Poor von Thadden, and poor misguided Ribbentrop. The Argentine Jews they struggled so hard to save from Himmler, Kaltenbrunner and Eichmann turned out to be of no interest at all to Perón and his colonels far away in South America.[111]

5

EXTORTION OF THE JEWS

Not only did Argentine diplomats benefit financially from the plight of the European Jews, but Argentina itself became a laundering centre for the money raised by the Nazis' own extortion racket. The Nazis issued exit visas to wealthy Jews in occupied countries against the deposit of large sums of foreign currency. Those threatened with deportation to concentration camps had to persuade friends or relatives in the Western Hemisphere to transfer the required ransom to banks in neutral Switzerland, Portugal or Argentina. Sometimes the ransoms were paid directly to the Reichsbank, at other times even to the German embassy in Buenos Aires. Behind the scheme were the officials in charge of the 'Final Solution', Heinrich Himmler and Adolf Eichmann, acting under the authorization of Adolf Hitler himself.

At first Hitler wanted to exchange 'foreign' Jews for German citizens interned in Palestine or the US, whom he imagined settling the newly occupied territories in the East. The Bergen-Belsen concentration camp was built near Hanover precisely in order to assemble Jews for such exchanges. As the war intensified and Germany's reserves began to dwindle, however, these schemes quickly degenerated into 'selling' Jews to obtain foreign currency. The Nazis preferred victims with sizeable assets abroad or with relatives in the

Americas who could be squeezed. When Jewish emigration was out-lawed in 1942, some Reich officials strongly continued to advocate the usefulness of such 'Jews for money' deals. Himmler and Eichmann, although less inclined to spare lives, also continued to engage in these activities. Ribbentrop's foreign ministry, meanwhile, was sidelined from the extortion racket and continued to lobby in favour of the original idea of exchanging Jews for German citizens, pestering Himmler and Eichmann to keep foreign Jews alive for this purpose.[112]

In December 1942, Hitler officially authorized Himmler to release individual Jews if enough currency could be obtained. The plan was to free only elderly Jews – no Polish Jews, who had seen too much, and no intellectuals, no matter how high the ransom offered. Hitler was endorsing a practice already prevalent in Eichmann's Office IV-B4 in Berlin, which had been selling exit permits at 100,000 Swiss francs each for Jews who combined the ideal conditions of age, money and a low 'security risk'. The payments from relatives and acquain-tances in the United States, Argentina and other South American countries were habitually routed through Swiss middlemen.

As the war dragged on, only Jews with Nazi connections were able to qualify for ransom. Sometimes these contacts passed through Himmler's secret service. By 1943 Reichsmarshal Hermann Göring was taking art works in exchange for the release of certain Jews, and during 1944, acting through Swiss and Argentine intermediaries, Himmler also received paintings in one documented case of a five-member family that left for Spain.[113]

A large number of the Jews who were victims of extortion lived in the Netherlands, where nearly 400 ransom demands amounting to some 35 million Swiss francs have been documented. At least three of the highest-ranking accomplices, Adolf Eichmann, SS Major-General Hans Fischböck and SS Captain Erich Rajakowitsch, later escaped to Argentina. All had played vital roles in Austria after its annexation by Hitler; Eichmann as head of the Office for Jewish Emigration in Vienna, Rajakowitsch as his most trusted aide, and Fischböck as min-ister of commerce, which involved drawing up anti-Jewish legislation.

Fischböck and Rajakowitsch took up similar posts in Holland. Rajakowitsch plundered a fortune in Jewish assets while Fischböck set up a foreign currency protection unit that worked closely with the Reichsbank and the RSHA in the plundering of Jewish assets and in Jewish extortion.[114]

When Eichmann ordered the deportation of 40,000 Dutch Jews in June 1942, his representatives in Holland set about the systematic extortion of the wealthier members of the community. Eichmann's office in the Netherlands kept a register of 'Angebotsjuden', Jews able to pay for their lives. It was known as the 'Frielingsdorfs Liste', after Margarete Frielingsdorf, the specialist in charge of such questions at Eichmann's office in The Hague. There were other 'lists' too, one of them administered by Jan Jacob Weissmann, who had an arrangement with Eichmann's representative whereby, in return for a hefty fee, he received applications from wealthy Jews. The dossiers he passed on to Frielingsdorf prevented the deportation to Bergen-Belsen of those who could get their names on the 'Weissmann list'. Another list-maker was Erich Puttkammer, who in return for gold, diamonds or jewels obtained special stamps (soon to be known as the 'Puttkammer stamp') from Fischböck's currency commando, sparing the wealthy Jews who could afford them from deportation to Westerbork transit camp. Puttkammer also allowed his account at the Rotterdamsche Bank in Amsterdam to be used to channel ransoms paid to the Nazis.[115]

Although the relevant documentation was destroyed by the fleeing Nazis at the end of the war, one ransom demand from Eichmann's department routed through Weissmann survives at the National Archives in Maryland. It demanded 120,000 Swiss francs for the family of Salomon Mayer. 'I request that the necessary amount of foreign exchange be transferred to the Foreign Exchange Section of the Reichshauptbank III C, Berlin,' reads the note of 21 October 1942, signed by Frielingsdorf. 'Upon receipt of the amount of foreign exchange the migration documents will be delivered.' The document was procured by the American consulate in Basel. Mayer was able to meet his ransom, plus an extra 50,000 francs along the way, and left

Holland in December 1943. The resultant sums were usually deposited at the Union de Banques Suisses in Zurich. To avoid Allied censorship, correspondence between Jews, intermediaries and banks went through Argentina and other third countries. About half the Jews wished to escape to the US, the other half to Argentina.[116]

The Ministry of Economic Warfare in London initiated the battle against the Nazi extortion scheme, inviting the US to join Britain in making public the facts and the identities of the persons involved. By October 1942 London had identified the two main intermediaries as Arthur Wiederkehr, a ruthless Zurich lawyer who raised 2 million francs in ransom money for the Nazis, and Walter Büchi, a 'young Aryan Swiss' who had a knack for delivering his clients into the hands of the Gestapo after collecting their money. They both worked in tandem with Eichmann's office in The Hague and with Fischböck's currency commando, and had personal contact with Eichmann in Berlin. The Argentine consulates at the Spanish port of San Sebastián and in Bilbao were involved in the business as well. They provided Argentine visas on the basis of which transit passes were issued by the Spanish consul in the Netherlands. Once German officials were notified that the payment had been made they issued a Nazi exit permit for the Jewish applicant.[117]

Most of the ransoms seem to have been handled by Wiederkehr, who shuttled between Zurich, Berlin and Holland on his errands and was considered by US diplomats in Switzerland to be 'one of the arch malefactors in this traffic'. The Swiss authorities viewed his activities tolerantly. His work was greatly simplified by the ease with which he was able to obtain courier letters from the Berne government and German visas for his travels. The Swiss police knew Wiederkehr 'very well and are fully acquainted with his activity', American diplomats in Berne heard, along with the rumour that he travelled under a Swiss diplomatic passport.[118]

Wiederkehr allegedly charged 125,000 francs for rescuing Jews from Holland. In the case of a Jewish furrier in Amsterdam he reportedly arranged for the transfer of the man's entire fortune in return for securing his escape to the US. His biggest coup seems to have been the Hirschler and Alexander families, valued at 500,000 Swiss francs each, ransoms extorted in direct combination with Berlin. Wiederkehr finally settled for 900,000 Argentine pesos payable in Buenos Aires.[119]

The Zurich lawyer's Nazi contacts were well placed for the job at hand. Wiederkehr discussed at least one ransom case personally with Eichmann, that of the banker Hans Kroch. He had escaped to Amsterdam, and through Wiederkehr had offered part of his fortune to the Germans in return for exit permits for his family. But Kroch's wife was arrested by the Gestapo trying to leave Holland without an exit permit and deported to Ravensbrück forced labour camp in Germany. Wiederkehr travelled to Berlin to put her case to Eichmann, who offered little hope, saying that persons in concentration camps could only be released after the end of the war. Wiederkehr advised Kroch to leave promptly with his daughters for Switzerland and to head from there to Argentina. The meeting with Eichmann had been arranged by SS officer Hermann Quetting, Obersturmbannführer of general economic affairs at the Reich Security Main Office, who had entrusted four ransom cases to Wiederkehr, including the Hirschler and Alexander extortion.[120]

Walter Büchi meanwhile was a Swiss liaison agent for Fischböck's foreign currency commando. He was intensely disliked by the British diplomats in Switzerland, who in their communications referred to him as 'a despicable person' and an 'unsavoury intermediary'. Büchi asked for 50,000 francs per person plus a 5 per cent commission for himself. Of the documented 26 ransom cases he was involved in, however, most were arrested by the Gestapo and sent to concentration camps after having paid Büchi in diamonds or foreign currency. Büchi caught the attention of the British when in the late summer of 1942 he talked the Swiss banker Paul Dreyfus into raising 5 million Swiss francs to ransom 700 Jews in Holland. Büchi had discussed the idea with Fischböck's currency commando, which saw an opportunity to raise foreign exchange for the Reichsbank, and then he apparently travelled to Berlin to fine-tune the details. Swiss banks were to keep the sum in escrow until the group of Jews reported to the Swiss consul in Lisbon.[121]

The idea did not work out, but this did not prevent Büchi and Wiederkehr from venturing into other fields, including obtaining a Rembrandt for Göring's collection, apparently in collusion with Göring's art supplier Alois Miedl. Wiederkehr was also reportedly involved in a case in which the Busch family of Amsterdam paid for their escape with paintings that went to Himmler, acting through the complicated mediation of a certain Clemens Oppenheimer, who obtained Argentine visas from the firm of Aguila in Buenos Aires.[122]

The communications of these Swiss intermediaries with their targets in the US, Argentina and other South American nations were handled by the Amsterdam tourist agency Hoyman & Schuurman, which triangulated the ransom demands through the Geneva booking agency Natural Lecoultre, apparently an unwitting partner in the gruesome business. Since it was impossible to cable direct from Amsterdam to the American continent, the Swiss agency forwarded the messages without asking questions, despite being puzzled that payment for the expensive telegrams came through with extraordinary rapidity and that the letters from Holland, sometimes marked with the numbers of four German censors, were delivered with unusual speed. These cables most often arrived out of the blue to relatives in the Americas, such as one received by Max Cain in Chile in October 1942: 'At request Travel Office Hoyman Schuurman Amsterdam ... necessity of emigrating for Harry Mendel 16 Okeghemstraat Amsterdam personally now extremely urgent ... exit permit for him obtainable when one hundred thousand Swiss francs free money paid in Switzerland ... for further details and information wire Doctor Wiederkehr.'[123]

Although the extortion racket had ramifications in almost all the neutral countries, including Spain and Portugal, the most energetic efforts to stamp it out came from the Allies in the two neutral countries most actively involved, Switzerland and Argentina. In 1942 British intelligence spotted the arrival in Buenos Aires of the enterprising Czech engineer Pavel Eisner. This businessman quickly made the acquaintance of 'high Argentine officials', drawing the attention of British

Security Coordination in New York, which had been tipped off by the Czech government in exile in London. Eisner was linked to an anti-Communist group set up in May 1942 by the head of the Russian Orthodox Church in Argentina, Archpriest Constantin Izrastzoff.

Concerned about its possible connection with the Nazi extortion scheme, British intelligence obtained the charter of the organization formed. It was headquartered at the blue-domed Orthodox church in Buenos Aires, and raised funds for the 'resurrection of Russia' and the ejection of Stalin. But until such ambitious plans could be effected, it planned to rescue 'nationalist' Russians in Europe, especially those in the former territory of the Soviet Union. Izrastzoff's plan included the appointment of a Red Cross representative to the directorship of the committee, foreshadowing the vital role the Red Cross would play in rescuing 'nationalists' after Hitler's defeat in Europe.[124]

Argentina's Immigration Office gave the Russian Orthodox organization ample leeway to bring large numbers of White Russians – 'whose morality is based on Christian anti-Marxist ideology' – into the country. This did not sit well with Argentina's diplomats, who suspected that Izrastzoff was somehow connected to the under-the-counter sale of landing permits to Jews. They especially mistrusted his 'formidable influence' at the Immigration Office, although their criticism was curbed by the belief that the Archpriest also acted under 'confidential orders from the Vatican'.[125]

Eisner was on close terms with the vice-president of the Russian committee, Sofia Lidska Krupensky, a woman with 'an unfavourable reputation' who claimed to be a Russian princess. It was Krupensky who opened doors in Argentine official circles for Eisner. The British suspected she was connected to the German embassy in Buenos Aires, the kind of link that made her practically a Nazi spy in Allied eyes. Eisner moved comfortably in Buenos Aires, approaching well-to-do exiled Czechs, saying he was in contact with a 'big business' group in Europe, and offering to purchase large concerns in the Nazi-occupied Czech territories – vanadium mines, for example. What British intelligence really wanted to uncover was the identity of Eisner's contact in Europe. This mystery man, a 'true enemy of the Nazis', Eisner claimed, was nonetheless linked 'with the most important officials of present-day Germany, who are indebted to him from the pre-Nazi time and feel indebted to him even now'. Eisner's contact offered to rescue even those Jews 'who have already been deported', at a fee ranging from 100,000 to 300,000 Argentine pesos for groups of up to five persons.[126]

Since before the war the Germans had been using Argentina to either acquire or launder badly needed foreign currency. Buenos Aires had become a preferred destination for 'the looted currency and securities seized in the invaded countries', according to a June 1943 FBI report. As the Nazis invaded new territories they plundered central banks and private businesses, looking especially for the dollar bills they needed for the purchase of vital war matériel. To launder this money, according to the FBI, 'every Axis agent arriving in Argentina brought large amounts of United States currency which was placed in circulation by the legitimate German business firms' in the country. From Buenos Aires, the looted bills were funnelled to the United States. The bureau believed Buenos Aires served 'as the Western Hemisphere outlet for the looted US banknotes that entered into commercial traffic in Switzerland'.

After 1942 the Jewish ransom schemes became a malignant new way of acquiring dollars in Argentina to finance Hitler's war. The Department of State knew by December 1942 that Germany was using Argentine financial institutions for the extortion schemes aimed at Jews living in Europe and that Argentine pesos deposited at one of the two German banks in Buenos Aires could buy exit permits for Jews in Germany. 'The authorization of ransom payments to the Nazis, like any other submission to blackmail, will merely result in increased demands and increased barbarity by the Nazis,' US Secretary of State Cordell Hull relayed in a message to Argentina in January 1943. 'This government trusts that the Argentine government will not make itself a party to this infamous traffic and will not grant such authorizations.'[127]

Washington and London finally clamped down on the Nazi extortion racket by releasing a lengthy public statement on 24 November

1942 unmasking the 'barbaric and inhuman practice', which carefully excluded any specific mention of the fact that Jews were its main targets. The Allies pointed out that the ransom demands were 'designed to provide foreign exchange for the furtherance of the German war effort'. The 'suspicion' that 'individual members of the Nazi party' personally profited from the racket was mentioned. The British Ministry of Economic Warfare shared with the Americans evidence it had obtained on the practice and warned there was 'good reason to believe that the Germans were contemplating operations of this kind on an increasing scale'. The Allies threatened to 'blacklist' any 'broker or agent' involved as well as victims who succumbed to the Nazi extortion. 'Persons . . . who pay ransom are warned that they are rendering themselves liable to treatment as enemies,' said the Allied statement. 'This may be a ruthless course but it is the only way open to us to check this form of blackmail,' said an internal paper of the British Ministry of Economic Warfare. 'In particular, the Jewish community throughout the world is likely to be deeply concerned.'[128]

Within a short time in Switzerland alone some 80 individuals and firms were singled out by the Allied Black List Committee. Among them was Wiederkehr, who quickly appeared before the British diplomats at Zurich pleading innocence of the charges. He proposed that in response to Germany's treatment of the Jews, the Allies should take reprisals against German nationals in Allied countries by deporting them somewhere with conditions similar to Poland. 'I know of no country under Allied control where such conditions obtain and even to satisfy Dr Wiederkehr I do not see why we should consider such a proposition,' commented a British diplomat wryly.[129]

A reporter in Zurich who went to see Wiederkehr found that he and other intermediaries had conveniently vanished. 'They did not, apparently, like the publicity given to their nefarious activities,' noted the Ministry of Economic Warfare. Sadly, also included were many relatives and business friends of Jews who, motivated by sincere humanitarian concern, had given in to ransom demands. 'While his Majesty's Government might, on humanitarian grounds, have been prepared to overlook isolated instances of payments made to the enemy in these circumstances, it is clear that the matter has reached the dimension of a regular organized traffic from which the enemy hopes to derive a market benefit,' said Lord Selborne in London.[130]

The Allied embassies in Buenos Aires began an all-out drive to stamp out the extortion. The interception of some 40 ransom telegrams exchanged between Argentina and Europe showed that the racket had reached alarming proportions. During early 1943 the British embassy alone called in approximately a hundred people in Buenos Aires who were victims of attempted extortion.[131]

One of these was a Mr Goldenberg, Austrian-born and the representative in Buenos Aires for Tracey Brothers Ltd of Manchester. He was being asked for 400,000 Swiss francs by the Dutch travel agents Hoyman & Schuurman for his brother and family who were at risk in Holland. Goldenberg was called in by the British embassy and warned against paying the ransom. He said he was communicating 'merely to leave the matter in suspense as long as possible'.

The same Amsterdam firm was demanding 100,000 Swiss francs from a man named Landauer. 'Some of the refugees I have had in to see me this week have told me there have been dozens of similar cases,' wrote Walter Simon of the British embassy to London. It was difficult to get details from the fearful refugees 'in case names concerned with information given us should ultimately become known to the enemy by one means or another'. All the same, the British were able to see a pattern develop, whereby Hoyman & Schuurman were acting in tandem with their branch in Geneva, Natural Lecoultre, and the travel agents Viajes Cafrance in Bilbao and San Sebastián. 'It is clear that this is the organization the Germans are employing in their campaign,' the diplomat concluded from his many interviews.

Argentine firms with Jewish connections were also the victims of Nazi extortion. The multinational Argentine grain-exporting corporation Bunge & Born was being blackmailed over the lives of two Dutch Jewish partners in Holland. Around October 1942 the firm was given 48 hours to hand over $50,000 to the German embassy in Buenos Aires. 'If payment was not forthcoming the two partners and their families would at once be sent to a concentration camp in Poland,' the Ministry of Economic Warfare reported. Bunge & Born requested approval of the payment from the British embassy in Buenos Aires, but London said that it would only encourage more Nazi blackmail. 'All attempts to obtain the Buenos Aires intermediary's name, from the Bunge & Born relatives here, have been unsuccessful,' the British embassy reported.[132]

The US approached Jewish leaders in at least two South American countries seeking a promise that they would advise members of their communities not to submit to these sorts of demands. In Buenos Aires, Adolfo Hirsch, a distinguished member of the local Jewish community who aided refugees in collaboration with the Joint Distribution Committee in New York, gave his support, pointing out that the transfer of ransom payments to Europe was being made outside normal banking channels by agents of the German Bank in Buenos Aires.[133]

In late 1943, Argentine Colonel Carlos Vélez arrived in Madrid. He had been sent by Perón on a secret mission to buy arms from the Nazis, but he was also on a personal mission for a friend. The colonel was a compulsive gambler, and his regular poker pal was Carlos Ketelhohn, a business partner of Perón's Nazi friend Ludwig Freude, whose half-Jewish mother had disappeared in Europe. During the long negotiations Vélez held in Madrid with special Nazi agent and arms salesman Reinhard Spitzy, the colonel brought up the matter of Ketelhohn's mother, even suggesting that her release was a condition for closing the arms deal.

The difficulty was how to find Ida Ketelhohn in the war-torn Europe of 1944. 'What I did was to start an investigation against her,' recalled former SS officer Spitzy 54 years later. 'In an authoritarian regime it's very difficult to help someone. It is easier to act against them. So I said she was dangerous and we very quickly located her in Romania.' With the help of SD chief Walter Schellenberg, Spitzy was able to bring Mrs Ketelhohn to Spain, where she stayed at the home of the Vélez family, spending entire days alone in her room while

Vélez tried to obtain for her a Navycert, the special British wartime pass required for crossing the Atlantic.

Finally Vélez took her to see the British military attaché, who nearly turned her away when Mrs Ketelhohn expressed the desire to return to Germany once the war was over. 'I was running a great risk because I had promised Schellenberg that I would return the woman to Germany, so in order to send her to Argentina I had to fake her death in Spain. If a German submarine had stopped her ship on the way to Argentina and they had found this woman who was supposedly dead with a British Navycert on a German passport, I would have been in bad trouble.'

Whatever hopes Spitzy may have had that his charitable act towards a half-Jewish woman would stand him in good stead when he fled to Argentina in 1948 were dashed shortly after his arrival in Buenos Aires: 'Carlos Ketelhohn met my wife at the dockside with a bunch of roses in his hands but then he proceeded to change the fifty gold pounds she had brought with her at the worst possible exchange rate,' said Spitzy.

Although Ketelhohn invited Spitzy to a lavish lunch at the exclusive Jockey Club, bastion of Argentina's oligarchy, and made him repeat over and over again the fantastic story of how he had rescued his mother, he failed to come through with any real material help for the Spitzy family in Buenos Aires. The first day he greeted Spitzy with open arms, but a month later he would receive him only in the corridor. After three months Spitzy stormed into his office. 'Look Ketelhohn, I've had enough, now you're going to pay me what I spent rescuing your mother or I will break your teeth in,' recalled Spitzy laughing. 'What a son of a bitch!'[134]

6

The Nazi Escape Begins

In the final days of World War Two a special agent of Heinrich Himmler's secret service, who spoke Spanish with a distinct Argentine accent, stepped off a plane in Madrid. Former SS Captain Carlos Fuldner, blond, blue-eyed and 34 years old, was a natural opportunist with a talent for deception. His arrival from Berlin on 10 March 1945, less than two months before Hitler's suicide, marked a fresh start for him and would soon provide a new lease of life for some of the most unsavoury criminals of the Nazi regime. Arriving on a mission not slated to begin 'until the end of the war', Fuldner was about to be reincarnated as the hub of an escape route that would remain open into the early 1950s. By the time he concluded his assignment, hundreds of German, Austrian, French, Belgian, Dutch, Slovakian and Croatian war criminals and Nazi collaborators had found safe homes in Argentina.

By late 1944 Allied POW camps in liberated Europe were already teeming with captives from the broken Nazi legions. Long before the end of the war a growing stream of fugitives had started to cross into neutral Spain, Switzerland and Portugal, Austria and Italy. Some sought refuge with the Catholic Church, others offered their anti-Communist skills to Allied intelligence. The fear of war tribunals was uppermost in the minds of SS veterans of the 'Final Solution'.

Criminals such as Adolf Eichmann sank into fits of depression when they realized defeat was at hand. Eichmann 'had millions of Jewish lives on his conscience', according to fellow SS officer Wilhelm Hoettl, who was witness to Eichmann's dread of postwar justice.

Such fears were not unfounded. On 17 December 1942 the three major Allies had already publicized their intent that 'those responsible for these crimes shall not escape retribution'. The Soviets had gone further and had held trials of captured Nazis involved in the killing of Jews as early as July 1943. By late 1944, the BBC had been periodically updating the names of individuals considered war criminals and reporting the fact that proceedings awaited them after the war. (Shortly after the end of the war, the Nuremberg tribunal declared both the SS and the Nazi party to be criminal organizations, rendering all their former members liable to investigation.) The impact of these broadcasts was felt even by top SS chiefs such as Ernst Kaltenbrunner, the head of the Reich Security Main Office. 'Kaltenbrunner had also once made the same sort of comment, i.e., that he was considered a war criminal by the Allies,' Hoettl stated in 1961.[135]

The big bosses at the Reich Security Main Office accused each other of secreting assets abroad for postwar survival. Kaltenbrunner and crack SD operative Otto Skorzeny accused Schellenberg of hoarding funds in Switzerland, while rumours spread that it was actually Kaltenbrunner, hiding in his native Austria, who was making provisions for his future. 'I know that Kaltenbrunner was down south especially towards the end and shortly before the defeat of Germany,' SD section chief Theodor Paeffgen told American interrogators after the war. 'His agent, Dr Hoettl, quite frequently went across the border into Switzerland or was near the Swiss border and it is my assumption that Kaltenbrunner transferred certain funds across to have a reserve in order to support his future political activities in Austria.'[136]

In April 1945, as the Red Army advanced on Berlin, the SS chiefs began concocting fake pasts for themselves. 'A high-ranking officer came who had brought hundreds of pages with all kinds of different printed letter-heads,' Eichmann would recount afterwards. The officers were issued fake 'testimonials' with fictitious, innocent-sounding wartime duties. 'I was the only one who did not care at all about such false testimonials,' said Eichmann after the war.[137]

Senior Nazis, apparently, also applied themselves to the question of escape routes. The task of preparing a route seems to have fallen naturally to the SD Foreign Intelligence Branch that Fuldner belonged to, and Nazi agents with Argentine connections suddenly found themselves at the helm of a hastily organized operation in Madrid.

During the last days of the war, while the Nazi hierarchy held out in Berlin against the advancing Allies, neutral Spain had become the main safe haven for fugitive Nazis and their French and Belgian collaborators fleeing from the liberated European nations. Several interesting characters would soon arrive in the Spanish capital: the parliamentary leader of the fascist Belgian Rexist party, Pierre Daye, and another Argentine-born agent of the SS secret service, the Frenchman Charles Lesca, both war criminals fleeing from justice; as well as the pro-Nazi former Romanian ambassador to Madrid, Radu Ghenea. All of them spent the end of the war in hiding in Madrid, helping intelligence agents and French and Belgian collaborators to flee, before escaping to Argentina themselves. All would meet with Perón in Buenos Aires. For over five decades, the rescue structure organized by these men, in association with Perón and aided by highly-placed Catholic Church dignitaries, remained secret. Until now. Over the course of the next five years its operations would move from Madrid to Buenos Aires, then to Sweden and Switzerland and Italy, and Fuldner, Lesca and Daye would thrive in their appointed task.

Fuldner was born in Buenos Aires on 16 December 1910 to German immigrants, and was to become an early adherent to the Nazi creed. In 1922 his father, Hugo Fuldner, packed his bags and returned to Germany with his wife and three sons. The family settled in Kassel. Young Fuldner finished secondary school and then attempted to study law but abandoned the course after four terms. Deciding that they were back in Germany for good, Hugo Fuldner had taken his children to the civil registry in Kassel in 1928 and signed them up as Prussian citizens. But because young Horst Carlos remained unsure which citizenship suited him best, in the end he would keep them both. Throughout his life he would be Horst to the Germans and Carlos in Argentina.

At age 20, while he was working for a firm called Kosmos-Export in Hamburg, the important matter of his obligatory Argentine military service needed to be sorted out. In October 1931, therefore, he showed up at the Argentine embassy in Berlin to present a letter stating that even though he still felt 'Argentine at heart' he wished to be exempted from military service as he now had German citizenship. The embassy replied with a curt note stating simply that 'Argentine nationality is not renounceable.' Young Fuldner suddenly became a military deserter as far as the Argentine authorities were concerned.

Around that time, as the surviving 33 pages of his SS file show, Fuldner was a member of the Young Stahlhelm (Steel Helmet) organization, a right-wing ex-servicemen's association. Also, more prosaically, but in key with his later chequered trajectory, he got into trouble for refusing to pay for a railway ticket.

Early in 1932, Fuldner was admitted into the SS, becoming member number 31,170 of Hitler's elite guard. He was 21 years old, 1.76 metres tall, wore shoe size 44 and gave his profession as 'export businessman'. He spoke German, Spanish, French and English. In March he was admitted to the Nazi party in Munich. He must have made a good impression, for he was promoted quickly through the SS ranks, rising to captain by September 1934. That year found Fuldner in East Prussia, where he worked for the SS 'newsletter', travelling frequently to Poland. He bought a new Mercedes-Benz and had some difficulty repaying the loan for it, running up a 5,000-mark debt with the SS. He was assigned administrative duties and was considered intelligent and efficient, a reputation apparently not yet tarnished by his shady business deals.

His personal life was a shambles. On 22 November 1934 he had married Hanna Kraus, a 21-year-old German woman, but within the year he abandoned his pregnant wife. According to friends he was extremely unhappy. Soon his taste for other people's money got him into serious trouble. After swindling a Munich businessman, a Hamburg shipping company, and apparently the SS to boot, Fuldner decided to get as far away as possible from Germany, where he faced charges of 'fraud, concealment and disloyalty'. On 12 October 1935, the Argentine SS captain disappeared from his apartment in Munich.

Fuldner had unearthed his expired Argentine passport and gone with it to the Argentine consulate in Hamburg. There, on 15 October, Bartolomé Daneri (the same diplomat who a few years later would complain so bitterly against not being allowed to charge Jews for visas) gave him a new Argentine document. Fuldner, in a 'fairly nervous state', told Daneri he had undergone a change of heart and now wished to return to Buenos Aires and undertake his military service. He planned to board an ocean liner at Lisbon. He was actually on the run from the SS, but the resourceful young man had still managed to procure the requisite 'certificate of good conduct' from the Munich police. Two days later Daneri was a little puzzled to receive a phone call from Fuldner's wife asking whether he had been at the consulate seeking a new Argentine passport. Fuldner had committed 'a few irregularities in the party', Hanna Kraus said, but she had managed to clear up the situation. She wanted to fly to Portugal to intercept her husband before he left Europe. 'She said she was willing to do everything possible to prevent her husband from reaching Buenos Aires,' Daneri reported later.

Fuldner meanwhile was putting as much distance as possible between himself and the SS, employing his new Argentine passport to cross from Germany to France and from there to Spain. At the Spanish–Portuguese border he switched passports and produced his German one for the Portuguese immigration officials. Fuldner was undergoing a crash course in passport tricks that would serve him well when rescuing SS comrades from postwar Europe ten years later. On 16 October he turned up at the office of the Argentine consul in Lisbon, Ramón Oliveira Cézar, a diplomat who would crack down on the granting of visas to Jews in France a few years later. Fuldner apparently required a stamp on his new Argentine passport and the consul, stating that Argentina did not allow dual citizenship, retained his German one – fortunately for this book, as it still survives in the Argentine Foreign Ministry archives and contains the only known picture of Fuldner.

The following day Fuldner boarded the steamship *Antonio Delfino* of the Hamburg-Südamerika line with a third-class ticket to Buenos Aires. For the moment he was safe, but the SS would not let him off that easy. Hitler's elite corps actually went to quite a lot of trouble to get Fuldner back. Ten days later, near the coast of Brazil and about a day's sailing from the port of Bahía, his ship was intercepted by the *Cap Norte*, a liner travelling in the opposite direction. A boat was lowered and a despondent Fuldner transferred to the Hamburg-bound ship. He complained bitterly to Captain Basse of the *Cap Norte*, invoking his Argentine citizenship and brandishing his Argentine passport. 'As far as I'm concerned, you are German,' said the unmovable captain. 'You are a member of the SS. You took a German oath.'

A desperate Fuldner fired off a series of telegrams to high-ranking SS officers, including Heinrich Himmler himself. When he received no reply he tried to commit suicide, after which Captain Basse decided it best to confine Fuldner to the ship's sick bay for the remainder of the journey. To top it all, Fuldner was penniless. Captain Basse had to lend him 15 marks to pay for a telegram while an uncle in Hamburg deposited 100 marks for him at the head offices of the Hamburg-Südamerika line. The young German-Argentine, despite the trouble he had caused, turned out to be a charming scoundrel. Captain Basse declared him 'well-mannered, cultured, refined and good-natured'. Fuldner was eventually forced to disembark at the port of Bremerhaven, where he was handed over to the Gestapo.

The German-Argentine was accused of desertion from the SS, stealing his own records, gambling, absconding with money and other charges. In January 1936 he was expelled from the SS. His death's-head ring was ritually melted down, the worst humiliation for a Nazi guard, and he was forced to cool off in jail. Shortly afterwards, on 26 May 1936, his only daughter Ingrid was born, and his luck seems to have turned, because in 1937 he was cleared of the fraud charges at least. The last few entries in his file date from 1938 and show Fuldner making an unsuccessful application to be reinstated in the SS.

What Fuldner did next remains uncertain. Allied intelligence, which included his name in a 'Hard-Core List of 201 Candidates for Repatriation from Spain' after the war, tried to piece together a picture of his career, but the image was anything but clear. 'Before the war he travelled all over South America, probably in Argentina but also in the United States,' said a 1945 secret American report. He apparently had a close connection with Spain, serving as a lieutenant and German–Spanish interpreter in the Blue Division, the corps of 20,000 soldiers sent by dictator Francisco Franco to fight alongside the Nazis on the Russian Front. He returned frequently to Berlin. At some point he joined the huge Nazi corporation Sofindus, which controlled widespread German business interests and provided cover and financing for the Nazi agents in Spain. True to character, Fuldner created trouble for himself even there and was 'dismissed for embezzlement'. In the last months of the war he travelled back and forth between Madrid and Berlin. An arrival by plane in Madrid was registered on 26 November 1944, then a return to Berlin in late December.

But by that crucial Monday in March 1945 when he climbed down the German plane's stepladder in Madrid, Fuldner seems to have been restored to his former rank. He was now on a 'special mission' for Himmler's secret service for which he carried both his German and Argentine passports, and to which he would add the particular brand of financial chicanery which had distinguished his career. In the coming years, many former Reich officials and some of the worst Nazi criminals, including Adolf Eichmann, would owe their lives to the Argentine SS captain. Was Fuldner's mission the result of a plan laid by Schellenberg and Himmler? There is precious little documentation available even today about Fuldner's activities in Madrid in the immediate postwar period, but his later activities suggest high-level Nazi involvement.

Fuldner's presence in Madrid puzzled even the German embassy. 'His activities were shrouded in uncertainty,' American intelligence reported: '. . . he once told [German Military Attaché Hans] Doerr he had nothing to do with the German embassy, and when pressed by Doerr to explain his presence here, he hinted vaguely that his job was to keep up relations between Spain and Germany after the war.' That was only half of it. 'Among the personnel in the embassy his name was linked with the Werewolf [the Nazi postwar resistance organization].'

Fuldner had come to Madrid bursting with cash and in charge of a planeload of art works that he wanted to sell, presumably to finance the escape operation. On his previous arrival from Berlin he had paid 45,000 pesetas cash down for a car. At the German embassy, where tensions were rising as the end drew closer, he met with diplomats Josef Schoof and Wilhelm Petersen, the latter a Nazi contact of Argentine nationalist Juan Carlos Goyeneche. Both diplomats later revealed to the Americans that Fuldner 'belongs to the SD', a claim that was verified by British intelligence.

Influential friends and members of the Spanish elite protected Fuldner. The 1945 report states: 'Subject was hidden for a time in El Escorial by Spanish friends of the Blue Division . . . is said to have stated that the most important move was to "save the present situation" . . . now lives with a family in Calle Duque de Sexto in Madrid . . . speaks Spanish perfectly with Argentine accent, knows bookkeeping, printing and many languages.'

Six months later, in July 1946, the Allies still hoped to capture Fuldner. He suffered some discomfort as the Spanish authorities began a half-hearted search for him, changing addresses frequently and staying for a while at the home of the Vizconde de Uzqueta, Gonzalo Serrano Fernandez de Villavicencio, a pro-German Blue Division member. He then moved in with a German woman, 'name unknown', at 33 Modesto Lafuente Street. 'Fuldner is being sought at present by the police, presumably for internment pending repatriation and, for this reason, recently has left Madrid and gone into hiding in the town of Tarrasa, near Barcelona,' says another secret 1946 American report. Every now and then the heat subsided and Fuldner would show himself in public. He was a personal friend of the Dominguín brothers, the most famous bullfighters in Spain.

Himmler's agent was also on good terms in Madrid with Pierre Daye, Radu Ghenea, and Spanish journalist and Blue Division veteran Víctor de la Serna. All four would meet in secret with Perón in Buenos Aires, when Fuldner would be put in charge of Perón's Nazi rescue team.[138]

Charles Lesca, who would become another key member of Perón's Odessa, opened the earliest pipeline for fleeing Nazis and their collaborators via Spain. Like Fuldner, Lesca had been born in Argentina. He straddled the Atlantic, with one foot in Buenos Aires, another in Paris, and fingers in Nazi pies in Berlin, Madrid and along the Franco-Spanish border. The 'serene ... magnificent' Lesca was fond of sporting 'a beige gabardine topcoat almost reddish of German make', American intelligence reported in 1945. An intimate collaborator of the Germans, he was in deep with 'the German General Staff and the Foreign Ministry' in Berlin.

One of Lesca's top contacts during the war was Otto Abetz, the Nazi ambassador to Paris who on 3 August 1940 was appointed by Hitler 'to seize and secure all public art treasures and private art treasures, and particularly art treasures belonging to Jews'. A true Nazi proconsul, Abetz plundered French museums, Jewish-owned galleries and private collections for Hitler, as well as participating in the much dirtier business of deporting foreign and French Jews to concentration camps. He was convicted of war crimes in 1949 and sentenced to 20 years' imprisonment. Lesca was also connected to the highest-ranking Vichy officials, including president Pierre Laval and the Vichy representative in occupied France, Fernand de Brinon.

Born in Buenos Aires on 19 February 1887, Lesca owned property there and also in France at Saint-Jean-de-Luz near Biarritz, where in 1920 he had married the Ecuadorian-born beauty María Levray. He attended university in France and was a volunteer in World War One. During the 1930s and 1940s, Lesca was on the directorates of various right-wing publications such as *Action Française*, *Frontières* and *Combats*. But he was best known as shareholder and editor of the violently anti-Semitic magazine *Je Suis Partout*.

Despite spending most of his life in France, Lesca kept in contact with Argentina, reporting in the pages of *Je Suis Partout* on political developments in the land of his birth. He returned to the country at least twice in the 1930s, the last time arriving in Buenos Aires on 22 August 1938 from Trieste, staying at the luxury Plaza Hotel and meeting with important Argentine nationalists, among them Cosme Beccar Varela. In Buenos Aires he obtained Argentine identity papers for himself and his wife, returning to Europe at the end of September. At some point during one of these visits he met a young military officer who had contacts of his own with Nazi intelligence in South America, Juan Perón.

Lesca's collaboration with the Nazis before Hitler occupied Paris got him into trouble with the French authorities. In March 1939 *Je Suis Partout* was closed down after being accused of defeatism in the face of the Nazi menace. Lesca himself was placed briefly under arrest in 1940, but Hitler's occupation of northern France that June resulted in his release and reappearance 'in the limelight', as one of his Nazi contacts told American interrogators after the war. The scurrilous *Je Suis Partout* was back on the street by February 1941, and Lesca even published an account of his incarceration under the title 'When Israel Takes Revenge'.

During the war, from his desk at the magazine, Lesca wove alliances with other Nazi collaborators, including the French-speaking Belgians of the pro-Nazi Rexist party. His main Belgian contact was Pierre Daye, a frequent visitor to Lesca's office at 186 rue de Rivoli in Paris.

In August 1944, shortly before the liberation of Paris, Lesca fled to Berlin, knowing what his fate would be without his Nazi protectors around. Thousands of French collaborationists followed the same route to Germany. Many were hired by Schellenberg to return to their homeland and engage in intelligence work for the Germans. They were sent back to France through Verona, Innsbruck and Milan. Lesca seems to have been one of them, moving from Berlin to his home at Saint-Jean-de-Luz near the Franco-Spanish border.

As early as October 1944, American intelligence heard that Lesca

was preparing to leave for Argentina, as he had 'large property there'.
The information was correct, for on 16 November the Argentine consulate at the nearby Spanish resort of San Sebastián issued two
passports for the Lesca couple. The border area near Biarritz was a
hive of Nazi intelligence activity during the war and the Argentine
consul in Madrid, Nazi collaborator Aquilino López, travelled frequently to Hendaye on the French side to deliver reports and receive
instructions from his German bosses. As the war drew to a close San
Sebastián became a transit point for fugitive Vichy officials. They
were assisted by a Spanish intelligence chief named Peña, a man
close to Franco, who had collaborated with German military intelligence while posing as an attaché at the Spanish embassy in Paris.
After the liberation of France, Peña followed a route similar to Lesca,
first fleeing to Berlin and then returning to Spain. In San Sebastián,
he recruited Frenchmen on the run for a secret service he was organizing under General Franco.

Lesca finally arrived in Madrid on a special Lufthansa plane in
December 1944 with his wife and two collaborators, and settled at 4
Víctor Hugo Street. He travelled under a false name and was carrying
a large amount of cash provided by Berlin, purportedly to establish
contacts for the negotiation of a separate peace with the Allies. But a
more likely version in view of Lesca's later trajectory was that the
funds were really for 'financing the Germans already in Spain and
those who would have to hide there in future', as one SS intelligence
agent told American interrogators after the war. Whether or not
Lesca's assigned mission was to oversee the escape of Nazi SD personnel, that is what he ended up doing. The Frenchman planned
nothing less than the systematic departure of all possible German
intelligence officers to Argentina. Upon his arrival he contacted the
German embassy, which provided him with 3 million pesetas to support fugitive French collaborators, while he began to work with Peña
to arrange the evacuation. Through his contacts with Spanish intelligence, Lesca was soon able to provide safe refuge and travel papers
for Nazi agents to escape to Argentina.

By 1946 American intelligence was attempting, without too much success, to infiltrate the 'Lesca–Peña Group'. Lesca was alleged to be part of 'a chain into France' and 'the courier travelling via Lufthansa to see Laval'. Members of the 'Lesca–Peña Group' included Daye and Ghenea. Other comrades included the Vichy press attaché Adalbert Laffon, who resigned from his post in protest against the new French government of General de Gaulle; a Frenchman named Robert Voineau, and another Frenchman, Paul Frechou, whose father lived in Argentina. A war criminal was on the list, Pierre Héricourt, a former associate of Action Française who had served as Vichy consul in Barcelona.

The group often gathered at the exclusive Horcher restaurant on Alfonso XII Street, installed there in 1943 by Berlin restaurateur Otto Horcher with the help, according to American intelligence, of Walter Schellenberg. To open his Madrid branch Horcher allegedly transferred 250,000 Swiss francs out of Germany to Nazi diplomats in Lisbon and later converted the Swiss notes to pesetas on the black market, an exercise in money laundering allegedly organized by another Schellenberg agent who ended up in Argentina, Walter Eugen Mosig. Schellenberg reportedly also helped Horcher transfer furnishings and silverware from Germany. The original Horcher restaurant on Berlin's Kurfürstendamm had been a regular meeting place for the Third Reich's hierarchy from Göring to Himmler. Unknown to most clients, it was planted with secret microphones to capture the conversations of foreign visitors. By 1946, in Madrid, Horcher allegedly had become extremely nervous because his name had appeared in the American press and 'like so many other colleagues, he had the intention of emigrating to Argentina'. But Horcher stayed and his restaurant, still managed by his descendants, remains one of the most exclusive in Madrid to this day.

Lesca's claim to having started up the first escape route to Argentina was supported by the intimate and personal relationship he professed to have with Perón. He revealed the friendship to Hans Sommer, an SS agent who knew Lesca from occupied Paris and who caught up with him 'at a small and inconspicuous restaurant in Madrid' around 27 March 1946, shortly after Perón had been elected to the presidency but two months before his inauguration. 'Lesca told me that he had known the new president Perón personally for many years and that they were close friends,' Sommer revealed on 18 July 1946 after falling into the hands of the Americans.

Perón's electoral victory had set the Nazi underground in Madrid buzzing with the news that the long-awaited evacuation of Nazi agents could finally get under way. Unfortunately, Sommer was unable to learn exact details of the Lesca–Perón link. 'I personally neither could nor wanted to revert time and again to the subject of Argentina, inasmuch as this was our first conversation and I did not want to raise doubt and suspicion in Lesca,' Sommer said. Lesca seemed to suggest he had met Perón during one of his trips to Argentina in the 1930s and that 'the friendship had started there'. He also believed that 'Lesca had recently been in communication with Perón through the Argentine embassy in Madrid.' The planned evacuation was uppermost in Lesca's mind. 'He himself would undoubtedly leave for Argentina soon,' Sommer asserted. During their meal, Lesca was called to the phone. When he came back he said: 'Yet another one who can't stay put in his hiding place. Everybody is asking when things will get going.'

Thanks to the assurances from Voineau regarding Sommer's '100 per cent reliability', Lesca agreed to see him again about a week later. This time Lesca was with spy chief Peña, who was travelling to San Sebastián, 'whence he brings the arriving French fugitives to the Spanish Intelligence Service'. Peña was particularly eager to hear what Sommer had to say about the 'Werewolf organization in Germany and in northern Italy.' The situation of various German officers hunted by the Americans was also discussed. Lesca was particularly concerned about the plight of Nazi war criminal and Luftwaffe General Eckart Krahmer. This was the German air attaché in Madrid who, in October 1944, had overseen the crossing from France into Spain of a convoy carrying 200 art works, including paintings by Rubens and Van Dyck, stolen by Göring. Betrayed by a fellow German, Krahmer had to be taken 'from his hiding place in Madrid to the rural estate of a Spanish officer' before he was successfully transported to Argentina. Fortunately, Spanish intelligence kept a 'black list' of Germans who had betrayed their comrades and such problems rarely repeated themselves, Sommer was told.

Sommer held out little hope that Lesca's group could be infiltrated: 'The men around Lesca are people who have known each other for years from their political warfare; they are fanatics who stick together, since for them there is no other way out. For a newcomer in Spain it would be impossible to enter those circles.' Asking the Spanish authorities for their arrest was equally pointless: 'The entire group is so closely tied up with the Spanish authorities, police and army, that . . . giving the address to the police is no longer of any use, as the circle will be warned by the police beforehand.' Lesca and his associates were convinced that Britain and the US would soon find themselves at war with their Soviet ally. 'These circles are of the opinion that the relations between the Big Three will grow worse all the time so that an armed conflict cannot be avoided,' Sommer said. 'The aforementioned circles would take the greatest possible advantage of any such crisis to realize their own purposes.'

He discovered that between 150 and 200 Germans were to be shipped from Cadiz, 'a few at a time', with Spanish papers provided by Franco. The first transports would start in August or September 1946. Coincidentally, around that time the American embassy in Buenos Aires started receiving reports that German agents from Spain were 'entering Argentina disguised as priests and deserters from Spanish ships'.

Another German-Argentine SD agent was the first to use Lesca's escape route. Carlos Reuter was a 53-year-old 'banker' who had been born in Hamburg, raised in Buenos Aires, and had left Buenos Aires for Germany in 1938 after acquiring Argentine citizenship. During the war he lived in occupied Paris. 'This Argentine was used . . . to recruit likely contacts for the German intelligence service among the Latin Americans living in France,' according to Sommer. One of those recruited by Reuter was consul Emilio de Matteis, an Argentine diplomat who ran a lucrative business selling visas to Jews in Marseille during the war. Reuter had been captured by the Americans during the liberation of Paris but 'talked himself free on the basis of his Argentine citizenship'. He fled to Madrid in December 1944, where he rendezvoused with Lesca at the Horcher restaurant. Reuter then did the trial run for Lesca's 'ratline'. He departed from the port of Bilbao in late January, arriving at Buenos Aires on 22 February 1946, two days before Perón's victory at the polls. It was a trouble-free passage. The 'banker' and his wife took up residence in the exclusive Barrio Norte neighbourhood of Buenos Aires. His task was now to prepare the ground for the mass emigration planned by Lesca. Sommer was convinced that 'Reuter was among those entrusted by the Germans with building up an intelligence organization for the future in South America.'[139]

In mid-1946 Lesca began preparing his own departure, bidding farewell to Daye and his other 'amis d'émigration' in Madrid. 'The great voyage has begun for us,' he wrote to Daye from Bilbao in August. There he visited the home of José Félix de Lequerica, Franco's foreign minister during 1944 and 1945, who feasted Lesca with 'un déjeuner succulent' accompanied by a 'voluptuous' Pommery wine. From Bilbao, Lesca travelled to San Sebastián and from there to Barcelona, where he boarded the *Cabo de Buena Esperanza* on 10 September, setting sail at last for his native Argentina.

All along the route American intelligence kept a close watch over him, and on 26 September the French government sent out warnings to the governments of Brazil and Uruguay, where the liner made stopovers. Lesca was carrying a pouch containing gold coins and diamonds, Paris said. The next day at the port of Rio de Janeiro the Brazilian authorities made the Frenchman disembark and his arrest seemed very probable. But the Brazilian authorities, taking into consideration the fact that the suspect held a valid Argentine passport, allowed Lesca to return to his ship, deciding that the extradition request was a matter of 'French domestic politics'.

Lesca's luck could not hold out for ever and during the next stop in Uruguay, a small country sandwiched between Brazil and Argentina with a more democratic tradition, the prospect of being shipped back to France to stand trial became eerily palpable. 'Friend of Laval and

Pétain Arrested,' read the evening papers in Buenos Aires on 2 October after Lesca and his wife were taken off the *Cabo de Buena Esperanza* with their 15 pieces of luggage. Uruguay had agreed to hold him pending the arrival of a formal extradition request from the French government and Lesca was lodged in a Montevideo cell. What happened next remains a mystery. Perhaps some of those diamonds and gold coins changed hands, but in any event the Lescas escaped. On 22 October, Mme Lesca arrived in Buenos Aires on board the ferry from Montevideo. Lesca may or may not have been with her, but he was certainly ensconced in Buenos Aires shortly afterwards.

Lesca lived in the upmarket neighbourhood of Barrio Norte at 2264 Santa Fe Avenue, third floor. The doorman was instructed to deny his presence but to receive any mail arriving in his name, especially 'if the envelope carries the seal of the Argentine army'. In Paris, meanwhile, an *in absentia* trial against Lesca on charges of 'intelligence with the enemy' was under way. On 20 January 1947 the French government presented a formal request for his extradition. Needless to say the request was ignored by Perón's government. A death sentence against Lesca was handed down by the Seine Court of Justice on 5 May 1947.

'You have perhaps heard that our mutual friend Carlos has in the last few days been promoted to the same exalted position as you,' Lesca wrote a few days later to Pierre Daye in Madrid, who had also recently been sentenced to death by a court in Brussels. 'You know him well enough to realize this has not disturbed his calm. Only his modesty has been slightly affected on seeing that the matter has appeared in some newspapers. He would have preferred this distinction to have passed unnoticed.'[140]

Charles Lesca was the pioneer who opened the route soon to be taken by a long series of other war criminals, but it was his dear friend Pierre Daye who would systematize their future method of escape. After his own escape to Buenos Aires, he connected himself directly to the Argentine presidential office, and implemented a rescue plan agreed in private conversations with Perón. Daye was the highest-ranking collaborator to organize the flight from Europe. His political acquaintances from his glory days were impressive. As a public official he had sipped tea with Adolf Hitler, received the blessing of Pope Pius XII and conferred with Nazi Foreign Minister Joachim von Ribbentrop. He knew Shah Reza Pahlevi, General Franco and King Leopold III of Belgium.

Born into an upper-class Brussels family, Daye was a compulsive traveller, visiting most of Europe, the Soviet Union, Africa and North America as a soldier, journalist and diplomat while still a young man. He was a volunteer in the Anglo-Belgian campaign in Western Africa in 1916, and was appointed to the Belgian military attaché's office in Washington from 1918 to 1919. By the time World War Two began there were probably few spots on the globe where he had not set foot. He was a brilliant intellectual and the author of various travel books and novels.

In 1925 the urge to wander took him to Argentina. Unable to convince his newspaper *Soir* to pay for the trip, Daye got himself enlisted as a crew member on board the 6,000-ton cargo boat *Eglantier* headed for Montevideo. As he confided in the unpublished memoirs written during his postwar exile in Buenos Aires, the Belgian found himself 'suddenly transported' from the world of letters in Brussels and Paris to cabin-sharing with 'rough sea fellows, who quickly became, for the space of three months, my friends'. Daye was captivated by their 'virile and popular coarseness', and felt this proximity was granting him new insight into the 'proletarian class'. Now he understood 'all the revolutions, including anarchy and Communism, because the people often cannot find another way to alleviate, for their own sake, and their children's, a terrible fate, which leaves them without hope at the hour of their death . . .'

Daye arrived in Buenos Aires on 3 September 1925. He was 33 years old and was described in the passenger list as a single Catholic diplomat. 'There is nothing as exciting for a young man with some romantic spirit as this way of discovering an exotic city, not in the fashion of the ordinary voyager, but through the back door,' he wrote years later. The Belgian plunged into the low life of Buenos Aires with gusto, at a time when booming meat exports had made Argentina one of the most prosperous nations in the world, its capital exploding with tango music and serviced by beautiful prostitutes imported from France and Eastern Europe. Daye was captivated most of all by the cheap brothel district of La Boca in southern Buenos Aires, with its tango bars and Italian immigrants, 'its dock hands, ruffians and young women who add their colour to one of the strangest underworlds in all of Latin America'. He was similarly hypnotized by the giant slaughter-houses that were the source of Argentina's wealth, 'red with blood and stinking with the smell of dead livestock soon to be frozen and shipped to Europe'. Daye was ecstatic over the freedom his new-found anonymity gave him. 'To feel at least once just a traveller, without a leather suitcase, wearing a cap, far from the palace hotels, mixing with a world of warmth and vibrant customs, familiar only to the reader of novels – what a sensation this was for me.'

Despite his taste for the underworld, Daye had an address book containing important contacts, and soon he was being entertained on the affluent north side of the city, visiting the green parks of Palermo, and taking boat cruises along the Tigre delta and the River Plate. Daye reached the top rung of Argentina's social ladder at the aristo-cratic Jockey Club, where he was struck by its 'onyx staircase' and its 'wine cellar holding 80,000 bottles'. He was invited to the opera at the Colón Theatre by 'beautiful women to whom I did not reveal my recent experiences or my lodgings'.

He was also invited to dinner at the home, appropriately enough, of the Fascist poet Leopoldo Lugones, a military fetishist whose author-itarian verse inspired decades of bloody dictatorial generals in Argentina. Daye was impressed by the man, if not so much by his writing. Lugones eventually committed suicide, but his policeman son was responsible for that uniquely Argentine innovation that con-verted the electric cattle prod of the abattoirs into the torture instrument of choice of successive dictatorships. His 'picana' was employed with equal relish first by Perón to terrorize his political opponents, then by the oligarchy against the Peronists. It was resur-rected with a vengeance by the generals of the 1970s, who wielded it

on a new generation of left-wing Peronists and Maoists. Among those
who felt its raw power was the 1970s guerrilla Pili Lugones, the grand-
daughter of the poet who had feasted Daye during his first visit to
Argentina.[141]

After his brief stay in Argentina, Daye returned to Europe. During
the 1930s his star ascended. He went from relative obscurity at the
Belgian embassy in Tehran to being a leading figure of the pro-Nazi
Belgian Rexist party. Soon he was rubbing shoulders in Berlin and
Nuremberg with Adolf Hitler, Rudolf Hess and Joachim von
Ribbentrop. In 1936 Léon Degrelle, the Rexist leader and 'adoptive
son' of the Führer, bestowed upon Daye the parliamentary leadership
of the party. Hess sent an invitation from the Führer to the
Nuremberg rally, that most quintessential of Nazi mass gatherings,
and Daye accepted enthusiastically. He attended along with 'a great
number of foreigners, Englishmen most noticeably'. The Thousand
Year Reich never seemed more solid than during the famous Nazi
'Parteitag' that September when Hitler saluted an endless procession of Nazi foot soldiers, Aryan prototypes of the New Order. 'I have
never concealed that I was extremely impressed by the spirit of faith,
enthusiasm and resolve . . . adorned in the colours of a triumphant revolution,' Daye wrote in his memoirs.

On 11 September, Hitler received Daye for tea. The Führer
appeared to him 'a little shy' but imbued with 'a simple dignity and
undeniable glamour . . . his heart is close to the people's heart. He
speaks. They feel.' The following day he met with Ribbentrop to discuss Belgian–German relations. In Brussels, democratic opponents
of the Rexist party began targeting Daye as someone who had sold out
to the Nazis. The parliamentarian was certainly enthusiastic about his
new-found friends. He had barely returned to Brussels than he and
Degrelle thundered off again to Berlin in a Rolls-Royce, this time pro-
voking a major scandal in the Belgian press. The trip included
breakfast at Ribbentrop's estate at Dahlem. Along the way, the speed-
ing Rolls flipped over near Hanover. Degrelle and Daye were
miraculously unscathed but Mme Degrelle was hospitalized. Daye
made use of the break to renew contact with an old acquaintance,

Otto Abetz, the future Nazi proconsul in occupied France. He was back again touring Germany in December, delivering lectures for the Rexist party. His postwar memoirs breathe admiration for National Socialism, 'one of the most essential phenomena of our era'. Daye met Hitler again in 1938. On this occasion Hess acted as the Führer's interpreter, 'in English, because I couldn't speak German and he didn't speak French'.

But all was not well with Daye, who had a writer's anxious temperament, and in 1939 he drifted away from Rexism and joined the Belgian Catholic Party. Returning to journalism in 1940 he became international editor of the *Nouveau Journal*. He was in Paris on 10 May 1940 when the Nazis invaded Belgium and was still in Paris when Hitler made his triumphant entry into the 'City of Light' in August. Now Daye grew more publicly pro-Nazi, advocating immediate collaboration with the overlords. He spent much of his time with Charles Lesca at the offices of *Je Suis Partout*, which had become the main press organ of collaborationism in occupied France, now and then writing an article for the publication. He also visited *Gringoire*, an equally anti-Semitic publication where he had friends.

With the Nazi occupation all restraints were removed from the anti-Semitic press. 'The Jews must be separated en bloc without care for the children,' wrote Daye's friend Robert Brasillach in *Je Suis Partout* on 25 September 1942. Not that Brasillach had shown any more self-control before the occupation. 'What court would dare condemn us if we denounced the extraordinary invasion of Paris and of France by monkeys? At the theatre? The hall is full of monkeys. The bus? The Metro? Monkeys . . . That which we call anti-Semitism . . . becomes every day a more urgent necessity,' Brasillach had written in 1939. Other French publications were less restrained. 'Death to the Jew! Death to villainy, duplicity, to the Russian Jew! Death to the Jewish argument! Death to Jewish usury! . . . Yes! We repeat! Let us repeat! Death! D.E.A.T.H. to the Jew!' declared *Au Pilori* on 14 March 1941. Daye found it all amusing, and reminisced fondly in his memoirs about those days at *Je Suis Partout*. One *Partout* journalist,

Lucien Rebatet, he recalled as 'hot-headed, gnashing, fiery, angry, ate Jews at every meal'.

When not at *Je Suis Partout* Daye could be found visiting his old friend Otto Abetz, now promoted to ambassador in Paris. Thus Daye spent his wartime days, walking from the offices of the century's most anti-Semitic French writers to those of the Nazis who were making their hateful wishes come true. He also continued travelling up and down the Reich, shuttling between Ribbentrop in Berlin and Pétain in Vichy. In Paris he renewed another old friendship, with the Spanish ambassador José Félix de Lequerica, a connection that would stand him in good stead when he was forced to escape to Madrid in 1944. Eventually Daye renewed his ties with the Rexist party and accepted the post of Belgian sports minister in 1943, the high point of his collaboration with the Nazi invaders of his country.[142]

Daye spent Christmas 1942 and early 1943 in Rome, meeting with senior Vatican officials including Pope Pius XII. Even at this early date, Daye sensed among the Italians a 'disaffection' with Fascism. At a dinner hosted by the Duchess of Villarosa, he complained later, 'I didn't hear anyone speak anything but English even though no English guests had been invited.' At the high-society Excelsior Hotel where Daye was lodged, an 'ostentatious Anglophilia' was evident. 'All this seemed fairly disturbing to me,' he wrote in his memoirs. In his pieces for *Nouveau Journal* and *Petit Parisien*, he conveyed 'as vaguely, as well-disguised as possible, that not all went well for Mussolini'. But in a secret report for King Leopold of Belgium, he was 'more precise'.

Firm Catholic believer that he was, the real motive of his Roman visit was to see the Pope. The Belgian collaborator was obsessed with finding out which of the two totalitarianisms the Church preferred, Nazism or Communism. On the morning of 6 January 1943, Daye rode an open carriage to the Vatican and was led through 'a succession of royal rooms, paintings by Raphael, the Renaissance uniforms of the Swiss Guards', to a private audience with Pius XII. Daye threw himself on his knees but was invited to rise again. The Pope opened the audience by asking for news of the Belgian royal family but abruptly changed the subject.

'General von Falkenhausen, the German military governor of Belgium, is a good man, isn't he?' the Pontiff pointedly asked Daye. (The Nazis arrested Alexander von Falkenhausen in 1944 for his participation in the 20 July plot to assassinate the Führer. After his liberation from Dachau by the Allies at the end of the war, a Belgian tribunal handed down a 12-year sentence against him. Later the sentence was reduced.)

'I've never met him personally but I believe he has surely shown good will in an extremely difficult situation,' Daye cautiously responded.

'Yes, but all the same he has closed our Nunciature in Brussels,' the Pope bitterly complained.

Pius XII then raised his arms and extended the papal blessing to Daye, who three years later would outdo Falkenhausen and receive an uncommuted death sentence for his collaboration with the Nazis. 'May God protect you, your family and Belgium. I bestow the Apostolic Blessing upon your country . . . your dear country and upon your King. In nomine patris . . .'

Unable to extract much clarity from the Pope regarding the Church's position in the war, a subject that remains murky over half a century later (not least because the Vatican refuses to this day to open its archives on the period), Daye spoke to a high Vatican officer in charge of international affairs whose name he glosses over in his memoirs. The Vatican preferred Communism, Daye was told, because Nazism was 'animated by a faith, a mysticism, infinitely more profound than Bolshevism' and therefore constituted the greater danger to the Catholic Church. Such an answer could hardly satisfy the Nazi collaborator, who kept demanding precision. 'The Church, you see, dear sir,' the slightly irritated prelate finally concluded, 'is like a cat wishing to cross a table covered in precious crystal without knocking over or smashing anything. It is obliged to be extremely supple and slither with the utmost prudence.'[143]

In Paris, Daye took on a responsibility that prefigured the role he would soon play in Argentina. Making use of his contacts with Otto Abetz and the Belgian legation, he began saving Belgians who had got into political trouble, arranging for their safe conduct out of the country, and even rescuing them from arrest by the Germans if necessary. 'It wasn't a case of politics,' Daye recalled later. 'Every Belgian citizen no matter what their opinion was well received.'

Although he was never rich, Daye managed to dine well in Paris thanks to invitations to Maxim's and the Tour d'Argent, 'reopened by the famous restaurateur Horcher of Berlin'. There Daye sat at tables with the stage celebrities Cécile Sorel and Maurice Chevalier, the Vichy representative Brinon, the Nazi ambassador Abetz, the Spanish ambassador Lequerica and a never-ending supply of 'ravishing women'. Among the clients, Daye saw, 'at a table garnished with purple tulips, Marshal Goering dressed completely in beige, with enormous stones on his fingers and a taciturn air.'[144]

Daye sensed early on the hopelessness of Hitler's position in the war. In January 1944, writing from Brussels where he was now minister for sports, he asked Spanish ambassador Lequerica for a visa for Spain. Three months later he arrived in Madrid. In keeping with his official capacity as Belgian sports minister, he then travelled to Barcelona to meet with 'General Moscardo, grand master of physical exercises'. But Daye sensed he was at the beginning of a long exile. General Eisenhower's landing in Normandy on 6 June sent a chill down his spine. 'That cunning Daye!' he imagined his friends in Brussels saying. 'He foresaw the blow. He could have warned us!' The German embassy in Madrid began demanding his 'urgent' return to Brussels, which made Daye even more wary. 'The tone sounded new,' he wrote in his memoirs. 'It became evident that with the latest catastrophic developments Berlin and Brussels had lost their nerve.'

The German retreat made a return through France a truly frightening prospect. 'The trains are being bombed, cars are being machine-gunned. Under the pretext of summary justice murders are being committed everywhere. The war of reconquest covers nearly all of France. It will soon spread to Belgium. Paris will inevitably be recovered some day soon, then Brussels,' Daye confided to his diary. 'I have all the best reasons in the world not to fall into the hands of excited, bloodthirsty madmen. Since nobody could guarantee my safety, I decided to stay.'

Daye was right. His return to Brussels would have meant certain death. By 25 August, Paris had been liberated. On 3 September, General Montgomery triumphantly entered Brussels at the head of Anglo-American forces and the roundup of Nazi collaborators began. 'Thank God I was in hospitable Spain,' Daye realized. 'I fear a time of chaos and violence. Excitation, crime, base revenge.'

Oddly enough, Daye chose the bar of the Anglo-American Club as the best place in which to weather this difficult period. There he discussed literature and politics with Walter Starkie, director of the British Council in Madrid. When evening fell Daye would leave his room at the exclusive Palace Hotel and prowl the night in Madrid, where he saw others like himself, equally lost. 'Illustrious men, outlaws, fugitives, from all countries. I know this or that one. I have common cause with them. They are from Berlin or London, Algiers or Paris, Rome or Lisbon.' Daye wandered to the Ritz, where he caught a glimpse of British ambassador Samuel Hoare dancing, celebrating the victories of the Allies. 'The nights are clear. I see the same stars the men in my country see, but this same minute they are under bombardment and have less peace than I do. I imagine also, through the ether, a triangle reconnecting me with what is left of myself.'

The war was hard on Daye's countrymen, but luck remained on his side. The Spanish foreign minister died unexpectedly and was replaced by his old friend, Ambassador Lequerica. But the news from France and Belgium remained horrifying. Paul Herten, the director of *Nouveau Journal*, had been tried and executed. The newspapers began carrying lists of collaborators. 'The names of so many friends!' Daye gasped. 'Vengeance above all else!'[145]

As the war neared its inevitable end Daye's mood became more gloomy. In the early winter of 1945 he was receiving letters clandestinely from fugitive Rexists who like Lesca had found refuge in Berlin. Expecting the worst, Daye bought a radio set and locked himself in his hotel room listening to the news from Belgium. Legal proceedings had been launched against him. 'I have often imagined with a slight shudder in my heart that, perhaps, I will hear announced over the speaker – that today, Pierre Daye has been condemned to death,' he confided to his diary.

Loneliness was not a problem, as Madrid was teeming with new fugitives and old friends who turned up at Daye's lodgings having been guided over the Pyrenees by Basque smugglers. Charles Lesca, 'solid, loyal and absolute, arrived with his wife, a truly great lady, by plane, and promptly joined the small group of French immigrants'. Around that same time Adalbert Laffon joined the group, along with Carlos Fuldner's friend, the Romanian ambassador Radu Ghenea. 'The Spanish Falangists heap attentions on us, and every now and then we meet Germans, Austrians, Italians or Croatians, all stoical under the avalanche of destiny.'

The hardest blow came on 8 February 1945, and Daye recorded it in his diary. 'As we left the table after having dined that evening at the usual *taberna* with the Lescas, we heard that, according to information on the radio, Robert Brasillach had been executed by a firing squad the day before yesterday . . . I stepped back inside to be alone with a pain that made me falter and erased all other thought from my mind.' After the liberation of France, *Je Suis Partout* had become the symbol of French collaborationism. The ardent anti-Semite Brasillach had been tried by the Haute Cour de Justice de la Seine, condemned to death and executed. General de Gaulle, who pardoned many condemned collaborators, refused to pardon Brasillach, despite the many pleas in his favour.

The little group of fugitives at the Horcher restaurant was joined by Spanish journalists and socialites, including Víctor de la Serna of *Informaciones*, Mariano Daranas of the big Madrid daily *ABC* and José Ignacio Escobar, the Marquis de las Marismas, director of *Acción Española* and *Época*, a good friend of Juan Carlos Goyeneche, Perón's wartime link with Berlin. Other members of this troupe included Abel Bonnard, the last minister of education of the Vichy regime, Manuel Aznar, the future Spanish ambassador to Buenos Aires, and the writer Eugenio d'Ors – who both stood as character witnesses for Daye's Spanish residence application.[146]

By February 1946, Daye had moved from the expensive Palace
Hotel to the more modest Victoria and entered completely into a new
role as rescuer of fellow collaborators fleeing from 'the tyranny that
reigns in Belgium'. His contacts among the sympathetic Spanish
authorities allowed him to pull comrades out of Spanish prisons and
refugee camps and find them employment. 'Some of them arrive
from Paris or Brussels on foot. These poor souls cross over the
Pyrenees, most of them without money, without papers, without luggage. The Belgian diplomatic and consular authorities . . . refuse to
look after them. So does the Red Cross. They are . . . fugitives, without rights, traitors.' Soon the word spread and Daye was swamped
with pleas for help. A war criminal himself, he now became 'a kind of
consul *in partibus* for non-orthodox Belgian refugees'. He visited 'the
camps, the hospitals, the prisons, I pestered government offices,
pleaded with the police . . . I have been able, sometimes, I believe, to
help a few brave young men.'

But the political tide was turning and Franco's dictatorship had
begun to make friendly gestures towards the Allies, which included a
half-hearted attempt to rid Spain of some of the more unsavoury war
criminals and Nazi collaborators in its midst. On 23 May 1946, Daye
started feeling the pressure when he was called to Seguridad headquarters and informed that it was time for him to 'prepare the
necessary documentation to quit Spanish soil'. Daye was furious. Was
the Spanish 'spirit of hospitality' completely gone? He fired off letters
to his influential friends: to the director of Seguridad, to Franco's
brother-in-law Serrano Suñer, to the Marquis de las Marismas, to
Serna. Hadn't he, Daye, fought in the Belgian parliament for diplomatic recognition of Franco's regime in the 1930s? Hadn't he been
Franco's guest in 1938 at the Generalísimo's headquarters in Burgos?
Hadn't he toured the battlefields of the Spanish Civil War that same
year with Lequerica at Franco's behest? 'What do they want to
become of me? In which country could I find refuge?' Daye raged.

He started to hear disquieting rumours: the Belgian government
had presented an extradition request for him, and the new foreign
minister Martín Artajo, who had succeeded Lequerica, was willing to

grant it in order to curry favour with the Allies. Daye's name was third on a 'black list' delivered to Madrid after the names of two other Belgian collaborators, Léon Degrelle and René Lagrou. (Degrelle remained untouched in Spain but Lagrou found his way to Argentina, participating in Daye's meetings with Perón.)

Eventually Daye had to accept that his days in Madrid were over. Charles Lesca's group of Nazi agents, enthusiastic over Perón's electoral triumph in Argentina, was packing its bags. Reuter was already in Buenos Aires paving the way. Daye was being hounded by the *New York Times* correspondent for an interview. It was only a matter of time before a Belgian court passed sentence on his life. He began to 'examine every way in which I could find refuge in another country where I could live more peacefully. But which country? France, the United States, England, all the Allied nations, all the territories where the Germans and Italians had been defeated, not to mention most of the terrified neutral countries, are closed to me.'

Daye finally worked up his courage and trundled off to the Argentine embassy to request a visa from the chargé d'affaires, Raúl de Labougle. (In contrast with his brother Eduardo Labougle, the former ambassador to Berlin, Raúl de Labougle in Madrid was a well-known Nazi sympathizer.) But it wasn't easy going for Daye this time. Perhaps he had left it too long. The arrest of Lesca in Montevideo had caused a storm which 'created a very unfavourable climate for my escape plans. Wasn't Lesca in charge of finding me . . . a landing permit?'

The Spanish Red Cross took an interest in Daye's case, while his friend Ghenea, who remained a daily visitor to the Romanian embassy in Madrid, obtained 'generously and secretly' a Romanian passport for Daye. Although moved by his friend's gesture, Daye finally threw it away, realizing that his 'total inability' to speak a word of Romanian was a dead give-away.

By December 1946, as the *in absentia* trial against him in Brussels gathered speed, Daye had sunk into a deep depression. His friend Lesca, who could have consoled him in this dark hour, was now safely in Argentina. Ever more alone, Daye stopped reading the Belgian press and got rid of the radio in his hotel room. Much of his time was spent jotting down in his diary a lengthy 'imaginary dialogue' between himself and his prosecutor in which he brilliantly shot down the accusations against him. 'I will not deny of course that in 1940 I took the decision to collaborate, France's defeat seemed unsalvageable, England's defeat probable, and German victory was assured.' What other choice was there? Daye asked his diary.

The answer came on 18 December 1946 when Daye was sentenced to 'execution by firing squad' by the Cours d'Assises in Brussels. He was also stripped of his citizenship and ordered to pay 5 million francs in damages to the Belgian state. The condemned man, cut off from all possible news sources, only found out on Christmas Eve. Outwardly unperturbed, he spent the night 'dining with a good strong appetite in the company of a few friends who had the kindness to toast my health and long life'.[147]

Following the verdict, Europe became unbearable. 'In the name of liberty they mean to turn us into legal outcasts, into pariahs, untouchables, something akin to the great excommunications of the Middle Ages. Good! We'll see how this ends . . .!' Daye's acquaintances began closing their doors in his face. He started leading a 'vegetative' existence, spending 'two or three days without talking to anyone'. Only a handful of friends remained loyal. One was the writer and Spanish Royal Academy member Eugenio d'Ors, who continued receiving Daye every Friday for literary lunches at his home on the old Sacramento road; another was the Marquis de las Marismas, who in early 1947 introduced Daye to certain important Argentines. Among them was the young Hipólito Paz, a foreign policy adviser and future foreign minister of President Perón who would become key to Daye's survival in Argentina.

Despite these brief oases things were getting much worse for the French and Belgian collaborators in Madrid, and they were being 'forced to depart towards the unknown'. In most cases, the 'unknown' turned out to be Argentina, and war criminals converged upon Buenos Aires. Now it was Daye's turn to escape. On 26 April, the third anniversary of his arrival in Madrid, he received news from the

Argentine embassy that his visa had finally been granted. With this, he was able to convince the Spanish passport office to grant him a 'stateless' passport, No. 596,506, for the sole purpose of travelling to Argentina. Consul Juan Heligón stamped the special passport at the Argentine embassy on 8 May, and the road was finally clear for the convicted war criminal. With his mother's surname added to his name, he now went as Pierre Daye-Adán, with an accent on the last 'a' for a more Spanish-sounding touch.

'It was with a sense of deliverance, of escape, a veritable joy in the heart, that I boarded the plane that would carry me to South America at the aerodrome in Barajas near Madrid, on the morning of 21 May 1947,' Daye wrote later. Following Lesca's misadventure, Daye had become convinced that air travel was the safest route. Should Belgian spies in Madrid notice his absence, he thought, they would barely have time during the 36 hours the flight lasted to warn the police in Brussels, who would have to issue an international warrant for his arrest.

'As the plane took off from Barajas . . . and a splendid rosy morning dawned over Madrid, I felt an infinite pleasure. After flying over Seville, while the plane rushed ahead towards Morocco, towards Cap Juby, Rio de Oros, to Villa Cisneros, the last Spanish outpost in Africa on the limit of the Senegalese desert, where we landed at breakfast time, among the *meharistes* with their faces veiled under a blue shadow. I started breathing better and better . . . As I felt the plane force itself through the sea air it seemed as though my chest opened, as though I grew younger.'

As the four-engine Douglas crossed the Atlantic at 400 kilometres an hour, flying at 3,000 metres altitude, Daye grew almost giddy with excitement. 'They can battle it out down there. They can even bomb each other. They may be looking for me in that troubled Europe . . . But they cannot reach me. I fly far from a world gone mad, towards peace. It's all over. I have escaped. I fly through the blue.'

The last stopover at Montevideo was uneventful; the Uruguayan police had not been alerted. Half an hour later, around midday, Daye walked down the plane's ladder in Buenos Aires. Three dear fellow war criminals were there to greet him – Charles Lesca, Georges Guilbaud, Robert Pincemin. With them was Perón's foreign policy adviser and former Nazi informer Mario Amadeo. The day remained forever etched in Daye's memory: 'Pedro D. Adán, radiant, landed at Morón aerodrome, under the sun in Buenos Aires, federal capital of welcoming Argentina.'[148]

7

CARDINAL RECOMMENDATIONS

The French-speaking war criminals and collaborators grouped around Charles Lesca and Pierre Daye in Spain were generously aided in their escape by the Vatican and by the Argentine Catholic Church. Indeed, it was through the personal intercession in Rome of French cardinal Eugène Tisserant and the newly consecrated Argentine cardinal Antonio Caggiano that these Latin and Catholic criminals were first able to flee Europe. The rescue effort began on 18 January 1946 when Caggiano boarded a sea-plane to fly to Rio de Janeiro with a small entourage of Argentine Church officials. From there they crossed by ship to Italy, where Pope Pius XII awaited them.

Caggiano was the bishop of the industrial city of Rosario and leader of the Argentine chapter of Catholic Action, a lay organization with Vatican support that had become the rallying point for a vibrant anti-Communist crusade in Argentina during the 1930s and 1940s. Catholic Action counted many staunch nationalists among its members, a large number of whom held important posts in Argentina's 1943–46 dictatorship. Not only did Caggiano's disciples form an integral part of Perón's complex and heterogeneous power base, Peronism itself was rooted in the brand of 'Catholic populism' with which the deeply political bishop had captured the hearts and minds of his city's

growing class of industrial workers. The mass rallies Caggiano organized during the late 1930s in support of decent housing and a
minimum wage brought together workers, nationalist activists, military officers and Catholic Action supporters in a mix that predated
Perón's by only a few years.

The bishop had been called to Rome by Pope Pius XII to be
anointed cardinal, only the second Argentine prelate to be elevated
to such a high position in the Vatican hierarchy. With him travelled
the aged and venerable bishop of Tucumán, Agustín Barrére,
another political creature obsessed with the fear that a
'Masonic–Communist plot' might undermine the Church's authority in Argentina. Barrére had old links to Action Française and ties
of friendship with Daye and Lesca. While Perón's regime of Axis-
leaning colonels began to disintegrate following the Allied victory
in 1945, Monsignor Barrére became particularly involved in
attempting to preserve the Church–State alliance that had evolved
during the preceding years of military and quasi-civilian rule in
Argentina.[149]

Setting the tone for their visit, Caggiano and Barrére were met in
Genoa in early February 1946 by Argentine consul Aquilino López,
the wartime collaborator of Himmler's secret service in Madrid who
had now been transferred to Naples. López had been instructed by
his ambassador in Rome to look after the two prelates and arrange
their overland trip to the Italian capital.[150]

Caggiano's arrival in Rome was marred by the prelate's sudden collapse with a bad bout of the flu, which required his admittance to the
Quisisana clinic for the month of March. Due to the scarcity of vital
products in postwar Italy, the Pope himself had to provide penicillin
for Caggiano's recovery, according to contemporary press coverage.
But surviving documents at the Argentine embassy in Rome show
that Caggiano's convalescence was secretly more fruitful than the
public state of his health suggested.[151]

On 25 and 26 March, supposedly convalescing at the clinic,
Caggiano was actually visiting the Pontifical Commission of

Assistance (PCA) at Villa San Francesco, and inviting the commission's president Pietro Luigi Martin to visit Argentina. The main task of this Vatican body was issuing identity papers to legitimate refugees, but after the war it also provided documents that helped a large number of Nazi fugitives escape to Argentina. The Croatian priest Krunoslav Draganovic, the Vatican representative who worked closely with Argentine officials in Italy to send war criminals over to Buenos Aires, often received identity papers for his 'clients' from the Commission.[152]

Argentina's offer to rescue French war criminals was made to the Vatican's expert on Russian affairs, Cardinal Tisserant, a man haunted by the dread of a Soviet takeover of Europe. 'Tisserant told me he firmly believes there is now a fifty-fifty chance Russia will provoke war this year,' special agent William Gowen of the US Army Counter Intelligence Corps reported to Washington in 1946 after an hour-long interview with the cardinal. Tisserant felt the Russians were in 'a favourable position to overrun Western Europe . . . which opportunity Russia realizes might not again occur'.[153]

Caggiano and Barrére informed Tisserant that 'the Government of the Argentine Republic was willing to receive French persons, whose political attitude during the recent war would expose them, should they return to France, to harsh measures and private revenge.' In other words, former Nazi collaborators. The idea of creating a pool of anti-Communist experts in South America to draw upon in case of a Russian cataclysm was presumably in the back of the minds of the three ecclesiastical dignitaries during these talks.[154]

Tisserant was so unabashedly anti-Communist that he believed 'Reds' did not deserve Christian burial. The French cardinal's position was a chilling precursor of the doctrine applied by Argentina's 1976/83 dictatorship, when rather than executing and burying their victims the country's generals imposed a secret policy of 'disappearances'. They threw thousands of people alive from military planes into the Atlantic Ocean, putting into practice what Tisserant had only dared preach in private among his peers. The Argentine Catholic Church turned a deaf ear to the desperate pleas for decent Christian burials from the relatives of the 'disappeared'. It was in fact a close collaborator of Cardinal Caggiano, military chaplain Emilio Grasselli, who compiled an index of the 'disappearances' as they occurred, not to help the victims so much as to gain more information about their connections. For a brief period at the start of the dictatorship, relatives of the 'disappeared' visited Monsignor Grasselli at the Stella Maris church in Buenos Aires, in the hope that through his military contacts the chaplain would aid them in their plight. But Grasselli's persistent questions about the names of 'friends' of their missing loved ones made the relatives suspect that his real purpose was to compile additional information so that the military could plan new abductions. In any case, Caggiano had made it quite clear where his sympathies lay in 1960 when he spoke out against the capture of Adolf Eichmann by Israel. 'Our obligation as Christians is to forgive him for what he's done,' Caggiano said regarding one of the main perpetrators of the Holocaust.[155]

Back in 1946, during March and April, the Argentine embassy in Rome began to receive a series of consecutive visa 'recommendations' for a large group of Frenchmen, including at least three confirmed war criminals. The pleas were routed through the Vatican to Caggiano, who forwarded them to the Argentine ambassador. This 'spiritual' support finally led to visas stamped on Red Cross passports by the Argentine consul in Rome, Emilio Bertolotto. On 15 March 1946, Bertolotto was instructed to stamp a tourist visa on the passport of French war criminal Marcel Boucher, 'dispensing with the health certificate and other documents' usually required by the Argentine authorities, in light of a 'special recommendation' from Caggiano. Two weeks later, on 1 April, two other criminals, Fernand de Menou and Robert Pincemin, along with five other Frenchmen, received tourist visas. Six of these seven Frenchmen held consecutively numbered passports issued by the Red Cross office in Rome. The consul this time was to also disregard the inconvenient fact that the 'tourists' had no return tickets and refrain again from demanding 'health certificates and other required documents bearing in mind the special recommendation of His Excellency Cardinal Antonio Caggiano'.[156]

During the remainder of March and April many more such 'special recommendations' for 'French gentlemen' from Caggiano and Barrére rained upon the consul's desk. The Spanish priest Vicente Lara Díaz, resident in Rome, who was to play a role in Pierre Daye's flight to Argentina, also received preferential treatment, this time recommended by 'high Vatican authorities and at the personal request of His Excellency Reverend Monsignor Agustín Barrére'.[157]

The flurry of recommendations subsided after Caggiano's 'convalescence' ended and he was finally able to don the robes of a cardinal at the church of San Lorenzo, a temple of the Franciscan order in Panisperma. The following day he held a farewell conference with Pope Pius XII and a few days later, together with Barrére and apparently the Spanish priest Lara Díaz, the new Argentine cardinal set off for Madrid, where more war criminals required divine intervention.[158]

Caggiano's reception in Spain was nothing short of heroic. Argentina had been shipping badly needed grains and foodstuffs on generous financial terms to Franco's dictatorship, which was still ostracized by the victorious Allies. The people of Spain were eager to show their gratitude. Crowds of the faithful thronged his path in Zaragoza, Toledo, Granada and other towns. On 22 April, Caggiano made a triumphant entry into Madrid in the company of Argentine chargé d'affaires Raúl Labougle, the pro-Nazi diplomat familiar to Daye and Lesca; they were flanked by the Argentine consul and Catholic Action leaders. Several thousand people gathered to greet the cardinal, cheering Argentina, Spain and Caggiano. They chanted religious hymns outside the Unión Católica residence on San Bernardo Street where he lodged.

The cardinal kept a busy schedule, meeting with Franco on 25 April and delivering a mass three days later at Toledo Cathedral, where he gave communion to 600 people. Finally, on 9 May, the clerical delegation headed back to Argentina, boarding the *Cabo Buena Esperanza* at Cadiz. A 'true multitude' of Catholic Action supporters was at the dock to cheer goodbye as Caggiano waved from the ship.

Below deck, French war criminal and fellow first-class passenger Emile Dewoitine welcomed the ship's departure with relief. Wanted in France for 'intelligence with the enemy' and 'endangering the

foreign security of the State', Dewoitine was one of Europe's leading
jet-plane designers. During the war he worked for the Nazis, Japan
and Spain, employing some 200 people at a special plant the
Germans had put at his disposal in Toulouse. With the liberation of
France in 1944, he fled to Madrid. There he came into contact with
Colonel Carlos Vélez, the emissary sent to Europe by Perón to
pledge Argentina's support for Hitler's cause, to purchase arms from
the Nazis and to hire 'technicians' for the Argentine military.

Dewoitine boarded the *Cabo Buena Esperanza* at Vigo with a Spanish
passport. On 28 May 1946, when the ship docked at the port of Buenos
Aires, the Frenchman became the first documented case of a certified
war criminal disembarking in Argentina. Dewoitine quickly joined
Perón's team of air force designers and by 7 August 1947 a working pro-
totype of his IA-27 'Pulqui' jet fighter made its first test flight, turning
Argentina into the fifth nation in the world to build an operational jet
aeroplane. In France, his crimes were considered serious enough to earn
him a 20-year forced labour sentence *in absentia* on 9 February 1948.[159]

Shortly afterwards, on 2 October, the *Buena Esperanza* returned to
South America, this time bearing three more French war criminals,
two of Caggiano's 'special recommendations', Menou and Pincemin,
and their comrade Charles Lesca. Menou and Pincemin disembarked
without any problems in Buenos Aires, presumably shaken by Lesca's
run-ins with the authorities in Rio de Janeiro and Montevideo. A
number of other Frenchmen recommended by Caggiano arrived on
the same ship.[160]

In Madrid, meanwhile, Pierre Daye sat down to fill in his application to the Argentine Immigration Office for a landing permit. Apart
from naming the two required character witnesses, provided by Lesca,
Daye could not help boasting of a higher endorsement: 'I could also
mention Monsignor Barrére, bishop of Tucumán, who is currently
kindly looking after my case and has spoken personally with His
Excellency President Perón; as well as Abbot Lara Díaz, at the
bishop's palace in Tucumán.'[161]

Through their efforts at the Vatican and their influential whispering in

Perón's ear, Caggiano and Barrére paved the way for some of the worst Nazi criminals and collaborators to escape to Argentina. Cardinal Tisserant continued to put in special requests for men on the run even after Caggiano's departure. 'During the last months I have been looking after certain compatriots, who have retreated from Germany to Italy and are living here in difficult circumstances,' Tisserant wrote the Argentine ambassador on 7 May 1946. As American intelligence knew, the French Nazi collaborators hiding in Rome were being fed at the Papal Mess on the Via Po.[162]

At around the same time, American diplomats in Madrid and Buenos Aires started to piece together details of an 'elaborately contrived escape plan' involving the Catholic Church and the Spanish security forces. Fingers pointed at the Spanish Commission of Charity and Aid for Refugees. A Father Juan Guim of the Jesuit order in Seville was mentioned. The rumours were confirmed by a German informant holding a Belgian passport who arrived in Buenos Aires for 'the study of the Communist movement'. He had the additional mission of providing 'aid and assistance' to fleeing Nazis. 'A Miss Goyeneche leads another group,' the American embassy in Buenos Aires reported, stating that this relative of Juan Carlos Goyeneche, Perón's wartime link with Himmler, headed a Catholic Action group.[163]

At a much higher level, an immigration agreement between the Pope and Perón's government was secretly under discussion. In June 1946, the Acting Vatican Secretary of State, Cardinal Giovanni Battista Montini, brought up the matter with the Argentine ambassador to the Vatican. Montini (the future Pope Paul VI) expressed Pope Pius XII's interest in arranging the emigration 'not only of Italians' to Argentina. The Pope considered Argentina the only country where emigrants could find 'a satisfactory solution to their needs'. The Holy Father was willing for 'the Vatican's experts to get in touch with the Argentine experts to arrange a plan of action'. The Argentine ambassador understood the Pope's interest to extend to the men penned in at Italy's POW camps – i.e. Nazi officers – and promptly informed Buenos Aires of the proposal.[164]

8

PERÓN'S ODESSA

Towards the end of his life Perón spelt out the motive behind his rescue of Nazi war criminals in lengthy memoirs dictated privately to a cassette recorder. In these solitary recollections the aged general confided to the winding spool how the Nuremberg trials of the leading Nazi officials in 1945 had outraged his monolithic sense of military honour, and how he had become determined to save as many of them as possible from Allied justice. 'In Nuremberg at that time something was taking place that I personally considered a disgrace and an unfortunate lesson for the future of humanity,' he related in his gruff voice. 'I became certain that the Argentine people also considered the Nuremberg process a disgrace, unworthy of the victors, who behaved as if they hadn't been victorious. Now we realize that they [the Allies] deserved to lose the war. During my government I often delivered speeches against Nuremberg, which is an outrage history will not forgive!'

These private tapes in which Perón came closest to baring his inner soul were recorded during the last years of his long exile in Spain, shortly before his triumphant return to Argentina to begin a new presidential term of office in October 1973. He died barely ten months later and the cassettes became his last major living testimony. During a farewell dinner in Spain he had given them to Spanish celebrity

Niní Montián, a 'friend of the family' who provided racy entertainment for the old general and his entourage in Madrid. The former actress had known Perón since at least 1949, when she met his wife Evita in Buenos Aires. She eventually sold the tapes to Torcuato Luca de Tena, publisher of the big Madrid daily *ABC*, who set a group of secretaries to transcribing them. 'It was like Ali Baba and the forty cassettes,' one participant recalled for this investigation.

Luca de Tena asked Spanish journalist Luis Calvo to co-author with him a book based on the tapes. It was published in Madrid in 1976, mingling extracts from the recordings with commentary. Interestingly enough, Calvo had been a correspondent for *ABC* and a secret Nazi spy in England during the war. The journalist was arrested by MI5 in London in 1942, and turned by British intelligence into a 'controlled agent' who fed fake information to the Germans until mid-1944. He was eventually released, apparently following pressure from the Vatican.

Thanks to these tapes Perón's extraordinary assessment of the Nuremberg trials was recorded for posterity; explaining the secret postwar Nazi immigration policy directed from the very heart of his presidency.[165]

The various Nazi trails that started in Europe converged in Buenos Aires behind the same balcony of the Casa Rosada from which pop singer Madonna sang 'Don't Cry for Me, Argentina' in the film *Evita*, five decades later. Behind the pink balustrades, near Perón's presidential office, was the Information Bureau, a presidential secret service under the control of Rodolfo Freude, a young, blond German-Argentine who had won not only the trust of Perón but also the friendship, at least at first, of Evita and her corrupt brother Juan Duarte.

The Argentine National Archives hold a large number of images in which young 'Rudi' Freude always walks a step behind Perón and Evita. Particularly noteworthy is a roll of film of 6 June 1947 in which he accompanies the First Lady to Morón airport. That day Evita boarded an Iberia DC-4 airliner on the first leg of her historic 'Rainbow Tour' of Europe. Standing on a podium behind Evita as she bids farewell to the assembled crowd, Freude is clearly on intimate terms with the couple. Towards the end of the reel Perón turns his head slightly to share a private comment with his secret service chief while Evita waves a white handkerchief to her admirers.

But all was not well between the First Lady and Freude. Once on the plane, stricken by her uncontrollable fear of flying, Evita wrote a farewell letter to Perón counselling him against his young spymaster. Freude's agents had apparently uncovered embarrassing secrets from her teenage years and revealed them to her husband. The resurrection of old ghosts was painful. 'I swear these are false charges,' wrote Evita. 'It's painful to love your friends and be repaid this way.' And there was more: 'Beware of Rudi, he likes to make money,' she wrote as she crossed the Atlantic.[166]

The provenance of the Freude family fortune had been a matter of concern to the Allies for some time before Evita put these thoughts on paper. Freude's father Ludwig, a long-time personal friend of Perón with proven Nazi links, had channelled large contributions from Argentina's German business community into Perón's 1945–46 presidential campaign, seeming to confirm the rumours that the colonel was in the pay of the Nazis. The millionaire, described as 'one of the 10 richest men in Latin America' by the *New York Times*, had been entrusted by the German embassy with a 'stay-behind' fund to finance Nazi intelligence activities after Argentina broke off diplomatic relations with the Reich in January 1944. In fact, after the break Ludwig Freude became the informal Nazi ambassador to Buenos Aires, consulted on matters of importance by the Swiss legation which took charge of German diplomatic interests in Argentina. This role was only a natural extension of the elder Freude's intimate association with the Nazi embassy since before the start of the war. The Freude mansion in the elegant Buenos Aires suburb of Belgrano had often served as a discreet meeting place for Argentine military officers and Nazi bigwigs. In Berlin SD chief Walter Schellenberg was convinced, or at least so he told his American interrogators after the war, that Ludwig Freude 'worked for Ribbentrop's secret service, Informationstelle III'.[167]

During 1945 Washington and London put intense pressure on Buenos Aires to repatriate Ludwig Freude to Germany for interrogation. For a few brief months the Nazi moneyman seemed to be in danger as the military dictatorship's grip slipped badly in the wake of the German defeat. Perón's colonels knew that sooner or later they would have to permit free elections – the only question was who their candidate would be. As the regime's multifaceted vice-president, war minister and labour secretary, Perón felt that he was ideally suited to the job.

On 6 August 1945 the cry for democracy forced the regime to lift a state of siege that had been in force for four years and Buenos Aires became a battleground for pro- and anti-Nazi demonstrators. Democratic-minded students clashed with the mounted police of the dictatorship in the streets of the city. The surrender of Japan in mid-August provoked particularly violent outbursts, pitching Nazi fanatics in favour of Perón's candidacy against those demanding the handover of government to the Supreme Court. 'The voice of the people of Argentina is being heard ... in the streets,' said American under-secretary for Latin American Affairs Nelson Rockefeller in a speech from Boston.[168]

During these outbursts the offices of the democratic newspaper *Crítica* were besieged by hundreds of armed soldiers escorting a Peronist mob. Glass lay shattered on the sidewalk and street sweepers were still hosing down large bloodstains in front of the building when Ludwig Freude turned up to speak to the paper's editor Raúl Damonte Taborda, a brave anti-Nazi crusader. 'I like you, you've put up a good fight against us,' said Freude. 'You defend your country and your ideals and we defend ours. But you must understand that to continue fighting under these circumstances will cause you the loss of your newspaper and who knows what other complications. Why don't you cut a deal with Perón? The Americans won't do anything to him, you'll see.'[169]

Behind his menacing words old man Freude was actually running a little scared. His cronies in Berlin had lost the war, he was obsessed with the fear that Germany would fall under Communist rule, and his protector Perón was losing the support of the senior generals who disliked Evita and mistrusted the uppity colonel's populist posturing. Washington had begun aiming its guns at Perón as well. 'To defeat [the Axis] we have paid a staggering price in blood and suffering. We shall not forget this lesson merely because petty tyrants are now assuming the disguise of spurious democracy,' said the American ambassador to Buenos Aires, Spruille Braden, in a public speech that was a clear dig at Perón's electoral ambitions.[170]

The combined assault was taking its toll. Perón's position was weak enough by 6 September that Argentine foreign minister Juan Cooke could promise the American ambassador that Ludwig Freude would finally be repatriated to Germany. On the following day the minister was almost able to keep his word. A police swoop nabbed Nazi businessmen Hans Leuters, Friedrich Frohwein and Ernst Schlueter, all three joint trustees of the Nazi spy fund with Freude, who was himself taken into custody. Freude's likely expulsion caused an alarmed Perón to telephone the head of the secret police, Major Oscar Contal: 'What are you going to do with that man? You've got to look after him. Consider what he represents, the head of the German community in Argentina!' Perón worked out a compromise. Ludwig Freude would not be officially arrested but he would be confined to his home under strict police custody. 'Perón protected Freude,' confirmed Contal in an interview for this book 52 years later.[171]

A few days later, on 11 September 1945, Argentina's military dictatorship finally caved in to Allied pressure and a decree was signed ordering the expulsion of Perón's German friend. But even while the colonel's political star was dimming he had remained one step ahead of his enemies. In anticipation of such a move Perón had obtained from a provincial judge a forged letter of Argentine citizenship which prevented Freude's expulsion, settling the matter in Freude's favour. On 19 September the Argentine foreign minister was forced to admit to the American ambassador that Ludwig Freude had too many friends in high places to be deported.[172]

Perón meanwhile was struggling for his own survival. That same day a gigantic 'March for the Constitution' drew 250,000 people to downtown Buenos Aires chanting 'Down With Despotism' and 'Death to Perón'. On 24 September the colonel was hit closer to home; a military rebellion against his government had to be crushed. Two days later a frightened Perón reimposed the state of siege, filling the country's gaols with non-Peronist military officers as well as with the pro-democratic journalists, politicians and university professors who had been calling for an end to the military dictatorship. Although not a word was published in the Argentine press about these arrests, nevertheless universities around the country staged a strike in protest. In response, Perón closed the universities. A group of the mothers and wives of Perón's political prisoners began marching around Plaza de Mayo in front of the Casa Rosada and were chased off with tear-gas, another story that didn't make the press. The rumour started to spread that the military regime and an extreme nationalist group were plotting a pogrom in Buenos Aires. Arms were distributed at synagogues around the city for self-defence.[173]

In an attempt to deflect the anger aimed against the dictatorship, his own fellow officers finally ousted Perón from office on 9 October. The once all-powerful colonel lost his three titles of vice-president, war minister and secretary of labour. At first Perón licked his wounds at Evita's flat on swanky Posadas Street, but by 11 October, fearing his life might be in danger, he decided to go underground. Ludwig Freude's son Rudi provided the perfect hiding place, Perón recalled in his taped memoirs decades later. 'Look, Colonel, if you're going to go away let me offer you my summer home Ostende, on one of the islands of the Tigre river, where you'll find total quiet,' volunteered Perón's young friend. 'The house has everything you need, including food. You go there and nobody will know where you are.'

That night Perón took the wheel of a Chevrolet motor car and with Evita at his side sped off from Posadas towards the northern suburbs of Buenos Aires. In the back seat were Rodolfo Freude and his inseparable friend, Evita's brother Juan Duarte. A couple of hours later Perón and Evita arrived on their own at Ostende island on the Tres Bocas river, where the Freudes had built a wooden chalet imported piece by piece from Germany.

'The only thing on the island was a house with a German caretaker who spoke Spanish pretty badly,' Perón would recall years later. 'He was called Otto and since he constantly said "Jawohl" we nicknamed him Otto Jawohl. We spent three days there devoted completely to ourselves. They were the only three days of real life we had together, three magnificent days of a hoped-for real honeymoon.'[174]

While Perón and Evita enjoyed their enforced privacy, the attempt to protect Ludwig Freude continued in Buenos Aires. A secret agent loyal to Perón stole the expulsion order against Freude from the steel safe of the secret police department and 'dressed as a mechanic, took it to Ludwig Freude's house'. There the presidential decree was 'burned in the billiard room fireplace in Freude's presence', a Nazi agent repatriated from Argentina told American interrogators in Germany a couple of years later.[175]

The pre-nuptial 'honeymoon' on Freude's island proved extremely brief. A military delegation soon arrived to arrest Perón. The colonel was pulled from a tearful Evita's arms and taken to an island prison in the middle of the River Plate. For a few days he entertained the gloomy possibility that his presidential ambitions had been definitely thwarted. But in reality the colonel's arrest had given him an aura of martyrdom and became the key to his legendary hold over the Argentine masses. An unprecedented wave of popular support for the downfallen workers' hero began to sweep the streets of Buenos Aires, culminating in a massive demonstration in front of the Casa Rosada demanding Perón's freedom. The nervous generals released him, begging him to address the crowd and calm down his supporters. That night of 17 October 1945, Perón gave a historic speech from the balcony of the Casa Rosada that would guarantee his supremacy over the Argentine people and seal the nation's fate to his own. 'All Power to Perón' headlined *The Times* of London, reporting the colonel's Phoenix-like rebirth from the flames.[176]

The events of October had cemented the already solid bond between Perón and the Freudes. Ludwig Freude now became the main conduit for German contributions to Perón's electoral campaign, while his son Rudi became the candidate's personal secretary. Together they would help Perón become president of Argentina. Meanwhile press stories and Allied intelligence reports pointed to Ludwig Freude's likely role as a front for Nazi assets. The US in particular, in a note to the military dictatorship, accused him of being 'one of the chiefs of the movement to place German capital in safe places in Argentina'. In this task he seems to have been aided by the leader of the Nazi spy ring in Argentina, SS Captain Siegfried Becker, briefly arrested at the end of the war by the Argentine police but cleared of charges once Perón became president in 1946. Becker had apparently put what was left of Himmler's spy network in Spain at Freude's disposal, as a channel for funds.[177]

While the elder Freude remained discreetly in the background, Rudi was seen everywhere next to Perón. One theory picked up by the American embassy was that Perón rescued the young German-Argentine from a tough military conscription in the navy by designating Rudi his orderly. The junior Freude quickly rose from menial chores such as shining Perón's boots to becoming the newly elected president's spy chief.[178]

The Nazi links of Perón's right-hand man were too flagrant to ignore. His brother-in-law Werner Koennecke, who lived next door to the Freude family mansion in the elegant Belgrano suburb of Buenos Aires, had been the accountant for the Nazi intelligence network in Argentina during the war. From an iron safe in an office in the German embassy he handed out money to Himmler's agents. Koennecke was arrested briefly by the Argentine police during the timid swoop on Nazi spies in 1944, but Perón and young Freude forced his release and no charges were ever pressed against him. He went on to become one of Freude's most trusted collaborators. The Freude clique's response to the threat of being incriminated in Nazi spying charges was to ransack the files of Argentina's secret police and destroy the patiently gathered evidence linking their family and Perón with Nazi activities in Argentina.[179]

Young Freude's reputation soon reached all the way to Europe, where fleeing Nazis began establishing contact with influential

Germans in South America as early as October 1945. By February 1946, before Perón had assumed the presidency and when Lesca was still at the Horcher restaurant in Madrid plotting the escape of Nazi agents, Nazi fugitives in Spain began to hear from Perón's new private secretary. 'Freude has sent them a messenger informing them that he will send orders shortly which they will execute without discussion,' the American embassy in Madrid reported to the State Department in Washington. 'Further, they have received news from Germany that they must obey Freude's orders.' Another American report mentioned that Ludwig Freude was 'financing Nazi resistance throughout the world'. Rumours abounded that Hitler's deputy Martin Bormann was in hiding in Argentina and working with Freude.[180]

Perón's resounding triumph in the presidential elections of 24 February 1946 set the stage for the massive evacuation of Nazi fugitives from Europe to Argentina. While this sinister traffic got under way Rodolfo Freude settled behind his desk in the Casa Rosada where he took charge of the presidential Information Bureau, and of the newly-created national Central State Intelligence (CIDE) as well. According to a former Freude agent interrogated by the military coup that ousted Perón from government in 1955, the main task of Freude's office was to collect intelligence on Communist activities. For this purpose secret agents had been posted at Argentine embassies in the American continent and Europe. The branch also spied on Perón's domestic opponents, and the president was briefed on its findings every Monday, Wednesday and Friday afternoon. One member of the opposition claimed that Freude's office also had the mission of 'harassing Jews and disturbing gatherings of opposition political parties with elements of the Nazi organisation'.[181]

It was Perón's intention to rescue as many Nazis as possible from the war crimes trials in Europe. To accomplish this mission, Freude's office developed a close link with the notoriously anti-Semitic anthropologist and author, and now Argentina's Immigration Commissioner Santiago Peralta. The month after Perón's inauguration, Peralta and a group of leading military officers created a 'Human Potential Commission' under the umbrella of the National Defence Council, to design Argentina's postwar immigration policy. Its surviving records are steeped in Communist paranoia, pseudo-scientific babble about the 'laws of blood' and stereotypical anti-Semitism. Peralta told the generals it was necessary to 'apply a selective criterion, seeking immigrants who will not form minorities lodged like cysts' in the body of the nation.

In 1946 the generals and Peralta created a National Ethnic Institute to prevent 'the formation of foreign communities or minorities'. This institute had long-term ambitions. It envisioned a 'scientific' and 'step-by-step' remodelling of Argentina's population over the duration of four generations. Also in the works were the drawing up of 'Argentina's human map' and a second 'secret' map tracing the nation's 'military anthropological features'. This Nazi-style racial blueprint was designed to 'guide the nation without interruption for centuries' and therefore could only be entrusted to the armed forces, not to politicians. By early 1947 Peralta and the generals began discussing specific measures to thwart the activities of 'Zionist' groups and the arrival of Jewish refugees who tried to enter Argentina from neighbouring countries such as Brazil, Uruguay, Peru and Chile.[182]

Out of this secret link between Freude and Peralta, Perón's Nazi rescue team was born. Its leading agents were flown in from Madrid during 1946 and 1947, many of them convicted war criminals themselves. Some were recruited into Freude's secret service, others became 'confidential advisers' at Immigration. The Argentine military establishment took in its fair share of them as well. Quite a few wore all three hats simultaneously. Peralta's forced resignation in June 1947, which followed a storm of protest against his overt anti-Semitism, not only failed to damage Perón's nascent Odessa network but breathed new energy into the Nazi schemers.

Pablo Diana, a former staff member of Perón's vice-presidency, replaced Peralta on 7 June 1947, the day after Evita departed on her tour of Europe. Perón told him that immigration policy was 'directed personally' by the 'First Magistrate' (i.e. Perón). Diana knew what was expected of him and proceeded to fine-tune the inherited machinery until it ran like clockwork.[183]

Perón's salvage team included:

• *Carlos Fuldner* The German–Argentine former SS captain and Himmler agent was Perón's main Nazi rescue operative. After his escape to Argentina in 1947 he became an agent of Freude's Information Bureau. He was also the main authority on German arrivals at Immigration, and recruited Nazi 'technicians' for the Argentine air force. He would arrange the safe passage to Argentina of major war criminals such as Adolf Eichmann, Josef Mengele, Erich Priebke, Josef Schwammberger and Gerhard Bohne.[184]

• *Jacques de Mahieu* This war criminal, a veteran of the Waffen-SS *Charlemagne* Division (33rd Waffen-Grenadier Division), recruited from French volunteers, was the first arrival by plane from Europe on 22 August 1946 and was probably the founding member of Peralta's team. He was rumoured to have fought alongside the Nazis on the Russian front. Mahieu was a theoretician of 'bio-politics' who scoffed at the idea of racial equality. He was on intimate terms with Perón but fell out of favour with Evita after he asked her to fire a Jewish secretary she employed. Evita refused. Mahieu nonetheless remained close to Perón, who named him national secretary of the influential Higher School of Peronist Leadership. During the 1960s he headed a Peronist Party branch on Talcahuano Street in Buenos Aires and still pulled strings at Immigration. A man of great influence over the Peronist far right, his lectures were attended by fanatics who on hearing the word 'Jew' roared back 'Soap! Soap!' enthusiastically. He was also a regular speaker, in flawless German, at the pagan solar solstice celebrations held by fugitive Nazis in Argentina. Mahieu even had disciples among young Peronist members of the Montoneros terrorist organization during the 1960s and 1970s. In 1989, shortly before his death, he campaigned for Peronist presidential candidate Carlos Menem.[185]

• *Gino Monti de Valsassina* The Italo-Croatian 'Count of Monti' was an ex-member of Hitler's Luftwaffe and a former spy for Nazi military intelligence. He escaped from Milan to Madrid 'under suspicious circumstances' in April 1945, according to one American report. From there he flew to Argentina on 4 January 1947, entering the country on 'official service'. Within a few months he had been granted a 'non-Argentine' passport by Perón, who sent him back to Spain to recruit 'Germans of high technical ability'. His beneficiaries covered a broad spectrum, from Nazi criminals such as Luftwaffe General Eckart Krahmer to the former arms dealer and special Nazi agent Reinhard Spitzy. Monti started helping wanted Nazis, including SS officers and former collaborators of General Krahmer, to board Argentine planes from Madrid towards the end of 1947. In Buenos Aires he worked closely with Rodolfo Freude, initiating landing permit applications for European fugitives, and making himself 'morally and materially responsible' for their arrival in Argentina. To finance himself, Monti was awarded a contract to furnish Evita's first-aid stations for the poor, an enterprise that ran out of steam because suppliers feared the First Lady's reputation for refusing to pay bills punctually, if at all.[186]

• *Branko Benzon* The wartime Croatian ambassador to Berlin and Budapest was rumoured to have enjoyed a personal relationship with Hitler and Göring. At the end of the war he arrived in Madrid on a German plane bringing back Spanish troops from Franco's Blue Division who had fought alongside the Nazis on the Russian Front. He left by air for Buenos Aires on 22 March 1947 bearing a Spanish passport under his own name. A cardiologist by profession, Benzon quickly found work both as 'technical adviser' to Perón's Public Health Ministry and at the German Hospital in Buenos Aires, settling down in a luxurious apartment at a classy address on Callao Avenue. He immediately joined the Peronist Party. The tall, good-looking Benzon became an intimate friend of Evita. As confidential adviser to Perón he was given ample power at Immigration, which he exercised on the one hand to aid Croatian criminals and on the other to harass Jews. His bold scrawl 'J. NO B.' ('Jew, no, Benzon') often marked landing permit applications by Jews for rejection. Benzon accompanied Perón into exile following the military coup that ousted the general from power in 1955.[187]

• *Georges Guilbaud* The next arrival on an Iberia flight from Madrid, on 13 May 1947, was another French war criminal with a death sentence on his head who was quickly adopted by Perón. Guilbaud had started his political life in France as a Marxist, then veered to the right to become a leader of the PPF. He was entrusted by Pierre Laval with organizing the Milice in northern France. In Buenos Aires he joined Freude's secret service and also became one of Perón's main economic aides, in charge of a reform of the Argentine banking sector. Guilbaud used his influence with Perón to aid fugitives brought to Argentina by his close friend and fellow war criminal Pierre Daye. In time Guilbaud made a fortune in his own right as head of the Piano financial house in Argentina, before moving to work in banking in Switzerland in the 1960s. His wife, Maud Sacquard de Belleroche, became a close friend of Argentina's First Couple and wrote the book *La Reine des Sans Chemises* about Evita.[188]

• *Pierre Daye* The Belgian war criminal arrived in Argentina barely one week after Guilbaud on 21 May 1947. Belgium's extradition request went ignored while Daye conferred with Perón at the Casa Rosada over setting up a special agency for the rescue of war criminals from Europe.

• *Léonard de Roover* This Belgian war criminal with a death sentence from the Brussels War Council arrived in Argentina on 4 July 1947. He was quickly recruited by the Information Bureau and became the link between Freude and Immigration, handling Freude's requests for landing permits. Roover fell out of favour when it was discovered that he was selling landing permits to Jews on the side, slipped in among the applications forwarded by the Casa Rosada.[189]

• *René Lagrou* The founder and well-known leader of the Algemene SS Vlaanderen (the Flemish SS) was captured by the Allies in France but managed to escape to Spain. Condemned to death by a war tribunal in Antwerp, he arrived in Argentina some time during July 1947. Under the false name Reinaldo van Groede he became a member of

Perón's Nazi team, with wide-ranging powers at Immigration. Some of the landing permits initiated by Perón's own presidential office carried his signature. He was also a major collaborator in Daye's rescue efforts. Shortly after his arrival Lagrou drew up a six-page proposal for the migration of some 2 million Belgians (comprising all wartime Nazi collaborators together with their families, friends and business partners) to Argentina. This 'elegant' solution, he argued, would 'save many precious lives and deliver to Argentina the healthiest and most valuable biological elements Europe possesses'.[190]

• *Herbert Helfrich*   A German Nazi recruited in Switzerland by Perón's military agents in Europe, Helfrich flew in from Zurich to Montevideo on a KLM flight, and then boarded the *General Alvear* to Buenos Aires on 25 July 1947. Barely two months later the Argentine army sent Helfrich back to Europe where, during the following two years at least, he operated in Germany and Switzerland smuggling Nazi 'technicians' to Argentina for Perón.[191]

• *Jan Durcansky*   This war criminal arrived from Genoa in August 1947 under the false name Giovanni Dubranka, along with his brother and fellow war criminal Ferdinand Durcansky. As regional leader in Bánská Bystrica in central Czechoslovakia he had been responsible for the mass murder of some 1,300 people between November 1944 and early 1945, including a large number of French and American prisoners of war. In one case 400 victims were made to kneel, and were then shot through the head and thrown into a burning quicklime oven; in another 750 people including women and children were machine-gunned in an open trench. In a third case 140 people were similarly killed and buried in an anti-tank trench. Barely two-and-a-half years later in Argentina, Durcansky was enrolled at Immigration, where he smoothed out landing permit and citizenship applications from fellow fugitives. His appointment was signed by Perón personally. The pint-sized Slovak was affectionately nicknamed 'Don Juan' by his workmates. A request for his extradition by Prague was turned down in 1960.[192]

• *Czeslaw Smolinski*   On the same day as Durcansky, a Pole who spoke German with an aristocratic 'hochdeutsch' accent arrived in Buenos Aires on board a Douglas DC-4 plane. Barely four months later he was back in Europe meeting with top Swiss officials as a personal representative of Perón. His mission was to measure Switzerland's willingness to serve as a transit point for Nazis recruited by the Argentine president. In Argentina meanwhile, the newly arrived mother and wife of former SS captain Carlos Fuldner, Perón's main Nazi rescue agent, found a safe haven at a farm owned by Smolinksi in Buenos Aires province.[193]

• *Radu Ghenea*   The intimate friend and collaborator of Carlos Fuldner and Pierre Daye arrived in Buenos Aires on board the *Monte Saja* on 4 October 1947. Shortly after his arrival Ghenea was meeting Perón at the Casa Rosada to arrange the escape of other war fugitives to Argentina.[194]

• *Víctor de la Serna*   An important Spanish journalist who fought alongside the Nazis on the Russian Front in Franco's Blue Division, Serna was a close friend and protector of Pierre Daye, Carlos Fuldner and other fugitive war criminals and collaborators in Madrid after the war. He was ushered into Perón's presence with Daye and Fuldner barely a month after arriving in Argentina on 7 November 1947. His close contacts with the Red Cross in Spain were undoubtedly considered an invaluable asset for the enterprise at hand.[195]

As these war criminals and Nazi collaborators arrived, Perón and Freude invited them to the Casa Rosada. The first group to be received included Benzon, Smolinski, Monti and Fuldner. Also at some of these meetings were Argentine Central Bank director Orlando Maroglio and Guilbaud. If the transfer of Nazi assets was discussed at these meetings Perón certainly had the right men in the room to plot the details. The commander-in-chief of the Argentine air force, Brigadier Bartolomé de la Colina, also sat in.[196]

In the best-documented of the meetings, in early December 1947, three convicted war criminals met simultaneously with the president. Ushered by Freude into Perón's office, Daye, Lagrou and Guilbaud joined Fuldner, Ghenea and Serna to plan the rescue of Nazi war criminals. The participants could hardly believe their luck. 'All these foreigners had been condemned to death in their respective countries,' recalled Daye in his unpublished memoirs afterwards. 'The President knew it and I admire his independence of opinion and the courage with which he received us in the national official palace.' Over fifty years later, despite the wealth of documentary evidence available, it still seems incredible that Perón could have plotted so brazenly with the war criminals themselves the greatest escape ever in the annals of crime.[197]

9

DIGGING FOR CLUES

A rgentina's main archive of documents about the Nazi rescue operation was located in the offices of the Information Bureau, the
nerve centre of Perón's Odessa. Unfortunately the files of this presidential intelligence service remain closed to researchers, despite the
fact that Argentina's 30-year state secrets limitation has more than
expired and that a 1992 presidential decree ordered the opening of all
Nazi-related records. It is also likely that Freude's files long ago
ceased to exist. Some claim that part of the Nazi rescue archive was
intentionally destroyed before Perón's ejection by a military coup in
1955 to prevent it from falling into the hands of his political enemies.
There is also evidence that another major cleanup occurred much
more recently, in 1996, when a new Peronist government was in
power.[198]

Perón's Odessa also used the secret archives of Argentina's
Immigration Office to store compromising documents. This government department today occupies the same sprawling riverside lot in
the port of Buenos Aires as it did during the 1940s. Next to the river,
behind a giant complex through which millions of immigrants arrived
at the end of the nineteenth century, stands the now derelict Hotel de
Inmigrantes. Once upon a time its giant-sized rooms offered state-
financed lodging to new immigrants until they could find jobs in

Argentina. The block-long building now houses the Immigration archive, or rather, a carefully purged version of it.

Researchers are usually granted access only to the voluminous passenger lists for sea, rail and air arrivals up to the 1970s, which are kept on its first floor. But by returning to the archive practically every day for five months, stating that I was working on postwar immigration in general without specifying any particular Nazi interest, I won the trust of the archive's caretakers and managed to obtain unaccompanied access to its off-limits 'Fleas' and 'Chela' sections on the second floor. The 'Fleas' section, as the name implies, is an unholy draughty nightmare of a place with broken windows. When I first started working there in 1998, it was filled with mountains of dusty old files piled on creaky shelves or strewn along the floor in no particular order. A litter of kittens was born on one mound of files while I worked there that year. At first I wore rubber gloves and a face mask; after a few days I was beyond caring. The neater 'Chela' section is named after an employee who took on the Herculean task of arranging in alphabetical order by year of arrival all the Immigration cards filled in by disembarking passengers from the 1920s to the 1970s. This constitutes a couple of city blocks of shelves stacked with tightly packed cards in what seem to be infinite sets of wooden boxes.

Painstaking work culling data from these passenger lists and cards produced a rich bounty of information regarding the arrival of Nazi criminals. For a start, Immigration opened a separate landing permit file for each immigrant, even for criminals such as Eichmann, Priebke and Mengele. These files included data from the moment an applicant first requested a landing permit, which was sometimes as long as two years before they would reach Argentina – this happened in the case of Eichmann for example. All subsequent paperwork was kept in them, including the testimony of character witnesses, and notes of whether the applicant figured in Allied-supplied Nazi lists, whether 'recommendations' had been made in their favour and, in politically sensitive cases, who specifically authorized their entry. Sometimes one file dealt with a large group of people. File 72513/46, for example, granted landing permits to some two thousand Croatians. This single file probably saved more war criminals than any other during Perón's presidency.

Entering the data thus obtained on a computer spreadsheet produced additional revelations. The files for war criminals Erich Priebke and Josef Mengele turned out to be consecutively numbered, 211712/48 and 211713/48 respectively, even though they arrived in Argentina on separate ships seven months apart. Since Immigration was opening files at a rate of over 500 a day during 1948, we can be 100 per cent certain that this was a simultaneous presentation by one person in favour of two major Nazi war criminals. Barely a month earlier, file 201430/48 had been opened by Fuldner for another important criminal, the SS mass murderer Josef Schwammberger. Eichmann's file 231489/48 was opened soon after, even though he delayed his arrival in Argentina until 1950. Fuldner's eventual close association with Eichmann, the fact that he was in Europe importing Nazis during 1948 when these applications were opened, the proximity of the dates and the consecutively numbered Priebke and Mengele files, are clear evidence that an organized system for the rescue of Nazi war criminals was in place and that Fuldner, acting either under his own or an assumed name, was at its centre.[199]

So far, so good. But after having identified them by name and number, next came the task of locating the files themselves. Earlier, in a different government archive, I had located one Immigration file marked 'Secret' belonging to a major Nazi collaborator, Yugoslav premier Milan Stojadinovic. This file provided details of Perón's close connection to the Argentine end of the Croatian ratline. What might Eichmann's file reveal?[200]

Weeks of wading through mountains of orange-coloured folders in the 'Fleas' section without turning up one single politically sensitive file made it clear that a secret hiding place existed elsewhere in the vast Immigration complex. There was no way to request these Nazi files without blowing my cover. Even so, the angry response my petition provoked from Immigration officials came as a shock. First I was accused of being secretly involved in a 'political' investigation. My 'impartiality' was called into question. Dark words were muttered against the Jews. An even more depressing reaction was to follow immediately afterwards: 'What do you want me to confess? Do you want me to tell you that Immigration ordered us to burn all those files two years ago? I'm never going to admit that!' barked the frightened caretaker.

Finally, after much insistence, on 26 October 1998, I was ushered into a personal interview with Immigration Commissioner Hugo Franco, a Peronist government official with close ties to the Catholic Church and with the chiefs of Argentina's 1976/83 military dictatorship. Flanked by one of his underlings, dressed in a light tan-coloured suit, Franco came out from behind his desk and relaxed into an armchair in his ample office. I was invited to sit across from him, a low coffee table between us. He did not smile. I explained the purpose of my investigation, pointing out that an Immigration document I had seen from 1949 suggested that the secret files in question were kept back then in the private archive of the Commissioner's office, i.e., the equivalent of Franco's own private archive. 'There's nothing, nothing, nothing,' was his staccato reply, setting the tone for the rest of the meeting. Franco claimed ignorance of the whereabouts of any of his department's Nazi-related files, and of his predecessors' archives, indeed he denied knowledge of any files from before the start of his own administration. 'I would have all those old documents burned if I could, they're just a headache for me, but I consulted with Congress and they won't let me,' he hissed between clenched teeth, the whole purpose of the interview obviously distasteful to him. Emphasizing how important it was for Argentina to exorcize its old Nazi ghosts failed to elicit any response. Pointing out that we were talking about individual files recording the exact escape routes followed by the most evil fugitives of the century barely raised an eyebrow.[201]

In the next few days a letter from me identifying the pertinent files by applicant and number was routed to Franco through the Argentine Foreign Ministry which, in the wake of the recent 'Nazi gold' revelations in Switzerland, had set up a commission to investigate charges of Argentina's own Nazi complicity. The written response from a lower-ranking Immigration official sounded hopeful. The files had not been destroyed and access was granted. Alas, when I arrived at Immigration on 4 December 1998 with letter in hand and accompanied by a member of the Foreign Ministry's commission, the reality proved heart-rending. 'Please come outside, we can't talk in here,' said the Immigration lawyer who had drafted Franco's response. Outside we went, to the large park in front of the Hotel de Immigrantes, under old trees where many a grateful Nazi criminal must first have walked in Argentina. 'Those files were extremely embarrassing. They were destroyed two years ago. That's all I can say. We obviously couldn't put that in writing in an official letter. I'm sure you'll understand.' The white shadow of the old hotel loomed behind us like a giant, beached whale. A family of Bolivians crossed the park clutching in dark hands their own residency applications. Right-wing groups had recently papered the walls of Buenos Aires with loud posters calling for restrictions against this influx of cheap labour from neighbouring countries. 'Argentina is way too generous,' muttered the fair-haired lawyer who had just sought our complicity over the burning of the Nazi files, eyeing the Bolivians with disgust.

Other Immigration officials confirmed the burning, adding details. The individual files containing the voluminous paperwork for the admission of Eichmann, Mengele, Priebke and others had been kept in a safe for secret documents until 1996, when they were all destroyed. A bonfire was lit behind the old hotel, on the edge of the dock, at night. Everything was gone. The Peronist cover-up had lasted right up to the end of the century.[202]

My long passage through Immigration was over, but no adventure would be complete without its epilogue. In the last days of December 1998 I was approached by the keymaster of the archive, the same official who only weeks earlier had accused me of not being 'neutral' in my research. In alarmed tones I was informed that orders had been received to burn all the remaining documents on the second floor. The old building was going to be turned into a museum-cum-shopping mall and there was no time and certainly no budget for moving the mass of papers. The keymaster may have been hard as nails on the surface but, as happens to many archivists, the old, dusty papers had cast a spell and to imagine them carted away in dump trucks was too horrifying for words.

'You have contacts in the press,' the keymaster pleaded. 'Couldn't you arrange the publication of a story to try and stop it?' We weren't talking Nazis now. The files in question register the arrival of the successive generations of immigrants from which most modern-day Argentines descend. I had seen thousands upon thousands of application forms with passport-sized photos of young Italian and Spanish mothers hopefully clutching children in their arms. Streams of their descendants regularly consult the Immigration archives today to trace their family history. It was worth a try. A story appeared on the front page of the Buenos Aires daily *Página/12* in January 1999. It was picked up by the radio stations and other media. The bosses at Immigration backed down, but not before making a disconsolate phone call to my home. 'How could you do this to us?' they whimpered. The documents, for a while, remained safe. But in 2001, when I returned for a second round of research, the thousands of orange files in the 'Fleas' section had disappeared.[203]

10

CRIMINAL WAYS

Although in Argentina much of the documentation for Perón's Odessa was intentionally destroyed in 1955 and the 1990s, the organization did leave evidence of its activities littered here and there throughout Argentina and Europe. In Berne, the Swiss Federal Archives hold the incriminating records which show how high-ranking Swiss officials allowed some 300 'illegal' Germans to pass through their territory en route to Argentina. In Brussels, the voluminous papers of Belgian war criminal Pierre Daye, divided between the Musée de la Littérature and the CEGES centre for World War Two studies, reveal the details of Perón's connivance in the Nazi rescue enterprise.

Another large cache remains sequestered in Argentina's police, military and intelligence archives. Fortunately for historians, Argentine officials, while immensely corrupt, were fussily observant of rules and regulations. Even in the case of secret Nazi immigrants they insisted on all the formalities being scrupulously complied with. This generated a large amount of paperwork that simply fell through the cracks of the country's under-financed and mismanaged archives, far from the reach of 'cleansing' operations. This bureaucratic mindset, coupled with the internecine war between Argentina's Foreign Ministry and its Immigration Office for control of immigration policy, led to procedures through which the secret doings of Perón's Nazi team remain visible to this day. Researchers need a long arm and a great deal of patience to get hold of these documents, but it's not an impossible task.

By World War Two, the officials had settled on a compromise solution to their power struggle, requiring that foreigners surmount two separate barriers in order to enter Argentina. First of all, a landing permit had to be obtained from Immigration, via an application presented by the interested party at an Argentine consulate in Europe or by a relative in Buenos Aires. In the case of Nazi war criminals and collaborators, a simple letter of reference from an associate of Perón's Information Bureau sufficed for a landing permit to be awarded in whatever name or alias was requested. Immigration would then send a wire to the respective Argentine consulate informing them that the application had been approved, and the consulate would call in the applicant to collect the permit. In the case of Nazi applicants, it would be collected by the member of Perón's Nazi team in Europe representing them. Very often the permits were picked up by Vatican representatives such as Draganovic or by agents of the Austrian bishop Alois Hudal.

After being awarded an Argentine permit under a false name, a Nazi could obtain a Red Cross 'travel document' under the same alias, taking a major step towards freedom. Intended for refugees who had lost their identification papers during the war, these 'travel documents' were to all intents and purposes the equivalent of a passport, and were admitted as such internationally. Thus armed with a landing permit and valid travel papers, the prospective immigrant could now return to the Argentine consulate to apply for an entry visa. The feud between the diplomats and Immigration continued even at this late stage, with consuls sometimes denying visas to travellers with valid landing permits, or Immigration permitting foreigners without valid visas to disembark in Buenos Aires. In most cases, however, Nazis on the run would leave the consulate with an Argentine visa stamped on their Red Cross papers. At the same time the consul would issue the immigrant with an 'identification certificate' which was used to obtain a *Cédula de Identidad* upon arrival in Buenos Aires – the standard ID issued by the Argentine police. The way was thus cleared for a successful escape to South America with nothing less than a complete change of identity thrown in.[204]

Armed now with a landing permit, Red Cross papers, an Argentine visa and his 'identification certificate', was our Nazi ready to board ship? No, there still remained one last rung of the ladder to climb. Perón had installed an organization in Italy known as DAIE, the Delegation for Argentine Immigration in Europe. Enjoying semi-diplomatic status, the DAIE had offices in Rome, where the paperwork was handled, and in Genoa, where prospective immigrants had to undergo a medical examination by Argentine doctors, who sometimes even rejected applicants with valid papers. Needless to say, exceptions were made at various points along this complicated route for Nazi VIPs.[205]

The accumulated paperwork was assembled in numbered files at the Immigration Office in Buenos Aires, usually one for each candidate, from the time the landing permit was first applied for until the moment of arrival in Buenos Aires. Sometimes these files remained active for a long time, and recorded the point at which Nazis changed the alias they had used to enter the country back to their real names.

During 1948, when the postwar wave of immigration to Argentina reached its highest point, some 500 new files were being opened daily to handle the rush. Immigration therefore 'privatized' its work by allotting quotas to be filled in at their own discretion by representatives of the Belgian, Croatian, French, German, Russian, Slovakian, Slovenian or Ukrainian communities in Argentina. These representatives were often war criminals or former collaborators themselves, hired as Immigration 'advisers' by Perón's government, always on the understanding that they would not submit Communists or Jews for admission.[206]

As we have seen, these Argentine 'Nazi' files survived until 1996, when their destruction in a large bonfire was ordered. Only one such document escaped the purge. It involves the case of a major Nazi collaborator whose admission to the country had to be cleared in 1947 by the Argentine Foreign Ministry, which neglected to return the paperwork to Immigration. The document rested safely in a separate archive, undisturbed by end-of-the-century Peronist pyromaniacs, and it clearly illustrates the methodology employed.

Secret File 87902/47 was opened on 20 March 1947 by the recently arrived Croatian collaborator Gino Monti de Valsassina. Upon entering Argentina the 'Count of Monti' had been drafted into Freude's Information Bureau and he promptly became one of Perón's main Nazi-recruiting agents, as well as a close friend of General Perón and Evita. The first page in the folder is a letter from Monti to Immigration Commissioner Santiago Peralta requesting a landing permit for Milan Stojadinovic, former premier of Yugoslavia, whose 'activities in Europe before and during the war' Monti had 'personally described' already to Peralta. Within five days Peralta wired instructions to the Argentine consulate in London (Stojadinovic was being held under British custody on the island of Mauritius in the Indian Ocean) to issue a landing permit for Monti's candidate 'with whatever documentation he presents'.

Stojadinovic's entry would have proceeded without a hitch had the US not discovered his intended move. Within a month Washington alerted Buenos Aires that the 'pro-Axis ex-premier of Yugoslavia is attempting to take up residence in the Western Hemisphere,' reminding Argentina of its obligation under the Act of Chapultepec to reject his entry. (The act had been signed in Mexico at the end of the war by all the American nations, binding them to refuse entry to Nazi criminals and collaborators to the Western Hemisphere.) The US was piqued by Stojadinovic's prewar espousal of the Third Reich, manifested in the visit to Berlin in January 1938 during which he held long conversations with Hitler and Göring and promised Yugoslavia's full support for the Nazi New Order. After the annexation of Austria by Germany, Stojadinovic had declared: 'Now we can feel secure with 120 million friends on our borders.' Under his leadership, Yugoslavia formed its own SS-style 'Green Shirt' storm troops and adopted the Nazi salute, while Stojadinovic took on the title of Vodja, the Yugoslavian equivalent of Führer. His government collapsed in 1939 and he was removed by Prince Regent Paul. The following year Stojadinovic was arrested after documents were found at his home linking him with Nazi 'Trojan Horse' activities. Prior to Hitler's invasion of Yugoslavia in April 1941 the former premier was smuggled into Greece and delivered to British authorities who placed him under confinement on Mauritius.

In view of the objection from Washington, the Argentine Foreign Ministry whispered a few words in Peralta's ear and a new telegram was sent off countermanding the original order and blocking Stojadinovic's entry. In mid-1947 however, following Evita's trip to Europe and the appointment of new Immigration Commissioner Pablo Diana, Perón's Nazi rescue organization got its second wind and the drive to rescue Stojadinovic gathered new strength. First, Monti wrote a new letter, which went straight into Stojadinovic's file, asking for entry papers for the Vodja's wife and two daughters, who had made it as far as Brazil, despite the fact that the only documentation they possessed was a set of 'already-expired Royal Yugoslavian passports'. Then came the clincher, a letter from Perón's intimate friend, the former Croatian ambassador to Berlin, Branko Benzon. Another recent arrival drafted into Freude's Information Bureau, he was a born charmer who had gone from meetings with Hitler to flirting with Evita. According to Benzon, the British authorities in Mauritius had 'withdrawn the vigilance' over Stojadinovic, making it a suitable moment to renew the application for a landing permit. On the same day Benzon presented his request, a telegram went off to the Argentine consulate in Cape Town, again granting Stojadinovic entry 'with whatever documentation he may possess'. The telegram did not go unnoticed by a well-intentioned but misguided official at the Foreign Ministry who sounded the alarm. He was quickly informed that Stojadinovic's admission had been agreed upon on 21 September 1947 at a meeting between the foreign minister and the new Immigration chief in Perón's office at the Casa Rosada. Stojadinovic finally disembarked at Buenos Aires on 2 April 1948 and was joined shortly afterwards by his wife and two daughters from Brazil.

This same complex but well-oiled machinery went into high gear during 1948 when Perón's Nazi rescue group began working in Europe, principally out of Berne and Genoa. In a period of under two months that year, Immigration files similar to Stojadinovic's were opened for four notorious SS officers: Adolf Eichmann, Josef Mengele, Josef Schwammberger and Erich Priebke. They arrived on separate ocean liners many months apart, but the paperwork for their journeys began together – in the case of Mengele and Priebke, simultaneously, as we have seen.[207]

Stojadinovic can't have arrived empty-handed, as he quickly settled into an apartment at an exclusive address in Belgrano 'R', one of the favourite spots in Buenos Aires for homesick Nazis. He quickly founded *El Economista*, which went on to become one of Argentina's most important financial dailies. Although his chequered past was never a matter of comment in Argentina, it seems to have come back to haunt him when Perón's government started falling apart in 1955. Stojadinovic hurriedly applied for Argentine citizenship, but Perón was overthrown before it could be granted. When he tried again in 1960, the former Vodja had to counter an Argentine police report that accused him of specializing 'in intelligence tasks among the Yugoslav community in Argentina', apparently in favour of the US, and of belonging to various 'Free Yugoslavia' groups. Stojadinovic survived the charges and became an Argentine citizen at last on 6 October 1960.

Stojadinovic's attempt to model the Yugoslavian state along Nazi lines earned him the label of a major collaborator. After the war, returning to Communist-ruled Yugoslavia would have certainly landed him in prison. Britain seems not to have cared particularly where he went as long as he was off her hands. Washington clearly tried its best to keep him out of the Western Hemisphere. But Perón was determined to welcome him with open arms, and it was the Argentine general who won the day.[208]

11

THE NORDIC ROUTE

In 1947 Perón's Information Bureau set up an escape route in north-ern Europe. Its purpose was to smuggle Nazi jet-plane designers out of Germany into Sweden and Denmark, and from there to Argentina to work on the president's ambitious aeronautics pro-gramme.

At the same time a parallel rescue effort was being bankrolled by German businessman Friedrich Schlottmann, owner of the giant Sedalana textile firm in Argentina. Schlottmann's route was operated by the intrepid 24-year-old German-Argentine Carlos Schulz, who travelled to Scandinavia to rescue as many fugitive Germans as possi-ble from postwar justice, brandishing Schlottmann's promise of employment in Argentina. Most of these Germans had fled to Denmark from the advancing Allied forces at the end of the war. Schulz brought with him a thousand landing permits issued by Perón's Immigration Office. He also carried letters of recommendation from the rabidly anti-Semitic Immigration Commissioner Santiago Peralta.

Presenting himself as the representative of an Evangelical church from the Argentine city of La Plata, the audacious Schulz was able to convince officials in Oslo to free imprisoned Nazis and permit their flight to Argentina. In Stockholm he obtained lists of fugitive Germans and wired these to Buenos Aires – they returned invariably approved for entry by Perón's Immigration Office. Argentine consuls then stamped visas on Red Cross passports obtained thanks to Schulz's landing permits. These passports were so crude that at times they even lacked the bearer's picture. (The Red Cross proved extremely accommodating to Nazi fugitives in northern Europe, its ambulances reportedly transporting Germans clandestinely across Scandinavian borders after the war.)[209]

Argentina's consuls asked no questions and worked hand in hand with Schulz during 1947. Some of them were in fact secret agents of Rodolfo Freude's Information Bureau, sent to Scandinavia to open the 'Nordic route'. Consul Carlos Piñeyro was entrusted with the task of filling out blank Argentine passports with Spanish-sounding aliases for Perón's Germans. Piñeyro was practically German himself. Born in Europe, he had served as Argentina's consul to Danzig through the 1930s, and had married a German national in Bulgaria in 1941. He was posted to Copenhagen at the end of the war. In 1947 he was called to the Casa Rosada for a few brief days for secret meetings with Freude and the president, then flown back to Denmark to carry out his mission under 'special orders' from Perón himself. The smuggling operation was also aided by Argentina's long-time consul in Denmark, Elzear Mouret.[210]

These Argentines hired the Danish SS officer Günther Toepke to smuggle Perón's Nazis from Germany into Denmark. From Copenhagen they usually went to Sweden, where they boarded commercial air flights to Geneva and then Buenos Aires. Despite his record, Toepke held a senior post in Denmark's intelligence service after the war, which made his moonlighting for Perón much easier. The Caritas representative in Denmark, the Prussian priest Georg Grimme, also spirited away fleeing Nazis to Argentina, with financial aid from Ludwig Freude. He later moved to Buenos Aires himself, where he wrote for the Nazi-leaning German-language daily *Freie Presse*. According to Schulz's own account, he rescued some one thousand Germans in northern Europe. The young German-Argentine checked their background as far as he could, to reassure Perón that there were no Communists among them.[211]

The Scandinavian authorities, however, had begun to lose patience with the blatant activities of the Argentines, and on 17 November 1947 Schulz was arrested during a surprise swoop in Stockholm. The young man defended himself in court in fluent German, and admitted that he was working in collaboration with Argentina's Immigration Office. Although a group of Swedish passport forgers, including a former SS officer, were eventually convicted, Schulz was freed on the understanding that he would leave the country as quickly as possible.[212]

At the same time, in Copenhagen, the capture of two Nazi scientists trying to leave the country with passports provided by the Argentine consuls Piñeyro and Mouret resulted in an acutely embarrassing diplomatic scandal. Toepke was arrested and Piñeyro, Mouret and the Argentine ambassador were discreetly invited to leave Denmark.[213]

But Schulz had one last trick up his sleeve. Before leaving Sweden he joined forces with German SS officer Ludwig Lienhardt, whose extradition from Sweden on war crimes charges had been demanded by the USSR. As a member of Alfred Rosenberg's East Ministry during the war, Lienhardt had been in charge of the forced resettlement of ethnic Swedes from Estonia, including a group of 3,400 people resettled during the final days of the war. Sweden had also ordered Lienhardt's expulsion, not wishing to hand him over to the Communists for trial, despite his grisly record. Tellingly, like the other leading Nazi-rescuers, Lienhardt had been an 'honorary collaborator' with Himmler's SD.[214]

Lienhardt's consortium represented Nazis from eight different European nations who, thanks to Schulz's intervention, obtained travel documents from the Argentine embassy in Stockholm for the most cinematic Nazi escape ever. On 30 December 1947 the group set sail from the port of Stockholm on board the *Falken*, an old training sailing ship that Lienhardt had acquired. The departure was widely covered by the Swedish press, which had been following the story of the ship's preparation for months. Two Soviet torpedo boats were reportedly sent by Moscow to intercept the *Falken*, but failed in their mission when blown off course by a giant storm in the Baltic Sea. It took seven months for Lienhardt and his crew to reach Argentina. They finally docked at Buenos Aires to a jubilant reception on 26 July 1948.

The restless Schulz did not stay on board for the duration of the trip. He disembarked during a forced stopover in London and promptly boarded a flight to Madrid. He continued his Nazi rescue operation from there, apparently through contact with Fuldner in Switzerland and Italy. Upon his return to Buenos Aires, Schulz was given a hero's welcome and taken on as aide-de-camp to Perón's close friend, Colonel Domingo Mercante, the governor of Buenos Aires province.[215]

One German that Piñeyro and Mouret were especially eager to get out of Europe was SS Captain Kurt Gross, the wartime head of Nazi espionage operations in Spain and South America. Gross had been privy to all the details of Goyeneche's meetings in Berlin, Hellmuth's failed mission to meet Hitler and the SD–GOU coup in Bolivia in December 1943. His Berlin office had frequently been visited by Argentina's military attachés, who communicated with Buenos Aires via the Nazi radio link. Nobody knew as much about the real link between Perón and Himmler's intelligence service as this man.

Gross had escaped to Denmark, crossing the border illegally in October 1945. He was arrested the following month, but then freed while his application for a Danish residence visa was processed. But in January 1947 he was placed in a detention camp and his visa request denied. Due to be deported on 17 October, he fled the camp the day before, and ran straight to Piñeyro and Mouret for help. Perón's envoys were willing to oblige, and some days later Gross approached the Copenhagen police with a document from the consulate stating that he was being granted entry to Argentina. The Danes acquiesced and Gross abandoned the country on 5 November 1947. Some kind of quid pro quo was at work, for the Danish Justice Ministry had advised the Copenhagen police 'not to treat this case too stringently, since the Argentines have done certain favours for us, especially in the case of some Ukrainians that we didn't want here whom they accepted.'

The Danish authorities were only too glad to offload their embarrassing guests and send them into Perón's open arms. And Perón must
have breathed a huge sigh of relief to know that Gross, with all his
secrets, was finally safely out of the reach of Allied interrogators.[216]

The most bizarre Nazi criminal to escape via Perón's Nordic route
was the 'Danish Mengele', Carl Vaernet, an SS doctor who claimed to
have found a 'cure' for homosexuality. In the 1930s Vaernet had
developed a pseudo-scientific therapy based on what he strangely
termed the 'reversal of hormonal polarity'. Himmler believed
Vaernet's therapy represented the 'Final Answer to the Homosexual
Question'.

In 1943 Vaernet signed a contract with the head of the Reich
Security Main Office, Ernst Kaltenbrunner, ceding patent rights for
his cure to the SS company Deutsche Heilmittel in exchange for
research funds, laboratory facilities and the use of concentration camp
internees as human guinea pigs. In 1944 Himmler put the 'pink triangle' population of Buchenwald at Vaernet's disposal. About 15
subjects were experimented on. Some were castrated and implanted
with the Danish doctor's 'artificial male sexual gland', a metal tube
that released testosterone into the groin over a prolonged period.
Vaernet claimed that as a result of his work some subjects had been
'reborn' as heterosexuals. Regarding the case of Buchenwald inmate
No. 21,686, Bernhard Steinhoff, a 55-year-old theologian, he reported
to Berlin that 'the operation wound has healed and there is no rejection of the implanted sexual gland . . . the person feels better and has
had dreams about ladies.' Apart from Himmler and Vaernet, nobody
seemed impressed. According to survivors' accounts, the SS doctors at
Buchenwald 'made terrible jokes' about Vaernet's experimentation.
Among the prisoners the implants were known as 'firestones'. In view
of the circumstances in which the experiments were conducted, it is
no surprise that Vaernet's subjects declared themselves cured when
questioned by the doctor.

At the end of the war Vaernet was imprisoned by the British occupation forces in Denmark and on 29 May 1945 Major R.F. Hemingway

informed the Danish Medical Association that the doctor 'would undoubtedly be punished as a war criminal'. But Perón's agents had another idea in mind, one that would conveniently rescue Copenhagen from an embarrassing trial involving operations on homosexual concentration camp prisoners by a Danish high-society doctor. After the British handed him over to the Danish authorities in the autumn of 1945, the plan for Vaernet's escape accelerated. Meanwhile, according to documents held at the Rigsarkivet national archives in Copenhagen, Vaernet tried to sell his Buchenwald hormone delivery system to British and American medical firms with the help of his eldest son and fellow doctor, Kjeld.

In January 1946 the doctor appealed to the Danish government for permission to travel to Stockholm to receive treatment for a feigned heart ailment. Not only did the Danish government agree, the Danish police even gave the doctor Swedish currency for his trip. Once in Stockholm, Vaernet was quickly spirited away by Perón's organization, most likely on a regular Stockholm–Geneva–Buenos Aires commercial flight, arriving in Argentina some time before March 1947. The doctor's family, apart from his eldest son Kjeld, followed on a Royal Mail ship. (After the war Kjeld Vaernet continued his medical practice in Denmark, performing lobotomies. He became the subject of media attention in the 1990s, but the doctor insisted his own work bore no relation to his father's work in Buchenwald.)

By August Carl Vaernet's application for Argentine citizenship stated that he was working as an endocrinologist under the 'direct orders' of Perón's health minister. From Buenos Aires he maintained contact with his son Kjeld through Carlos Schulz. After a few years Vaernet opened a private practice at 2251 Uriarte Street, but he never regained the social status he had enjoyed in prewar Denmark. Ostracized by the local Danish community, and unable to speak proper Spanish, the 'Danish Mengele' lived in constant fear of being discovered by Nazi-hunters. He suffered a series of personal mishaps, including being run over by a taxi in 1955, which left him severely injured, with 15 fractures. That same year his wife was electrocuted in a freak train accident and died.

Vaernet's ultimate fate remained a lasting mystery in Denmark. In 1949 a Danish court closed his case, declaring that he was believed to be hiding in Brazil, despite all the evidence, including press articles, pointing to Argentina. There the matter stood until 1999, when a Danish gay rights activist traced Vaernet's grandson, who had never been informed of the doctor's real role during the war. 'I hope that at least the pain of the relatives can be mitigated a little,' wrote his shocked grandchild. 'I also hope that the mistakes of the past will prevent our generation and those of the future from committing crimes against humanity, or from discriminating against or pursuing people on account of their religion, the colour of their skin or their sexuality.' Christian Vaernet reported that his grandfather had died of an unknown fever on 25 November 1965. He is buried at the British Cemetery in Buenos Aires, row 11.A.120.[217]

The early German arrivals aided by Schulz, Piñeyro and Mouret had provided a solid base in Argentina for the continuation of the Nazi rescue effort. Lienhardt's *Falken*, now turned into a floating head-quarters, enjoyed a long afterlife as a meeting place for the group of Nazis around Mengele's protector Hans-Ulrich Rudel. This group, known as the *Kameradenwerk*, sent food packages from Argentina to high-ranking prisoners such as Rudolf Hess and Admiral Karl Dönitz. In some cases Rudel's group even paid the legal defence fees of former Nazis under trial in Europe.

As well as Rudel and Lienhardt, the *Kameradenwerk* included other notorious Nazis such as the Gestapo criminal Kurt Christmann, the Austrian criminal Fridolin Guth, and apparently also Perón's long-time friend and former Nazi spy in Chile, August Siebrecht. These *Falken* conspirators maintained close contact with the former Poglavnik (Leader) of Croatia, Ante Pavelic; the former head of the Italian Fascist party, Carlo Scorza; the son of Il Duce, Vittorio Mussolini; and with Konstantin Freiherr von Neurath, the son of Hitler's foreign minister – all of them hiding in Argentina under Perón's protection.

A peculiar offshoot of the *Falken* and its journey was the German branch of the Peronist Movement for Foreigners (MPE), an organization set up in the dying days of the administration. The movement gathered Peronist supporters from among 32 foreign communities in Argentina, united under the leadership of a certain Gustav Müller. The German Group of the MPE was set up in February 1955 under the presidency of Lienhardt and promptly sent off a warm note to the embattled Perón promising to repay 'loyalty for loyalty'! Plans included the formation of an armed battalion of a hundred Nazi troops. But perceiving the increasingly fragile situation of the Peronist government, Lienhardt met personally with Perón, only a few days before the general's downfall, and decided to disband his 'German Legion'.

The withdrawal proved fortunate, for the leaders of the 1955 revolution that unseated Perón promptly summoned Lienhardt for explanations. The SS officer was saved by a telegram he was able to brandish which was dated shortly before Perón's overthrow, declaring the dissolution of his German Group.[218]

Perón's 'Nordic route' was practically shut down in November 1947 following Schulz's arrest in Sweden and the quiet expulsion of Argentina's diplomats from Denmark. The collapse of this escape tunnel probably explains the sudden appearance of Fuldner and his agents in Europe the following month for the opening of a 'southern route' through Switzerland and Italy, which was to operate smoothly during 1948.

12

THE SWISS CONNECTION

Perón's secret conferences with war criminals and Nazi collaborators in the Casa Rosada set the stage for the boldest venture yet by his Odessa-style organization: the opening of a clandestine bureau in Switzerland. Ostensibly created to recruit German 'technicians' for Argentina's military projects, the office was run by bona fide Nazis and enjoyed the veiled support of anti-Semitic members of the Swiss government. By the admission of one of its own members, the bureau was really set up to rescue persons who 'should be before the Nuremberg court rather than in Argentina'. This murky alliance of former Nazi agents, Swiss officials and Argentine diplomats assisted an evil procession to safety. Some went under an alias, heavily disguised, others brazenly flaunted passports bearing their own names. All had their journey eased by the secret brotherhood whose tentacles reached from sheltered Buenos Aires to war-devastated Europe.

During her 'Rainbow Tour' of the Old Continent in mid-1947, Eva Perón generated a great deal of good will among important decision-makers in Spain, Switzerland and the Vatican. These leaders soon proved disposed not only to turn a blind eye to the doings of Perón's agents but also to aid them in their task. Rumours that Evita had met in Madrid with SS Colonel Otto Skorzeny and in Rome with the Croatian priest and Nazi-smuggler Father Krunoslav Draganovic are difficult to confirm. But Perón's wife did meet with General Franco and Pope Pius XII, and before returning to Argentina she was able to send out a reassuring message to fugitive Nazis that help was on the way.

Argentine military officers of German descent had begun to reach Europe as early as 1945 to prepare the escape. By late 1947, the rescue missions from Italy to Sweden were active as roving scouts sent from Buenos Aires scoured the continent seeking out deserving candidates. Official cover was provided by Argentina's embassies, where agents of Freude's Information Bureau took up fake posts as diplomats.

The nerve centre of the operation was established in Berne where the rescuers obtained a green light from the Swiss chief of police and the minister of justice as long as they kept a low profile. As a matter of fact, Swiss officials seemed relieved to have somewhere to offload their growing influx of Nazis, although they apparently charged under the table for their discretion. Perón's agents also enticed them with the promise that, in return for Swiss transit visas for German 'technicians', berths could be made available for the war victims on their territory, who could be dispatched on the very same ships used to smuggle Nazis to Argentina.

A personal friend of Perón, retired army major Benito Llambí, who formed part of the secret GOU lodge that ruled Argentina until 1946, headed the Argentine legation in Berne and was in on the game. Cover for the Nazi schemers took the form of an 'Argentine Emigration Centre' opened at 49 Marktgasse. There, Carlos Fuldner plotted the escape routes out of Allied-occupied Germany. Eichmann and Mengele escaped with the organization's help. Other criminals such as Dr Gerhard Bohne, administrator of Hitler's euthanasia programme, Erich Priebke, involved in the Ardeatine Caves murders in Rome, and Josef Schwammberger, responsible for mass killings of Jews in Poland, were also helped by Perón's minions.

In the immediate postwar period, the Argentine military pursued ambitious plans to build weapons factories, jet fighter planes, and even to develop nuclear capabilities. Perón had long cherished the dream of turning Argentina into a military-industrial power in its own right. In mid-1945 an Argentine officer of German descent, Colonel Julio Hennekens, was already combing Europe for technicians. Unable to reach Sweden, a preferred transit point for Nazis bound for Argentina, Hennekens was rerouted to London; there he enrolled a group of Polish engineers who had worked for the British military aviation industry during the war and who began arriving in Argentina by late 1946.[219]

Another officer, Colonel Rodolfo Jeckeln, was more successful at recruiting real Nazis. Buenos Aires dispatched him to Berne in June 1947 with 150,000 Swiss francs. A fluent German speaker, he had been an assiduous visitor of German arms factories in the pre-Hitler era. He was also intimately connected with the Nazi-tainted Austrian arms manufacturer and multimillionaire Fritz Mandl, who had fled to Argentina during the war and had become a major contributor to Perón's electoral campaign. In Switzerland, Jeckeln was one of the guests of honour at a reception hosted for Eva Perón at the Hotel de Ville in Lucerne on 5 August 1947 during her visit to Switzerland. By November he was signing a contract to hire Berlin University chemist Hans J. Schumacher, who was later joined in Argentina by five fellow war industry experts and Nazi party members. At least one of them, Dr Peter Brodersen of Frankfurt University, possessed the additional distinction of being a member of the SS.[220]

But Colonel Jeckeln's star recruit turned out to be Herbert Helfrich, a Nazi architect who became a major cog in Perón's rescue machine. Helfrich had joined the Nazi party in 1933 and rose to director of public works during Hitler's Reich. He was involved in the building of the Munich–Berlin autobahn and was responsible for major military projects such as the fortifications in Normandy and along the northern German coast. He was also associated with the secret V-2 rocket project at Peenemünde, where he built launch pads for the Nazi missiles that rained on London during the war. Among his friends he counted Wernher von Braun, the V-2 designer later hired by NASA to build rockets for the American space programme, and Georg Weiss, another guided missile scientist who helped Helfrich to rescue Nazis for Argentina.

How Nazi experts like Helfrich came to be discovered by Perón is difficult to know at this late date. Helfrich claimed to have been invited to Argentina by Perón himself at the start of the war. Perón had undergone military training in Fascist Italy between 1939 and 1941 and spent a long time in Rome. Some independent historians speculate that Perón travelled to Berlin during this period. Peronist historians on the other hand argue against such a trip, stating correctly that no documentary evidence has been found to support it. Perón himself, contradicting his supporters, frequently claimed that he had visited Germany and he professed to be particularly impressed by Hitler's autobahns, of which Helfrich happened to be an architect. Intriguingly enough, Helfrich's brief Nazi party file gives a Rome address, Via Milano 5, along with his Berlin address, perhaps suggesting an Italian rendezvous.

The end of the war found Helfrich at his post in Berlin while his wife and three children waited at Schlosswalter castle near the Italian border in Austria, where many other fugitives were being sheltered by an Austrian nobleman. After being contacted by Colonel Jeckeln, Helfrich flew from Switzerland to South America via KLM, a tried and tested airline for fugitive Nazis, arriving in Buenos Aires with his family on 25 July 1947. He had travelled on an official Argentine passport made out in his real name. Soon he was attending lunchtime barbecues at Perón's presidential residence in Buenos Aires.[221]

Barely two months after arriving in Argentina, Helfrich was sent back to Switzerland as a secret agent for Freude's Information Bureau. His aim, in what became known as the 'Helfrich Mission', was to rescue as many fellow Nazis as possible from Germany by using his generous funds to bribe Swiss officials. (Helfrich was not above charging the Nazis for his services, according to at least one testimony.) He enjoyed the support of Enrique Moss, a career Argentine diplomat of Germanic descent who had been posted to the Argentine embassy in Berlin during the war. Married into a family of Zurich bankers, Moss had been one of the organizers of Evita's 1947 visit to Switzerland, and secretly doubled as a recruiting agent of Nazi brains for the

Argentine army. 'Moss had been out of the country so long he practically wasn't Argentine any more,' recalled Guillermo Speroni, a fellow Argentine diplomat posted in Berne at the time, over 50 years later.[222]

It was Moss's job to sort out the paperwork and finance the transportation of Nazi experts and their families, a process that required regular transfers of large sums of money from Buenos Aires. To this end, Moss had obtained the Marktgasse offices. Helfrich travelled into Allied-controlled Germany to set up an illegal escape network for Nazis who could not obtain the necessary exit permit from the occupation authorities. He himself possessed such a document, either real or forged, which allowed him to cross the Swiss–German border with ease. But since many of his candidates could hardly expect to obtain one, they had to be smuggled into Switzerland, travelling from there to Argentina either directly via KLM or through Italy and by ship from Genoa. Some candidates were smuggled straight to Italy through Austria. Special cases went to Rome to board flights on Perón's recently created FAMA state airline.

Helfrich's clandestine network inside the former Reich included a base in Cologne, headed by a Herr Westerhof, and another in Aach bei Singen, led by a Herr Ellinghausen, where guided-missile scientist Weiss also operated. Helfrich's activities, begun slightly before Moss had secured the Marktgasse cover, had got him into trouble with the Swiss authorities. He had been arrested in Berne some time in late 1947 or early 1948 but was quickly released through the intercession of a friend, Lieutenant Colonel Paul Schaufelberger, a Swiss intelligence officer apparently in the pay of Marktgasse.[223]

The arrival of Fuldner in Europe in December 1947 threw Argentina's Nazi-rescue machinery into high gear. Based in Genoa at Perón's recently created Delegation for Argentine Immigration in Europe (DAIE), Fuldner presented himself as an Immigration official, bearing an official passport inscribed with the title 'Special Envoy of the President'. Secretly, he was on a mission for Freude's Information Bureau and the Argentine air force, combining the smuggling of 'technicians' with the rescue of fellow SS officers. Freude had asked Argentine legation chief Llambí to give Fuldner all the necessary assistance he needed in Switzerland.[224]

First of all Fuldner sought a secret understanding with the Swiss authorities to overlook and assist wherever possible the goings-on at Marktgasse. Fortunately for the former SS captain, the highest officials in the land were well disposed towards him. During the war, Swiss justice minister Eduard von Steiger had slammed shut his country's borders against the Jews. Afterwards he displayed remarkable leniency towards fugitive Nazis on their way to Argentina. While Fuldner obtained a broad assurance, in high-level talks with Steiger, that Perón's rescue efforts would not be interfered with, the details of Switzerland's collaboration were worked out with the minister's right-hand man, the notoriously anti-Semitic Swiss chief of police, Heinrich Rothmund.[225]

Fuldner's past as a Himmler agent did not close doors to him in Berne. SD chief Walter Schellenberg, serving time in 1947 following his conviction at Nuremberg, could boast close friends within the Swiss military and intelligence services. In postwar interrogations, he admitted that during the war he had travelled to Switzerland on various occasions for talks with the Swiss army commander-in-chief, General Henri Guisan, and the Swiss intelligence chief, Colonel Roger Masson. After the war, these contacts ended the careers of Guisan and Masson, but in early 1943 Justice Minister Steiger was very eager to join the game and sent Rothmund to negotiate a secret agreement of his own with Himmler.[226]

That had not been Rothmund's first contact with the SS. In 1938 he had been taken on a tour of the Oranienburg forced labour camp outside Berlin where thousands of Jews, homosexuals and opponents of the Nazis met their death during the war. Rothmund agreed with the Nazis about the existence of a 'Jewish problem' but did not necessarily see extermination as the solution. He therefore proposed to the camp's officers the Swiss method of 'opposing from the outset any Jewish particularism' by forcing the Jews to lose their identity in the larger social melting pot. 'The method currently applied in Germany seems to me wrong and dangerous for all of us,' Rothmund told his hosts, 'because it ends up by throwing the Jews at our throats.' The Nazi bosses listened 'courteously and attentively', he reported to Berne.[227]

Precisely what kind of 'solution' Rothmund had in mind was made evident on 20 February 1939 when he imposed a special tax on Switzerland's Jewish community to cover costs incurred by Jewish refugees entering the country. Speaking to a police conference in August 1941, once the war was fully under way, Rothmund openly expressed his feelings against Jews: 'Today we have roughly 6,000 Jewish refugees in Switzerland. They constitute a danger to our country . . . All Jews are to be sent back across the border.'[228]

During 1938, in negotiations with Berlin, Switzerland had convinced the Nazi regime to mark the passports of German Jews with a 'J' stamp so that Swiss border guards could know exactly who to turn away. As the war progressed, it was Rothmund and Steiger who were responsible for ensuring that Switzerland's borders remained sealed against 'J' passport-holders. On 13 August 1942, Rothmund instructed Swiss border posts to strictly apply the existent regulations against Jewish refugees, in what is universally considered one of the darkest pages of Switzerland's wartime history. Spectral figures began to haunt the frontier posts. For these lost souls fleeing from Hitler's concentration camps it was impossible to move forward, impossible to go back. Many committed suicide in full view of the Swiss border guards. The resulting public outcry and the appeal for mercy from some of his more sensitive advisers completely failed to move Rothmund. As word spread throughout occupied Europe that Switzerland's gates had been closed against them, countless Jews in Germany, Holland, France, Belgium and the Eastern countries decided not to risk an already perilous journey, condemning themselves to certain death at the hands of the Nazis. Rothmund and Steiger had by omission become accessories to one of the greatest crimes in human history.[229]

Despite his glaring racism, Steiger became president of Switzerland in 1945. As president he did permit some last-minute negotiations with Schellenberg over the release of Jews from Hitler's concentration camps. Schellenberg managed to bring together Himmler and former

Swiss president Jean-Marie Musy secretly during the last days of the war to discuss the initiative. Himmler wanted tractors, cars and medicines in return for the Jews, but Schellenberg convinced him to settle for foreign currency, to be held in trust by Musy. The first and only transport of 1,200 Jews went smoothly in February. 'Musy acknowledged the receipt of the five million Swiss francs, which were paid to him as trustee at the end of February 1945,' according to Schellenberg. As part of the deal 'an article was published by President von Steiger in Berne, and another appeared in the *New York Times*.'[230]

During that same month President Roosevelt had asked Steiger to block all transit between his country and the Reich and in particular to prevent Nazis from escaping into Switzerland. But three years later Steiger was meeting with Fuldner, himself a 'hard-core Nazi' wanted for arrest by the US, who was on a mission to bring about exactly the opposite.

Rothmund meanwhile, despite his appalling wartime record, went on to become, from April 1945 until September 1947, the Swiss delegate to the International Refugee Organization (IRO) which had as its charter the rehabilitation and resettlement of the victims of Nazism throughout Europe. To finance its activities, this international body received a large amount of non-monetary Nazi gold – that is, gold looted from concentration camp victims by the SS and recovered after the war by the Allies.

Feelings in Buenos Aires about the IRO were divided between those government officials who saw it as a bulwark against the Communist takeover of Europe and those who considered it a tool of the Jews for infiltrating Argentina. Perhaps because of this, Rothmund got mixed signals from Argentina's diplomats in Berne who displayed a distinct lack of enthusiasm when it came to permitting Jewish refugees in Switzerland to travel to their country.[231]

On 23 December 1947 Czeslaw Smolinski arrived at Rothmund's office. The Swiss chief of police needed hospitable nations to accept the large number of war refugees under his care, and had been told that Perón's secret Polish agent might be able to lend a hand. In early

1946 these refugees amounted to 9,440 people, and Rothmund kept a strict account of them, with separate columns for 'Jewish' and 'non-Jewish' refugees, the Jews making up somewhat under half of the total.[232]

Smolinski began by claiming he was an Argentine citizen who had lived in Argentina for the past 30 years, a bare-faced lie, since he had only escaped from Europe four months earlier and did not obtain citizenship until 1951. He told Rothmund in a rather roundabout way that he was on a fact-finding mission and was reporting directly to the Argentine president. Smolinski was well aware that Argentina's gates had been closed to refugees from Switzerland. The former Immigration commissioner, 'Herr Peralta', had been a 'race theoretician' who had fortunately now been forced to resign, Smolinski explained, and the change augured well for Rothmund's refugees. Smolinski agreed that Argentina's diplomats were way too cautious when it came to granting landing permits, explaining that they feared any small mistake could put their jobs on the line. In other words, they were scared to grant visas to Jews.

The interview was going rather better than Rothmund had expected. Smolinski offered to speed matters up by allowing landing permits to be obtained directly from Buenos Aires. He could even arrange the president's personal intercession. 'Perón is very spontaneous and omnipotent and often acts above the law and writes his own decrees,' Smolinski said. 'Perhaps I can obtain one of those written decrees to support emigration from Switzerland.' This was music to Rothmund's ears. 'Herr Smolinski, who is not Jewish and who made it clear that Argentina (save a few exceptions) will not accept any Jews, gave the impression of being very open (to taking refugees),' an exultant Rothmund wrote in a three-page memo to Steiger that same day. Rothmund's Jews were not acceptable to Argentina, but at least some of the other half of his charges might be placed there.

Smolinski kept his word; within a few days of his return to Buenos Aires, Rothmund received landing permits for the emigration of 127 displaced persons to Argentina. The Swiss diplomatic representative in Buenos Aires, Eduard Feer, was equally thrilled. Soon enough Smolinski and new Immigration Commissioner Pablo Diana were dining at the Swiss legation. Smolinski was nominally employed as an Immigration agent of the Argentine Central Bank, Feer reported to Rothmund, but the important fact was that he was one of the 'circle of friends' of the president. 'He belongs to that group of recently nationalized Europeans whose intelligence and worldly straightforwardness are greatly valued here, especially by a person of initiative like President Perón, but who are still not Argentine enough to act openly in politics.' The door opened by Smolinski, which cut Argentina's troublesome diplomats in Berne out of the loop, especially pleased the Swiss representative. 'All the same, I have never dared intercede for Israelites, since it is well known that President Perón pursues a strict anti-Semitic line in Immigration,' Feer alerted Rothmund.[233]

Following Smolinski's providential appearance, Rothmund began to hold frequent conversations with the 'Argentines' at Marktgasse, conferences he fortunately recorded in lengthy and detailed memos for Steiger. Together with Smolinski and Fuldner, Gualterio Ahrens, another freshly arrived Argentine colonel of Germanic descent, started knocking on doors in Berne, arranging the illegal flight of 24 German 'technicians' hired by Argentina's military industry. The main problem was obtaining the necessary documents for these men to safely cross the border into Switzerland and then proceed to South America.

The Swiss proved eager to collude. In January 1948, Henri Tzaut of the Berne police reassured Ahrens that a Swiss consulate inside Germany could grant transit visas for the fugitives. That still left the Nazis in question without valid passports for their journey to Argentina – for obvious reasons unobtainable from the Allied authorities in Germany. Ahrens therefore approached Hans Frölicher, the notoriously pro-Nazi wartime Swiss diplomatic representative in Berlin, to see if the German Interests Office in Berne could issue the passports. Frölicher was non-committal but promised to consult Rothmund. Ahrens confided to Frölicher that he could arrange for Argentine papers to be issued to the Nazis in Berne in any case. The biggest problem, crossing the Allied-controlled German–Swiss border without exit permits, remained unsolved, at least by legal means. Luckily, Ahrens told his Swiss interlocutors, an agent had been found who knew ways to cross the frontier. Ahrens had received many requests from Germans eager to depart, the 'majority' highly qualified technicians, as Rothmund noted in a memo on the subject. The police chief conveniently failed to ponder the probable records of the remaining 'minority' he was about to save from justice.[234]

On 18 February 1948, after dinner with Moss and Ahrens, Rothmund was told over coffee by the Argentine colonel that many of those in question were Nazi party members who would have to be smuggled into Switzerland. Despite telephone consultations the following morning with the Swiss ministers for immigration and politics, who argued against an informal arrangement with the Argentines, Rothmund decided to run with the Marktgasse crew. During the negotiations that followed he agreed to grant Swiss transit visas to Perón's Nazis, even those who 'would not be able to obtain an exit permit from the Allies' in Germany, and excluding only 'political personalities'. He warned, though, that Switzerland did not want a repeat of the scandal that had erupted only three months before when the Argentine-run Nazi-smuggling ring had been uncovered in Sweden.

It was simply 'a matter of organization', Rothmund figured. Switzerland was willing to be a 'transit country' for Perón's recruits 'as long as the preparations in Germany are carried out as agreed'. He instructed Swiss border officials to make exceptions for Nazis smuggled out by Perón's agents. As it turned out, it proved impossible to differentiate between 'technicians' and 'political personalities'. The real beauty of the arrangement for the Marktgasse conspirators was that once inside Switzerland their Nazis could leave Europe without interference from the Allied authorities, since the Swiss did not require proof from departing Germans that they had left their country legally. Ahrens reassured Rothmund that his candidates would receive Argentine landing permits immediately upon their arrival in Switzerland, promising that 'in general' his candidates would be 'technicians'. Moss reassured Rothmund that any candidate Switzerland objected to would be struck from their list. Like Smolinski, Ahrens said he would be travelling to Buenos Aires soon and that he hoped to inform Perón personally of their talks.[235]

The United States had known full well since at least mid-1947 that Switzerland was turning a blind eye to the illegal transit of Nazis. For some nine months US diplomats in Europe investigated the escape route from Switzerland to Argentina via the KLM airline. To their great surprise they found themselves unable to stanch the flow; the traffic was simply too profitable for both the airline and certain Swiss government officials.

On 1 March 1948 the State Department received a lengthy and extremely disturbing report from the American embassy in The Hague. It had ascertained that 'the Swiss government was not only anxious to get rid of German nationals, legally or illegally within their borders, but further that they made a considerable profit in getting rid of them. It would seem . . . that too many questions were not asked of German nationals in Switzerland as to whether they were in the country legally or not, provided these German nationals wished to proceed to another country, preferably Argentina . . . These German nationals have paid Swiss officials as much as 200,000 francs for the temporary residence document they are required to have before being processed for transport via KLM to the Argentine.'

The investigation had begun in July 1947, when the American consulate in Zurich was informed by an employee of Swissair, which acted as the booking agent for KLM, that 'a number of German citizens who have no papers other than the Swiss *Ersatzpass* [a Swiss certificate of identity issued to displaced persons], an Argentine visa and no transit visas' were leaving Zurich via KLM to Buenos Aires. Among those who had made the journey were four members of the powerful German–Argentine Schlottmann family, the millionaire clan behind the massive Nazi-smuggling operation uncovered in Sweden. So close were the family's links with the Nazi escape network that a visit to a Schlottmann executive was the first move made by Josef Mengele upon his arrival in Argentina in 1949.

In a rescue operation of the kind Marktgasse later excelled at, clan leader Friedrich Schlottmann had sent one of his employees, Max Suter, from Argentina in early 1947 to smuggle two of his daughters out of Germany. Suter was refused entry to Germany by the Allied authorities in Berne but was finally able to acquire an entry permit in Paris, travelling from there to Berlin. Despite his best efforts, the Allies continued to refuse exit permits for the Schlottmann sisters, 'but as a result of Suter's other activity the two women nevertheless appeared in Switzerland in the Spring', as the American consulate in Zurich discreetly put it. By late March they had both left for Buenos Aires via KLM.

The difficulty had lain in the Nazi connections of the sisters' husbands. According to the Americans, Russian-born Rüdiger Schultz had left his home in Argentina in 1939 to join the Wehrmacht, reportedly transferring to an SS division. Smuggled out of Germany with his wife, Schultz obtained a landing permit from the Argentine legation in Berne, which in turn allowed him to obtain an *Ersatzpass*. With this he was able to purchase a KLM ticket, leaving Berne on 21 June 1947. His brother-in-law Horst Deckert likewise entered Switzerland illegally in the spring of 1947, after being detained for three days by the Swiss police on the German–Swiss border, and left Switzerland for Argentina via KLM on 5 July. The American consulate in Zurich considered Deckert 'at least a Nazi enthusiast'. While neither of the two was a member of the Nazi party or could be classified as a war criminal (although they were certainly denied exit permits by the Allies), their escape route was similar to that of important Nazis such as Herbert Helfrich, who left Switzerland via KLM around the same time.

The Nazi traffic was voluminous. The American consulate in Zurich was able to determine that during two weeks in October 1947 alone the Argentine legation in Berne had issued landing permits to at least ten illegal German entrants into Switzerland. KLM tickets for some 'immigrants' were even being paid for by the Argentine embassy in Rome.

An appeal to Berne to block the traffic was rebuffed. 'Since the Swiss authorities do not require exit visas they will not concern themselves with Germans travelling to Argentina unless, of course, they were informed that certain individuals had entered Switzerland illegally,' the American embassy in Berne reported. 'As a necessary condition to any action on the part of the Swiss authorities it would be necessary to name the individuals.' Such identification before the fact was impossible, as the Swiss very well knew.

The Americans therefore turned to the Dutch government, asking it to pressure KLM to supply the passenger lists for flights leaving Zurich, so that they could identify likely Nazis and prevent their departure. A meeting set up by the Dutch foreign ministry with KLM vice-president Slotemaker in The Hague proved deeply disappointing. 'KLM wants this business for purely commercial reasons, regardless of the type of persons being transported,' the American diplomats concluded. A Dutch government official privately told the embassy that KLM representatives in South America were actively seeking out Nazi clients.

The Dutch government was reluctant to order KLM to hand over passenger lists in Switzerland, 'especially in view of the apparent situation that the Swiss government is not discouraging this illegal immigration and Swissair is the booking office for KLM in Zurich'. The Dutch cynically suggested that the US should provide photographs of suspects to be screened by French and Brazilian migration officials during the one-hour stopovers in Dakar and Rio de Janeiro. 'They stated that KLM would be cooperative to the extent of not complaining about delays specifically caused by the security checks suggested.'

Finally, the US called it a day. 'The only real solution to the problem would seem to be involved in getting the cooperation of the Swiss authorities,' the diplomats resolved. That cooperation, they realized, would never be forthcoming. 'Principally because the Swiss police authorities are more than willing to have these unwelcome visitors leave the country as soon as possible.'[236]

In return for his cooperation, Rothmund was offered the opportunity to interrogate the Nazi 'experts' smuggled through Switzerland by

Perón for any information that might be of interest to the Swiss authorities. As an additional sweetener, Fuldner offered berths for 15 war refugees at the end of March on one of the ships he employed to ferry Nazis from Genoa. But the arrangement nearly collapsed when towards the end of March, and despite reassurances to the contrary, the Marktgasse crew made one of Rothmund's worst nightmares come true. A Swiss employee of the Marktgasse office, Samuel Pomeranz, managed to get himself arrested while attempting to smuggle a Nazi 'technician', Erich Bachem, through the border at Lake Constance in the northern canton of Schaffhausen. If the press got wind of the story, a scandal like the one in Sweden could blow up in Rothmund's face.

Rothmund was forced to telephone the Schaffhausen police to sort out the mess. He reassured the officials that Bachem was not only on his way to Argentina but that the Swiss military authorities wished to interrogate him, which was why the Swiss consulate in Stuttgart had been instructed to issue him an entry visa. Pomeranz might have neglected to pick up the visa but had acted in 'good faith', said Rothmund. Pressured by their superior, the Schaffhausen police reluctantly allowed Bachem into Switzerland but told Pomeranz they didn't want to see him around Lake Constance again. Pomeranz complained bitterly. He had commitments with many other 'clients', various Poles among them, who wished to be smuggled out of Germany. He had already been paid for these jobs and could not afford to renege on them.

As a result of the arrest, Rothmund had his wrist slapped by the Swiss minister for politics, Alfred Zehnder, who viewed the goings-on at Marktgasse with extreme distaste. The chief of police was forced to summon the 'Argentines' for a scolding. 'As I had the intention of behaving somewhat strongly with Herr Pomeranz due to the events on the northern border I turned down his offer of arriving in the company of Herr Fuldner,' Rothmund wrote in yet another incredibly detailed memo. But whatever his initial intention, the police chief was swept off his feet by Pomeranz. 'First of all, I would like to make it clear that Herr Pomeranz made a very good impression on me,' he wrote after the meeting, all his initial anger having subsided. His brusque demand for an explanation had been met with 'disarming ease' by Pomeranz, who proceeded to explain the inner workings of the Marktgasse bureau. Smolinski was a 'well-intentioned, sensitive idealist'. Ahrens was strictly a soldier with 'limited vision'. Moss and Helfrich worked together but Moss collaborated only with technicians hired by Argentina's military-industrial complex, leaving Helfrich a wide-open field for other cases. And last but not least, Pomeranz gave Rothmund the lowdown on Perón's 'special delegate', Carlos Fuldner.

The conversation left Rothmund in two minds. On the one hand he had become determined to 'grant Swiss visas only to those who have obtained [Allied] exit permits', while on the other he wished to 'reserve the right to grant exceptions for exclusively humanitarian cases such as Herr Smolinski's relatives'. Above all, he seemed uncomfortable with the fact that Helfrich's efficient organization was being disbanded. Smuggling Nazis through Allied controls was now the responsibility of Pomeranz, who despite all evidence to the contrary insisted he had the matter 'under control', while pleading that if he couldn't continue receiving people in Switzerland 'then the thing in Germany will dissolve'. In a last attempt to put his foot down, Rothmund said he wanted the smuggling organization in Germany disbanded.

But Pomeranz had tricks up his sleeve, and he now raised the Communist spectre. If Argentina didn't get the 'technicians', he warned the chief of police, then the Soviets would. Didn't Rothmund know that even as they spoke a shipload of Nazi experts was about to leave the port of Kiel supposedly bound for Argentina? Pomeranz himself had found this out in Germany. The candidates were even taking Spanish lessons from their recruiters, who all spoke Spanish. What they didn't know was that it was all a Communist ploy. Once at sea, the ship would head for Russia instead and the experts fall into Communist hands. It had happened once before, when a trainload of German scientists who thought they were on their way to board a ship to Buenos Aires found themselves steaming into the Soviet

Union instead. Why, even the British had duped a group of German technicians and engineers who believed they were going to Argentina! Rothmund paused. The Marktgasse crew had won a reprieve.[237]

The Lake Constance incident resulted in a series of meetings that failed abysmally to draw the Marktgasse crew into line. Rothmund reminded the 'Argentines' that they had promised not to cause any Nazi-smuggling scandals. They for their part seemed contrite and promised to mend their ways, but once they were out of Rothmund's sight they went their merry way as before.

On 9 April and again on the morning of 15 April, for example, Moss and Helfrich were called in for strong words from Rothmund. At these meetings, Moss played the 'good guy', Helfrich the 'bad guy'. The bureau had to spend more time aiding war victims and less time rescuing Nazis, Rothmund said. There were some 9,000 refugees awaiting visas in Switzerland, he implored, of whom less than 4,000 were Jewish. Surely Argentina could spare room for some of them? Helfrich said he had been arguing this exact point with the Argentine authorities during his recent visit to Buenos Aires, and that the president of the Argentine Central Bank, Miguel Miranda, would soon be in Switzerland to discuss the matter in person. The German added lamely that he had been present in Genoa when Rothmund's 15 war refugees had finally embarked for Buenos Aires. Unfortunately only 13 had actually managed to board ship, and they weren't in any case 'quality' material, so it was unlikely their arrival would lend any impetus to immigration from Switzerland. Rothmund couldn't believe his ears. He fumed that Fuldner had not given him enough time to make a proper selection. In any case, what Rothmund really wanted to say was that the illegal smuggling of 'technicians' was not a priority for Switzerland by any means. 'I told Herr Moss again that he must ask his government to get in touch with the Allies to make sure that those Germans with a special interest in emigrating to Argentina obtain an exit permit.' Moss, as 'confused and distracted' as ever, could only venture that he was leaving for Buenos Aires on Saturday. He would be back in three weeks, hopefully with fresh orders from his government. Again, Rothmund was outwitted and Marktgasse had obtained another reprieve.[238]

In reality, Rothmund was acting with one hand tied behind his back. That same afternoon of 15 April, a higher-level meeting took place with his boss, Justice Minister Eduard von Steiger. Into the minister's office trooped the Argentine diplomatic head of mission, Benito Llambí, former SS captain Carlos Fuldner, and Argentine diplomat Guillermo Speroni. Llambí expressed Argentina's keen interest in accepting war refugees. Fuldner wanted a complete and detailed list of all the refugees in Switzerland in order to make a proper selection, and stressed that it was important for ethnic origin to be explicitly stated in each case. 'Argentina has had a very bad experience with refugees from the cities of the East,' the SS man explained, in obvious reference to Jewish immigrants. Speroni added that the list would be forwarded to the Argentine government for immediate consideration.

Steiger welcomed the offer and said it would be simple enough for Rothmund's department to provide such a document. And that was it. The Argentines must have breathed a huge sigh of relief as they left. The minister had by omission granted an official endorsement to Perón's operation in Switzerland, of which Steiger was fully aware. He had certainly erased whatever impression Rothmund might have made on Moss that morning. The arrests of Helfrich and Pomeranz were blithely ignored. Not a word was uttered about Nazis smuggled illegally out of Germany, nor any mention made of that troubling office on Marktgasse, which therefore stayed open, ready for business as usual.[239]

Neither Rothmund nor Steiger had really had any intention of closing down Marktgasse. A wink and a nod from the ministry of justice had made the Nazis' saviours untouchable, even though their presence had started to draw the attention of other Swiss cabinet members and even of fellow European governments.[240]

In early June, Rothmund again had to calm down Zehnder, who wanted Marktgasse closed down. Rothmund begged for time, claiming that Llambí and Fuldner now felt the 'practical' end of business should move to Genoa, while 'diplomatic questions continue to be addressed through the legation in Berne'.[241]

By now Rothmund was totally plugged into Fuldner's Nazi ratline. When the chief of police travelled to Rome for Swiss–Italian immigration talks in mid-June, Fuldner played his trump card, arranging a meeting for him with the Vatican's top Nazi smuggler, Father Draganovic. Writing from the Hotel Schweizerhof in Berne, Fuldner regretted he could not join Rothmund in Rome, 'far from the daily worries of being on service . . . It would have been wonderful to . . . consider some questions that concern your fatherland and my home country. In so far as these important questions for my country regard immigration, I have been fortunate to meet splendid people in Europe, whose friendship and disinterested work have been of inestimable help.' Fuldner informed Rothmund that 'I wanted to introduce you to two of these gentlemen, Monsignor Professor Dr Draganovic, a Croatian priest at the Vatican, and Dr Octavian Rosu, president of the Union of Expatriate Romanians. Both gentlemen have rendered great services to my country, providing passages to South America for hundreds of people, from all European nations, freeing them from the misery of being refugees, which in Italy is especially acute. Despite my absence I know that meeting these gentlemen will be extremely pleasurable. You will get a profound, personal and direct vision of how a solution is being sought in Italy to the human emergency of tens of thousands of refugees. Both gentlemen live only for this task.'[242]

Given the tight connection between Rothmund and Fuldner, it is perhaps not very surprising that even the damning and detailed evidence uncovered independently two months later by the Berne secret police failed to damage Marktgasse. The bureau was nothing if not a false front. The investigators had not found a single case in which Marktgasse had helped war refugees or Swiss residents travel to Argentina. Instead it found plentiful evidence that Nazi fugitives were being brought illegally into Switzerland from both Austria and Germany. Following Pomeranz's scrape with the law, the Nazis were now met at the German border by one Max Bubb and brought to

Berne by a certain Albert Steiner. The Berne police went as far as to interrogate Schaufelberger, the Swiss secret agent who had extricated Helfrich from his early scrape in Berne. 'The Argentine Emigration Centre in Berne follows an agreement with Dr Rothmund,' stated Schaufelberger. Industrialists inside Germany and Austria were financing the escape network, the Berne police discovered. Still Marktgasse survived.[243]

In September 1948, Fuldner wrapped up his European business and embarked for Argentina, where he still had a massive job to do arranging the reception of the many Nazis he had brought to safety. In what may have been no coincidence, a fellow passenger was Hubert von Blucher. This young German was connected to the evacuation of the gold bullion and currency reserves of the Berlin Reichsbank in the last days of the war. The evacuation had been personally approved by Hitler in his bunker on 9 April, and the task of transferring the treasure from Berlin to Hitler's Alpine Fortress in Bavaria was entrusted to SS Colonel Friedrich Rauch, a Nazi war criminal who would himself eventually end up in Argentina. The colonel transported the treasure to southern Germany by train, carried it by mule-back into the mountains and buried it. Part of the treasure was hidden in the vegetable beds of the Blucher family home in Garmisch. The garden was dug up by US troops in August 1945, but despite a lengthy investigation, the full amount of the hidden treasure was never recovered.[244]

Behind him Fuldner had left such a trail of unpaid debts and deception that even Rothmund was hard put to defend him. The Berne police, who seemed intent on complicating Rothmund's arrangement with Marktgasse, had started to pursue a simple lead, a car crash Fuldner had had driving his Ford through the streets of Berne. It turned out that there was no record of the inveterate swindler's entry to the country. Repeated summons by the Berne police failed to impress Fuldner, who felt protected by his official Argentine passport with its 'Special Presidential Envoy' inscription. What really puzzled the police was that although he had failed to regularize his own situation, Fuldner had put in a permanent residency application for his secretary Barbara Weiss de Janko, who had recently arrived from Austria. (In Argentina, Weiss formed part of the inner court around German Colonel Franz Pfeiffer, also involved in the Reichsbank gold raid). When summoned for interviews, Fuldner excused himself, saying that he was leaving for Italy and would phone back on his return. But despite passing through Berne twice in September, Fuldner never checked in.

In mid-October, the Berne police decided to pay Fuldner a visit instead. They were not amused by what they found – though it had its comical side. At the apartment Fuldner and his wife had rented at Weststrasse there was no sign of Perón's special deputy, only a very distraught Fraulein Anna Siegwart, who informed them that Fuldner's behaviour had been 'to say the least, strange'. The landlady had been particularly offended by Fuldner's wife, Hanna Kraus, a convinced Nazi who contended that Switzerland was really part of Germany, causing angry arguments between the two women. Like someone out of a spy novel, Fuldner had had a diplomatic plate on his car which he would display or hide under a leather cover depending on the occasion. 'It's camouflage for the Russians,' Fuldner said. 'I'm never safe from the Russians.'

Unfortunately for the police, Fuldner had already sailed from Genoa, saying he would be back in November. Behind him he had left 2,800 francs' worth of unpaid phone calls that Siegwart tried to collect from his aunt in Berne, a lady by the name of Lydia Hopf, who paid with a cheque that, characteristically, bounced. Fortunately for this book, Siegwart thought to ask Fuldner's aunt for his address in Buenos Aires, which she learned was Peña 2484, fourth floor, apartment A. Jotted down by the Berne police, the address has survived to prove indisputably Fuldner's responsibility for the rescue of one particular major war criminal who found refuge in Argentina.

The Berne police also learned that Fuldner had turned Siegwart's address into a safe house for the illegal Germans he had been smuggling into Switzerland. Their perpetual comings and goings had alarmed the landlady. Occasionally there were so many that some had to camp out on the patio, where their behaviour was so rowdy that Fuldner had to intervene to quieten them down. Finally it was Pomeranz who settled Fuldner's outstanding debts, not only with the landlady but also with the Schweizerhof Hotel. Less lucky was the salesman who appeared after Fuldner's departure with a bill for six typewriters specially fitted with Spanish-language keyboards. Fuldner had put in an urgent order for them and the man's employees had stayed up all night adapting the machines. The poor soul was devastated, Siegwart told the police.[245]

Rothmund and the worried Berne police decided to consult, each in their own way, the Swiss legation in Buenos Aires about Fuldner's reputation. While the Berne police wanted Fuldner barred from Switzerland, Rothmund simply wanted him told off for his uncivil behaviour. Legation chief Eduard Feer, who had already discussed the Fuldner case with Rothmund over the phone, had surprisingly little trouble raking up additional dirt, as the return of Perón's agent had started some very well-informed tongues wagging. By 15 November, Feer began bombarding the Berne police, Zehnder and Rothmund with dramatic cautions against Fuldner.

The Swiss diplomatic representative embarked on nothing less than an all-out campaign to stamp out 'the trio of Fuldner, Helfrich and Weiss'. These men, Feer discovered a little late in the day, were 'scheming adventurers and 110% Nazis', members of the 'very active groups of Argentine Nazis'. He confirmed Fuldner's link with Perón's Casa Rosada. 'The current sponsor of these three men is a certain Dr Freude, the personal secretary of President Perón, who is a very important person in the current regime. It would be extraordinarily delicate to act against Carlos Fuldner without risking hurting the feelings of the very influential Dr Freude.' The diplomat ruled out approaching Fuldner personally, as Rothmund had suggested. Given his 'haughty and scheming' character, this would only make him feel 'more important' than he already was. Instead Feer suggested 'preventing all three – Fuldner, Helfrich and Weiss – from continuing their activities in Switzerland'. The proper way to end their game,

Feer proposed, was for Rothmund to call in Llambí in Berne for a few words, since Feer understood that Fuldner was not in Llambí's good books.[256]

Feer's sources of information were Pomeranz and Smolinski. Pomeranz had arrived in Buenos Aires on a plane ticket paid for by Smolinski because 'things had got too hot for him in Switzerland', and had decided to pay a visit to the Swiss legation. He did not have a pretty story to tell. 'Pomeranz spent approximately an hour with me . . . In this short period, he presented a picture of intrigues and mutual deception by the three Argentine agents Fuldner, Helfrich and Dr Weiss, which is difficult to fathom,' Feer wrote in a new 'For Your Eyes Only' note to Rothmund. Pomeranz also claimed that Fuldner, Helfrich and Weiss had enjoyed the collaboration of Swiss secret agent Schaufelberger, who was at least guilty of 'passive bribery' and had provided them with arms in Switzerland. 'Those three have access to special funds for bribery,' said Feer. 'And, of course, they can claim in Buenos Aires that they had to pay this or that member of the Swiss government for services rendered.' Feer also learned all about Fuldner's Roman connections. While the IRO could help Rothmund by organizing the transport of Jewish and non-German displaced persons, it was Draganovic who held 'all the most important threads for the shipment of refugees', Feer reported. 'Monsignor Draganovic has been specifically instructed by the Vatican to get Catholics out of the Russian sphere of influence,' he explained. Feer suggested to Rothmund that the Swiss legation in Rome would have 'no problem' approaching Draganovic for aid in ridding Switzerland of its refugees.

But most impressive of all was hearing Fuldner's real mission spelt out in black and white. 'Pomeranz also confirms that Fuldner, during his short stay in Switzerland, managed to bring approximately 300 persons to Argentina from Germany . . . Among those are supposedly forty technicians destined for the Argentine Air Ministry . . . Smolinski added that many of those people should be before the Nuremberg court rather than in Argentina.' Not knowing the full story, the diplomat theorized that Perón's government was not really interested in these 'political' immigrants but that it was 'the 110% Nazis who work as Immigration agents' who had foisted them on Perón.[247]

Rothmund meanwhile, despite the evidence showering onto his desk about the real activities of Perón's special agent, continued to give Fuldner the benefit of the doubt. After reading Feer's alarming reports, the police chief drafted a rambling but incredibly candid reply justifying Fuldner's actions. The 'disagreeable' Pomeranz knew too much about the smuggling of illegal Germans. 'Fuldner always clearly stated that anything Pomeranz said could have dire consequences not only for Argentina but also for Fuldner personally,' Rothmund wrote. 'Fuldner believes Pomeranz can do less damage in Argentina than in Europe.' That was why Fuldner had arranged Pomeranz's trip to Buenos Aires, where Pomeranz hoped to open a business. Rothmund's reply revealed too much about Fuldner's affairs, and he must have realized it, for he filed it away unsent among his papers.[248]

According to the surviving documentation, Fuldner does not seem to have returned to Switzerland, but despite all warnings to the contrary, Helfrich and Weiss certainly did. The Gestapo missile scientist now travelled on an Argentine passport, passing briefly through Switzerland on his way to Paris, where the Berne police tracked him down on the phone. Weiss referred them to Schaufelberger who, he said, could give them all the details they needed about him. Helfrich, too, was back in Berne in January 1949, meeting once more with Swiss officials.[249]

By March 1949 even the French government had begun to demand a police inspection of Marktgasse, along with a probe into the Caritas Catholic aid office in Berne. Fortunately for Perón's Nazis, the French request landed on the desk of Jacques Albert Cuttat, a wartime Swiss legation deputy chief in Buenos Aires, co-organizer of Evita's trip to Switzerland and a personal friend of Argentine legation chief Llambí. Between 1939 and 1945, Cuttat had gold bars deposited at Argentina's Central Bank, and following Argentina's break of relations with Hitler in 1944, when Switzerland took over the representation of German diplomatic interests in Argentina, he allowed the Nazi diplomats to keep on using their embassy's premises in Buenos Aires to send coded telegrams to Berlin. Now, in response to the French request for an investigation, Cuttat telephoned the French embassy and made it quite clear that Marktgasse would not be touched. The French should investigate the Caritas office in Paris instead.[250]

Such loyalty to the cause from sympathetic Swiss officials was no doubt much appreciated by Perón's agents, but Marktgasse's days were numbered and in the spring of 1949 the 'Argentine Emigration Centre' was finally shut down. The office had served its purpose by now anyhow, and Fuldner had his hands busy in Argentina finding employment and safe identities for his Nazi newcomers. These men continued to disembark from Genoa until 1950, in almost all cases with landing permits applied for during 1948 by Fuldner and Perón's Information Bureau.

What was the final balance between the war refugees Switzerland managed to dispatch to Argentina and the number of Nazi fugitives it allowed Fuldner to rescue? Rather pitiful, by Rothmund's own account. If we are to believe Pomeranz's figure, Fuldner helped some 300 Nazis escape to Argentina, of whom only 40 were genuine technicians. Rothmund, on the other hand, found by 1950 that of the 127 refugees Smolinski had obtained landing permits for, only 34 were able to make the trip because of last-minute obstruction from Argentina's diplomats. Out of a further 200 permits granted as a result of Fuldner's meeting with Steiger, only 49 more had actually sailed for Argentina. The Nazis had won by well over three to one.[251]

Another well-known Swiss character mixed up in Argentina's Nazi-rescue efforts was the ubiquitous Colonel Henri Guisan, a 'great friend' of Benito Llambí and son of General Guisan, the Nazi-tainted wartime commander-in-chief of the Swiss army. After the war, the younger Guisan started to visit Argentina, establishing himself there during Perón's government. 'I met him in Buenos Aires in 1946,' recalled his widow María Schwank for a Swiss television documentary in 1998. 'He was always travelling between Switzerland and Argentina, helping Germans emigrate there. He gave them passports and papers so they could enter Argentina legally.'

During the war, the young colonel had been connected to the German agent Wilhelm Eggen, an SS captain who bought timber in Switzerland for the Waffen SS. As a member of the board of directors of the Swiss timber firm Extroc SA, the younger Guisan supplied wooden constructions for the Dachau and Oranienburg concentration camps up until 1944.

It was Guisan who introduced Eggen to Swiss secret agent Paul Meyer, a colourful businessman-cum-spy who lived in a castle named Wolfsburg and wrote novels under the *nom de plume* Wolf Schwertenbach. Acting under the orders of the elder Guisan, Meyer arranged the meetings between Swiss intelligence chief Roger Masson and SD chief Walter Schellenberg, some in Berlin, some in Meyer's Wolfsburg castle, which resulted in the elder Guisan's fall from grace after the war. Although Guisan later argued that the intention behind these contacts was to dissuade the Germans from invading Switzerland, there was speculation by the press and even Allied intelligence about the use of this connection for concealing Nazi funds in Switzerland.

In 1947, the younger Guisan put Llambí in touch with a group of Nazi rocket scientists who had worked for Wernher von Braun's missile team. What Guisan offered was nothing less than the blueprints of the ultra-secret V-3 missile, successor to the V-2 that Hitler had used to bomb London. Llambí himself travelled to Paris on 7 March 1947 to meet with a mysterious man named L. Halmos who was the contact agent for the Nazi scientists. These experts wished to be smuggled out of the Russian-occupied part of Germany where they had hidden their precious blueprints.

Nothing seems to have come of the V-3 offer, which Llambí said, in memoirs published shortly before his death, had failed to interest Perón's government. Guisan himself was involved in shady deals in Argentina, establishing several arms-trading firms. Recalling those days, his widow said: 'I had to attend to business associates of my former husband I'd rather not shake hands with. When they started to talk business I had to leave the room.'[252]

There are still secrets concerning Perón's operations in Switzerland that are not revealed by the documents extant over five decades later. A relative of the Argentine president, for example, Edgardo Benavente Perón, was posted in Berne on mysterious duties, shuttling between the Swiss capital and Rome. A deep undercover agent of the Casa Rosada, Jorge Oscar Jorge, who traversed Europe in the company of an Argentine priest rescuing Nazis, had his own links in Switzerland and met with Rothmund in 1950 in the company of Ernesto Heer, a Swiss citizen who enjoyed Argentine diplomatic status and aided the Marktgasse crew.

The actual smuggling operations remain obscure. One example of a 'technician' who was spirited out of Germany survives only in the memory of the Argentine diplomat involved, retired ambassador Guillermo Speroni, who was then first secretary at the legation. Perón's Ministry of Health informed Speroni that a German 'foot and mouth' expert was willing to work for Argentina. The man, named Dr Otto Walimann, was a difficult case because he and his family were stuck inside the Russian-occupied half of Berlin. Speroni was able to slip him out with the help of a Swiss colonel who handled the Berlin end of the operation. For the journey through France the Argentine diplomat enlisted the aid of the French military attaché in Switzerland. 'I waited at the railway station in Berne with the Swiss colonel as Walimann and his family arrived in a closed wagon,' recalled Speroni for this book. 'They didn't open the windows until the train stopped, and then continued on their way to Genoa.'[253]

By similar means, serious Nazi criminals were spirited out of their hiding places in Germany and Austria on their way to Italy. Others were already hiding in Italy by the time Fuldner got to them. All benefited from the wide web Perón had thrown across Europe, each filament controlled from Buenos Aires.

13

THE BELGIAN WAY

No sooner had Pierre Daye descended from his Iberia flight to Buenos Aires on 21 May 1947 than Brussels demanded his arrest. As it turned out, this was never to happen. It was not only German-speaking Nazis who obtained refuge from Perón after the war. Over 100 French and Belgian certified war criminals fled to Argentina, not counting the many other French-speaking Nazi collaborators whose exact wartime responsibilities have yet to be determined. Starting in May 1946, when Emile Dewoitine became the first French war criminal to arrive in Argentina aboard the ship that carried Cardinal Caggiano back from Italy, this group of Latin and Catholic Nazi idealists received a warm welcome from Argentina's leaders. Their flight was coordinated by the group gathered around Daye and Charles Lesca. Working with other Nazi collaborators from the wartime Catholic regimes of Slovakia and Croatia, Daye's group enjoyed the support of Argentine and Belgian church dignitaries. Protected by Perón and therefore immune to extradition for the crimes committed during the Nazi occupation of their respective nations, the members of Daye's organization meshed seamlessly with the Nazi team assembled at Perón's Information Bureau to conduct one of the slickest escape operations of modern times.[254]

Argentina was asked to place Daye 'at the disposal of the Belgian

authorities on board a Belgian ship' for repatriation. The Belgian government reminded Argentina of its obligations under the Act of
Chapultepec. Perón's Foreign Ministry was provided with a recent
photograph of Daye and his correct address at the Lafayette Hotel in
downtown Buenos Aires. The Belgian legation pointed out that the
former parliamentary leader of the Christus Rex faction had been
condemned to death on 12 December 1946 for his flagrant wartime
collaboration with the Germans. From the start, Perón's government
dragged its feet on the case. A month after its original approach,
having had no response, Brussels was forced to renew the appeal, this
time adding three other notorious Belgian war criminals to the list.
Two of them, Jan Lecomte and Gérard Ruysschaert, had arrived bearing Spanish passports on 15 May 1947 aboard the *Cabo Buena
Esperanza*, the same ship that brought Daye's close friend José María
Areilza as Franco's new ambassador to Argentina. The third, Rudolf
Clayes, disembarked on 7 June from the *Campana*, a ship that also
brought at least three confirmed Croatian war criminals to Argentina.
Small wonder that the Belgian legation felt compelled to end the list
of new arrivals with a disquieting 'etc.'

The well-informed French ambassador, Wladimir d'Ormesson, had
alerted the Belgians to Daye's presence. Daye himself had been very
quickly warned of the move against him. More offended than frightened, he seethed with anger against the head of the Belgian legation,
Marcel-Henri Jaspar, an old political acquaintance from the mid-
1930s. In revenge, whenever the two crossed paths 'on the street, at a
restaurant, at the Jockey Club where I was occasionally invited for
breakfast, I amused myself . . . pretending I didn't see him,' Daye
gloated in the extensive unpublished memoirs he wrote in Buenos
Aires. In a more practical vein, Daye's Argentine contacts quietly
ensured that the extradition request was not acted on, and he soon felt
secure enough to 'laugh inwardly' at Jaspar's attempt to ensnare him.

It wasn't that the Argentine authorities couldn't find him, for even
before the renewal of the extradition request Foreign Minister Juan
Bramuglia had a detailed Federal Police report on his desk that
included Daye's new address at an apartment in the Viggiano

building at 785 Corrientes Avenue. Initially excited at identifying
their target, the tone of these reports quickly started veering in
favour of the war criminal. By late September, even though all four
Belgians had been located, the minister was being told that the real
purpose of Daye's visit was to 'write a book about the Argentine
Republic' that would 'make known its greatness to the world'. And of
course, the police pointed out Daye's close association with the new
Spanish ambassador Areilza. By October the ministry had decided to
await a third request for Daye's arrest before making any drastic deci-
sions. And by December extradition was out of the question, for by
then Daye was being ushered into the president's office in the Casa
Rosada as an honoured guest. 'What would he [Jaspar] have thought,'
Daye pondered in his memoirs, 'had he known that . . . at the same
time he wanted me arrested, I was about to be received by General
Perón?'[255]

Perón's growing community of war fugitives shared two basic tenets
with Argentina's president: a lofty disdain for the democratic and
Communist alternatives that had emerged victorious from World War
Two and a firm belief that a third world war was imminent. Perón and
Evita attended secret conferences at the Immigration Office during
which Argentina's role in the imagined cataclysm was discussed, and
the Nazi runaways foresaw a glorious return to their former rank once
it had occurred. 'Here, everybody thinks 1948 will be the year of the
war,' Daye wrote to a fellow fugitive in Madrid.[256]
     In Europe, Hitler's former collaborators also expected a glorious
return to their former rank. 'In two, three, five years, great hours will
come,' Léon Degrelle, the leader of the disbanded Belgian Rexist
party, wrote to Daye from his hideout in Spain. 'You shall see, my old
Pierre, you shall see, we will accomplish formidable tasks. Everything
so far has been nothing but patrol work, reconnaissance, scuffling.
Real life has yet to begin. I firmly believe this.' The response from
Buenos Aires was no less spirited. 'The future is ours,' Daye wrote in
letters carried by mysterious couriers to Degrelle's secret sanctuary.
'Experience and misfortune have moulded us. The martyrs, necessary

to every superior cause, will see their names triumphantly rehabili-
tated.' The 'highest spheres' in Argentina expected a 'tragedy',
foreseeing that either 'all of Western Europe will pass to Bolshevism
or war will erupt between the United States and Russia'.

Meanwhile, safe and sound in South America, Daye began to see
similarities between the pro-Nazi Belgian Rexism of the 1930s, which
he had considered a viable alternative to both 'capitalism of the far
right and the Communism of the far left', and Perón's own Third
Position, a political concept the president had started discussing privately in mid-1947 with his future foreign minister, Hipólito Paz.
This was the same Paz who had met Daye at the home of the Marquis
de las Marismas in Madrid earlier that same year. They were reintro-
duced in Buenos Aires by Spanish ambassador Areilza, and Daye
visited Paz at the Beaux-Arts Museum, where Perón's young adviser
had his office. Another foreign policy expert intimately linked to
Daye was Mario Amadeo, who had been there to welcome Daye on
the tarmac of Buenos Aires airport. The diplomat sat on Perón's
Postwar Council, a body drawing up recommendations on a broad
spectrum of issues, including Argentina's position on the war crime
trials being conducted by the Allies.

Impressed by Perón's nascent middle way between the two major
postwar political alternatives, along with a small group of fugitives
'who find themselves in my same situation', Daye saw that Perón's
initiative offered 'firm ground, a solid base' for a return to the political arena. The core members of his group seem to have been his old
Madrid acquaintances Carlos Fuldner and Radu Ghenea. 'We have
started meeting to envisage the eventual creation of a totally new
movement,' Daye confided to his memoirs.[257]

Pampered and feted in Buenos Aires, Daye began to 'recover a
serenity that I was on the verge of losing in Western Europe'. The
large fellowship of expatriate Nazis, Belgian Rexists, Italian Fascists
and Spanish Falangists, together with members and officials of the
Romanian Iron Guard, the Hungarian Arrow Cross, the French Vichy
government and the Croatian Ustashi, held Daye in high esteem, and
formed a tight mutual support group under Perón's protection.

Spanish ambassador Areilza in particular smoothed Daye's path, even allowing him to use the embassy's diplomatic pouch for communicating with his comrades in Madrid. 'The beautiful Spanish Embassy has replaced the Belgian Legation which disowns me,' Daye wrote. He also had close contact with the 'always magnificent' Charles Lesca, with Marc Augier, a writer sentenced to death in France who became Evita's ski instructor, and the 'excellent and Utopian Réne Lagrou', who busied himself with his plan to ship some 2 million Belgian Nazi collaborators and their families to Argentina. There were as well many 'charming North Americans and beautiful and aristocratic Argentines' among Daye's new acquaintances, whose names he discreetly left out of his memoirs.

Walking along a Buenos Aires street shortly after his arrival, Daye was astonished to see in a bookshop window a Spanish-language translation of his novel *Stanley*. Unbeknownst to him, the rights had been acquired by an Argentine publisher. 'All of a sudden I possessed, without having sought it, the best of intellectual calling cards.' Daye quickly distributed copies among his Argentine hosts – the list he drew up only four months after arriving reveals how quickly he had plugged into the highest Peronist circles. It included three key presidential staff members, as well as Juan Carlos Goyeneche and Amadeo, now at the forefront of nationalist support for Perón's government.

When he was not meeting with his Third Position group, Daye did the social rounds. He had tea with Mussolini's former ambassador to Madrid, Eugenio Morreale, and with the anti-Semitic Austrian Prince Ernst-Rüdiger Starhemberg. Once the vice-chancellor of his country during the Dollfuss regime, Starhemberg had been reduced to the role of 'gentleman farmer' on the fertile Pampas. 'I thus discovered little by little that in this country there lived discreetly a large number of personalities whose names had resounded for a moment on the stage of contemporary history, and who were now in hiding, awaiting their hour to return,' Daye wrote. Before long he would be meeting regularly with Milan Stojadinovic, the former Nazi-leaning Vodja of prewar Yugoslavia, who had 'a charming wife, of a rare beauty'. In the same breath, Daye could boast of his conversations with the former Poglavnik of the Free State of Croatia, Ante Pavelic, 'a lot more brutal and less charming', with the blood of some half a million Serbs, Gypsies and Jews on his hands.[258]

While nurturing this growing network, Daye also made haste to resume his Good Samaritan work. His first efforts in Buenos Aires were on behalf of two notorious Belgian Nazi collaborators, Léonard de Roover and Jules van Daele, who were travelling to South America on Peruvian visas and only had transit passes for Argentina. Roover already had reason to be grateful, as Daye had arranged a soft landing for him in Madrid in late 1945. Now he was escaping Europe with a death sentence on his head. Daye was only half successful. He obtained permanent residency in Argentina for Roover, who disembarked from the *Monte Ayala* in Buenos Aires on 4 July 1947, but Daele had to continue overland on his original visa to Peru. In Argentina, Roover was quickly conscripted into the Nazi-rescue team at Freude's Information Bureau, where he became a vital link between the Casa Rosada and Immigration.[259]

'In more ways than one our era resembles the Renaissance, when a man cannot know whether tomorrow he will not be imprisoned, hanged or in flight, or hidden in some foreign land and drafting his memoirs to pass the time,' Daye mused. 'It is an era of adventurers, with all the risks and all the opportunities. An era with the attraction of a full, strong existence, of the passionate human game.'[260]

During two consecutive days in early December 1947 General Perón invited Daye and his Third Position group for sessions in the spacious office at the Casa Rosada where the president usually held his cabinet meetings. The group of six consisted of Daye, Lagrou, Georges Guilbaud, Ghenea, Spanish journalist Víctor de la Serna and Carlos Fuldner. They were steered in by Rodolfo Freude. This was a tight group who knew each other from the early postwar days in Madrid. Over half a century later, an American intelligence document obtained through the Freedom of Information Act shows what a careful watch Washington kept on them.[261]

The 1947 document gives brief descriptions of some of the people linked to Lesca. These mini-reports culled from an obviously richer intelligence archive show how deeply interlocked the Nazi group that met with Perón really was. The document paints an unflattering portrait of Daye, far removed from the sanitized image he presents in his memoirs, showing that in Madrid he subsisted on '3,000 a month' provided by Nazi agents. Until the end of the war Daye drew up intelligence reports for the German embassy in Madrid based on information obtained from 'his spies at the Palace Hotel'. He was being 'run' by the German attaché Otto Pickham, 'in charge of liaison with political refugees of pro-Nazi tendencies'. Daye was believed to be 'engaged in the purchase of jewels' with Lesca. During 1946 he started being seen in the company of French war criminal Georges Guilbaud and his mistress.

Guilbaud had a long history of providing special services to authoritarian rulers before becoming Perón's 'financial adviser'. A close confidant of Vichy president Pierre Laval and Marshal Pétain, he had travelled to Lisbon in 1943 to salt away funds for Laval 'and his pals'. (During 1944, shortly before the liberation of France, American intelligence learned also that Laval was channelling funds to Argentina through Madrid and that a 'Frenchman or Belgian' had arrived in Buenos Aires to launder part of the Vichy leader's booty in gold, jewels and real estate.) At the end of the war, on 23 April 1945, Guilbaud escaped from Italy to Spain on a Savoia plane from Milan, placed on the flight at the insistence of the German ambassador.

Ghenea had remained quietly in Spain until late 1944 when, hired by Spanish intelligence, he suddenly took a large flat and began to entertain lavishly. American intelligence found that due to his country's recent break with Hitler's Axis, the Germans planned to set Ghenea up 'as a representative of a dissident Romanian government'.

After serving on the Russian Front alongside Hitler's troops in Franco's Blue Division, Víctor de la Serna had made 'several trips to Germany'. His namesake father in mid-1945 bought 'a large block of stock' in the influential Madrid daily *Informaciones*, apparently with

Nazi money. The Americans did not like the Sernas. 'Father is a well-known collaborator, son is even worse,' said one report. It added ungraciously: 'Son is more stupid than the father.' He was flown in from Madrid for the meeting at the Casa Rosada on one of Perón's FAMA planes.[262]

Daye's group had been invited to meet Perón by Freude, 'who had heard about us – about our adventures and our intention to help refugees establish themselves in Argentina,' Daye recorded in his memoirs. Perón and Freude were particularly interested in the group's objective of creating 'a movement to unite all those in the world who do not support either of the two formulas offered to the masses: American democratic capitalism, which declares itself the champion of freedom and the defender of private property, and Bolshevik Russian Communism, destroyer of private capitalism but also destroyer of all individual freedom'.

The first meeting was a midday session during which 'a storm surrounded the Casa Rosada with such lightning and thunder as if at that hour on a new Sinai the Law of God was being handed down to the world'. The second meeting the following day started at seven o'clock on a clear, bright morning and lasted three hours. The gathering of so many condemned war criminals at the presidential palace astonished the participants. 'Decidedly, the world evolves,' Daye wrote. 'Ah, if only some diplomats knew!'

Despite having met the most powerful leaders of his time, from Hitler to Pope Pius XII, from Franco to Shah Reza Pahlevi, Daye was impressed by Perón's stately demeanour. 'He's a large, solid man, well set, who seems to be about fifty years of age. His hair is black and thick, his eyes smiling, he speaks clearly, precisely, with good sense and a surprising lack of caution . . . His sober gestures seemed to be invested with a kind of unctuousness at times, in the ecclesiastical fashion.' The general was sure of his own power, considering himself (a little too confidently, Daye noted) the 'absolute master' of Argentina.

The group was aware it held opinions that had become 'forbidden and persecuted'. It was flattered to confirm that 'the chief head of state of the continent of South America understands us and approves many of our ideas'. Daye was especially excited by Perón's espousal of a middle way between capitalism and Communism. The shared belief that a third world war was imminent shadowed the meeting. Perón announced he would remain neutral as long as possible. 'Argentina is weak,' Perón said. 'She must await her hour.' Making clear his absolute opposition to Communism, Perón insisted he was 'neither Russian nor North American', anticipating the cry that would be taken up by his left-wing supporters during the mass gatherings greeting his return from exile in 1973: 'Neither Marxists nor Capitalists. Peronists!'

Perón expressed enthusiasm for 'some kind of movement of popular international unity and for aid to be given to European refugees through immigration'. He offered the material support for such an enterprise. 'It is not necessary to resurrect precisely that which perished with the war,' Perón said, 'but we still have wisdom to create anew.' As they parted, the group of war criminals and Nazi collaborators expressed deep gratitude for 'the touching hospitality' they had received in Argentina, and pledged full support for Perón's 'great enterprise'.[263]

Emboldened by the meeting, Daye and his group set about their most ambitious political project: obtaining a 'Christian' amnesty for the Nazi criminals sentenced during the postwar trials in Europe. With Argentina about to take a seat on the Security Council of the United Nations, the opportunity seemed almost God-sent. Most important of all, the initiative had received Perón's enthusiastic support. (At the Vatican, a 'Nazi amnesty' was also being considered by Cardinal Montini at the insistence of Bishop Hudal. In May 1949, Montini was able to inform Hudal that he had obtained the Pope's consent for a 'wide-ranging amnesty', although the idea was eventually discarded due to strong resistance from Germany's bishops.)[264]

As strange as it may seem with hindsight, in 1948 Perón was reaping rich dividends from lobbying the UN in favour of a pardon for Franco's Spain, which had been ostracized by the international community for its support of Hitler during the war. In 1946, when the General Assembly issued a recommendation for all nations to break off diplomatic relations with Franco, Argentina's ambassador to the UN, José Arce, voted against it. In the months that followed, most countries followed the recommendation and turned their backs on Madrid. Perón alone resisted the boycott. This explains the enthusiastic reception Evita received when she visited Spain in 1947. In the words of Spanish ambassador Areilza, Buenos Aires became Franco's 'submarine periscope' to the world. But by November 1947, when the Communist bloc wished to intensify the ostracism of Spain, the Cold War had set in, and a new vote at the UN failed to confirm the previous year's resolution. Now the US voted against the Communists. In Spain there was jubilation, and the press even speculated that inclusion in the Marshall Plan was not unthinkable. Daye's group met with Perón in the afterglow of this recent success.[265]

These fugitives elicited greater warmth from the general than the accredited diplomats of their respective nations did. The evident hostility between Perón and the French and Belgian diplomats, who had become a magnet for Argentina's anti-Peronist liberals, had left the door wide open for the officials of formerly Nazi-occupied nations such as Daye and Guilbaud to become 'parallel' ambassadors at the Casa Rosada.

Fired up by the defeat of Nazism, the envoys of the liberated nations found themselves in a country dominated by military officers who had stamped out all attempts to celebrate Hitler's end. When Soviet troops entered Berlin on 23 April 1945, Perón's military government banned the 'sounding of sirens, whistles or fireworks' and Argentine radio stations were forbidden to transmit the three words 'Berlin has fallen.' A few days later, when students in Buenos Aires disregarded the order, many were wounded and some killed in a combined attack by police, military conscripts and nationalist youth groups.[266]

France's post-Vichy ambassador, Wladimir d'Ormesson, had committed the unpardonable mistake upon his arrival of siding with the Democratic Union, the political coalition that Perón subsequently defeated in the 1946 presidential elections. The general was not amused. Belgian legation chief Jaspar had not fared any better and was kept waiting for a solid month before Perón received him. The dislike for the official representatives of countries that had fallen under Soviet domination was even stronger, and Croatian fugitives in Argentina received special favours from Perón. They were elevated to the rank of personal friends or became members of his personal body-guard. To the diplomats of the liberated nations, Perón's Third Position was an anathema redolent of Hitler's corporate-minded New Order. The reports they sent home fumed with indignation at the presence in Perón's court of the very same criminals whose extradition they were unsuccessfully requesting.[267]

Following the meeting at the Casa Rosada, Daye's group gave Rodolfo Freude a note for Perón laced with the kind of flattery that the general would have liked to receive from the official diplomats. His Third Position reflected 'the deep aspiration of the immense majority of the people of Europe who dread the prospect of a new world war', the group said, representing itself as perfectly placed to publicize Perón's achievements in Europe and attract 'a new elite immigration'. The group offered to place its European contacts and 'accumulated experience' in the 'anti-Communist struggle' at the service of the 'Argentine National Revolution'.[268]

Related to this was the group's bid for 'a general amnesty throughout Europe in favour of all those sentenced or accused after the war', as Daye explained in a letter to *Informaciones* editor Serna, who had returned to Madrid after the meeting with Perón. Daye wanted the journalist to lead a Spanish press campaign in favour of the 'Nazi amnesty'. Their mutual friend, Ambassador Areilza, had already broached the matter with Perón and the president 'showed enthusiasm for the idea and has decided to pursue it personally'. The possibility of a direct pronouncement by Perón was being investigated, but the preferred approach was for Argentina to propose the 'internal reconciliation' of Europe at the Security Council of the United Nations, where Ambassador Arce was scheduled to take a seat in 1948. 'Peace will not really exist until we put an end to hatred,' Daye proclaimed.[269]

In the week following the meeting with Perón, Daye's group drew up a working paper outlining the proposed amnesty, full of praise for Argentina's wartime neutrality and the 'moral gains' it had accrued. The country's election to the Security Council not only rewarded Perón's opposition to Russia but also his 'less visible' opposition to the US, a country that they claimed envied 'the growing stature of the principal republic in Latin America'. This was the kind of talk Perón enjoyed, not the awkward extradition requests he was receiving from the French and Belgian representatives.

Real peace required 'an end to the wave of hatred that has swept across the world, and Europe in particular, after the end of the war'. The 'veritable season of judges' started by the Nuremberg trials had failed to distinguish between real criminals and those who had been merely anti-Communists. On the eve of the Third World War, Europe could not afford to keep these men in prison. 'Could Argentina not therefore solemnly demand that the United Nations adopt measures conducive to the proclamation of a general amnesty that would put an end to the hatred?' Daye's group inquired in its customary rapturous prose. 'In a time without a conscience, Argentina could become the bearer of the Christian Conscience of the world.'[270]

Despite their enthusiasm and Perón's endorsement, the Nazi amnesty never made it off the drawing board. Lobbying in favour of Franco's Spain, the 'Mother Country' with its centuries-old ties of religion and race to Argentina, was one thing. Proposing an amnesty for condemned Nazi criminals, no matter how appealing the notion may have been to Perón's military code of honour, was quite another. Even the die-hard nationalists among Perón's foreign policy advisers must have frowned at the mere mention of such a suicidal venture.[271]

The meeting with Perón nonetheless opened the way for a mass escape. Contact with the presidential office continued on a 'constant and regular basis' and the escape operation was now on a firm footing thanks to financing provided by 'the great friend you met with us', Daye reported to Serna. Arrivals were being housed at a reception centre in Buenos Aires that could hold up to 60 people while jobs and permanent residences were found for them. Daye asked Serna to draw up lists of candidates in Spain, indicating which of them needed 'to be saved most urgently'. Fuldner was helping out too.[272]

The landing permits Daye required were usually requested at the Casa Rosada by Perón's financial adviser Georges Guilbaud, and were routed from there to Immigration by Roover, who presented them in the name of Freude's Information Bureau. Other presentations were made by Lagrou, who as a member of Freude's secret service initiated a large number of files under the alias Reinaldo van Groede. Daye also kept in personal contact with Immigration Commissioner Pablo Diana.[273]

During 1948 Daye's old *Je Suis Partout* colleague Charles Lesca, who had first opened the 'ratline' out of Spain in 1944, continued playing an important role, recommending fugitives and handling part of the workload. Individuals recommended by French jet-plane designer Emile Dewoitine also received preferential treatment. Daye and Lesca maintained their contact with Bishop Barrére, who had played such a vital role in the Tisserant–Caggiano talks at the Vatican, sending new arrivals into his safe-keeping in the northern province of Tucumán.[274]

Most arrived on standard ocean liners. Others came on smaller ships, motorboats and sailboats, packed tightly with nothing but war criminals. Dutch SS man Willem Sassen, who would become Eichmann's confidant in Argentina, travelled under the alias Jacobus Janssen on the schooner *Adelaar*, which sailed from Dublin in September 1948, after receiving an *in absentia* death sentence from a Belgian court. There were only nine passengers on board: Sassen, two Belgian war criminals (Willem Smekens and Achille Hollants) and the men's families. Typically, the landing permit applications for these three fugitives were processed by Argentina's Immigration Office at the same time as others sponsored by Perón's presidential office.[275]

Another audacious transatlantic crossing was made by the sailboat *Thyl Uilenspiegel*, which was also packed with Belgian war criminals.

Among them was Adolf De Braekeleer, who was charged with large-scale 'economic collaboration' with the Nazis during the occupation of Belgium. With a fake passport in the name of Florentin Gilissen, De Braekeleer fled to Paris with his mistress Mariette Van Damme, finally reaching the Argentine consulate in Barcelona in March 1948. There, apparently in exchange for a large sum of money, he obtained a landing permit, and arrived in Buenos Aires on 18 July 1948, barely a month after receiving an *in absentia* 20-year sentence in Brussels.

De Braekeleer did amazingly well in Argentina, entering into shady business deals with Argentine government officials. Together with Guilbaud, he managed the luxurious Hotel Crillón, directly across from the Argentine Foreign Ministry in downtown Buenos Aires. Publicly, he presented himself as a 'political refugee', but privately storms were brewing. In a moment of vindictiveness his mistress blurted out the claim that De Braekeleer was a double agent for the Soviets. The judge handling his citizenship application promptly received a letter from the Argentine secret service, not only raising the alleged Communist connection but also accusing De Braekeleer of attempting to bribe Argentine officials.

De Braekeleer's response shows which way the wind blew among Argentine officialdom. In a letter to the secret service that survives in his citizenship application, he vehemently denied the Communist charge, proclaiming instead that he had been a fervent admirer of Hitler, that he had earned by his own estimate some 250 million francs from the Nazis during the war, and that he had been sentenced to 20 years in prison for it. He added that he was now planning to develop 250,000 hectares of land in the wine-growing province of Mendoza. Endorsing his pro-Nazi sentiment, scores of letters from other Belgians (and even some Germans) hiding in Argentina flooded the judge's desk, all openly declaring their collaborationist past and attesting to De Braekeleer's pro-German sympathies. Topping off the bulky file was a letter from a senior Belgian Catholic Church dignitary to Cardinal Caggiano, attesting to the worth of De Braekeleer's supporters. So much heartfelt pro-Hitlerism made a good impression. Argentina's secret service apologized to the judge for its earlier, clearly mistaken, assessment, and on 3 June 1954 De Braekeleer was cere-moniously handed his Argentine passport.[276]

By mid-1948 arrivals had grown so numerous that 'following the wish expressed by President Perón', and with a little help from the Catholic Church, Daye and his entourage set up SARE, the Society in Argentina for the Reception of Europeans. The organization estab-lished its headquarters at 1358 Canning Street, a grand colonial-style building owned by the archbishopric of Buenos Aires. Today, SARE's old rescue HQ has been gutted to accommodate the makeshift Church of Our Lady of Perpetual Succour.[277]

The archbishop at the time was Argentina's Cardinal Primate Santiago Luis Copello, a sympathizer of the Vichy regime, supporter of Franco and regular visitor at the German embassy in Buenos Aires during the war. The cardinal shared Perón's intense dislike for both 'atheistic Communism' and capitalism. In 1947, Perón had appointed him his 'Papal Legate', a vaguely defined position which meant the cardinal acted as Perón's go-between with the Vatican. According to Daye's personal papers, Copello was not averse to meeting personally with French-speaking supporters of Perón's Third Position. In 1951, when Marshal Pétain died, Daye's friends at the Cathedral of Buenos Aires organized a funeral service for the Vichy leader. A catafalque was adorned with the French flag and hundreds of burning candles lit the nave. The mass was presided over by Cardinal Copello, robed in purple.[278]

SARE's statutes were drawn up on 29 June 1948 during a meeting at Ghenea's home attended by fugitive representatives of various for-merly Nazi-occupied nations: Daye and Lagrou for Belgium, Robert Pincemin for France and Ferdinand Durcansky for Slovakia. Men named as Haas and Hinrichsen represented Germany and Austria, Italy was represented by Morreale, and another key player was the Croatian diplomat Branko Benzon. Hungary was represented by Monsignor Ferenc Luttor, a diplomat at the Vatican during the war. He had arrived in Argentina in April 1947 on an Italian liner packed with Croatian fugitives, with the words 'Holy See' written boldly across his travel papers. In Rome after the war, the Monsignor had run a brisk business obtaining fake papers for fugitives through his 'Pontifical Assistance for Hungarians' office at Piazza dei Massimi No. 4.[279]

For its logo, SARE chose the image of a lifebelt encircling a map of Europe, which it stamped on the masthead of the application forms it printed up for its prospective immigrants. In October 1948, Immigration Commissioner Diana officially recognized the society, authorizing it to accept landing permit applications 'within the selective guidelines you already know'.[280]

SARE's objective was 'to procure for our endangered friends on the Old Continent visas and resources for immigration to Argentina', Daye wrote in his memoirs. 'The country's government has quickly shown the most humane understanding. It has recognized us officially and by its generosity – as well as its desire to obtain select immigration – it has allowed us to save thousands of friends and even strangers.' True, many of those he rescued had been served death sentences, but this did not make them any the less 'good, honest young men'.[281]

The private papers of Daye preserved today at the CEGES archive in Brussels contain the names of well over 100 such Belgian and French individuals that Daye personally helped escape to Argentina. SARE's total tally is no doubt much higher, since Daye did not handle cases from the other various nationalities represented by the organization. National boundaries were strictly respected along the lines fixed by Immigration. When a request for landing permits for three Germans landed on his desk, for example, Daye scribbled 'Remit to Carlos Fuldner' on the note.[282]

After a successful start in Argentina – evading extradition, meeting with Perón, setting up SARE – 1949 began on a sorrowful note for Daye when his friend Charles Lesca suddenly passed away on 11 January. The Franco-Argentine had been almost a father figure to Daye, from publishing Daye's articles in *Je Suis Partout* until the day he became the first person Daye saw as he descended the plane steps to freedom in Argentina. It must have been a heavy blow, and the otherwise expansive Daye could barely bring himself to mention Lesca's death in his memoirs.[283]

In retrospect, Lesca's death seems to portend the difficulties that lay ahead for Daye's Nazi-rescue operation. In 1949 Perón started to withdraw quietly from the business. Although the general never completely severed contact with the Nazi network (he continued to be surrounded by his Croatian bodyguards and let himself be photographed with Mengele's protector Hans-Ulrich Rudel during his last presidency in the early 1970s), after Lesca's death relations between Freude's Information Bureau and Immigration mysteriously ground to a halt.

The first intimation that something was wrong came in February 1949, when the door to the office of Immigration Commissioner Diana was unceremoniously slammed in Daye's face for the first time. Then the commissioner himself vanished. 'Don Pablo has disappeared,' an alarmed Daye wrote in February to French war criminal Jacques de Mahieu, the expert in 'biopolitics' whom Perón had appointed to a professorship at Cuyo University in northern Argentina. 'Impossible as yet to make precise inquiries, confusion reigns.'[284]

Unknown to the SARE fraternity, the long-running battle between Argentina's Foreign Ministry and Immigration had flared up again, and dislodged Diana in the process. The rivalry was being fuelled by the pervasive anti-Semitism among Argentina's diplomats, furious about 'the crime being committed against our Fatherland' by the authorization of too many landing permits in favour of 'thieves, murderers, Communists, vagabonds, Jews'. The diplomats in Europe felt better placed to judge applicants than the Immigration clerks in faraway Buenos Aires. Their pent-up frustration exploded in a long report recording their grievances put together by a nationalist senator who toured Europe in early 1949. To block the entry of persons they considered 'human scum', the diplomats at the consulate in Paris had started refusing visas even to those who had obtained valid landing permits from Immigration, going as far as withholding their passports to stop them from travelling. Specially commissioned by Foreign Minister Bramuglia to inform Perón of the 'undesirables' obtaining landing permits, Senator Alejandro Mathus-Hoyos talked with Argentina's diplomats in France, Belgium, Poland and Italy, and came away shocked by the 'riffraff' emigrating to Argentina. He was also disturbed by rumours about the behaviour of Perón's DAIE officials in Italy (presumably Fuldner's group), who were allegedly involved in 'scandals' with 'prostitutes and low-life characters'.[285]

The Argentine consul in Beirut was particularly angered by the fact that applicants he advised against, on the grounds that they were 'Israelites' or other 'evidently undesirable elements', still received landing permits from Buenos Aires thanks to an 'organization' which, he alleged, collected bribes for these exceptions.[286]

Despite their upper-class contempt for the more plebeian bureaucrats at Immigration, Argentina's diplomats were not immaculate themselves when it came to squeezing Jews, and their anger was fuelled as much by being excluded from a lucrative venture as by any real concern about the nature of the human material heading across the Atlantic. One example of the hypocrisy of Argentina's diplomatic service was a report by the country's consul in Vienna, José Ramón Virasoro. This diplomat prided himself on denying visas to Jewish refugees while advocating the mass emigration to Argentina of anti-Communist elements escaping from the Soviet-occupied nations – postwar shorthand for former Nazi collaborators. But shortly after his report denounced the irregularities at Immigration, Virasoro himself faced charges of selling Argentine passports in Vienna. By 1952 he was dismissed from the diplomatic service for his involvement in drug-trafficking, illegal foreign exchange dealings and gold smuggling.[287]

Another more personal factor may have compounded the move against Diana, for the new Immigration overseer brought in by Perón was the former GOU mastermind Colonel Enrique González, trained in the Panzer units of General Guderian. Intimately connected to Himmler's secret service during the war, González was dismissed from the GOU dictatorship in 1944 after his plan to send a special

German-Argentine envoy to meet with Hitler in Berlin backfired. His agent was arrested by the British authorities in Trinidad. At the time, González was convinced that the 'betrayer' of the plan had been Ludwig Freude, and pledged that he would 'take strong measures against those he believed guilty as soon as the circumstances permitted'.[288]

When a secret inquest was opened in 1949 against Immigration Commissioner Pablo Diana on charges by Argentina's diplomats that he was too lenient granting landing permits to Jews, it seems finally to have afforded González his opportunity for revenge. The investigation set out by training its guns on Rodolfo Freude's Information Bureau, and the first persons called to testify were four Argentine collaborators of Freude who carried documentation back and forth between the Casa Rosada and Immigration.[289]

The inquest found itself quickly unmasking the activities of Freude's special Nazi 'advisers'. The examiners of the Ethnic Institute, whose objective had been to safeguard Argentina against a flood of Jewish arrivals, found themselves instead drawing up lists of the names (or aliases) of the Nazi collaborators Daye, Lagrou, Guilbaud, Ghenea, Serna and Fuldner, and other unsavoury characters such as Count Monti, Count Menou, Benzon and the Russian Orthodox Archpriest Izrastzoff.[290]

Although Freude himself was never called to testify, Fuldner was. The former SS captain readily admitted the true nature of his work and stated point-blank that he acted under Perón's direct orders. He offered a brief description of the meetings with war criminals and collaborators hosted by the president at the Casa Rosada. Higher orders from Perón explained the blatant irregularities evident in the landing permits he had handled, Fuldner said, pointing out that 'powerful and secret reasons of state' made such short cuts necessary. 'The special character of his secret missions could cause problems of conscience for some officials, for which reason he is forbidden from going into details or talking openly about them,' the inquest stenographer recorded.

Fuldner appealed to the 'exceptional period that humanity and, inseparable from the world's destiny, our own Fatherland' were going through, to excuse his mission in Europe. What others might have considered a conscience-troubling enterprise actually required special 'norms and regulations', especially in 'sectors such as Immigration which find their control, their stability, their justification, and their purity only in the higher interests of the nation'. Fortunately for all concerned, Fuldner had enjoyed the opportunity of hearing these interests 'interpreted by His Excellency the President of the Nation', and had seen them materialized in 'measures . . . which in no country and at no time have been regarded as outside the law, but certainly above regulations'. Fuldner's clumsy mix of arrogant Nazi jargon and Argentine mystification may not wash five decades on, but it impressed the inquest officials.[291]

The chief officials at Immigration confirmed the existence of a secret arrangement with the Information Bureau for the granting of landing permits to German and Japanese war criminals even in cases where their documentation was deficient. The number of such applications was so large that Immigration even coined the abbreviation 'Doc. Def.' for them.[292]

No mention was made of the background or wartime responsibilities of Perón's 'advisers' or the persons they rescued. The interrogations skirted the issue with consummate skill, sometimes employing simple euphemisms such as 'technicians', sometimes more roundabout surrogates such as 'German subjects, especially devotees of the last regular government'. The word 'Nazi' was studiously avoided and does not appear once in the 529 pages of transcript.[293]

With almost scholarly delight, the Ethnic Institute continued to map out in detail how the Information Bureau went about obtaining landing permits for 'Doc. Def.' applicants, only to conclude that the 'irregularities' committed by Fuldner and the rest of Freude's agents conformed to secret presidential instructions and therefore fell outside the inquest's scope.[294]

The Immigration officials accused of admitting Jews, on the other hand, felt the full impact of the investigation. Diana and his deputies were dismissed from service under a decree signed by Perón. They tried to defend themselves as best they could from the charge of being soft on the Jews, but file after file was produced showing that too many exceptions had been made.[295]

Embarrassingly for the inquest, it turned out that the vast majority of the exceptions for Jews had been ordered by Perón himself, who applied his mercy selectively, favouring landing permit applications from loyal Peronist Jewish leaders above those from non-Peronist Jews. Confronted with Immigration file 205612/48, for example, granting entry to Neuch Rubinstein and his wife 'despite the fact that the beneficiaries are of advanced age and profess the Israelite religion and can consequently be considered defective and useless immigration', the official who authorized their entry was able to point out that Perón favoured the admission of elderly Jews, 'firstly, to soften the widely held perception of racial persecution, and secondly and fundamentally, because being elderly persons they can leave no descendants and the [Jewish] community does not increase'.[296]

Regarding the original suspicion that some Jews had obtained landing permits through Freude's secret service, Diana assured the Ethnic Institute that Freude himself strictly controlled his agency's lists to make sure they did not include 'those people the country is not interested in'. Despite all precautions, however, Freude's Belgian agent Léonard de Roover was caught slipping landing permits for Jews among the applications for Nazis he delivered from the Casa Rosada. Roover was hurriedly dismissed, and disappeared with a large bundle of landing permits for Nazi collaborators awaiting rescue in Europe, forcing Daye to initiate their applications again from scratch.[297]

But the cumulative pressure of thousands of Jews desperate to abandon war-torn Europe proved too strong for Perón's stopguards. Daye himself succumbed to it in 1951 while still aiding Nazi fugitives from Brussels and Paris who wished to settle in Argentina. The major difference was that now Daye's candidates included some Jews, who falsely declared themselves Catholics to gain admission. 'What strikes me is that now nobody wants to talk openly about the Jewish question,' Daye confided to his diary. 'Not for good, or evil . . . There is a kind of strange restraint. The Israelite is taboo . . . I have, here, one or two very good Jewish friends, who treat me with a correctness not shown by my erstwhile compatriots, imbued in baptismal water for twenty generations.'[298]

Daye's new life took a bad turn when he lost his post as assistant professor of French Literature at the University of La Plata, some 50 kilometres south of Buenos Aires. In 1948 the professor had begun commuting twice weekly to lecture a class made up mostly of 'jeunes filles', who proved 'attentive and charming'. But his career was abruptly halted when a small coup staged by rival academics unseated him from his position. Appeals to the university's authorities for reinstatement went unheeded, and even a visit to the Casa Rosada, where a colonel on Perón's staff promised to repair the 'abuse' against 'a foreigner of such unequalled qualities', drew a blank.[299]

As often before in his life, a stroke of luck saved Daye. In an overnight cabinet switch his Madrid acquaintance Hipólito Paz became Perón's new foreign minister, after the previous minister Bramuglia fell out of favour with Evita. Although Paz's foreign policy was based on patching up wartime differences between Perón and Washington, his appointment only reinforced the protective ring around the war criminal. Daye and Paz exchanged warm greetings and the Belgian's university career was put back on track by a letter of recommendation from Paz that earned him the chair in French Civilization at La Plata.[300]

By then Daye had accepted the fact that Buenos Aires had become his 'fixed port' and that the death sentence against him in Belgium removed all hope of ever returning to Europe. With a little help from Perón's staff, he therefore set about becoming an Argentine citizen. Presidential aide Atilio Ravanetti walked him through the paperwork, helping him obtain a certificate of good conduct from the same Federal Police that had earlier located and identified him for extradition. Daye mailed this certificate to the Casa Rosada on 26 October 1949, and met with Ravanetti ten days later at the Buenos Aires Law Courts, where his citizenship was granted in double-quick time. 'It is truly a passage from one world to another,' Daye wrote of his new nationality. 'A transformation that has astonished rather than pleased me.'[301]

If Daye's rescue efforts declined, his political ambitions did not. In mid-1949 he participated in the creation of a Centre of Nationalist Forces, an international initiative including Italian Fascists, Belgian Rexists and Croatian Ustashi. The Centre's plans were based on the expectation of World War Three, which it considered inevitable and necessary for the annihilation of its declared enemies, Communism and capitalism. Each nation was considered 'a biological and spiritual reality . . . ruled by its own spiritual and divine laws'. Among the Italians involved was the Franciscan Father Eusebio, a fanatical soldier-priest who had stood by Mussolini till the end. The Italian Fascists in Argentina were financed with the help of Vittorio Mussolini, Il Duce's son, who, standing alongside Hitler in Berlin, had greeted his father after his rescue by Skorzeny in 1943. The younger Mussolini had escaped to Argentina in 1947 with the aid of the Catholic Church. The Ustashi were represented by none other than Ante Pavelic, the Poglavnik of wartime Croatia, perhaps the highest-ranking war criminal sheltered by Perón, who in Argentina had become, even in Daye's eyes, 'a gloomy and tormented figure'.[302]

Daye moved to a new address, a small flat near the railroad tracks at 4537 Guemes Street in a dreary section of Palermo, and for the first time he was able to feel he had a home again. While not luxurious, the apartment allowed him to assemble 'the debris from my past': five paintings, books from his library and the part of his archives that relatives smuggled out of Belgium for him. But, now that his initial honeymoon with Argentina was over, Daye became depressed. He missed his family home in Brussels, and he was bitter over the confiscation of all his property by the Belgian state. His existence had become 'monotonous'. Much of his time was spent corresponding with old friends in Europe, going over the events of the war. Trying to make sense of his situation, he lovingly copied these exchanges into his memoirs, which eventually ran to some 1,700 pages.[303]

Other fugitives didn't fare much better. The German general Krahmer, rescued from Spain by Count Monti, tended a remote farm in the Pampas, Vittorio Mussolini had gone into the textiles business, the Hungarian Count Teleki manned the reception of a Buenos Aires hotel, Prince Gorchakov was employed at a Jewish import–export business, former Marseille mayor Simon Sabiani, who had been condemned to death in France, provided legal advice from a bar on Lavalle Street, former Luftwaffe ace von S... piloted the plane of an Argentine cabinet minister, and so the list went on, including a fellow Belgian who delivered wild animals to the circuses and zoos of Argentina. 'I've got three ostriches and seven boa serpents in there,' the fugitive shouted at Daye from his lorry one day. 'A cargo arriving tomorrow is bringing me a panther, three zebras and a baby elephant. And I have to feed the whole lot. What a job!' In the back of all their minds burned the hope that a new world war ('when the bombs start to fall again on the European countries that chased them out') would be their ticket home. 'They impatiently await, without daring to express it out loud, that restorative event,' Daye whispered into his diary.[304]

Then, as often happened in his life, things got miraculously better. One day in September 1950, Daye's phone rang. 'Don't you recognize me?' asked the voice at the end of the line. To his utter astonishment, it was Jaspar, the Belgian legation chief who only three years earlier had attempted to extradite him to face his death sentence back home. Over lunch at Amerio, a discreet Italian restaurant, Daye was surprised at the 'unquestionable pleasure' he felt meeting his old colleague from the 1930s. 'That he took the initiative to renew our relationship and invite me proves his independence of spirit, his good heart, and perhaps even, his flair,' he wrote afterwards. 'If only a photographer from the Belgian press could have spotted us!' It was a breath of fresh air to be able to discuss Belgian politics again, remember old friends, exchange gossip about Perón. The extradition request was an inconsequential detail. 'I assured him that in his place I would have done the same.'[305]

Reanimated, a few days later Daye attended a lecture by his old friend the Spanish writer Eugenio d'Ors, who was visiting Buenos Aires. Suddenly Daye felt good again. Buenos Aires had little to envy

New York in terms of its cultural life, Argentina was 'young and rich' and Perón was leading an unprecedented social revolution, he wrote in his diary. Where else but in 'brilliant Buenos Aires' would he have had the chance to introduce two notorious fugitives such as the former Yugoslavian premier Milan Stojadinovic and the former secretary-general of the Italian Fascist party Carlos Scorza to one another?

Scorza was now the editor of an influential magazine, *Dinámica Social*, which was publishing extracts in Spanish from Daye's new book, *Suicide of the Bourgeoisie*, while Stojadinovic ('Stoja' to his friends) was a financial adviser to the province of Buenos Aires. The Serb, the Italian and the Belgian fugitives discussed, in Spanish, American policy in Korea. Daye was ecstatic, surrounded by 'la crème des réfugiés d'Europe!' The writers who contributed to *Dinámica Social* used to meet at a coffee shop named La Fragata on Corrientes Avenue. Stojadinovic was often seen there with Vittorio Mussolini. In November 1950 a cocktail party organized by the magazine brought them all together – Stojadinovic, Guilbaud, Daye, Scorza, d'Ors – in honour of the British Fascist leader Sir Oswald Mosley, who had just flown in from London and was staying at the expensive Hotel Lancaster. Daye held a long conversation with Mosley, 'a handsome man, large, slender, distinguished', whom he had met once before in London in 1930.[306]

Daye was mesmerized by Eva Perón, whom he compared to St Teresa of Avila. She impelled him to compose rapturous lists of her qualities; her heart of flame, that unbending will, a lay saint lacking all sense of ridicule, 'beautiful, young, elegant, audacious, strong, tireless, loving; and perhaps, dying'. Although he had not met Evita personally, there was something about her that reminded Daye of his own Christus Rex leader Léon Degrelle, 'devoured by passion, insatiable'. Knowing the rumour about her fatal cancer, he wondered nervously how 'the sentimental adventure of Peronism' would continue once Evita, 'covered in pearls and diamonds', had left the scene. Upon her death in July 1952 he was stunned by the devotion her memory inspired among the working class. 'Sincere to the point of madness, untouched by doubt, sweet with the weak and harsh to the great', Daye had no doubt that Evita had been 'the most remarkable woman ever produced by Latin America'. He expected that in time the people of Argentina would have her 'proclaimed a saint, and the Church will have to place Eva Perón upon the altar'.[307]

Her death succeeded other disheartening news. Earlier in 1952, Daye's diplomat friend Jaspar, in reparation for his earlier attempt to extradite him, had offered to do what he could to influence the Belgian government to pardon him. Daye therefore penned an appeal to Belgian justice minister Joseph Pholien. He dared not ask for a full amnesty, but sought instead only a gentleman's agreement to be permitted to travel to Europe, outside Belgium, without risking an extradition request. He also asked for the proceeds of the sale of his property by the Belgian courts to be credited to his name. 'I have no Belgian blood on my hands and no German money in my pockets,' he claimed, incredibly for a man who had welcomed the invasion of his own country by the murderous Nazis. In Brussels, Jaspar took up the matter personally with Pholien twice, but the minister lost his post in a cabinet shuffle before any serious consideration could be given to Daye's appeal.[308]

In 1953 Daye made sure to send Perón a copy of his newly published *Suicide of the Bourgeoisie* (Perón thanked him effusively for the book in a letter), but his enthusiasm for the general had started to wane. 'This Third Position Perón talks about: it already exists, it is Fascism, or National Socialism, or Rexism,' he told Guilbaud. Perón's financial adviser added his own twist to Daye's train of thought, theorizing that Perón's war against Argentina's oligarchy, his antagonism towards the United States and his programme for the nationalization of industry showed a secret socialist streak. Guilbaud was of the opinion that Perón perhaps represented a new ideology, something the Frenchman dubbed 'National Communism'.[309]

After Evita's death, disenchantment with Perón set in. Argentina's military and the Catholic Church in particular had grown tired of the widespread corruption and the personality cult Perón promoted. He renamed cities, provinces, streets and railway stations after himself and his dead wife, and stood idly by while his minions lined their pockets from state coffers.

Daye had begun writing a column for *El Economista*, the prestigious Buenos Aires daily that Stojadinovic founded with a former leader of the Spanish Falange, Cecilio Benitez de Castro, and the Argentine journalist Juan Zenon Etchenique, a man who used to ordain masses in memory of Hitler in Buenos Aires. On 16 June 1955, as Daye left Stojadinovic's offices near the Casa Rosada after delivering his weekly article, the Belgian was lost in a reverie about Argentina, 'this country where calm is only apparent, without peace, submissive yet ignorant of discipline'. Heading for the underground entrance, his thoughts were suddenly interrupted by a sound he had not heard in well over a decade, a sound that 'froze' him in his steps. It was 'a kind of muffled whistle, the heavy rumble of a train advancing at top speed, a thunderous din . . .' It took him only seconds to realize that the Casa Rosada was being bombed by aircraft flying over the Plaza de Mayo. A revolution against Perón had started! In a dreamlike haze, Daye saw huge clouds of black smoke rise over the Casa Rosada. 'My wartime experience had taught me that above all one must not panic,' he thought as he descended to the underground. 'I could hear the thunder of the bombs as they fell, near or far, and how the planes dived in terrifying swoops.' That night as he dined with Lesca's widow, word arrived that a fellow Belgian war criminal, Henri Collard-Bovy, had survived an attack on a trolley bus in which many passengers had died. Collard-Bovy escaped with only slight wounds to his right leg.[310]

But the revolt failed. Perón saved his life by hiding in the bombproof basement of the nearby Army High Command. By late afternoon, all the ringleaders had been arrested. The cost in human lives had been high: 350 dead and over 600 wounded, mostly civilians struck by the bombs in the Plaza de Mayo area. Angry Peronists took their revenge, setting fire to the city's Catholic churches, including the cathedral.

It was the beginning of the end for Perón. Lost without Evita, engaged in a debilitating battle with the Catholic Church, his government had started to flounder. Perón himself had become a pathetic figure, a lecher pushing 60 years of age who spent ever greater amounts of time with the teenagers of his UES High School Students Union, organizing 'Existentialist Carnivals' or scooting around the city of Buenos Aires on Italian motorbikes with the giggling girls. In fact, as the planes headed towards the Casa Rosada on the day of the failed revolution, they were being watched from the rooftop of the nearby presidential residence by 16-year-old UES student Nelly Rivas, a girl Perón had seduced two years earlier, bringing her to live with him and even allowing her occasionally to wear Evita's jewels. Now three planes swooped towards the presidential residence itself. Rivas watched transfixed as a bomb hit a wall of the palace, bounced off and failed to detonate. The bombs that followed did explode and a stunned Rivas was quickly removed to safety.

Perón's respite did not last long. The last time Rivas saw the general was on 19 September 1955, packing bags while his aides stuffed huge dossiers into a blazing fire in the chimney of the presidential residence. 'Poor Perón, who started out doing so much good before he became a ridiculous dictator,' Daye mused to his Argentine nationalist friend Amadeo. Daye blamed Evita's death for the general's downfall. Perón had gone 'crazy', undone by his lust for young girls and the corruption in his government.

Rivas and the other UES girls who had partied with Perón were thoroughly interrogated by the military dictatorship that followed. Their testimony was typed on hundreds of pages of thin onionskin paper and left in the basement archives of the Lower House of Congress, until they were unearthed during the research for this book well over 40 years later. The generals and lawyers doing the questioning were desperately eager to hear the details of Perón's sexual preferences. The fact that the general had no children, despite being twice married, obsessed them. Was it true Perón was impotent? That he employed 'other substitutes' for satisfying women? Wasn't it also true that he occasionally practised sex with men? The young girls ran rings around their panting, middle-aged inquisitors. In the transcripts their roles are almost reversed: the generals and lawyers come across as gawking teens, while the UES girls reveal practically nothing. One UES student did make vague allusions to Perón's 'unnatural practices', but Rivas stated only that she had sex with Perón once every 15 days, refusing to elaborate on his rumoured preferences.

'And once every 15 days was enough for you?'

'That's my own business,' the girl demurred.

No, Perón did not use contraceptives, he simply 'didn't consummate the act', Rivas said.[311]

Many of the war criminals and Nazi collaborators who had been protected by Perón fled Argentina after his downfall. Daye, on the other hand, landed on his feet again. The first military government that followed Perón was a strongly nationalist and Catholic regime, and Amadeo became its foreign minister. Another Daye acquaintance, Juan Carlos Goyeneche, was appointed the culture and press secretary of the new Casa Rosada. The advancement of these old friends sparked some brief life into the old network. Radu Ghenea, now working for Volkswagen in Peru, wrote to Goyeneche asking him and Amadeo to intercede in the case of an old Iron Guard fugitive in Argentina who had fallen on hard times.[312]

The dream was short-lived, however. Partly because of the Peronist-Nazi stigma attached to Amadeo and Goyeneche, a palace coup unseated the nationalists and a new military government stepped in, determined to erase all vestiges of Perón's existence. Disillusioned with the anti-Peronist revolution much more quickly than he had lost faith in Perón himself, Daye sank into a dark depression. 'The pain of exile is bitter,' he wrote to his lawyer in Brussels in 1956. 'I love Belgium, land of my ancestors for centuries, land of my childhood, my formative years, my life.' The hope of returning to some other European nation taunted him continually – Sweden, Switzerland, Spain, he even considered giving himself up to prison in Belgium. 'Some believe that the time for a definitive explanation has arrived,' he wrote to another friend. 'Ten years after my sentencing and after nine years in South America, I believe I do have that right!' But the obvious difficulty in obtaining the kind of hearing Daye felt

entitled to finally dissuaded him from such a voluntary return. Even
his relatives in Brussels pointed out the impossibility of ever justifying to the Belgian public, now that the full truth about the Nazi
concentration camps was known, his desire for a German victory at
the start of the war.[313]

14

THE SLOVAK COMMITTEE

Ferdinand Durcansky, a leading member of the murderous wartime Slovak regime of Monsignor Jozef Tiso, attended the inaugural session of the Nazi-rescue organization SARE in 1948. His presence demonstrates the society's links to the Vatican, the Catholic Church in Argentina and Belgium, Perón's secret service and even to British intelligence. As we shall see, Durcansky had close ties to all of these organizations and could not have survived the war safely without them.

In the late 1930s, Durcansky had been at the centre of the Nazi conspiracy that split Czechoslovakia into its component parts. During a meeting with Hermann Göring in the winter of 1938/39, he promised loyalty to the Führer in return for Hitler's support for an independent Slovakia, and guaranteed that 'the Jewish problem will be solved as it was in Germany'. But Durcansky's negotiations with the Nazis raised suspicions in Prague, which sent troops to Bratislava and deposed Tiso's regime on 10 March 1939. Durcansky escaped to Vienna and then Berlin. From the German capital, he called on the collaborationist Hlinka Guard to rise against Prague. Arms were brought across the border from Austria and distributed among the German minority, who proceeded to occupy government buildings in Bratislava.

On 13 March, Tiso was flown to Berlin, where he and Durcansky held overnight meetings with Hitler and Ribbentrop. The Nazi leaders demanded that Slovakia break away from Prague and handed them a declaration of independence already drafted in the Slovak language. Back in Bratislava the following day, Tiso read the declaration to the Slovak diet, paving the way for Hitler's invasion of the separate Czech state on 15 March.[314]

Slovakia was not occupied by Hitler's troops until 1944, and Monsignor Tiso became a Nazi puppet ruler. His Catholic regime kept Durcansky's promise to implement the 'Final Solution', first drafting anti-Semitic legislation that eventually required Jews to wear yellow stars. In 1940, Eichmann's representative SS Captain Dieter Wisliceny arrived in Bratislava as an adviser on Jewish affairs. By October 1942, some 58,000 of Slovakia's 90,000 Jews had been deported to Nazi concentration camps, and by the end of the war only 15,000 were left alive. As minister of the interior and foreign affairs, Durcansky played a vital role in their extermination. He was also responsible for a decree authorizing the establishment of 'protective camps' which were really death camps, inside Slovakia itself.[315]

In 1945, with his brother Jan Durcansky, who had participated in the mass killings by the Hlinka Guard after the German annexation in 1944, Durcansky managed to escape into the French-occupied zone of Austria, accompanied by other prominent members of Tiso's regime. An attempt to extradite him failed when the brothers fled to Rome. There ('persecuted by Communist spies', as Jan Durcansky would declare later) they assumed the aliases Mandor Wilcsek and Giovanni Dubravsca.[316]

The new Czechoslovak government sought Britain's endorsement for Durcansky's extradition from Italy. London hesitated, fearing that 'this may be connected with a future request for the extradition of the Czech National Committee', as the Foreign Office stated in an internal memo in February 1946. The War Office was even less enthusiastic, stating in May incredibly that 'Durcansky is not, as far as we are aware, a war criminal.' Washington on the other hand had

f Hitler with his Argentine-born
ulture Minister Richard Walther
.

The secret Argentine envoy and SD
collaborator Juan Carlos Goyeneche
(AGN).

pictured with Italian Crown Prince Umberto in the Italian Alps, *c.* 1940 (AGN).

Walter Schellenberg, head of Himmler's Ausland-SD, the SS Foreign Intelligence service (photo from Schellenberg's SS file at NARA).

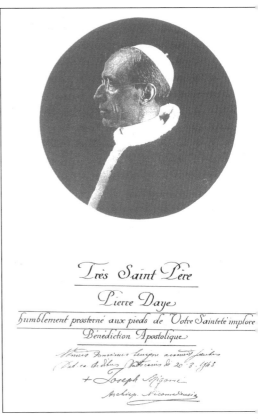

Notorious Belgian Nazi collaborator Pierre D was received by Pope Pius XII on 6 January and brought back this Vatican memento of th interview (ML).

A Fascist-style parade during Perón's 1943-46 GOU dictatorship (Mundo Libre)

...ón addresses a meeting of the Circle of Catholic Workers during his GOU regime ...N).

...iago Peralta, Perón's anti-Semitic ...nigration Commissioner (AGN).

The notorious Nazi collaborator and secret SD operative Charles Lesca (ML).

Cardinal Antonio Caggiano (second from right) and Bishop Agustín Barrére (first from right) arrive back in Buenos Aires on 28 May 1946, after secret talks at the Vatican (AGN).

Pierre Daye in Buenos Aires in 1948, when he headed the Perón-sponsored SARE organization (ML).

Pierre Daye (extreme left) and Charl Lesca (second from right, with his wi in Spain, 1945 (ML).

Perón and Evita with Rodolfo Freude, head of Perón's secret service, the Information Bureau (AGN).

n (centre) and Rodolfo Freude (extreme right) greet Evita at Morón airport on
ecember 1946 (AGN).

The German-Argentine
SS Captain Carlos Horst
Fuldner, 1935 (MRE).

Branko Benzon, Croatia's
wartime ambassador to
Berlin, 1947 (DNM).

The Croatian Poglavr
and major war crimin:
Ante Pavelic, disguise
behind beard and glas
1948 (DNM).

The SS arch-criminal Adolf
Eichmann, 1950 (ICRC).

An Argentine landing permit, in
case granting entry in 1948 to
special SD agent Reinhard Spitz

schwitz doctor Josef
ngele, 1949 (ICRC).

SS Captain Erich
Priebke, 1948 (ICRC).

SS General Hans
Fischböck, 1951 (ICRC).

ón with a group of UES girls
ing the final stretch of his
sidency in the mid-1950s (AGN).

ón puttering around Buenos Aires
his Vespa motorbike, 1955 (AGN).

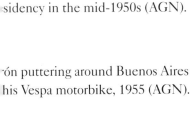

Ante Pavelic and his wife in Buenos Aires, 1957 (AGN).

Wartime SD collaborator Mario Amadeo in 1978 with Argentine dictator Jorge Vid‹ (AGN).

quickly acceded to a request for Durcansky's extradition from the US-occupied sector of Germany, where he was believed to have been hiding during March.[317]

Even though the American State Department enthusiastically supported a swift arrest of Durcansky by the Allied Commission in Italy, on 14 June the British Foreign Office formally turned down Prague's appeal on the grounds that he was not a war criminal. In its note to the Czechoslovak embassy in London the Foreign Office put the matter, literally, in God's hands, stating that Durcansky had taken refuge 'in the Vatican City', and London ironically suggested that 'the Czechoslovak government may feel disposed to raise the matter of his extradition with the authorities of the Holy See.'[318]

But Durcansky was every inch a war criminal, and on 18 September 1946 the UN War Crimes Commission in London placed him on its 'A' wanted list. Durcansky was charged with 'murder and massacres, systematic terrorism, torture of civilians, deliberate starvation of civilians, internment of civilians under inhuman conditions, forced labour of civilians in connection with the military operations of the enemy, confiscation of property and indiscriminate mass arrest', all of this linked to 'serious crimes committed against the Jews'.[319]

Living in Rome under the cover of the Vatican, Durcansky now set about plotting the restoration of a Catholic totalitarian regime in Slovakia. This anti-Communist scheme was supported by British intelligence and the Holy See (in a complicated game that eventually backfired and brought about instead the replacement of the postwar democratic Czechoslovak government by Communists). Durcansky and the Franciscan priest Rudolf Dilong, a close collaborator of Monsignor Tiso who had fled through Austria with Durcansky, set up the Slovak Action Committee in Rome. In late 1946, Durcansky disappeared momentarily from view. He reportedly travelled to Spain, where another Vatican-protected Slovak, the former ambassador to the Holy See, Karol Sidor, was in hiding.[320]

In 1947, the press claimed that Durcansky was in contact with his country's underground movement and broadcasting daily to Slovakia from Italy. He was also charged by Prague with sending agents into

Czechoslovakia to murder government officials. In June, leaflets were distributed claiming that a new government would soon take power with Durcansky as premier. When the conspiracy was cracked in September, Durcansky was pinpointed as its 'main instigator' and documents surfaced showing that scores of Slovak politicians formed part of his ring. The ensuing purge and its attendant political débâcle opened the way for a Communist regime in Czechoslovakia. Years later it transpired that during this fiasco Durcansky had been part of Intermarium, a British-controlled anti-Communist group master-minded by Kim Philby, the notorious British SIS operative who was actually a double agent for the Soviets.[321]

Meanwhile, Czechoslovakia had condemned Durcansky to death after an *in absentia* trial. Either because he was shaken by the sentence or in order to distance himself from the Slovak conspiracy, he quit Europe in the first wave of the massive flight of former Tiso func-tionaries, who continued arriving in Argentina into the early 1950s. The Durcansky brothers left from Genoa with Father Dilong on the *Maria C* ocean liner. They travelled third class under their Wilcsek and Dubravsca aliases, landing at the port of Buenos Aires on 11 August 1947. (Their ship was packed with dubious Croatians, at least two of whom would soon take up posts in the rescue chain out of Europe.) The travelling papers of the Durcansky brothers were apparently not in order and the Argentine authorities held them on board for two days before allowing them to land. Also held was Stefan Polakovic, secretary-general of the Slovak Action Committee, who had crossed the Atlantic with Durcansky under the alias Giuseppe Horvath.[322]

The Slovaks settled in quickly, making contact with Perón's net-work of Nazi agents. Jan Durcansky, whose war crimes record was even more grisly than his brother's, became an official in the Certifications department at Immigration. He guided arrivals through the bureaucratic procedure for obtaining identification papers, help-ing them to switch their aliases back to their real names and acquire Argentine citizenship.[323]

Ferdinand Durcansky slotted into Perón's secret police, and by

December he had proved his worth with a report on the pro-Communist activities of the Czechoslovak embassy in Buenos Aires. Its highly detailed eight pages included the 'revelation' that the ambassador was a converted Jew. Perón's virulently anti-Communist and generally anti-Semitic secret police took Durcansky seriously and distributed his report to the Foreign Ministry and Argentine military intelligence, along with an account of the war criminal's activities in Buenos Aires. Perón's agents were aware of Durcansky's classification as a war criminal by the UN, and pointed out that he feared Argentina might surrender him for extradition. Only Reverend Dilong, who had travelled with Durcansky and was living under Franciscan protection at the Church of the Mercedarian Order in Buenos Aires, knew his real hiding place. Durcansky forwarded his reports to Perón's secret police through Federico Müller-Ludwig, editor of the pro-Nazi German-language daily *Freie Presse*.[324]

Although these former Slovak officials were now far away from their homeland, their struggle for the dismemberment of Czechoslovakia continued. Their Slovak Action Committee rekindled the cause on 12 January 1948, when Durcansky and Polakovic wrote to their compatriots back home calling on them to rise against Prague or else be considered 'agents of international Communism serving Moscow's aim of world domination'. The Czechoslovak authorities were understandably perturbed, and in March an appeal was renewed at the UN War Crimes Commission for Durcansky's arrest. Additional evidence had surfaced during the second round of 'Wilhelmstrasse' trials at Nuremberg, showing that Durcansky had been in the pay of Himmler's secret service since at least November 1938, and this had been added to the existing charges. 'Is it not a serious fact that a man who has been listed as a war criminal – not for political activity against the new regime, but for crimes committed during the German occupation – and who, as the Americans showed, was in the pay of the SS and SD, should now be at large, posing abroad as a political leader while in reality plotting against my country?' the Czechoslovak representative pleaded.[325]

The emotional tone was employed to win London's support for a new extradition request. 'The Czechoslovak government has asked the Argentine government to ascertain the whereabouts of Durcansky, to arrest and extradite him,' the Czechoslovak embassy in London wrote to the Foreign Office. For the extradition to succeed it was 'essential' for Czechoslovakia to 'secure the assistance of one of the Western Great Powers'. Embarrassingly for London, the UN War Crimes Commission's unanimous vote to put Durcansky on its 'A' list had been taken during a session presided over by the British representative, Sir Robert Craigie. The Czechoslovak government wanted Britain to inform Argentina that it had 'also voted' for his inclusion. But Durcansky's connection to British intelligence made it difficult to comply with Prague's wish. Finally, on 5 July 1948 Foreign Secretary Ernest Bevin informed the Czechoslovak ambassador that Britain would not 'intervene directly with the Argentine government' in favour of Durcansky's extradition.[326]

Washington, on the other hand, took an extremely dim view of Durcansky's Nazi-rescue operation in Buenos Aires. While London shielded the war criminal, the CIA was busy compiling a thick dossier on the activities of a man it considered 'guilty of the gruesome Calvary of the Slovak Jews'. The American file contained shocking confirmation that the 'Slovak populist emigration' Durcansky promoted was 'supported by the Vatican' and that the financial means were being provided by 'church dignitaries, especially in Belgium and Argentina'.[327]

The CIA reference to support from Argentine and Belgian Catholic Church leaders finds corroboration in the fact that SARE's headquarters were owned by the archbishopric of Buenos Aires. With such backers, Durcansky was indeed untouchable. In 1948 his Slovak Action Committee set about presenting a series of collective applications for landing permits at the Immigration Office. As a result, a wave of Tiso's Catholic Fascists headed for Argentina, where they formed the largest Slovak community in South America, numbering some 30,000 during Perón's administration.[328]

In 1949 both Ferdinand and his brother Jan Durcansky felt confident enough in their new surroundings to abandon their aliases and switch back to their real names. In late 1950 Ferdinand was spirited out of Argentina by his British protector Kim Philby and deposited in Canada. He returned to Buenos Aires in 1952 to acquire Argentine citizenship, a step also taken by his brother. He finally settled in Canada, where he became a revered figure among the Slovak Fascist community, working for the Catholic-dominated Anti-Bolshevik Bloc of Nations and occasionally giving anti-Semitic speeches. His brother Jan continued to live in Argentina until 1960, when an attempt by Czechoslovakia to extradite him for the mass killings he was involved in during 1944 was rejected by Buenos Aires. Released after a month's arrest, Jan Durcansky quickly left for North America.[329]

15

FLIGHT OF THE USTASHI

If the German Nazis with their godless ideology and their gas chambers industrialized the business of genocide, the wartime Ustasha regime in Croatia was led by deeply Catholic men who employed medieval methods to conduct their programme of extermination. Mass shootings, clubbing and decapitation were the methods by which they pursued their aim of a racially pure and 100 per cent Catholic state. By the end of the war some 700,000 people had perished in the Ustasha death camps at Jasenovac and elsewhere. The regime's fury was directed primarily against the Orthodox Serb population, but Jews and Gypsies were also included in the death roll.

The creation of the kingdom of Yugoslavia after World War One had brought together Croats, Serbs and Slovenians under the rule of King Alexander. The Ustasha movement resisted this integration and became the standard-bearer of the Croatian cause, led by the deeply nationalistic Ante Pavelic. In 1934 Ustasha terrorists murdered King Alexander, one of many bloody acts committed in the name of a separate Croatian state, in a struggle that enjoyed the support of Fascist Italy and Nazi Germany.

During World War Two, Yugoslavia was carved up by the Axis powers and Pavelic became the Poglavnik, or Führer, of an independent

Croatia. The Allies denounced the dismemberment of Yugoslavia and refused to recognize Pavelic's regime. But Pavelic received carte blanche to implement his murderous policies during a meeting with Hitler in June 1941. Hitler outlined a series of racial measures, plans he described as 'momentarily painful' but preferable to 'permanent suffering'. If Croatia was to be strong, Hitler said, 'a nationally intolerant policy must be pursued for fifty years, because too much tolerance on such issues can only do harm.'[330]

Pavelic had anticipated Hitler's wishes, and in the first few days following the declaration of Croatian independence on 10 April 1941, Zagreb passed a series of racial laws that included the 'Aryanization' of Jewish property. In Croatia, not only were the Jews forced to wear an armband with the Star of David and the letter 'Z' (*Zidov*: Jew), but Serbs were also ordered to wear blue armbands with the letter 'P' (*Pravoslavni*: Orthodox).

Concentration camps were set up across Croatia and Bosnia, with the camp system at Jasenovac as the main killing centre. The regime's racial policy was stated in the bluntest and simplest of terms on 22 July 1941: 'For the rest, Serbs, Jews and Gypsies, we have three million bullets. We shall kill one third of all Serbs. We shall deport another third, and the rest of them will be forced to become Roman Catholic,' said Mile Budak, Pavelic's minister of education, in a widely publicized speech.

The Vatican may have failed to condemn the murderous racial policies of the Nazis, but it certainly did not endorse them, whereas the Roman Catholic Church in Croatia became an ardent supporter of Pavelic's crimes. In May 1941 the Church organ *Hrvatska Straza* gave a warm welcome to the racial legislation, deeming it necessary for 'the protection of our honour and blood'. Some bishops were equally supportive. 'There exist limits to love,' said the archbishop of Sarajevo, Ivan Saric, praising the new laws and affirming that it would be 'stupid and unworthy of Christ's disciples to think that the struggle against evil could be waged in a noble way and with gloves on'. The Croatian regime's leading racial theorist, Ivo Guberina, was a Roman Catholic priest who combined concepts of religious 'purification' and 'racial hygiene' with a call for Croatia to be 'cleansed of foreign elements'.[331]

Unlike their Nazi masters, the Croatians carried out their Holocaust in broad daylight. The *Katolicki Tjednik* newspaper stated on 31 August 1941: 'Now God has decided to use other means. He will set up missions, European missions, world missions. They will be upheld not by priests, but by army commanders, led by Hitler. The sermons will be heard with the help of cannons, tanks and bombers. The language of these sermons will be international.'

But the Nazi authorities in Croatia were actually horrified at the extent and the nature of the killing. By August 1941, the office of General Edmund Glaise von Horstenau, the German army representative in Croatia, reported to Berlin that 200,000 Serbs had 'fallen as victims of animal instincts whipped up by Ustasha leaders'.[332]

On 17 February 1942 Himmler received a detailed report on the 'atrocities carried out by Ustasha units in Croatia against the Orthodox population'. His agents told Himmler that the Ustashi committed their deeds 'in a bestial manner not only against males of conscript age, but especially against helpless old people, women and children. The number of the Orthodox that the Croatians have massacred and sadistically tortured to death is about 300,000.'[333]

German foreign minister Joachim von Ribbentrop received a similar report stating that 'the persecution of Serbs has not stopped, and even cautious estimates indicate that at least several hundred thousand people have been killed. The irresponsible elements have committed atrocities such as could be expected only from a rabid Bolshevik horde.'[334]

Germany demanded that the most brutal Ustasha executioners be removed from office. There is evidence suggesting that the midwar Ustashi political crisis this induced led to the first escape route out of Croatia to Argentina. An American intelligence report of 25 November 1943 showed how links were being established between Perón's military dictatorship and Pavelic. 'It has been reported that the Pavelic government has purchased sixty Argentine passports for evacuation purposes,' states the document. 'Funds have been transferred to Argentina. Minor officials, it is said, will go to Slovakia.'[335]

Argentina's early provision of passports to Pavelic was not an unusual transaction. At the time Perón was making full use of his secret pact with Nazi intelligence to topple the government of neighbouring Bolivia. In return for collaboration in this coup, Mario Amadeo was supplying the Nazi spy service with blank Argentine passports. The simultaneous procurement of Argentine passports by Pavelic and the Nazi spies in Argentina certainly demonstrates how prevalent the practice was long before the war had ended.[336]

We have seen already that the Croatian priest Father Krunoslav Draganovic became the Vatican's most successful Nazi-smuggler after the war. Draganovic was considered by American intelligence an 'alter ego' of Pavelic, and was himself an Ustasha colonel and war criminal. Until 1943 he had been a leading figure in Pavelic's Ministry of Internal Colonization, the agency in charge of confiscating Serb property in Bosnia and Herzegovina, and he had participated in the 'relocation' of Serbs and Jews. His Nazi-smuggling services after the war were even employed by the Allied occupying forces in Italy, who blithely ignored a request for his extradition from the newly reunited Yugoslavia in 1947.[337]

Draganovic had been sent to Rome in August 1943, during the tense period between Mussolini's expulsion and the German occupation of the city. Before leaving Croatia, he had become involved in the dispute over Eugen 'Dido' Kvaternik, the chief of Pavelic's Order and Security office, which was in charge of the persecution of Serbs, Jews and Gypsies. Kvaternik was considered a pathological killer even by Ustashi standards, and Himmler, objecting to his idea of killing 2 million Serbs, forced his exile from Croatia. 'Dido' and his father Slavko Kvaternik, Pavelic's second-in-command, complied and waited out the end of the war in the Nazi puppet state of Slovakia. By the time he was exiled, the younger Kvaternik had started to doubt that the Germans could win the war, but was pleased that, regardless of the outcome, 'there will be no more Serbs in Croatia'.

Draganovic sided with the Germans, accusing Kvaternik of being 'a madman and a lunatic' and of having a Jewish mother to boot – despite which he had shown 'extraordinary cruelty in his treatment of Jews'. Following the 1943 feud, Draganovic was 'kicked upstairs' to Rome. His arrival in the city coincided with Pavelic's purchase of Argentine passports from Perón. In Rome, Draganovic acted as Pavelic's unofficial representative, and when the Nazis entered the city he was entrusted with the archives of the Croatian legation, which he hid in the Vatican. On a more sinister note, considering their likely origin, the prelate also became the custodian of valuables smuggled out of Croatia by the fleeing Ustashi.

Draganovic was sponsored by Croatia's Archbishop Aloysius Stepinac, and had ostensibly arrived to represent the Croatian Red Cross and negotiate with the Italian and German authorities over the release of some 10,000 internees held in Italian war camps. But his relief work was a screen, and itself highly suspect. Many of those he 'rescued' never made it back to Croatia but were seized at Trieste by the Germans and carried off for forced labour.

Draganovic's real task was to employ his good Vatican connections to seek an arrangement with the Western powers that would prevent Croatia from falling under Soviet control. In January 1944, while Rome was still under German occupation, he made contact with the British representative at the Vatican, and submitted a memorandum to the Foreign Office proposing 'the formation of a Danube confederation consisting of Austria, Slovenia, Croatia, Czechoslovakia and parts of Hungary'. Like the Nazi intelligence chiefs acting through the Argentine Juan Carlos Goyeneche in 1943, the Croatians wanted to drive a wedge between the Allies by seeking a separate peace with the West against the Soviets. Draganovic was not entirely unsuccessful in this endeavour; he inspired British intelligence secretly to recruit Croatian criminals as anti-Communist 'freedom fighters' after the war.

Approaches by Pavelic officials seeking Western support to prevent a Soviet occupation of Croatia were not uncommon at the time. In 1944 Lieutenant Colonel Ivan Babic flew to Bari, Italy, on a secret mission to try to convince the British to land on the Dalmatian coast and block the advance of the Red Army. Babic had already attempted a similar negotiation with the Americans in 1943. Like others who participated in these unsuccessful approaches, he would find refuge in Argentina after the war.

By 1944, Croatia's Nazi puppet regime was crumbling. Pavelic was threatened from the outside by advancing Soviet troops and from the inside by the Communist partisans of Josip Broz Tito. Knowing what their likely fate would be following Hitler's defeat, the Ustasha leaders began secretly planning for the massive evacuation of their government with the treasure they had plundered from their victims.

Having interrogated Draganovic five times after the Allied liberation of Rome but while Pavelic still held power in Croatia, American intelligence reached the conclusion that the prelate's real mission was 'to attempt a political re-insurance of the Ustasha party'. But unlike the British, who seemed to respond more favourably to his overtures, the Americans did not like Draganovic, at least at first. As far as the US was concerned, by claiming to be a Croatian citizen the priest was claiming 'to belong to a nation not recognized by the Allied powers, and factually at war with them'.

As he admitted to the Americans, who had him classified as a Nazi collaborator, Draganovic had established contact with the Germans while working for the Red Cross in Serbia in 1941 and again in Italy in 1943 and 1944. This was shaky enough ground as the war drew to an end. It is therefore understandable that the priest failed to mention another more intimate connection: his younger brother, Kresimir Draganovic, was a member of the Croatian embassy in Berlin. The diplomat disappeared after the war, apparently into the British zone in Germany. Some time later, like many of his brother's fugitives, Kresimir Draganovic obtained a Red Cross passport and escaped to Argentina.[338]

Just before the German collapse and after Tito's government had been recognized by the Allies, pincered by the Soviets to the East and the British to the West, Pavelic fled towards Austria in May 1945.

Along with almost the entire Ustasha leadership, the Poglavnik was now submerged in a wave of humanity fleeing from the advancing Communists. For Pavelic, once the powerful ruler of a Fascist Christian nation, there were dark days ahead. But the Ustashi had begun preparing for the inevitable far in advance. Since early 1944 they had been placing large amounts of gold and liquid currency in safe accounts in Switzerland. By one estimate the Croatians managed to stash away 2,400 kilos of gold and other valuables in Berne before the end of the war. Two such transfers have been confirmed so far: 358 kilos of gold were transferred to the Swiss National Bank in May 1944 and a further 980 kilos in August. (The latter amount had apparently been pillaged from the Central Bank of the Kingdom of Yugoslavia in 1941 and hidden outside Croatia.) The Croatians had hoped to place these two large gold deposits under Nazi safe-keeping, a plan that failed when the Swiss National Bank refused to transfer the gold to Germany in October and again refused to transfer it back to Zagreb in December.[339]

While these gold transfers were taking place, Pavelic began negotiating a protected exile for himself and his family with Himmler. The evidence is available in documents captured from Himmler's intelligence service now stored at the US National Archives. On 5 December 1944, Konstantin Kammerhofer, Himmler's personal representative and the senior German military commander in Croatia, informed Berlin that the Croatian *Ausweichmassnahmen* (Nazi jargon for 'alternative methods' of withdrawal or, more realistically, outright 'flight') was under way. Pavelic's wife, one of his daughters and other relatives were abandoning Croatia for Semmering, Austria, in six days. The considerate Kammerhofer requested and received permission to welcome 'Frau Pavelitsch' with a bouquet of flowers in Himmler's name. This did not prevent Pavelic from indulging in a show of bravado in a greeting he wired Himmler on the last day of the year: 'Excellency, for the New Year, I and Croatia wish you the very best. Croatia's soldiers will remain at the side and under the leadership of the Greater German Reich without hesitation, faithfully until the final victory.'[340]

But victory was far from Pavelic's mind as he ran for Austria four months later. To finance his escape, in early May 1945 the remaining gold reserves of the Croatian Treasury, consisting of 45 cases of gold of unknown value, were divided into two parts. The smaller portion, 13 cases, was to be sent abroad with Pavelic. The remaining cases were taken to Zagreb's Franciscan monastery. As well as gold bars, they were said to contain wedding rings, jewels, gold coins and gold teeth extracted from Pavelic's victims. At first the monks hid them behind a specially built wall in a burial vault under the church altar, and later in a hole dug under the confessional for the deaf in the same monastery. There the gruesome treasure would remain, protected by the Catholic Church, until 1946 when the cases were recovered by Tito's regime.[341]

Some gold may have been moved directly from Zagreb to the Vatican. In the last days of the war, the Ustasha foreign ministry archives were entrusted to Archbishop Stepinac, who placed them in the cellar of his palace in Zagreb. These archives consisted of eight sealed boxes that were forwarded to Draganovic at San Girolamo in Rome. By at least one account they also contained gold taken from the Ustashi's victims.[342]

Little is known about Pavelic's exact escape route from Croatia. He seems to have fled with a party of up to 1,500 panicked Ustashi from Zagreb through the Slovenian town of Maribor to Austria, presumably optimistic about his reception by the British and Catholic authorities there. In the prewar era British intelligence had maintained links with Pavelic's terrorist organization even after its murder of King Alexander. Pope Pius XII had shown special deference towards the Poglavnik, receiving him in a private audience in 1941 when his regime's atrocities were already well under way. Even after the war Pavelic continued to enjoy some good will in both quarters, but it would never be more than secret sympathy and it would come at a price. Eventually he would be forced to abandon Europe for Argentina if he wished to avoid extradition to Yugoslavia.[343]

Having failed in the attempt to put his gold under safe-keeping in Berlin, and knowing the difficulties that lay ahead, the Poglavnik

brought with him to Austria a significant slice of the Croatian State
Treasury, derived in part at least from the assets plundered from his
victims. Pavelic's loot consisted of gold (estimates of the amount vary
between 350 and 500 kilos), a large cache of diamonds and a sizeable
amount of foreign currency, all transported in two lorries to Austria.
Once safely across the border, the party of Croatians reportedly
handed part of their gold over to the British, 'and so saved themselves', as one American intelligence document succinctly put it.[344]

British documents about Pavelic's escape remain off-limits to
researchers, but as far as the Americans were able to ascertain the
Poglavnik 'was protected by the British in British-guarded and requi-
sitioned quarters for a two-week period. Due to the insecurity of his
position and due to the inevitable embarrassment of the British
Command, he then left these quarters but remained in the British
Occupation Zone for at least two to three months more, still in contact
with the British.'[345]

During the next few months, and over the coming years, Pavelic
would use the stolen gold to obtain favours from the British, maintain
his organization in Italy, finance the anti-Communist guerrilla and terrorist activities of his Krizari, or Crusaders, in Yugoslavia and sustain his
supporters in Argentina. The intrigues that surrounded the treasure's
transport to Rome and eventually to Buenos Aires, and the losses it suffered along the way, were known to a handful of the top-ranking
Ustashi who fled with Pavelic. By 1951, disagreements over its distribution had created noisy brawls among these fugitive anti-Communist
'freedom fighters' in Buenos Aires, most notably between Pavelic and
his wartime foreign minister Stjepan Peric. Echoes of the disputes
floated up to the CIA in Washington, and this information, contained in
recently declassified CIA documents, spliced together with other intelligence reports and the recent work of some independent researchers
provides an idea of the ultimate fate of the Ustasha treasure.

On its way to Austria, Pavelic's gold suffered various 'distributions'
and 'withdrawals' and even armed robbery. But there were still 350
kilos of gold and 1,100 carats of diamonds left, along with other valuables such as foreign currency, when the loot was 'buried in the

vicinity of an Austrian village', according to one American intelligence report. Another stated it had been 'concealed in a wall near Salzburg'. Yet another that it was secreted near Wolfsberg. At this stage, the task of guarding it was entrusted to a small group consisting of the former Ustasha economics minister Lovro Susic, Pavelic's confidant General Ante Moskov, and Bozidar Kavran, leader of the Krizari network. Of the three, only Susic would make it to Argentina alive. An inventory was drawn up and copies shared with two lesser custodians, Franc Saric and an Ustashi named Musa.[346]

In the early summer of 1945 Draganovic was on a tour of northern Italy and the Austrian–Yugoslav border. He met with Susic, who asked him to carry 40 kilos of gold bars from the cache, concealed in two packing cases, back with him to Rome. Draganovic complied and was appointed by Susic to a three-member committee to control this portion of the treasure. The gold was to be shared with two Ustasha war criminals, former agriculture minister Stjepan Hefer and General Vilko Pecnikar, the 'clerical, anti-Hebrew, anti-Serb, pro-Austrian' son-in-law of Pavelic, a general of the Ustasha gendarmerie who had worked in close collaboration with the Gestapo. For the next two years Draganovic hid Hefer and Pecnikar in Rome. Pecnikar made use of the stolen treasure for anti-Tito terrorist activity. He also published a Croatian newspaper that attacked the Allies and promised Pavelic's early return to Zagreb. Eventually, with Draganovic's help, Hefer and Pecnikar found their way to Argentina.[347]

Some of the Ustasha loot seems to have fallen prey to the greed of individual Croatians and certain British officers. Following orders from Pavelic, Moskov and Saric dug up the main body of the treasure buried in Austria. They enrolled the help of Ante Codina (one of the organizers of the assassination of King Alexander), Ustasha Captain Marko Cavic, Ustasha Colonel Mara Pavelic and a former Croatian Nazi spy named Tomljenovic. In the process, the British separated a portion of the gold from the 350 kilos left and entrusted it to Moskov to transport to Italy. Along the way, on 27 April 1947, Moskov was handed over to Yugoslavia to be tried for war crimes. The fate of his cache remains a mystery. 'No one can ask Saric to account for this gold since he can justify himself by claiming that the British appropriated the entire amount,' stated the Croatians who knew the facts first-hand in Buenos Aires.[348]

Parts of the puzzle were filled in by American agents in Europe who had done their own investigation into the treasure. A top-secret 1947 report by the Rome Detachment of the US Army Counter Intelligence Corps stated that 'British Lieutenant Colonel Johnson was placed in charge of two lorries laden with the supposed property of the Catholic Church in the British Zone of Austria. These two lorries, accompanied by a number of priests and the British officer, then entered Italy and went to an unknown destination.'[349]

Another document supports the claim that part of Pavelic's loot disappeared into the hands of British authorities. It is an October 1946 report from the SSU (a US War Department intelligence service) to the American Treasury, drafted by Emerson Bigelow, an expert in providing funds for overt and covert US intelligence operations during the war. According to Bigelow, Pavelic had removed a total of 350 million Swiss francs from Croatia, largely in the form of gold coins. 'Of the funds brought from the former Independent Croat State where Jews and Serbs were plundered to support the Ustasha organization in exile, an estimated 150 million Swiss francs were impounded by British authorities at the Austrian–Swiss frontier,' wrote Bigelow. 'The balance of approximately 200 million Swiss francs was originally held in the Vatican for safe-keeping. According to rumour, a considerable portion of this latter amount has been sent to Spain and Argentina through the Vatican's 'pipeline', but it is quite possible this is merely a smoke-screen to cover the fact that the treasure remains in its original repository.'[350]

Some time in 1948 the fugitive Ustashi were able to get their hands on secret loot that they had stashed away in Swiss bank accounts. The delicate operation was entrusted to Slovenian Bishop Gregory Rozman, a notorious anti-Semite and war criminal. Despite well-founded grounds for Rozman's extradition following his flight to Austria at the end of the war, Yugoslavia was unable to defeat the combined resistance of the Vatican, Britain and the US, who proved unwilling to hand over such a high-ranking Church dignitary to the Communists. In the company of another war criminal, Catholic Action Bishop Ivan Saric, Rozman travelled 'undercover' to Berne. There the Ustashi were reaping huge dividends from the postwar economic situation, turning the stolen gold into dollars at the exorbitant black market rate, accounting for the funds they employed to 'aid refugees of the Catholic religion' at the depressed official rate, and pocketing the difference. As US intelligence learned in March 1948, 'Rozman is going to Berne to take care of these finances. The money is in a Swiss bank, and he plans to have most of it sent through to Italy and from there to the Ustashi in Argentina.'[351]

For the fleeing Ustashi, all paths met at San Girolamo, a Croatian monastery at 132 Via Tomacelli, just outside the Vatican City. As US intelligence found, 'many of the more prominent Ustashi war criminals and Quislings' were living at the monastery, which was 'honeycombed with cells of Ustasha operatives'. Protected by the Catholic Church, these Croatians considered themselves a government in exile. Even their intelligence agencies remained in operation. 'All this activity seems to stem from the Vatican, through the Monastery of San Girolamo, to Fermo, the chief Croat camp in Italy,' American intelligence reported in early 1947.

Draganovic was believed to head the operation and was considered the public face of Ante Pavelic, whose whereabouts remained a tightly guarded secret. 'It is his task to coordinate and direct Ustasha activity in Italy,' American intelligence concluded. 'He provides them with moral and material help and in particular, he is able to send to America all those who collaborated with the Germans.' Draganovic's support of the Ustashi stemmed from 'a deep-rooted conviction that the ideas espoused by this arch-nationalist organization, half logical, half lunatic, are basically sound concepts'.

Many of the Croatian cabinet ministers hiding at San Girolamo had escaped from the Afragola POW camp. Now they shuttled several times a week between the Vatican and the monastery in a chauffeur-driven car bearing diplomatic plates. 'It issues forth from the Vatican and discharges its passengers inside the monastery,' stated American intelligence.

Access to San Girolamo was tightly controlled. The Ustasha guards checked the IDs of visitors, submitting them to a body search and exhaustive interrogations, including questions about how they had heard there were Croatians living at the monastery. 'All doors from one room to another are locked and those that are not have an armed guard in front of them and a password is necessary to go from one room to another,' American intelligence found. 'The whole area is guarded by armed Ustasha youths in civilian clothes and the Ustasha salute is exchanged continually.'

The Americans were able to infiltrate a counter-operative into the monastery who drew up a list of the ten most prominent criminals lodged there. The agent, posing as a Croatian, confirmed that the war criminals effectively commuted between San Girolamo and the Vatican. He even overheard a phone conversation between Draganovic and former Croatian economy minister Lovro Susic, who was calling from the Vatican.

'Draganovic's sponsorship of these Croat Quislings definitely links him up with the plan of the Vatican to shield these ex-Ustasha national-ists until such time as they are able to procure for them the proper documents to enable them to go to South America,' wrote the intelli-gence officer commanding the San Girolamo operation. 'The Vatican, undoubtedly banking on the strong anti-Communist feelings of these men, is endeavouring to infiltrate them into South America in any way possible to counteract the spread of the Red doctrine.' Not long after this 1947 report was filed, at least six of the ten Croatian criminals discovered at the monastery were taking ship at Genoa, bound for Argentina.[352]

The first Croatians to reach Buenos Aires were the priest Peter Ciklic and his brother Ljubomir, on 6 April 1946. Travelling on Red Cross passports, the Ciklic brothers left Paris to take a ship from Spain. Upon arrival they headed for the office of the archbishop of Buenos Aires, where they were expected. According to American intelligence, in 1946 Draganovic arranged the departure of some 50 Ustasha criminals via the Iberian Peninsula. But by the end of the year the Spanish route had largely been abandoned. On 27 December 1946 Draganovic sent his first large contingent directly from Genoa to Argentina, on the Italian liner *Andrea Gritti*. Practically the entire former Croatian government would be transported by Draganovic to Argentina over the next few years.[353]

'He is helped in this activity by his numerous contacts with the embassies and legations of South America in Italy and with the International Red Cross,' stated American intelligence, adding that Draganovic also counted on 'the approval of the Pontifical Welfare Commission for Refugees.'[354]

The mass escape of the criminal Ustashi was initiated in late 1946, when Draganovic obtained a blanket landing permit from Peron's government for 250 Croatians. He acted through the Franciscan Father Blas Stefanic of the Bari Basilica in Buenos Aires, who had arrived in the city in 1935. Working alongside three other Franciscans, he soon became an anti-Communist campaigner and a pillar of the Croatian community in Argentina. There is no doubt that the Franciscans ran the escape line. As a rule, fleeing Ustashi gave the Croatian Franciscan community in the town of José Ingenieros as their intended place of residence when completing their visa applications at the Argentine consulate in Rome. At least one notorious Ustasha criminal, Father Vladimir Bilobrk, who called on Croatians to use pick-axes, hoes and scythes to slaughter Serbs, simply wrote down Stefanic's name as his local reference.

When Draganovic's first group of Croatians disembarked from the *Andrea Gritti* on 25 January 1947, it was thanks to a thick brown dossier, Immigration File 72513/46, that Stefanic had opened on 13 December 1946 in the name of Caritas Croata Argentina. This document alone would be extended a number of times to admit some 2,000 Croatians, not all of them war criminals, by the end of the decade. By one knowledgeable estimate, a total of some 5,000 Croatians settled in Argentina in the postwar period, 2,000 travelling from Hamburg, 2,000 from Munich and 1,000 from Rome. Other estimates place the number at anywhere between 10,000 and 35,000.[355]

Like many other Nazi-related documents at Argentina's Immigration Office, the Caritas Croata file seems to have gone up in smoke in the mysterious 1996 bonfire. All the same, painstaking work culling data from the surviving passenger lists turned up the names of 150 of those who left Europe because of it. At least twelve of these have been positively identified as war criminals, while five others have names that match those of known war criminals. A simple extrapolation would suggest that at least 200 war criminals entered Argentina under the Caritas Croata file alone.[356]

Draganovic wasted no time in sending the main Ustasha leaders to safety across the Atlantic. Among the first to leave from Genoa in January 1947 were three major war criminals who had been hiding under his care in Rome: Mile Starcevic, Stjepan Hefer and Dr Vjekoslav Vrancic. Starcevic had been Pavelic's minister of education. Hefer, his minister of agriculture, had smuggled the 40 kilos of gold into Rome with Draganovic in 1945. Prior to his death in Spain in 1959, Pavelic named Hefer his political successor.

Perhaps the worst of the three was the Hitler-decorated Vrancic. As under-secretary of the Ustasha interior ministry, he oversaw Pavelic's concentration camps and the repressive police apparatus. He had flown to Italy to attempt to surrender to the British in May 1945 in the company of naval captain Andre Vrkljan, another Croatian who would end up in Argentina. Both men were arrested but Vrancic escaped British custody and hid under Draganovic's wing. In Argentina he was named vice-president of Pavelic's 'government in exile' and became involved in terrorist activities with Argentina's ultra-nationalist groups. This did not prevent him from being granted a professorship at Buenos Aires University.[357]

With the blank landing permits furnished by the Caritas Croata file it was easy enough for Draganovic to fake the identity of his fugitives. Once it was rolling, the system was simplicity itself and it interlocked with Perón's other escape routes. Draganovic received requests for Argentine landing permits from his agents in Hamburg, Munich and Rome. The lists of real names and aliases were then wired by him to Caritas Croata in Buenos Aires, which acted as an informal embassy for the Ustasha movement out of offices provided by the Argentine Catholic Church. It fell to the head of Caritas Croata, Marko Sinovcic, to take these lists to the Immigration Office, where they received automatic approval, no questions asked. These landing permits were then used by Draganovic as proof of identity to secure passports under fake names from the Red Cross offices in Rome and Genoa.[358]

Sinovcic had himself been an early beneficiary of this mechanism. He took control of the Buenos Aires end of the network immediately upon arrival, as he recalled in an interview for this book 50 years later. The story of his flight was similar to that of many other Croatians. Having worked as a propaganda officer at the Croatian consulate at Fiume, Sinovcic escaped to Austria at the end of the war. He fell into Soviet hands but was liberated by the British and hidden in a convent in Florence. He was aided by one of Draganovic's closest collaborators, the Franciscan Father Dominic Mandic, who paid for his ticket to Argentina. Sinovcic arrived in Buenos Aires on 11 August 1947 on board the *Maria C.* The most notorious of his fellow travellers were the brothers Jan and Ferdinand Durcansky, the Slovak mass murderers who would soon be running their own escape network.[359]

Sinovcic was eventually replaced as Draganovic's link to the Immigration Office by Pavelic's former ambassador to Berlin, Branko Benzon. In Argentina, Benzon joined the Peronist party and became the virtual leader of the Croatian fugitive community. Together with his close partner Cirilo Cudina, a former Ustasha major who became a permanent fixture at Immigration, Benzon invariably met new arrivals at the port of Buenos Aires.[360]

Also waiting at the dock would be Andro Vrkljan, the Black Sea naval commander who had flown to Italy with Vrancic at the end of the war to attempt negotiations with Britain. British Field Security had arrested the two would-be peace emissaries as they reached Forli in a Mercedes-Benz car. They were held for a time in British camps while Yugoslavia unsuccessfully attempted their extradition. Vrancic was quickly delivered not to Tito but into the arms of Draganovic. The less fortunate Vrkljan, who spoke good English, bounced in and out of prison camps and British labour units where his translation skills were required. The threat of extradition to Yugoslavia reared its head each time his name was mentioned on Radio Belgrade. In May 1947, he was among various Croatian prisoners whose release was demanded by Draganovic. In an angry letter, the prelate complained to the Allied authorities that Vrkljan's 'democratic rights are not being respected'. The prelate's appeal seems to have worked, for Vrkljan soon stood alongside Benzon and Cudina awaiting fresh Croatian arrivals at the port of Buenos Aires.[361]

Perón found employment for the Croatians in his ambitious construction projects. Many went to 'Evita City' (a new town designed so that its street map resembled the profile of the First Lady's face), or helped build the new international airport for Buenos Aires. It was up to Benzon to direct arrivals to these sites. Sometimes Public Works Minister Juan Pistarini, the same military officer who could not be restrained from making the Nazi salute during his prewar visits to Berlin, drove up to the port personally and loaded the arriving Croatians onto buses that took them directly to the construction projects.[362]

One example of how suspect Croatians prospered in Argentina is Ivo Rojnica, the wartime commander of Dubrovnik and a man whose long and chequered career is practically a lesson in the evasion of justice. Following the German occupation of Croatia, Rojnica had signed the first racist legislation in Dubrovnik, and was a close collaborator of the Gestapo under the alias 'Ante'. According to certain accounts, some of the valuables plundered from the victims of the Ustashi were stored by Rojnica in 'an enormous warehouse' and formed the basis of his wealth later on. He escaped to Trieste after the war, where he hid under the name Ivan Rajcinovic. This did not prevent his arrest by the British authorities when he was recognized by the widow of a Jewish victim he had allegedly evacuated to Jasenovac concentration camp. The new Communist authorities in Yugoslavia sent a detailed file of Rojnica's crimes to London. It was too late, however, for by the time it arrived he had escaped. With the help of the Holy See and the Argentine government he arrived in Argentina on 2 April 1947, as a stowaway on the *Maria C*.[363]

During Perón's government, Rojnica took out Argentine citizenship under his Rajcinovic alias, and became a textile industry magnate. In the 1970s he was suspected of financing plane hijackings by Croatian terrorists in the US and Europe. A visit he made to New Zealand in the company of Vrancic almost ended in disaster for them both in 1977. Their capture was requested by Yugoslavia and it was only by invoking Argentine citizenship and getting the help of the Argentine embassy that they were able to return to Buenos Aires.[364]

Incredibly, in 1991, following the collapse of the Communist regime in Yugoslavia, Argentine President Carlos Menem accepted Rojnica's appointment as ambassador of the newly independent Croatia. The post had been offered to Rojnica by Croatian president Franjo Tudjman, author of a book that dismissed the estimate of 700,000 deaths in the Croatian Holocaust as 'mythical' and put the 'real' figure at 60,000. A scandal ensued the following year when the Wiesenthal Centre pleaded with Argentina for the arrest of both Rojnica and Vrancic, revealing their wartime records to the public. The plea went unheeded even when the story reverberated in the international press, including a *New York Times* editorial in November 1993. In Zagreb, meanwhile, the press published a 1941 order signed by Rojnica forbidding all Jews and Serbs to appear on the streets from 7pm to 7am – the first step towards death camps. Reached in Argentina, Rojnica was quoted as stating: 'Everything I did in 1941 I would do again.'

Hounded from all sides, Rojnica remained in charge of the Croatian diplomatic representation from the shadows, personally handing over the post to his successor in January 1994. A renewed plea by the Wiesenthal Centre for his arrest was ignored by both Argentina and Croatia in 1998. In Argentina, press reports suggested that contributions by the wealthy former Ustashi to Menem's electoral campaign explained his 'diplomatic immunity'.[365]

Only one Ustasha criminal was eventually extradited from Argentina. In the 1940s and 1950s Peron's government ignored repeated requests for the arrest of Pavelic and his helpers, but the international outcry that followed a 1998 television interview in Argentina with former Jasenovac commander Dinko Sakic made another refusal unthinkable. Sakic had been tricked into speaking by an enterprising journalist who knocked at the door of the 76-year-old Ustashi's home in the quiet Atlantic beach resort of Santa Teresita. 'Jasenovac was only a work camp and the Jews managed their own affairs there,' Sakic told the camera. Barely a year later, in October 1999, a Zagreb court sentenced the Ustasha murderer to 20 years in prison for crimes against humanity.

Sakic was only 24 years old when he inherited the command of Jasenovac from his brother-in-law Vjekoslav Luburic in the final days of the war. Luburic, a bloodthirsty madman by all accounts, had spun out of control. In December 1944, he began intercepting German trains and supply columns passing through the Jasenovac area, and forcibly removing and shooting the anti-Communist Serb soldiers who fought alongside the Nazis. The response from Berlin was thunderous. Nazi Foreign Minister Ribbentrop informed Pavelic that such an affront against Germany's troops required the arrest and exemplary punishment of those responsible.[366]

Luburic made it alive to Argentina, and during those last few months of the war Sakic ran Jasenovac. He and his wife then fled to Austria. They eventually crossed the border to Italy in 1946, ending up in the Fermo prison camp. But in mid-1947, the criminal 'Dido' Kvaternik, also imprisoned at Fermo and secretary to the British camp commander, warned Sakic that his name appeared circled in red on a list of wanted war criminals. Sakic fled for Rome. There he came into contact with Father Josip Bujanovic, 'Popa Jolu', a Ustasha murderer closely connected to Pavelic who arranged for Sakic's safe-keeping in a series of monasteries outside the Eternal City. It was the Franciscan Father Mandic who finally arranged for Sakic's ticket to be paid for by Pavelic's moneyman Ivo Heinrich, who was already in Argentina. After difficult negotiations with Draganovic, who disliked him because of his association with the uncontrollable Luburic, Sakic was included on the prelate's Caritas Croata list and he boarded the *Tucumán* liner from Genoa in December 1947. His first stop upon arrival was Heinrich's home on Ugarteche Street in Buenos Aires, where he received a warm greeting and 150 pesos in cash.[367]

Pavelic's whereabouts for the first 18 months after the war remain a mystery. London invariably met requests by Yugoslavia for his extradition from the British Zone of Austria, where Tito suspected he was hiding, with puzzlement. An angry Tito insisted that Pavelic had been held prisoner by the troops of British Field Marshal Alexander, that he was disguised as a monk at a monastery in Klagenfurt, that Yugoslavia had even given the British the name of the street where Pavelic lived 'in complete freedom'. The Foreign Office shrugged its shoulders and sent off disingenuous letters to the Americans and the Soviets, asking whether they had seen the Poglavnik. Tito's press insisted that the West could find Pavelic if it wanted to but that he was being groomed for an anti-Communist crusade against Yugoslavia.[368]

Pavelic stayed in Austria for a full year, moving on to Rome in April 1946 in the company of Ustasha Lieutenant Dragutin Dosen, a 'leading light' at San Girolamo and a senior officer of the Poglavnik's Personal Bodyguard. Both men were disguised in the robes of Roman Catholic priests. They took refuge at the Collegio Pio Pontificio at 3 Via Gioacchino Belli, in the Prati district of Rome, a stone's throw from the Vatican walls – this address corresponded to the Vatican's Pontificial Latin American College. According to an American intelligence report, this was 'the only college in Rome enjoying complete extraterritoriality, and which can be entered only by presenting the proper credential. Presumably the Papal seal is needed because it is said that this is the only college in Rome directly under the administration of the Pope.'[369]

The Americans started piecing together a disturbing picture of Vatican complicity. In May 1946, Pavelic hid 'close to Rome in a building which is under the jurisdiction of the Vatican'. This was Castel Gandolfo, the location of the Pope's summer residence, where Pavelic had been housed together with a former minister of the Nazi Romanian government. The Americans also learned that Pavelic held 'frequent meetings with Monsignor Montini', the future Pope Paul VI.[370]

On 9 November 1946 London informed Washington that five war criminals wanted by Yugoslavia had found refuge behind Vatican walls, at the Oriental Institute in Rome, the Pope's agency specializing in East European affairs. 'It would create a most unfortunate impression if the British authorities decided to arrest these men on Vatican property without any prior notice to the Vatican authorities,' said London. The Americans cynically agreed to the British proposal that, where Pavelic was concerned, 'the Yugoslav government should apply to the Vatican, to whom they have an accredited representative'.

By the end of the year Pavelic had apparently moved to San Girolamo and, according to rumours, was set to board the *Andrea Gritti* at Genoa on 27 December, with the first group of Croatians leaving for Argentina under the Caritas Croata file. But in January 1947 American agents discovered he was still in Rome and had moved again, this time to the Dominican monastery of Saint Sabina, 'in the extraterritorial walled-in compound on the left bank of the Tiber at Lungo Tevere Aventino, Rome'.[371]

The Americans now started closing in on Pavelic. They took the obvious step of tracking down his wife. They also traced whoever was collecting the rent on a home Pavelic owned in Florence and went through the records of his two daughters at the Annunciata School in the same city. They attempted to interview the Pavelic family's domestic help. But the inherent difficulty in locating the Poglavnik was driven home in April 1947 when the agents learned that 'each time the "Allied Officials" were about to capture the Pavelics, they were moved elsewhere by Allied personnel who were hiding them, and who were each time rewarded by the Pavelics with jewellery and money.'[372]

Between March and June, Pavelic seems to have moved continually between the Vatican college on Via Gioacchino Belli and various apartments. He now held a Spanish passport in the name of Padre Gomez, 'a Spanish Minister of Religion', and was planning to leave shortly for Spain on a trip 'arranged for by some Jesuits in the Vatican'. Meanwhile his wife, two daughters and son-in-law, the Ustasha General Pecnikar, were reportedly residing at San Girolamo.[373]

The Americans had certainly obtained enough information to proceed with Pavelic's arrest. Nervous negotiations between London and Washington had been under way for some months to work out the correct procedure. Neither government wanted to embarrass the Vatican, and neither government actually meant to arrest the Poglavnik, who was still considered useful in the fight against Tito's Communist regime. Nonetheless, on 7 August 1947 instructions were sent to a combined group of British and US agents to plan Pavelic's arrest 'at a suitable moment when he leaves the Vatican precincts'.[374]

The agents went into high gear and by the next day had extremely precise information of Pavelic's whereabouts. The Poglavnik was hiding as 'an ex-Hungarian general under the name of Giuseppe', sporting 'a small pointed beard and . . . hair cut short at the sides after the fashion of a German army officer'. (The information was correct, for that is exactly how Pavelic looked in the photograph affixed to the 1948 landing document that survives in Argentina's Immigration Office archives.) Pavelic now resided 'on Church property under the protection of the Vatican' on the second floor of 17-C Via Giacomo Venezian. 'On entering the building you go along a long and dark corridor,' stated the instructions for the agents handling the operation. 'At the end of the corridor there are two stairs, one to the left and one to the right. You must take the right. On the right the rooms are numbered 1, 2, 3, etc. If you knock once or twice at door No. 3 an unimportant person will come out. But if you knock three times at door No. 3, door No. 2 will open. It leads to the room where Pavelic lives.' About twelve Ustasha bodyguards protected the Poglavnik. His visitors included the custodian of the Ustasha treasure, Susic. 'When Pavelic goes out he uses a car with a Vatican (SCV) number plate.'[375]

But the arrest was never carried out. The American agents working on the case had already received contradictory 'Hands Off' instructions in July. The likely embarrassment to the Vatican and the adverse effect on the recruitment of former Nazis for the Cold War weighed too heavily in the final balance – certainly heavier than procuring justice for Pavelic's hundreds of thousands of victims.[376]

Afterwards the Americans working on the case put their thoughts on Pavelic in writing. First of all, they warned that 'numbers of Croatian guerrillas in Yugoslavia' were 'fighting and dying in his name' in Western-backed efforts to weaken Tito's Communist regime. They went on: 'Today, in the eyes of the Vatican, Pavelic is a militant Catholic, a man who erred, but who erred fighting for Catholicism. It is for this reason that Subject now enjoys Vatican protection . . . Pavelic is known to be in contact with the Vatican which sees in him the militant Catholic who yesterday fought the Orthodox Church and today is fighting Communist atheism . . . For the reasons given above he is receiving the protection of the Vatican whose view of the entire "Pavelic Question" is that, since the Croat State does not exist and since the Tito regime cannot be expected to give anybody a fair trial, the Subject should not be turned over to the present Yugoslav regime . . . The extradition of Pavelic would only weaken the forces fighting atheism and aid Communism . . . Pavelic's crimes of the past cannot be forgotten, but he can only be tried by Croats representing a Christian and Democratic Government, the Vatican maintains. While Pavelic is allegedly responsible for the death of 150,000 persons, Tito is the agent of Stalin, who is responsible for the deaths of tens of millions of persons in the Ukraine, White Russia, Poland, the Baltic and the Balkan States over a period of 25 years.'[377]

Pavelic was also too closely implicated with British anti-Communist operations, the agents felt, going into a long chronicle of Pavelic's sojourn under British custody in Austria and the appropriation of part of his stolen treasure by the British authorities there. 'It is the opinion of these agents that the Subject has been closely linked to the British in the past and still is, though to what degree is unknown . . . Monsignor Juretic . . . recently stated in regard to Pavelic's present status that, "he has got all his faith in the British" . . . These agents recommend that no direct police action be taken against him on the part of the American Military Authorities. Such action would force his extradition to Tito and would bolster the present British anti-American campaign waged among the political émigrés in Western Europe . . . If, however, contact can be established through the Vatican, as these agents believe quite possible, and proof can be collected concerning British protection and cooperation with Subject, then the British could be forced to arrest and extradite him themselves.'[378]

Barely two weeks after drafting the above report the same agents made 'indirect contact' with Pavelic. The Poglavnik was recovering from an operation but 'an interview can be arranged with Subject on extraterritorial ground when the condition of his health permits his movement.' All the same, the agents held out little hope of ever being able to arrest the war criminal: 'Pavelic's contacts are so high and his present position is so compromising to the Vatican that any extradition of Subject would deal a staggering blow to the Roman Catholic Church.'[379]

Despite his half-hearted promise to confer in secret with the Americans, Pavelic seems to have chosen a safer course. After these last reports from Rome, American intelligence goes strangely quiet over Pavelic and does not pick up his trail again until after his arrival in Argentina in November 1948. Where did Pavelic go in the meantime? One possibility is that Perón's secret agent Carlos Fuldner, along with Pierre Daye's rescue organization, took Pavelic in hand in early 1948. A mysterious letter from Daye's contact in Madrid, the well-known Franco supporter and Nazi sympathizer Víctor de la Serna, suggests this may have been so. The Spaniard had been organizing the flight of Belgian and French war criminals to Argentina as the Madrid end of Daye's SARE organization.

In March 1948, a mysterious 'motor car' ready for shipment across the Atlantic had to be camouflaged after certain Argentines 'leaked' information about the operation. Serna immediately sent a coded letter to Daye in Buenos Aires obviously referring to an important political figure whose escape had been thwarted. 'We've nonetheless painted the fins and placed big headlights on it which make it look different for anyone who has not seen it run too often in the many European races in which it participated,' said the letter from Madrid.

Fuldner was upset, and wired a message to Serna from Genoa imploring him not to inform his representatives in Spain about the hitch. 'Too many people know about this and my first measure has been to move the car elsewhere,' Serna reported to Daye. Funds were being sent by Fuldner to cover the added expenditure. 'Balkan interference has ruined many things,' Serna concluded.[380]

All through the summer of 1948 a special court met at the old Zagreb Fair to put on trial 57 members of Pavelic's Krizari 'freedom fighters'. The attempt to undermine Tito's regime by infiltrating anti-Communist rebels into Yugoslavia had ended in disaster. One after another the defendants, mostly Ustasha war criminals who had been sheltered at San Girolamo, confessed that Pavelic and Draganovic led the Krizari, and substantiated the accusation that the Vatican together with US and British intelligence had supported the terrorist campaign. As summer faded, so must have Pavelic's hopes of returning in glory to Zagreb. It must also have seemed clear to those who had secretly protected him that Pavelic had outlived his usefulness. Suddenly the Poglavnik was nothing but a dinosaur from a bygone age, one that didn't fit into the new realities of the Cold War.[381]

A few months before his departure, Pavelic returned to Castel Gandolfo, this time to a monastery near the Pope's summer residence. There he sat out the Krizari trials in close proximity to God's representative on Earth. He probably read the series of articles published in late September in the Italian newspaper *La Repubblica* revealing the Vatican's role in his concealment. Even the Via Giacomo Venezian address where he had hid the year before was revealed.[382]

With a heavy heart the leader of the Ustashi headed for the port of Genoa and on 11 October 1948 he boarded a first-class compartment on the *Sestriere*, a ship that would take him to a country at least as fanatically Catholic as his former Croatia. He carried Red Cross passport 74369 made out in the name of Pal Aranyos, a widowed Hungarian engineer with three children whose ages roughly corresponded with those of his own children. (Pavelic's wife and two of his children had preceded him across the Atlantic, arriving in Buenos Aires on 3 May 1948 on the *Ugolino Vivaldi* from Genoa, under the Flego alias.)[383]

It is unclear exactly who arranged the details of Pavelic's flight. According to a 1948 CIA report, Pavelic reached Genoa with Draganovic's help. The first published version of his escape in the

1950s claimed that the Croatian priest had accompanied Pavelic all the way to Argentina, remaining in the country with him for a full year. The best-researched version to date, the Aarons and Loftus book *Unholy Trinity*, concluded that Draganovic had provided Pavelic with a Red Cross passport but had been excluded from the final travel arrangements. According to the authors, Pavelic had entrusted the last leg of his trip to his fellow war criminal, Father Josip Bujanovic. Arrangements were formalized by Ustasha officer Daniel Crljen, who reportedly participated in ultra-secret negotiations under Vatican auspices, boarding a plane to Argentina 'to confer with General Perón on the organization of an Ustasha elite movement in the Argentine'.[384]

The real escape combines elements of all the previous versions and was explained in an interview for this book by the former head of Caritas Croata Argentina, Marko Sinovcic. Pavelic mistrusted Draganovic's connections with British and American intelligence and made his own travel arrangements. Draganovic did travel to Buenos Aires, but he did so late in 1949, a year after Pavelic, setting himself up for a brief period at Sinovcic's Caritas Croata office. There he received visits from the Croatians in Argentina, but Pavelic refused to meet with him.[385]

The evidence now available supports Sinovcic's first-hand account. Pavelic's travel papers bear no sign of Draganovic's collaboration. He did not travel under the Caritas Croata file and his wife and children travelled under unrelated individual Immigration Office files. In fact, as the *Sestriere*'s passenger list shows, Pavelic did not travel under any Immigration Office file at all. Nor did he obtain any Argentine travel documentation before departure. His Argentine Identification Certificate, the mandatory form he should have filled in at the Argentine consulate in Rome, Pavelic completed six days after disembarking in Buenos Aires. His photo, in which he is easily identifiable behind a silly goatee, fancy moustache and thick round glasses (the 'fins and headlights' of the previous year?), is still affixed to the surviving copy of the Aranyos certificate at the Immigration Office archive today. Since the form was not completed in Italy, the lines reserved for the Red Cross to authenticate the passport bearer's identity remain blank. Pavelic did not even possess an Argentine landing permit. Everything indicates that the Croatian leader was whisked off the ship in Buenos Aires by Perón's agents, no questions asked, probably on a launch before the *Sestriere* docked. And his passport may have been a forgery. According to present-day Red Cross officials in Geneva, passport application number 74369 was not made out in the name of Pavelic or Aranyos or even Antonio Serdar, the other alias the Poglavnik is known to have employed in Argentina.[386]

When Pavelic arrived at the port of Buenos Aires on 6 November 1948, he was taken to an unglamorous three-storey apartment building at 2525 Olazabal Street in the Belgrano neighbourhood. His formal reception was left to his wartime ambassador in Berlin, Branko Benzon, who 'speaking in the name of the Argentine government, extended full help and collaboration', a secret CIA source reported only a few days later. Benzon, 'the leader of the Ustasha colony in Argentina, had ingratiated himself with President Perón and the Argentine government and was able to be of considerable assistance to the Ustasha members who have arrived and are continuing to reach the Argentine,' another report stated.

After holding two long conferences with Benzon, Pavelic was reunited with some of his main collaborators, who had been informed of his imminent arrival by Draganovic. Awaiting him were Vrancic, the former Sarajevo administrator Ivica Frkovic, his personal representative in Bosnia in charge of deportations Oskar Turina and his agriculture minister Jozo Dumandzic. Also present was Susic, the custodian of Pavelic's gold in Austria. According to the CIA, these men jointly held the keys to the Ustasha gold that presumably still lay stashed away somewhere in the Vatican.

Also in the reception committee was Vinko Nikolic, member of the Ustasha Supreme Command and a poet who wrote wartime odes of allegiance to the Poglavnik. A close collaborator of Draganovic, Nikolic and another Ustasha, Ivo Omrcanin, had met with Pope Pius XII in June 1946. Nikolic had founded the bi-weekly Buenos Aires newspaper *Hrvatska*, and greeted the Poglavnik together with his co-editor Franjo Nevistic and the war criminal Father Vlado Bilobrk.

Pavelic urged his men to pull together and work for the restoration of the independent state of Croatia. He then left with Vrancic for the interior of the country, either for the central province of Córdoba or the southern town of Tandil, both of which harboured large pockets of Nazi fugitives. 'Source states that Pavelic is convinced that he has a mission to perform, and that he and his followers still regard him as the Poglavnik,' the CIA was informed.[387]

How much of the stolen gold finally reached Pavelic in Buenos Aires and how was it transported? According to a 1951 CIA report, a group of disenchanted Ustasha fugitives in Argentina raged that year against the 'perfidious and fantastic theft of the Croatian treasure' by Pavelic. These men believed that a total of 250 kilograms and all 1,100 carats of the diamonds were routed to Argentina through an unnamed banker contacted by Tomljenovic in Brazil. Pavelic's accusers were angered by the 'several pieces of gold that various Croatians have seen in Codina's possession in Buenos Aires', as well as by the comfortable standard of living the Poglavnik's family enjoyed. They claimed that Pavelic sold the gold through 'his principal bank adviser', Ivo Heinrich, a Croatian Jew who converted to Christianity on the eve of the war.[388]

After the war, Heinrich was held by the British and accused by Tito's government of 'the death of numerous people in Jasenovac concentration camp, including the death of his first wife, who was a Jewess'. Draganovic stepped in to plead his case to the Allies in 1947, arguing that the charges were 'the revenge of Jews against a converted Jew'.[389]

In reality, Heinrich was Pavelic's moneyman and the financier of the Ustasha escape network. Remembered in Ustasha accounts as a 'Viennese Jew', he had been born around 1904 in Karlovac, Croatia. Under the aegis of concentration camp commander Vjekoslav Luburic, he had proved himself an invaluable financial fixer during the war. With Luburic's help he escaped to Hungary with a vast amount of treasure when Pavelic's government collapsed, and proceeded to multiply this fortune in postwar Switzerland. He moved on to Rome, and provided his miraculous financial services to Draganovic's helper, Father Dominic Mandic, who used the money to rescue Franciscan priests from Communist Yugoslavia. Heinrich and his second wife escaped to Argentina using one of Draganovic's landing permits, and they arrived in Buenos Aires on 31 July 1947 after travelling first class aboard the *Vulcania*. From Argentina, Heinrich paid for the fares and travelling expenses of dozens of Croatian war criminals, receiving them with open arms and a generous wallet upon their arrival in Argentina.[390]

In Buenos Aires, Pavelic shared his treasure with a select circle of four men he considered his ministers-in-exile. 'He pays them to reward them for their loyalty, but at the same time he lets the burden of the responsibility for the theft of the gold fall upon a larger number of persons in order to lessen the burden which might fall upon him,' stated Pavelic's accusers. The four had been among Pavelic's most important aides during the war: his agriculture minister Jozo Dumandzic, his mining minister Ivica Frkovic, his deputy foreign minister Vjekoslav Vrancic and Oskar Turina, who was in charge of deportations in Bosnia. All four had been there to greet the Poglavnik upon his arrival in Buenos Aires in 1948. Only a few months later, in mid-1949, they were joined by a man who certainly had the know-how to be a key player in the gold operation, the last president of the Croatian Bank in Zagreb, Franjo Cvijic, whose travel documents were reportedly arranged by Father Draganovic.[391]

In 1952, the CIA received new information about Pavelic's gold, confirming once again the facts of the case. A high-ranking source within the Croatian community in Buenos Aires reported that Pavelic's appointed custodians Ante Cudina and Marko Cavic had left for Europe in October 1951 to transfer 250 kilos of gold to Argentina. The hoard came from 'twelve cases of gold and jewels' sent by Pavelic to Austria before the fall of Croatia. 'Source does not know the outcome of this mission,' stated the CIA report, 'but within the last few days Pavelic has been offering to sell on the Buenos Aires market 200 kilos of gold through his intermediary, Juan Heinrich.'[392]

16

A Roman 'Sanctuary'

The massive evacuation of war criminals from Europe was a task that exceeded even the combined resources of Perón's secret service and the group of former Nazi agents and collaborators gathered around it. Thousands of former Nazi, Rexist, Vichy and Ustasha officials – some of them major criminals, others passive accomplices to crime – had to be clandestinely provided with aliases, travel documents, money, lodging and a ticket to South America. As we have seen thus far, it was only the Catholic Church that was able to braid the strands of such a gargantuan endeavour. The Croatian escape line, Fuldner's operations in Europe, Daye's SARE in Buenos Aires – all of these intersected in Rome, the ultimate guarantor of their various efforts. And once the realities of the Cold War had set in, even the United States turned to the Church to help it hide one of its own Nazis in South America in 1951.

Perhaps the clearest example of the Church's central role was a letter drafted on 31 August 1948 by Bishop Alois Hudal to President Juan Perón, requesting 5,000 visas for German and Austrian 'soldiers', probably the single largest such appeal made to the Argentine general. These were not refugees, Hudal explained, they were anti-Communist fighters whose wartime 'sacrifice' had saved Europe from Soviet domination. In other words, in Hudal's shorthand, they were German and Austrian Nazis. The bishop's letter was drafted while Perón's special agent Carlos Fuldner was wrapping up his Nazi rescue mission in Italy, after having obtained the collaboration of other Hudal-related agents, including the notorious Croatian Father Krunoslav Draganovic, for the rescue of major war criminals.[393]

As rector of the Santa Maria dell'Anima church at Via della Pace 20 in Rome and as Spiritual Director of the German community in Italy, the Austrian-born Hudal had been an enthusiastic supporter of Hitler, holding religious services for the Nazi occupiers in Italy. He boasted a Golden Nazi party membership badge and, until the liberation of Rome, drove around the Vatican with a Greater Germany flag flying on his official car.[394]

Like other Nazi collaborators who later helped war criminals escape to Argentina, Hudal had attempted to reconcile Christianity with Hitlerism. In his 1936 book *The Foundations of National Socialism*, he criticized certain anti-Christian aspects of Nazi philosophy, but concluded that on the whole Hitler was preparing the ground for the consolidation of a Christian Europe, a train of thought shared by Argentina's nationalist clergy. The bishop even sent a copy of his strongly anti-Semitic book to Hitler with the handwritten dedication: 'To the architect of German greatness.'[395]

Following the liberation of Rome, Hudal became 'the greatest and best friend' of the fugitive Nazis streaming through Italy, and would eventually be associated with the escape of the most notorious Nazi criminals. He began to piece together his network in 1944 when Pope Pius XII's Pontifical Commission of Assistance (PCA) was divided into some 20 regional subcommittees. The Austrian section, Assistenza Austriaca, was placed under his control.[396]

Ironically, some of the financing for Hudal's escape network came from the United States. The American National Catholic Welfare Conference (NCWC) supported various Catholic organizations in Europe during the postwar period and its Italian delegate distributed contributions among the regional subcommittees of the PCA, providing Hudal with substantial funds for his 'humanitarian' aid. Among those who participated in the NCWC's meetings in Rome was none other than Father Draganovic.[397]

By December 1944, as the Nazis fled from the advancing Allied troops all over Europe, the Vatican had named Hudal its special representative to visit German internees at the 'civilian' camps in Italy, which were crawling with fugitive Nazi officers hiding among the real refugees. His visits were allowed even though American officials had strong reservations regarding Hudal's Nazi loyalties.[398]

Among those who later expressed their gratitude to Hudal was Luftwaffe hero Hans-Ulrich Rudel, the postwar friend of Perón and of Paraguayan dictator Alfredo Stroessner, and secret benefactor of Josef Mengele in Argentina. Thanks to Hudal, 'Rome became a sanctuary and salvation for many victims of persecution after the "liberation". More than a few of our comrades found the path to freedom through Rome, because Rome is full of men of good will,' wrote Rudel.[399]

Hudal openly admitted his role. 'I thank God that he opened my eyes and granted me the unmerited grace of being able to visit and comfort many victims in their prisons and concentration camps in the postwar period, and of having been able to snatch not a few of them from the hands of their torturers, aiding their escape to happier countries with false identity papers,' he wrote in his book *Roman Diary* years later. 'I felt duty bound after 1945 to devote my whole charitable work mainly to former National Socialists and Fascists, especially the so called "war criminals".'[400]

Hudal's main assistant in sending incriminated Nazis from Genoa to Argentina was Captain Reinhard Kops, a Nazi military intelligence officer and anti-Masonic 'expert' who had seen duty in the Balkans and Hungary. The end of the war found Kops in Klagenfurt, Austria, escaping from SD agents trying to carry out a death sentence against him – allegedly for sparing 25 Hungarian Jews from deportation to Auschwitz in October 1944 by giving them false IDs as members of his intelligence unit. Kops was saved by General Leo Rupnik, president of the puppet Slovenian buffer state created by the Nazis towards the end of the war to prevent the westward advance of the Communist troops overrunning Croatia.[401]

As a member of Nazi intelligence, in 1945 Kops was subjected to 'automatic arrest' by the occupying British authorities in Klagenfurt. After spending a year in custody, he fled to Frankfurt, where he bought Allied documents in the name of Hans Mahler. Kops went down to Rome to aid Hudal, liaising with various other Croatian and Hungarian prelates also involved in transporting war criminals to safety in Argentina.

In late 1947 Hudal hosted a Christmas celebration for a group of 200 Nazi fugitives living under his protection, Kops among them. The guests included Austrian and German diplomats and certain Italian officials. At one point during the evening, a high-ranking prelate, head of an important religious order, was invited by Hudal to make a telling toast to the assembly: 'You can rest assured the police will not find you here, it is not the first time people have lived in the catacombs of Rome.'

Kops was recruited to handle the desperate Nazis who poured into Rome seeking the divine assistance of the Catholic Church. Hudal explained to Kops that it was important for security reasons to separate the more notorious war criminals from the other fugitives, remarking on the assistance provided by Perón's recently opened Delegation for Argentine Immigration in Europe (DAIE) in such cases. As Kops had already heard, the DAIE enjoyed a highly favourable reputation among fugitive Nazis in Italy.[402]

Kops was nominally employed at the library of the Casa Generalizia of the German-dominated Salvatorian Order, at Via della Conciliazione 51, the wide new road built by Mussolini before the war, directly outside the portals of St Peter's Square. The job provided ample cover for his Nazi rescue activities, as he remarked in his memoirs decades later.[403]

Kops found an excellent tutor in Franz Ruffinengo, a former Italian officer who had seen combat duty in Mussolini's army and who now worked at the DAIE in Genoa. Captured by the Americans, this good-looking and affable south Tyrolean, who spoke fluent German, French, Spanish, English and Italian, charmed his Allied masters. 'He is a person of high intelligence and education and is thoroughly versed in secretarial duties,' read his release papers in January 1946.

'Is thoroughly trustworthy.' In hindsight the American assessment seems naïve. The Austrian-born linguist had amassed a considerable amount of experience sending Nazis to Argentina by the time Kops arrived on the scene. Ruffinengo worked in close contact with Father Draganovic, who was a regular visitor at Perón's office in Genoa. He scanned the passenger lists of departing ships, to find last-minute cancellations that could be filled by Draganovic's and Hudal's fugitives. 'I clutched in Rome the hand Franz extended to me from Genoa,' Kops would recall 40 years later.[404]

Hudal had meanwhile struck a secret deal with the Italian police. Instead of arresting wanted Nazis, the Carabinieri agreed to direct them to churches, convents and monasteries specified by Hudal. The arrangement was particularly useful in Genoa, where the Allies kept the Italian police under close watch. (But the patience of even the lax Carabinieri had a limit. A blow was delivered to the agreement when a group of 110 young Nazis burst into German war songs from the deck of a departing ship in Genoa, taunting the powerless Carabinieri standing at the wharf. Unfortunately for the enthusiastic Nazis, the ship suffered a technical mishap and was forced to return to dock, delivering the would-be fugitives into the hands of the irate Italians.)[405]

Two Hudal associates in Rome who also helped Nazis on the run were Monsignor Heinemann and Monsignor Karl Bayer. Heinemann tended the Nazi flock, albeit with some distaste, at Hudal's Santa Maria dell'Anima church. He also shared space with Monsignor Bayer at Via Piave 23, next-door to the wartime German embassy to the Holy See. Unlike Heinemann, Bayer was well loved by Nazis such as Kops. Interviewed many years later by author Gitta Sereny, he recalled how he and Hudal had helped Nazis with the Vatican's support. 'The Pope did provide money for this; in driblets sometimes, but it did come,' Bayer said.[406]

A 1947 American intelligence report described Bayer as in charge of 'the German refugee action of the Vatican'. He was in 'close contact with the elements who have been using the former German Embassy to the Vatican at Via Piave 21 as a lodging or forwarding address. He has further been most useful in supplying food and letters from the Vatican which has been of tremendous help in this chain.' At the former Nazi embassy, fugitives also received false discharge permits from the Italian POW camps.[407]

According to American intelligence, Monsignor Bayer formed part of a chain led by Dr Willy Nix, head of the nominally anti-Nazi Free German Committee in Italy. But in reality, Nix helped Nazi prisoners who had escaped from Italian war camps, finding them new homes in South America and dispatching them through Genoa with Red Cross passports.

In August 1946 American intelligence infiltrated Nix's chain with an undercover agent who posed as a German fugitive. The chain provided the fake Nazi with a letter from the prominent Vatican scholar Monsignor Antonino Romeo, which identified him under a false name, and it then obtained a passport for him under this alias from the Red Cross. Material aid was given at Villa San Francesco, a gigantic religious palace located among various embassies at Via dei Monti Parioli 64, where a Father Filiberto provided 'food, lodging and contacts with German and Vatican officials'. Once sufficient intelligence had been gathered, American agents arrested a group of Nix's 'clients' and subjected them to lengthy interrogations. Nix's helpers reportedly included Baron von Frohlichstal, a man with 'strong Vatican connections' who helped all Germans regardless of their political colour. 'It was found that the chain of Dr Nix to Frohlichstal to Padre Bayer to a Harald Embcke, who provided escapees with concentration camp documents, ended up with persons like Baronessa Carbonelli or Padre Don Carlos of the Vatican, who succeeded in providing jobs for the escapees in South America,' American intelligence concluded.

By early 1947 Nix had attracted the attention of the Italian secret police, probably because of a rumour that his chain had been infiltrated by Communist elements. 'Yet only a matter of minutes before Dr Nix's actual apprehension, he was able to learn of his imminent arrest and fled to the Vatican where he is now residing,' the Americans learned. 'It has always been suspected that Dr Nix was operating under the benevolent protection of the Vatican. His flight and present sanctuary in Vatican City is positive proof of this fact.'[408]

The Nazis who arrived in Genoa, the point of departure to Argentina, were well served by high-ranking Catholic dignitaries there. The Pontifical Commission of Assistance even had an office at the city's main railway station. The source of this support was Genoa's Archbishop Giuseppe Siri, who had founded the National Committee for Emigration to Argentina and the diocesan committee Auxilium, both of which aided fugitives. According to a 1947 American intelligence report, the archbishop headed 'an international organization whose purpose is to arrange for the emigration of anti-Communist Europeans to South America ... This general classification of anti-Communists would obviously cover all persons politically compromised with the Communists, namely Fascists and Ustashi and other similar groups.'[409]

Kops plugged in easily to this Nazi rescue organization, and worked in liaison with Perón's DAIE offices at Via Albaro 38. He lived in an apartment with a group of German and Croatian fugitives protected by Monsignor Karlo Petranovic, an Auxilium representative who acted as Draganovic's agent at the Italian port. Petranovic was himself a war criminal and Ustasha captain who had been deputy to the local Ustasha leader at Ogulin, a district that saw the extermination of some 2,000 Serbs during the war. The Monsignor organized and instigated many of these murders, personally directing the arrest and execution of 70 prominent Serbs. He fled to Austria with the rest of the Ustasha leadership in 1945, moving later to Italy, where he was taken under Draganovic's wing. A request for his extradition by Yugoslavia was ignored by the British authorities in 1947.[410]

British intelligence nonetheless placed Petranovic under surveillance, noting that he was 'helping Croat émigrés, and in particular, Ustashi, escape to the Argentine'. Among the 'listed war criminals' shipped by Petranovic were the first high-ranking

Croatian criminals who arrived in Argentina in early 1947, the group that included Stjepan Hefer, Mile Starcevic and Vjekoslav Vrancic.[411]

Petranovic was one of the few clergymen who suffered direct Allied interference. London had learned that the commander of the Ustasha Air Force Vladimir Kren was 'being looked after in Genoa by Father Petranovic, a trusted collaborator of Draganovic'. Kren was about to board the *Philippa*, a ship that sailed the Genoa–Buenos Aires route, as part of a large group of war criminals travelling under the Caritas Croata file that Draganovic had secured from Perón. It was probably because of the heinous nature of his crimes that Kren was slated to become one of the few Ustashi turned over to Communist justice. In January 1941 he had fled to occupied Austria and betrayed to the Germans the secret location of Yugoslavia's military airfields. This led to the swift annihilation of the Yugoslav air force by Nazi bombers, directed by Kren himself. He was arrested on 4 March 1947 with eight of Petranovic's other fugitives as he tried to embark under the alias Marko Rubini. When Petranovic heard about the arrests he made an impassioned but futile plea to the British officer in charge to 'let these people go'.

The British operation was only partly successful. The *Philippa* departed from Genoa carrying at least 23 other war criminals whose extradition was required by the Yugoslav chargé d'affaires in Rome. They all arrived safely in Buenos Aires under the Caritas Croata seal on 1 April. As for Kren, he was extradited, tried and executed in Yugoslavia in 1948.[412]

Another clergyman linked to Kops was the Hungarian Father Edoardo Dömöter of San Antonio parish in Genoa. This was the priest who would sign Adolf Eichmann's Red Cross passport application two years later. Like Petranovic, Siri and Draganovic, Dömöter worked closely with Bishop Hudal. The Hungarian priest extended his help to 'all foreigners, especially Germans', confiding to Hudal that he ran the risk of being arrested by the police. Kops knew these priests well, and reported his impressions of them to Hudal. He was disappointed that Draganovic and Petranovic catered almost exclusively to their Croatian fellows when so many Germans were badly in need of aid. Draganovic and Dömöter in particular pursued their own loyalties, Kops felt, although Dömöter was credited with having a genuine soft spot for hard-core Nazis.[413]

Perón wisely sent a man of the cloth to set up his DAIE immigration service, which opened its main office in Rome in December 1946. The Salesian Army Chaplain José Clemente Silva, brother of Perón's close friend, the ultra-nationalist General Oscar Silva, had orders to organize the immigration of 4 million Europeans, at the rate of 30,000 a month, to boost the economic and social revolution Perón envisaged for his country.

In Argentina the few democratic press organs sharply questioned the appointment of a Catholic priest, fearing he would discriminate against non-Catholics. In the Vatican, however, the Salesian brotherhood opened doors. From the start the DAIE worked closely with the Catholic Church in Italy, both in sending *bona fide* emigrants and in the rescue of war criminals. The stated goal of the immigration of millions of European workers was never met. The priest's undercover assignment was more successful. DAIE officials handling arrivals at the port of Buenos Aires soon learned to distinguish 'special' Nazi cases from the general run of passengers. Former DAIE official José Otero, interviewed for this book, clearly remembered the large number of 'Greys', who entered via special channels, disembarking separately from the ocean liners, sometimes picked up by special launches before the ships docked.[414]

Interestingly, DAIE terminology seems to have filtered down from secret British and American operations. The Allies made strict distinctions between 'Blacks' (indefensible war criminals), 'Greys' (collaborators) and 'Whites' (Jews and other war victims). In practice, however, the fine line between 'Greys' and 'Blacks' became blurred. The American ambassador in Yugoslavia, John Moors Cabot, who had previously served as ambassador in Buenos Aires, was not fooled. 'Some arrangement has been worked out with Vatican and Argentina,' he cabled indignantly to the American Secretary of State in mid-1947.

'We are conniving with Vatican and Argentina to get guilty people to haven in latter country.'[415]

Cabot's sermonizing was severely reprimanded. 'Argentina, in taking some of the "Greys", takes persons Yugoslavia would like to have, but takes them with the approval of US authorities,' barked Washington. A British secret document put it more bluntly. 'His Majesty's Government have asked the Vatican to assist in getting the "Greys" to South America, although they were certainly wanted by the Yugoslav government,' states a 1947 document of the British embassy before the Holy See.[416]

In Argentina, the DAIE officials knew exactly who they were giving access to. 'They were German and non-German Nazis,' Otero recalled.[417]

It was not difficult for Kops to arrange his own escape to Argentina, but it did take time to procure the necessary money and travel documents. When the occasion for a simultaneous application for six Argentine landing permits arose, Kops wired Buenos Aires his own alias and that of five other Nazis he felt faced 'the highest risk of death'. Some 30 days later Perón's Immigration Office wired back the authorizations. Kops distributed the documents among his chosen comrades, leaving it up to them to make their own separate travel arrangements. (Judging by their consecutive Argentine Immigration file numbers, one of the five seems to have been the SS criminal 'Francisco' Vötterl.) Kops's well-documented escape is especially illuminating because it coincides with that window in 1948 when Fuldner was at the DAIE in Italy and major criminals such as Eichmann, Mengele, Priebke and Schwammberger obtained Argentine landing permits all within the space of some dozen weeks.[418]

Kops arrived in Buenos Aires on board the *Santa Cruz* from Genoa on 4 September 1948. He was greeted at the port by Eugene Rupnik, the son of the puppet president of Slovenia who had saved Kops from the Nazi execution squad in Austria. A former Slovenian officer himself, now employed at the Argentine Immigration Office, Rupnik quickly arranged free lodging at the Immigration hotel, and introduced Kops to Argentine police officers who, within hours of arrival, provided him with an Argentine ID.[419]

The Slovenian also gave Kops a few pointers on Argentine survival strategy. Although Perón and Evita were staunch defenders of the Nazi fugitives, Rupnik said, 'Masonic' elements had infiltrated the Peronist movement and were passing intelligence to the Allies about new arrivals. Certain precautions were necessary. Not speaking German in public was the first and most obvious. Reading the Nazi-leaning *Freie Presse* or even the moderate *Argentinisches Tageblatt* was out. The only newspaper it was safe to peruse was Argentina's German-language Jewish daily. Kops swallowed hard each time he had to flip through its pages.[420]

Kops had been preceded on 3 May 1948 by his friend and mentor Franz Ruffinengo, who decided to cash in on his experience at Perón's DAIE by opening up a travel agency in Argentina. He soon became well known among Nazis on both sides of the ocean. It was the brilliant success of Ruffinengo's travel agency that started rumours of 'the so-called Odessa organization', Kops confided in his memoirs decades later.[421]

Kops blended in remarkably well, and his initial fear of being discovered by Allied intelligence soon vanished. He was now known as Juan Maler. He quickly found employment at *Der Weg*, a monthly magazine written and read by Nazi fugitives in South America that also enjoyed wide distribution in Germany. From Argentina, he continued his correspondence with Hudal. The magazine heaped lavish praise on the Austrian bishop for the 'greatness of soul, clear authority and daring willingness to help' he had shown in the postwar years.

Der Weg also kept contact with leading Nazi war criminals such as Josef Mengele and Adolf Eichmann. Hitler's Argentine-born agriculture Minister Richard Walther Darré, author of the neo-Nazi bible *Blood and Soil* and a racial theorist second only in importance to Alfred Rosenberg, was a contributor, writing under the alias Carl Carlsson. Even after being sentenced at Nuremberg, Darré kept in touch with the magazine's editors. *Der Weg* also published collaborations by

Johann von Leers, the rabidly anti-Semitic collaborator of Propaganda Minister Josef Goebbels, and Wilfred von Oven, Goebbels' private secretary. And it made room for French and Belgian Nazis close to Perón such as Pierre Daye, Jacques de Mahieu and Marc Augier. British Fascist Oswald Mosley was another friend of the publication.

It was produced from the Dürer-Haus bookshop, owned by Ludwig Freude, at 542 Sarmiento Street in downtown Buenos Aires. Dürer-Haus had bought up the stock of a bookshop that had belonged to a member of the Nazi wartime spy ring in Buenos Aires. The magazine's editors were actively involved in helping new arrivals and sending food packages to comrades in Germany. Dürer-Haus even acted as a major reception point for landing permit applications that were forwarded to Perón's Immigration Office for prompt dispatch.

The public face of *Der Weg* was Luftwaffe ace Hans-Ulrich Rudel, heavily involved while writing for the magazine in setting up his *Kameradenwerk*. Kops and Rudel, and a long list of other Nazis officers, maintained a regular correspondence with Hudal from Argentina. Kops was even able to convince the Austrian bishop to write an article for *Der Weg* in 1949 that earned Hudal a severe reprimand from the Vatican authorities because of the magazine's unabashed anti-Semitic and pro-Nazi line.

Der Weg became increasingly successful, and its circulation reached a high point of some 20,000 copies, boosted by subscribers in Germany and Austria. As its circulation grew, so did its reputation as the organ of a 'Fourth Reich' in Argentina. Finally, in May 1949, the Chief Publication Branch of the American occupying authorities banned the magazine in Germany. Shortly afterwards the ban was extended to Austria, although the magazine continued to circulate clandestinely in both countries until its final closure in 1958. The ban in Europe received considerable publicity in Argentina, but while other more democratic publications suffered persecution and had their paper supplies cut off by Perón, *Der Weg* flourished.

The correspondence between Hudal and Kops during those years underlines the obsessions shared by the bishop, the Nazi fugitives and Argentina's ruling military class: Communism, 'Jewish

Capitalism', the perceived evils of democracy, and the inevitability of a third world war. In 1951 Kops and Hudal discussed elaborate plans to smuggle Nazis from Europe to Colombia. Occasionally Hudal arranged money transfers to Kops, acting as the intermediary for mysterious backers in Italy.[422]

According to eye-witness accounts, including reports from Jews who travelled on the same ships, a great number of Nazi and Ustasha officers entered Argentina disguised as priests. One confirmed case involved a major war criminal who travelled to Argentina in the borrowed robes of a Spanish Carmelite monk.[423]

SS Captain Walter Kutschmann had been responsible for the murder of thousands of Jews in Poland during the early part of the war and is suspected of having participated later in deportations from France. He was undoubtedly one of the most brutal war criminals to escape to Argentina.

After his killing duties in Poland were completed, Kutschmann was stationed in occupied France in 1943, ostensibly as a Border Police Commissioner. In reality, he was the chief of Himmler's spy service at Hendaye, the French town where the Argentine diplomats in Spain who collaborated with the SD went to deliver their reports. After the war, American officials received anonymous reports that Kutschmann had 'deported many French from Hendaye as hostages, the majority of whom never returned'.

The SS captain was the contact man for one of Himmler's most special secret agents, the famous French fashion designer Coco Chanel. In her late fifties, in occupied Paris, Chanel had taken 46-year-old SS officer Hans Guther von Dinklage as her lover. (Chanel was a close friend of Walter Schellenberg, to the extent that when a penniless Schellenberg died of cancer in Milan in 1952, she paid for the funeral service.) Kutschmann made frequent trips into Spain with Chanel. 'On one occasion, Kutschmann was told to deliver a large sum of money to Mme. Chanel in Madrid,' SD agent Hans Sommer told American interrogators after the war.[424]

After the liberation of France, Kutschmann was ordered to report for battle duty on the Russian front. Instead, he skipped across the border to Spain, where he could expect a warmer welcome, having fought on the Falange's side during the Spanish Civil War. Kutschmann went first to Barcelona, running from Nazi agents who had orders to remove him from Spain by air. Berlin even placed a request for his extradition with the Spanish Ministry of War, on charges of embezzling customs funds at Hendaye. Next he fled to Zarauz near San Sebastián, driving a blue convertible two-seater. He impressed the locals with his 'brisk military walk'; he arrived with one large heavy suitcase and left with seven.

British intelligence meanwhile considered Kutschmann a 'gangster of the worst type' and learned that the SS man boasted in Spain of having been 'personally responsible for the death of 15,000 Jews in Russia and Poland'. When finally incarcerated at the Spanish prison camp at Miranda, Kutschmann said he had been on the run since the failed attempt on Hitler's life, in which he claimed to have participated. Kutschmann was quickly released, this time into the arms of a Spanish girl in the Gestapo's service at Biarritz, moving into the Hotel Terminus at San Sebastián.[425]

By the time American officials tried to pick up his trail in 1946 it had grown cold, even though the SS criminal was number 182 on a list of wanted Nazis that Spain was asked to repatriate to Germany. Kutschmann had been taken in by the Carmelite Fathers at Plaza España in Madrid. On 29 May 1947 the Seville police granted him Spanish passport number 59/47 in the name of Carmelite Father Pedro Olmo, a real member of the order who lived at Plaza España. Kutschmann also obtained a special clergy ID (No. 2307) issued by the Spanish Foreign Ministry. His identity switch complete, he boarded the *Monte Ambato*, disembarking at Buenos Aires on 16 January 1948.[426]

Upon arrival Kutschmann went directly to 2345 Charcas Street, an apartment building one block from the Church of the Carmelite Fathers in Buenos Aires. As well as heavenly protection, even at this early stage the SS criminal enjoyed the direct assistance of the Casa Rosada. His application for a taxi licence was seconded by Dr Fernando Imperatrice, an official of Perón's presidential staff.[427]

Shortly after, on 30 November, Kutschmann married and moved suddenly up the job ladder, securing a managerial post at Osram, a German company that had opened a branch in Argentina in 1943. Kutschmann kept contact with his old SS pals. One of the character witnesses in his Argentine citizenship application in 1950 was the wife of Eduard Roschmann, the 'Butcher of Riga', responsible for the death of some 30,000 Jews in Latvia.[428]

(Roschmann had reached Argentina from Genoa bearing a Red Cross passport on 2 October 1948, through the auspices of Bishop Hudal. He managed to stay out of the limelight for 28 years until Germany finally requested his extradition. Argentina's military dictatorship arrested him on 1 July 1977, only to let him slip through its hands 24 hours later. Roschmann escaped to neighbouring Paraguay, where he was admitted into a hospital in the capital city of Asunción, dying of heart failure on 10 August. His corpse disappeared mysteriously a few days later. 'Six men came and took his body away,' was all the hospital authorities could say.)[429]

Kutschmann was still working at Osram in June 1975 when Simon Wiesenthal revealed that the SS criminal lived in Buenos Aires under the Olmo alias. Despite an arrest warrant issued by German Interpol, no formal extradition proceedings were started. Kutschmann and some of his friends called a press conference at the Osram offices announcing they would make 'sensational revelations' in the next few days, but the revelations never came and Kutschmann disappeared from view until the final days of Argentina's 1976–83 dictatorship. During the military regime a trial against Kutschmann on charges of misrepresentation in his Argentine citizenship application ground to a halt when the court lost the case dossier. It was found five years later . . . in the judge's safe.[430]

It wasn't until 1983 that Kutschmann was tracked down again, this time by two journalists who discovered his whereabouts simply by ringing the doorbell at his flat in the beach town of Miramar. Catching the SS criminal off guard, they managed to get a few statements and a picture. The past was still on Kutschmann's mind: 'I know a car could drive by one day with relatives of those Poles they say I killed.

I know they can stick twenty bullets in me. I'm ready. Some people insist I'm a monster, that my hands are bloodied, that I'm a criminal. My conscience is clean. If it is my fate to die with twenty bullets in me, I accept it.'[431]

Kutschmann revealed also that he was now involved in 'animal protection'. The grisly truth behind this apparently innocent remark was that in 1973 his wife Geralda Braumler had formed the AAA 'Friends of the Animals Association'. Membership was restricted to those who advocated euthanasia for stray dogs, an effort the AAA aided by donating small gas chambers to various municipalities in the province of Buenos Aires.[432]

Despite having been tracked down by journalists, Kutschmann was still not arrested. The Argentine authorities proved singularly incapable of positively identifying the war criminal, even though the picture on Olmo's Argentine ID was taken from the same negative as the one in Kutschmann's SS file. Finally, in November 1985, Argentina accepted Germany's extradition request and Kutschmann was taken into custody. He would not live to stand trial, dying of a heart attack in a Buenos Aires hospital on 30 August 1986. He was buried under his Pedro Olmo alias, despite the proof obtained by the extradition court that the real Carmelite brother of that name had died in Spain in 1969. A few days later a makeshift bomb exploded over Kutschmann's grave, releasing pamphlets signed by the non-existent 'OSW' (Organization Simon Wiesenthal) – anti-Semitic provocation of a kind only too frequent in Argentina.[433]

Father Silva was not the only clergyman sent by Perón to rescue Nazis in Europe. A much more secret mission, precious few details of which are known, was carried out by Friar José Pratto, an obscure priest who had been elevated to the post of Ecclesiastic Adjutant, becoming Perón's personal representative to the Pope. Pratto belonged to the Mercedarians, an order founded in the thirteenth century for the rescuing of captives. Perón had grown devoted to the order during his stay in Rome in 1940, and upon his return to Argentina he made contact with Pratto. The priest formed part of the extreme nationalist groups conspiring with Perón prior to the coup he led in 1943. One of the first acts of Perón's military dictatorship was to proclaim the effigy of the order's revered Lady of Mercy a 'General' of the Argentine army.

After 1946, the friar had an office close to Perón's at the Casa Rosada. Between 1948 and 1952 he was seconded by a young secretary, Horacio Carballal, whose job description included picking up Nazis at Buenos Aires airport. 'Pratto would send me to the airport in a presidential automobile,' Carballal recalled in an interview for this book. Wielding a card that read 'Assistant to the Ecclesiastic Adjutant', Carballal was whisked through airport security. 'My job was to conduct these Germans to addresses I was given in the neighbourhood of Belgrano. Then I never saw them again.'

In mid-1949, Friar Pratto was sent to Europe on a secret six-month mission in the company of 'Ambassador' Jorge Oscar Jorge, an even more obscure figure of whom little is known except that as a child he was raised by the Mercedarians. Bearing diplomatic passports, Perón's special emissaries were based at the Argentine embassy in Rome, from where they branched out on lengthy tours of France, Belgium, Germany and Switzerland. In Italy, Pratto met with Pope Pius XII and with the bishop of Milan. Old DAIE hand Franz Ruffinengo simultaneously returned to Europe, touring Italy, Belgium and France. The silence around these missions remains almost total. Former DAIE officials and retired Argentine diplomats recall little. 'Their mission was top secret. They rescued Nazis for Perón.' In 1950, Jorge turned up in Berne for meetings with Swiss police chief Heinrich Rothmund and other Swiss officials linked to Fuldner's mysterious Marktgasse office. Eventually something went horribly wrong. Around 1952 Pratto suddenly disappeared from view amid rumours that he had pocketed funds sent to the Vatican by Perón.[434]

Perhaps the last major Nazi criminal to pass through the Catholic Church's hands on his way to Argentina was SS mass murderer Klaus Barbie, the Gestapo chief responsible for exterminating an uncountable number of Jews in occupied France. The 'Butcher of Lyon' was handed over to Draganovic by American secret service agents at the railway station in Genoa in early March 1951. Barbie had acted as an anti-Communist informer for American intelligence after the war. Now the agents were returning the favour by paying Draganovic 1,400 dollars to tuck their Nazi discreetly away in South America.

At the station Draganovic told Barbie, who had his hopes set on Argentina and even had a letter of recommendation for the Argentine government, that he was being sent to Bolivia instead. 'Draganovic knew a priest in Cochabamba,' Barbie would recall years later. The priest booked Barbie in at Via Lomellini 6, a hotel where Eichmann had supposedly stayed the year before. On 16 March, Draganovic took Barbie to the Bolivian consulate in Genoa, which promptly extended him an entry visa. The next stop was the Red Cross, where that same day Draganovic signed Barbie's passport application under the alias Klaus Altmann.

It was the turn of Perón's DAIE three days later. To Barbie's utter consternation, his arrival with Draganovic was greeted with a lively 'Heil Hitler' by the Argentine officials. At first the SS officer feared a trap, but later he realized that the reception was genuine. Barbie emerged with the required transit visas to pass through Argentina en route to Bolivia, granted through two consecutively numbered Immigration files, one for himself, the second for his wife and children. (Fellow Germans travelling with Barbie also received consecutive file numbers.)

Draganovic showed Barbie a good time in Genoa. The SS man and the Ustasha colonel toured nightclubs and restaurants together. Barbie finally boarded the liner *Corrientes* with a group of other Nazis in Genoa on 22 March 1951, arriving in Buenos Aires three weeks later and spending only a brief time in the city before he went on to Bolivia. When he asked Draganovic why he was aiding his escape, the priest replied: 'We've got to keep a sort of reserve on which we can draw in the future.'[435]

Exactly 25 years later, some 20,000 people began to be silently murdered in the Nazi-style extermination camps set up by an Argentine military dictatorship that enjoyed the support of the

Catholic Church, that professed allegiance to the 'Christian way of life' and proclaimed itself to be the 'Moral Reserve of the Western World', in a chilling echo of Draganovic's parting words to Barbie.[436]

Only a single account survives of Pope Pius XII being questioned about his apparent support of Perón's pro-Nazi policy. It comes from an unlikely source, the producer of the hippie-era musical *Hair*. In the 1950s, Michael Butler was not yet a show business impresario. As heir to a wealthy Catholic family from Chicago, he had high Vatican connections, as well as a line open to Perón.

'I was really fearful Perón represented the greatest threat to the peace of the Western hemisphere,' Butler recalled for this book. 'He had the active support of the Pope. Furthermore, by rumour and our intelligence, we were besieged by stories that Argentina had become the hideaway for many prominent Nazis. These rumours added fuel to the tales of the Vatican's disregard for the fate of Jews in the Nazi era. We wanted to change that. As I was actively involved with the Vatican in some negotiations, I became the natural candidate to try to sway their position.'

Butler eventually met Perón himself after the general's overthrow in 1955. 'I spent a day with him in Caracas, Venezuela. I must say, like so many of his type, he was a charmer. I was running a trading company, and we did some business in Argentina, primarily with Butler Paper. We mostly talked about social conditions in South America.'

As Butler recalls, he was 'stonewalled' by Pius XII when he asked about Perón. 'The Pope granted me two audiences. He was quite surprised when I suddenly brought up the subject of Perón. He stated that they were not supporting the Peronist movement, putting down the constant and persistent flood of intelligence to the contrary. This first audience ended in some acrimony. The next one was even more disappointing and quite disquieting.'[437]

The opening of the postwar archives of the Red Cross has finally ended the debate as to whether or not Nazi criminals were aided by the Catholic Church in their escape to Argentina. Taken together with the other archival sources, the verdict is abundantly clear. Cardinals such as Montini, Tisserant and Caggiano masterminded their escape. Bishops and archbishops such as Hudal, Siri and Barrére implemented the necessary procedures. Priests such as Draganovic, Heinemann and Dömöter signed their passport applications. In the face of such incontrovertible evidence the question of whether Pope Pius XII was fully informed is not only immaterial, it is alarmingly naïve.

In 1947, American intelligence had already determined that 'an examination of the records in Geneva of all passports issued by the International Red Cross would reveal startling and unbelievable facts.' Today the examination of those records is possible. Even more importantly, cross-checking the information they contain with the relevant records in other American, Argentine and Swiss archives provides a full picture of the Catholic Church's conscious involvement in securing sanctuary for war criminals.[438]

One detail that comes into focus is how the generous Caritas Croata quota extended by Perón's government in 1946 ensured safe conduct not only for hundreds of incriminated Croatians, but also for incriminated German Nazis. Such was the case with SS officer Friedrich Rauch, who masterminded the evacuation of the reserves of the Berlin Reichsbank to Hitler's alpine fortress in 1945. Rauch's coup had the Führer's personal approval and was meant to finance a postwar Fourth Reich. Despite an intensive investigation, the Allies never recovered the full amount of the hidden gold. Nor could they interrogate Rauch about it, for on 17 February 1948 he reached safety in Argentina disguised as a Yugoslav named Ivan Pavic, travelling under Draganovic's Immigration file 72513/46. He arrived on board the *Cabo Buena Esperanza*, a ship from Genoa that carried numerous Croatians and at least one Belgian war criminal. To Argentina's Immigration officials he stated his profession, almost tongue-in-cheek, as 'economist'. By 1954 he had legally changed back to his real name, thanks to the special legislation passed by Perón for clandestine 'immigrants'. Soon he had obtained a valid passport from the German embassy, travelling extensively in Germany and Europe until 1971 at least, after which time he reportedly settled in Austria.[439]

Another SS thief aided by Draganovic was Hans Fischböck, the Eichmann aide and finance minister in Holland who appropriated large amounts of Jewish property during the Nazi occupation. During the war, Fischböck also participated in the extortion of Jews living on the American continent. While arranging his departure, Draganovic booked him into Via Lomellini 6, where Eichmann and Barbie also received shelter. Draganovic personally signed Fischböck's Red Cross passport application, certifying the SS officer's fake identity of Jakob Schramm, and his 'photograph, signature and digital imprint'. Bearing this passport, Fischböck arrived in Buenos Aires on 2 February 1951, feeling secure enough under Perón's protection to revert to his real name two years later.[440]

The cooperation between Montini, Hudal and Draganovic is best illustrated by the case of Brunswick district-inspector Bernhard Heilig, convicted in 1947 for ordering the execution of his own troops for 'defeatist' behaviour. Heilig escaped prison in Germany and made his way to Italy. On 11 November 1949 he showed up at Via Gregoriana 28, the office of the International Red Cross in Rome. His application bore the signatures of both Draganovic and Monsignor Heinemann, the German representative at Hudal's Santa Maria dell'Anima church. At the same time, he appealed for help to Father Bruno Wüstenberg, a German aide to Acting Vatican Secretary of State Cardinal Montini, the future Pope Paul VI. Heilig asked for Vatican money to purchase a visa and a transatlantic ticket. Wüstenberg declined but passed his case back to Hudal. Upon arrival in Argentina in 1951 his economic problems ended, for he immediately found employment next to Adolf Eichmann at Fuldner's CAPRI firm in the northern province of Tucumán.[441]

Equally illustrative is the case of Eichmann adjutant Franz Stangl, the commandant of the Treblinka extermination camp, second only to Auschwitz in the scale of slaughter it achieved, where some 900,000 people are estimated to have been murdered. Captured by the Americans in 1945, Stangl 'escaped' from an Austrian prison camp in

1947, wending his way down to Rome looking for Hudal. When they finally met, Hudal walked up to the dedicated butcher with both hands extended. 'You must be Franz Stangl,' the bishop said. 'I've been expecting you.' Stangl was extradited from Brazil years later. In an interview in his German prison, he recalled Hudal's help. The bishop arranged 'quarters in Rome where I was to stay till my papers came through. And he gave me a bit more money – I had almost nothing left.'[442]

A full list of Nazi criminals known to have been aided by these Church dignitaries would be too long to detail here, and shorter than the unrecorded total. We have already seen how they helped Eichmann escape. Then there was the 'Butcher of Riga', Eduard Roschmann, aided by Hudal. And the SS officer Friedolin Guth, assigned to killing partisans in France, aided by both Hudal and Draganovic. Another SS officer, Erich Priebke, condemned in Italy in 1998 for the Ardeatine Caves massacre, had his passport application endorsed by the Pontifical Commission of Assistance. The SS mass killer Gerhard Bohne, one of the men in charge of Hitler's euthanasia programme, was also endorsed by the PCA and by Draganovic. And the list goes on.[443]

It is now beyond dispute that these clergymen synchronized their operations closely with Nazi agents such as Reinhard Kops. It is also clear that their endeavours were enthusiastically aided by the Nazi-saluting officials at Perón's DAIE. Moral justification flowed from leading Church figures such as the anti-Communist French Cardinal Eugène Tisserant and the like-minded Argentine Cardinal Antonio Caggiano. It may be impossible to pin the rescue of any individual war criminal on the Pope's office, but it can no longer be doubted that the Vatican as an institution exerted its influence to clear the way for fugitive Nazis. It is also abundantly clear that Argentina was chosen by the Church as 'the largest recipient' for these criminals.

'In those Latin American countries where the Church is a controlling or dominating factor, the Vatican has brought pressure to bear which has resulted in the foreign missions of those countries taking an attitude almost favouring the entry into their country of former Nazi and former Fascists or other political groups, so long as they are anti-Communist,' stated an American intelligence report in 1947. 'The justification of the Vatican for its participation in this illegal traffic is simply the propagation of the faith. It is the Vatican's desire to assist any person, regardless of nationality or political beliefs, as long as that person can prove himself to be a Catholic. This of course from the practical point of view is a dangerous practice. The Vatican further justifies its participation by its desire to infiltrate not only European countries but Latin American ones as well with people of all political beliefs as long as they are anti-Communist and pro-Catholic Church.'[444]

At least American intelligence had not erred when it surmised that, when it came to providing sanctuary to incriminated Nazis, it was only the bottom line that mattered to the Vatican. In every Nazi passport application signed by Draganovic, Heinemann and Dömöter, the stated religion was 'Catholic'.

17

ERICH PRIEBKE

In 1948 Erich Priebke badly needed somewhere to hide. His immediate wartime superior, SS Lieutenant Colonel Herbert Kappler, had just been condemned to life imprisonment by a Roman court for the murder of 335 Italian citizens in the Ardeatine Caves, a mass carnage in which Priebke had played a key role. Other distressing shadows floated near him. They included the roundup of over 2,000 Roman Jews for extermination at Auschwitz, the extraction of 50 kilograms of gold from the city's Jewish community, and the massive quantity of gold plundered from the Banca d'Italia following the Nazi occupation of Rome.

Priebke had joined the SS in 1936 at the age of 23, after having worked since he was 16 at various hotels in Italy, Germany and England. Although his last stint was at the Splanade in Berlin, preceded by the Savoy in London, his happiest times were spent at the Savoia and Europa hotels in Rapallo and Liguria. 'Those two years in Italy were the most beautiful in my life,' he recalled much later. 'An owner of one of those hotels was a single man and he practically adopted me as his son, teaching me many things about the business.' Due to his uncanny flair for languages Priebke became a fluent English and Italian speaker.

Once in the SS this ability earned him a transfer to the Gestapo office that liaised with foreign police departments, reinforcing what became for him a long association with Italy. When Mussolini visited Germany in 1937, Priebke formed part of his bodyguard. The following year, the young SS officer travelled as one of Hitler's translators during the Führer's visit to Rome, returning to Italy shortly afterwards with Field Marshal Hermann Göring. His career blossomed and Priebke rose to become head of his liaison office in Berlin.

In 1940 the young officer was back in Italy, this time accompanying Reinhard Heydrich, the initiator of Hitler's 'Final Solution'. When the police attaché at the German embassy in Rome, Herbert Kappler, requested General Heydrich to assign him a deputy, Priebke was sent. Considered a 'Nazi robot', Kappler years later recalled that his responsibilities had been 'to explore the organizational structure of the Italian police, to exchange information pertaining to international Communism, or rather to international Communist organizations, to provide information in cases of political and military espionage which might interest Italy and Germany'.

Priebke acted nominally as link man with the Italian Fascist police, but secretly he was the Nazis' go-between with the Vatican, his main intermediary a German priest who liaised with the Nazis on behalf of the Pope. 'My task was handling relations with the Vatican. I was helped by Father Pankratius Pfeiffer, with whom I had contact in Rome during the war,' Priebke would admit afterwards. But the SS officer and his wife Alice apparently had Church connections that rose well above Pfeiffer's level and that ultimately gained them an audience with the Bishop of Rome himself. 'We are deeply religious, in 1942 we were granted a private audience with Pope Pius XII,' he revealed in a 1996 press interview.[445]

While Mussolini remained in power, Lieutenant Priebke led a relatively quiet existence. But following Il Duce's ejection from office by the Italian Fascist Council in July 1943 'everything changed'. The Italians had grown tired of the war. Mussolini was placed under arrest at an undisclosed location and a pro-Allied government headed by Marshal Pietro Badoglio took office. The Fascist dream was over. Hitler reacted angrily to what he considered Italy's ingratitude towards Mussolini, ordering German troops to march on the Eternal City. Anticipating what was to come, Priebke sent his wife and two children back to their native Berlin.[446]

Rome was entered on 10 September 1943 by General Albert Kesselring. Four days later, except for the few blocks of Vatican territory, the entire city was in Hitler's hands. Suddenly Kappler was elevated to Gestapo chief. Priebke claimed in later years that he ceased being Kappler's second-in-command following the occupation. While it is true that a couple of higher-ranking SS officers were now transferred under Kappler's orders, Priebke, at 30 years of age and with three years' experience in Italy, could boast well-oiled contacts in Rome not equalled by the new captains. Also, according to his SS file, he was in line for promotion to captain himself, putting him on a hypothetically equal footing with the new arrivals. Priebke remained Kappler's most experienced officer in Rome and he now ranked third or fourth in the Gestapo line of command. The real change was that suddenly his job included the arrest, torture and execution of Communists and Italian partisans.

During early September Priebke reportedly took part in the frantic search for Mussolini's whereabouts. Hitler had entrusted crack SS agent Otto Skorzeny with liberating Il Duce and delivering him to Berlin. Skorzeny made straight for Rome, where he sought Kappler's help with the intelligence-gathering to locate where Badoglio's government had imprisoned Mussolini. Apparently Priebke's excellent command of the Italian language worked in Mussolini's favour, and in one of the most daring commando operations of the war, Hitler's wish was soon achieved.

The creator of Fascism was rescued from his confinement in the Gran Sasso by Skorzeny on 12 September. Hitler's commando dropped down silently in a glider on the fortified ski resort in the Apennine mountains, snatched Mussolini from his Italian guards and whisked him off to Austria in a small Storch aircraft. Mussolini was taken to meet Hitler and a few days later installed as the head of the Nazi puppet state of Salò, a slice of territory carved out of northern Italy. Priebke reputedly earned the Iron Cross for his part in the intelligence work and was finally promoted to captain of the SS at the end of the year. One of the soldiers who reportedly also participated in the operation was Reinhard Kops. Ironically, it was Kops who eventually betrayed Priebke's presence in Argentina in 1994. The hero of Mussolini's rescue, Otto Skorzeny, would himself arrive in Argentina in 1949.[447]

After seizing Rome, the Nazis went on a treasure hunt. On 20 September 1943 the Banca d'Italia (the Italian Central Bank) was plundered, and some 118 bars of gold extracted and presumably sent to Berlin. A much bloodier search for riches would soon follow as the Third Reich extended its Holocaust to include Italy's Jews.

Some time in late September, Kappler was ordered to arrange the arrest and deportation of Rome's 7,000 Jews. 'I remember particularly a telegram signed by Himmler, in which the need was stressed to solve the Jewish Question also in the city of Rome,' he recounted in 1961 when he was called as a witness in the trial of Adolf Eichmann in Jerusalem. 'I remember this because on that occasion I heard for the first time the term *Endlösung der Judenfrage* [Final Solution of the Jewish Question].'

Kappler began with the gold. He called in the leaders of the Jewish community and demanded a ransom of 50 kilograms of the precious metal. The collection began on 27 September at Rome's synagogue on the banks of the Tiber. The gathering of the gold quickly became a public event. Many Romans, Jews and Christians alike, brought jewellery and medals as donations. An appeal for aid from the Vatican, however, brought forth only the half-hearted offer of a 'loan', but Kappler's quota was finally met without dipping into the Vatican's coffers.

The metal was smelted down and ten bars were delivered by an SS major to Ernst Kaltenbrunner in Berlin. Some witnesses claim that there were originally twelve bars, but that two disappeared into Kappler's pockets. 'I sent the gold to Kaltenbrunner, because at that time our espionage services did not have sufficient funds, and there was urgent need to provide them with additional means,' Kappler explained during the Eichmann trial. By playing up the value of the Jews as a source of finance for the Nazis, Kappler claimed he hoped to delay their deportation. He also suggested to Berlin that Rome's Jews might be a possible source of intelligence on 'the international Jewish financial conspiracy'.

A short time later, Eichmann sent Kappler his personal representative, a specialist who had already shown particular zest working on the 'Jewish Question' with police attachés in France and Bulgaria. SS Captain Theodor Dannecker bore a written order for the 'search operation against Jews' signed by the Gestapo chief, SS General Heinrich Müller. The human hunt now began in earnest. News of the impending catastrophe had already spread through the city and many people were able to go to ground. All the same, well over 1,200 people were taken between 16 and 17 October. After the release of foreign nationals and the children of mixed marriages, some 1,000 Roman Jews were loaded onto a train bound for Auschwitz. Until the liberation of Rome by the Allies eight months later the deportations continued as house-to-house searches yielded up more hidden Jews. A total of some 2,100 men, women and children were sent from Rome to their deaths in Nazi concentration camps while Kappler, backed by Priebke, headed the Gestapo there.

Throughout the operation ('from October until May 1944', by his own account) Priebke monitored the open but strangely mute line to the Vatican. No secret message from Pope Pius XII came down it. Not a single public word was uttered by the Holy Father on the genocide occurring literally on his doorstep. (On 4 November 1943, Priebke had met with Father Pfeiffer to reassure the Vatican that the SS would not enter religious institutions in search of 'fugitives', giving the Vatican the green light to grant sanctuary to Jews within its small borders.) In all, 7,500 Jews were deported from Italy during the German occupation, of whom just over 600 returned.[448]

If Priebke's role in the deportation of Italy's Jews remains doubtful, the same cannot be said about his part in the Ardeatine Caves massacre, the Nazi crime with the strongest reverberations in postwar

Italy. Priebke now operated out of Gestapo headquarters, a detention and torture centre in a nondescript modern apartment building on Via Tasso (now Rome's 'Liberation Museum'), just a few blocks from the German embassy. The street was sealed off with barricades and SS troops, and some 40 makeshift cells were fitted in, housing Italian partisans, Communists and Jews. The Gestapo's victims carved the walls with graffiti proclaiming 'Viva Italia!'

Despite all its horrors, for some unfortunate prisoners Via Tasso was merely a holding pen prior to their deportation to the infinitely more dismal Auschwitz concentration camp. Although Priebke always denied participating in torture sessions, exactly the opposite seems true. 'It can be safely affirmed that Priebke played a primary role in the German command at Via Tasso, participating in police operations, arrests, interrogations and tortures,' the Roman military court that tried him ruled on 22 July 1997. Apparently brass knuckles were his instrument of choice, distinguishing Priebke from the more technologically-minded Nazi torturers who applied electric current to their victims' genitals. During the German occupation, as Via Tasso's go-between with the Vatican, he handled the clemency requests transmitted by Father Pfeiffer. The German priest 'used to intercede in favour of certain detainees, he managed to get Kappler to release prisoners,' Priebke recalled decades later.

On 23 March 1944 a company of German soldiers marching along Via Rassela in Rome were victims of a bomb attack by Communist partisans, resulting in the death of 33 men. Priebke was in his office at Via Tasso when he heard the news. Hitler's response was immediate and lethal. 'For every German soldier, ten Italians had to die,' Priebke himself related in 1994. Hitler wanted his order executed within 24 hours. To fill the quota Priebke combed the Via Tasso files for 330 Italians who had been sentenced to death by the Germans and were awaiting execution. 'The whole of that night we searched the records and could not find sufficient persons to make up the number required,' Priebke related to Allied interrogators in 1946. A further search was made for people who had been arrested but not yet convicted. Still the number proved too small. Finally, the difference was made up with 73 Jews awaiting deportation and 50 prisoners from the city's gaols provided by Rome police chief Angelo Caruso. Father Pfeiffer is alleged to have pleaded with Priebke for the reprisal to be called off.

The following day, 24 March, Kappler, Priebke, 90 Nazi troops and some 12 officers led their assigned victims to an entrance to the Ardeatine Caves outside Rome. The victims ranged from 14 to 75 years of age and represented a cross-section of Roman society, from bankers to waiters, and musicians to resistance fighters. Priebke called out their names from his list as they were dragged into the dark mouth of the cave. The killing started at three o'clock in the afternoon.

'All were tied with rope with their hands behind their backs, and when their names were called they walked into the cave in groups of five,' Priebke related to Allied interrogators on 28 August 1946. 'I went in with the second or third party and killed a man with an Italian machine pistol, towards the end I killed another man with the same machine pistol. The executions finished when it was getting dark in the evening. During the evening some German officers came to the cave and after the shooting the caves were blown in.'

The true extent of the horror was revealed after the liberation of Rome, when the caves were opened and Italian forensic experts began their work. A total of 335 bodies were found, five more than Hitler's order demanded. Why? As was proven in the trials that followed, the usually efficient SS men had bungled their count. Upon discovering the mistake Kappler held a conference among his officers. It was decided that the five extra men could not be allowed to live on as witnesses. By the end of the evening Kappler was forced to hand out alcohol among his executioners, who could no longer stomach the growing pile of corpses inside the cave. As the spirits began to take effect, their aim faltered badly. Forensic experts found that various victims had suffered multiple non-lethal bullet wounds instead of a clean shot through the back of the head, and had suffered slow deaths among the pile of bodies.[449]

The Ardeatine massacre, supposedly meant to reaffirm the authority of the Nazis, was actually an act of cruel bravado by an invader ready to take flight. On 4 June 1944, the Allies entered Rome and chased the Germans out of the city. Running from the victorious British and American troops, Priebke retreated to Verona. He continued serving in the Gestapo there until 31 August 1944, when his SS file shows he received an urgent personal call from Himmler to go to Berlin for unspecified duties. There has been much speculation about this summons. Priebke claimed in a press interview in 1996 that he went to accompany a relative of Mussolini who needed to be interned in a German hospital. But there are other reports, denied by Priebke, which state that he participated in the roundup of Italy's Jews during this final period of the war. These reports suggest that he signed deportation orders for at least two Italian Jews, Isaac Tagliacozzo and Mario Sonnino, and that as early as 1940 he had already been assigned to Adolf Eichmann's department of 'Jewish Affairs', although his SS file does not support these claims. By November, in any case, Priebke was back in Italy, in Bolzano now, living at Via Diaz 250.[450]

At the end of the war, on 13 May 1945, Priebke was arrested and taken to the Afragola prison camp. In August 1946 he was interrogated there about his role in the Ardeatine killings. Later he was moved to the British-run camp at Rimini, on the Adriatic. During these months the Ardeatine Caves massacre was acting as a lightning rod for much of Italy's pent-up anger against its former Nazi occupiers. The revelations about the case were permanently in the news, and most of the German officers involved were imprisoned and lined up for trial. Priebke was one of the few to avoid this fate.

Incredibly, Rimini's commanders ignored the Italian arrest warrant issued in his name on 25 November 1946, only three months after his interrogation, and failed to hand Priebke over to Italian justice, even though he had been perfectly identified and had plainly admitted his crucial participation. During the New Year's Eve celebrations at the camp, taking advantage of the drunken condition of his British guards, the SS captain cut through the barbed-wire fence. He ran straight into the arms of the Catholic Church, as Priebke himself related in Argentina in 1995 before his extradition to Italy. 'Five of us managed to escape: three non-commissioned officers, another officer and myself. We went to the bishop's palace and that's where our flight really began.'[451]

Breakouts were a routine occurrence at Rimini. 'There were escapes every night from that camp, we were 220,000 German soldiers,' Priebke said in another interview in 1996. 'I took the train to Vipiteno, where I met with my wife, buying the ticket that night at the station, changing trains at Bologna. I was scared at first, it's true. We stayed there two years . . . But no one came to arrest me.'[452]

This serene reunion in the Alto Adige, after his wife and two children had lived out the end of the war in bombed-out Berlin, was too bucolic to last. During 1948 the revelations arising from the Ardeatine Caves trial continued to reverberate throughout Italy. After the shock of Kappler's conviction, it was undoubtedly wiser to start a new life elsewhere. 'Help came from a Franciscan father whose name I don't remember. He said he couldn't send me to Germany but he could offer me Argentina. I said all right and left for Genoa,' Priebke told the Italian newspaper *La Repubblica* almost 50 years later.[453]

Escape was now possible because some time in the summer of 1948, while Fuldner was handing out landing permits at the DAIE office in Genoa, an application for Priebke was entered at Immigration in Buenos Aires under the alias Otto Pape. Magically, an application for fellow SS officer and Auschwitz doctor Josef Mengele was entered on the same day. As we have seen, the landing permit applications of these two criminals carried the consecutive files numbers 211712/48 and 211713/48, at a time when over 500 new files were being opened daily at Immigration. Since the vital documents apparently no longer exist, it may prove impossible to determine exactly how these applications were routed. An educated guess based on the research for this book would be that Fuldner wired them together from Genoa to Freude's office in the Casa Rosada, thus resulting in consecutive numbers when Immigration opened files for them in Buenos Aires. Whatever the actual details, the broad picture is clear. If there is one point more than any other at which Perón's Nazi rescue organization resembles the fictional Odessa of novels and film, this moment when two notorious SS criminals obtained Argentine papers simultaneously is certainly it.[454]

On 26 July 1948, the Pontifical Commission of Assistance in Rome issued Priebke a Vatican identity document (PCA 9538/99) under his Pape alias. On the same day, this Vatican ID was used to obtain a Red Cross passport for him. 'The problem was that I couldn't travel under my own passport and that is why Bishop Alois Hudal in the Vatican helped me, handing me a blank passport with the Red Cross insignia,' he said later. When Priebke's presence was uncovered in Argentina in 1994, the Vatican's official historian confirmed the Austrian's bishop's assistance. 'Perhaps Priebke contacted Monsignor Hudal who, being a friend of the Nazis after the war, may have written a letter to Perón's ambassador,' said Jesuit father and historian Robert Graham. The Vatican spokesman also admitted that Hudal might have provided 'money and letters of recommendation' for the SS captain, as he certainly did for other war criminals.[455]

Priebke's next stop before boarding ship would have been the Argentine consulate to have a visa stamped on his Red Cross passport. Then he just had to make the mandatory visit to the DAIE office at Via Albaro 38, where Argentine doctors conducted health checks on prospective immigrants. Some VIPs and Nazi criminals could dispense with this last hurdle, others were accompanied by the Croatian priest Krunoslav Draganovic, the Vatican's Argentine-connected Nazi-saviour.[456]

The 'Pape' family boarded the *San Giorgio* steamship at the port of Genoa on 23 October 1948, travelling third class and arriving in Buenos Aires three weeks later. Upon disembarking, Priebke stated his profession as 'butler'. His first job in Buenos Aires was actually washing dishes at a hotel. He later progressed to waiting tables at the Adam restaurant, where German beer was served round the clock.[457]

A large number of the war criminals and former collaborators around Perón had been rescued from Europe with 'deficient documentation' and were living under aliases. In July 1949, therefore, to tie up this particular loose end of his Nazi immigration policy, Perón granted a 'general amnesty' for foreigners who had entered the country 'illegally'. Dispensing with Congress and using instead the kind of presidential decree his agent Smolinski had boasted about to Swiss police chief Rothmund, Perón made Argentine identity papers available to all comers.

The procedure was simplicity itself: no embarrassing questions asked about wartime responsibilities, no proviso made for background checks, name-switches were awarded simply by signing on the dotted line. The only requirement was two character witnesses and some proof of entry prior to the cut-off date of 8 July 1949. Ostensibly presented as a humanitarian gesture towards all arrivals, the real beneficiaries of the decree were the Nazi fugitives who had travelled incognito, a ruse rarely employed by innocent war refugees. (While Peronist historians tend to argue that the decree favoured Jews, a patient perusal of the passenger lists at Immigration, where the name-switches were registered, revealed few switches for refugees but an abundance for war criminals and collaborators.) In any case, no precautions were taken to distinguish between the two categories, which weighted the scales in the Nazis' favour.[458]

A swarm of eager candidates soon lined up at Immigration to reclaim their real identities. To guide them through the process they found a warm, sympathetic official who certainly knew the ropes. Slovakian war criminal Jan Durcansky had himself entered Argentina under an alias and switched back to his real name. Now he helped many a new arrival to do the same at Immigration. Among those who regained their real identities was Otto Pape, who for this purpose, on 6 October 1949, stated he had 'lived at the German embassy in Rome until the end of the war and left for the Argentine Republic through the intercession of the Catholic organizations'. Priebke presented his Red Cross passport made out under the Pape alias and his real German ministerial passport number 249, issued in Berlin during 1941. The Legal Affairs Director at Immigration who signed the SS captain's name-switch looked at both and did not so much as blink.[459]

In 1954, Priebke left crowded Buenos Aires and moved with his

family to the peaceful Andean ski resort of Bariloche, an idyllic moun-
tain retreat in the southern region of Patagonia noted for its
resemblance to Switzerland. Bariloche had become the Mecca for
Nazi fugitives the world over. Hudal's assistant Reinhard Kops had
settled there, setting up a publishing enterprise that mailed Nazi literature to all corners of the globe. Freude also possessed a home
there, and Josef Mengele was rumoured to visit often. A short hop
across the Andes more Nazi fugitives were hiding in Chile, a country
on a par with Argentina when it came to providing hospitality to criminals.

In Italy, Kappler continued serving his life sentence, but Priebke
was to all intents and purposes forgotten. Oblivious to his presence in
Argentina, in the early 1960s the Italian military court that had handled Kappler's trial 'provisionally' filed away the case against the
runaway SS captain. Priebke prospered. He travelled frequently, to
Italy, Germany and the United States, renewing his passport periodically at the German embassy in Buenos Aires. Erich Priebke soon
became 'Don Erico' to his Argentine neighbours. He was considered
a model citizen and was a respected public figure, director of
Bariloche's German–Argentine Cultural Association, as well as of its
German School, which boasted 1,100 students, some of them Jewish.
The cold cuts he sold at his 'Vienna' delicatessen were the best in
town.

His role in the Ardeatine Caves massacre was public knowledge.
Priebke himself openly admitted it to anyone who cared to ask,
always sticking to the story that he had only shot two men. He even
confirmed his participation in a bestselling book published in Buenos
Aires by Bariloche writer Esteban Buch in 1991. In it, Priebke preferred to reminisce about his arrival in Argentina rather than about the
Nazi occupation of Rome. 'In those days Argentina was a kind of par-
adise to us,' Priebke told Buch. 'Nobody since I've been here has ever
said a word about politics. It's completely taboo, and that's how our
people behave.'[460]

All that changed drastically in early 1994 when an American television crew arrived in Argentina looking for Reinhard Kops. The

Wiesenthal Centre had discovered that Hudal's former collaborator was living in Bariloche and had alerted ABC's *Primetime* news programme. Doorstepped by renowned American journalist Sam Donaldson, a fear-stricken Kops ratted on his comrade, indicating to Donaldson that he should go after Priebke, a real war criminal, instead. The crew accosted the surprisingly vigorous 80-year-old Priebke as he walked, keys in hand, towards his car on a quiet street in Bariloche. Donaldson confronted the former SS captain with the facts of the Ardeatine Caves massacre. Priebke foolishly confirmed his participation on camera, admitting that he had shot two Italians. 'That kind of thing happened, you know,' a straight-backed Priebke said in perfect English. 'At that time, an order was an order, young man. You see?'[461]

The screening of Priebke's straightforward admission on American television caused an international uproar. The Italian vice-consul in Bariloche, who had known all along of Priebke's presence but didn't have the nerve to tattle on him, resigned from his post in shame. In May, an Italian extradition request landed in Buenos Aires and in November 1995 Priebke was put on a plane back to Rome, finally behind bars 51 years after the deed. The Argentine policemen who had held him under house arrest pending the extradition hugged him tearfully at the foot of the plane's steps.[462]

A series of trials and appeals followed until 7 March 1998, when Priebke was sentenced to life imprisonment, to be served under house arrest. During the proceedings the Catholic Church once again provided him with protection, admitting him under police guard at the San Bonaventura monastery outside Rome. The international press published claims that the monastery had lodged a number of Nazi criminals in the postwar period, including Adolf Eichmann.[463]

Through it all, Priebke remained totally lucid but vaguely uncomprehending, oblivious to the issues at stake. To the Italian judges he held up his 'life membership of the Argentine Automobile Club' as proof of character. 'I was never an anti-Semite,' he declared. 'I grew up in Berlin where I had Jewish friends and my wife's best friend was Jewish.' This from a man who had been a member of the SS for nine years, a Nazi party member for twelve, and who self-admittedly helped round up 73 Jews to fill Hitler's quota at the Ardeatine Caves.[464]

In an embarrassing postscript, once Italy had solicited Priebke's arrest in Argentina, Germany put in a tardy extradition request of its own. Soon it transpired that the three senior prosecutors of the Dortmund war crimes unit that held the files on the Priebke case between 1947 and 1973 had all been wartime members of the Nazi party. In 1996 Dortmund senior prosecutor Hermann Weissing shame-facedly admitted that his unit had always possessed the documents it needed to indict the SS captain. In particular, they had the evidence from the 1948 trial in Rome. But the Italian documents had been shelved in 1971 without ever being translated or even evaluated. 'I always lived under my real name without hiding from anyone,' Priebke rightly said in an Italian press interview in 1996. 'If they had wished to arrest me they could have done so all along.'[465]

18

GERHARD BOHNE

The clearest example of a Nazi responsible for crimes against humanity who was brought into Argentina disguised as a 'technician' for Perón's military industry was Dr Gerhard Bohne, an SS officer who played a leading role in Hitler's euthanasia programme. Interestingly enough, his is also one of the very few cases in which the formality of a landing permit was dispensed with. The fact that after he disembarked in Buenos Aires the euthanasia specialist went straight to Carlos Fuldner's apartment perhaps explains his special treatment. Furthermore, Bohne is one of the few Nazi criminals to have openly admitted he was given 'money and identity papers' by Perón's helpers.[466]

In the year he came to power, 1933, Hitler enforced the compulsory sterilization of persons suffering from what the Nazis considered hereditary diseases. The list covered congenital mental deficiency, schizophrenia, manic-depression, epilepsy, Huntington's disease, blindness, deafness, severe physical abnormalities and chronic alcoholism. Some 2 million people are reported to have been sterilized during the Third Reich under Hitler's order. By the end of the decade a great deal of propaganda had been printed in the Nazi press pointing out the exact cost of caring for the mentally and physically handicapped. The Nazis attempted to condition the population to believe that the state's resources could be better employed elsewhere. The quick, economic solution? Exterminate.

The plan for the murder of incurably ill citizens was code-named Aktion T4, and run from offices inside Hitler's Chancellery at Tiergarten 4. The medical division was run by Dr Werner Heyde, while the administrative nuts and bolts were entrusted to Dr Bohne, a doctor of law in his late thirties who became the head of RAG, the Reich's Work Group of Sanatoriums and Nursing Homes. The RAG had a 'killing capacity' of 70,000 people, an estimated 20 per cent of all the inmates at its 'homes'. Patients chosen for extermination were told they were being taken to showers, then stripped of their clothes and led to gas chambers inside the institutions, where their bodies were subsequently cremated.

As it turned out, Bohne got quite close to his goal. By August 1941, when Aktion T4 was cancelled, a total of 62,273 Germans with incurable diseases, mental patients and other handicapped citizens had been delivered to the RAG gas chambers. Hitler's euthanasia programme had been a test run for the mass extermination camps of the SS, which were often staffed by T4 veterans. But the failure of the Aktion T4 bosses to keep their work secret created a surge of public displeasure. The plan proved too distasteful an endeavour for even Nazified Germany to swallow. It was therefore cancelled before Hitler could realize his plan to eliminate all 'genetically damaged' citizens.

Left at the helm of a drifting ship, the punctilious Bohne fell into disgrace in July 1943 after submitting a report to his Nazi superiors which accused the RAG of irregular gold trading, fraud, corruption and black marketeering. Bohne contended that the 'Work Group' was being kept alive only for the personal enrichment of its managers. The SS and the Nazi party, while admitting the validity of some of Bohne's accusations, took the view that his divulging them was unacceptable, and that it revealed a serious character flaw. The Nazi bigwigs frowned on Bohne's inability to keep a secret and resented his displaying the Nazi system in a bad light. The euthanasia expert was thrown out of the party and Himmler recommended he should be cast out of the SS as well.[467]

Eventually Bohne was sent to the battlefront, where he was captured by American troops. At the end of the war, his crimes against humanity undetected, the 'doctor' was released, and promptly resumed his legal practice in Düsseldorf. It was not a position with a future, given his past, and the former RAG chief was contacted by Perón's rescue organization in 1948. At the time, Fuldner was shuttling between Italy, Switzerland and Austria arranging the transport of Nazi aviation experts for the Argentine air force. During 1947, Perón had managed to spirit the director of the Bremen Focke-Wulf factory, Kurt Tank, out of Germany through Denmark, before the Danish government closed that route. Once in Argentina, Tank quickly replaced French war criminal Emile Dewoitine as the new head of Perón's jet fighter project. One of Tank's conditions was that his senior assistants should be brought across the Atlantic to aid him in the task.

In the spring of 1948, aviation expert Hans-Gerd Eyting was approached in Germany by former Focke-Wulf colleagues who invited him to work with Tank in Argentina. To speed up the arrival of the experts, Fuldner had turned to Father Draganovic. Eyting and two fellow aviation engineers were soon en route. As Eyting told the story in 1990, their first contact was a certain 'Dr Bohne' in Munich, almost certainly Gerhard Bohne. The good doctor directed the trio to a Croatian tavern in the city where a mysterious man in a leather overcoat who called himself Lavic awaited them. This Croatian agent had managed to bribe American officers at a frontier post, and he brought the Nazi 'technicians' through the Austrian border to Salzburg in jeeps driven by American soldiers. There he booked the group into a hotel and handed them Red Cross passports for 'displaced' Croatians personally signed by Draganovic, with Italian residence permits for each of them inside. All the Germans had to do was glue their photographs to the passports and sign their (false) names. Eyting became Antonio Kohavic.

The group continued through Milan and Genoa to Rome, where they were taken under the wing of Ivo Omrcanin, a former Ustasha official who spoke perfect German. Despite protests by the Italian government to the Western powers about his activities, Omrcanin continued as Draganovic's right-hand man and even met with Pope Pius XII during 1946. Many years later he settled in Washington and claimed to have sent 'thousands' of German scientists and technicians down the ratline to South America.

Eyting and his companions were lodged at the Centocelle convent for Croatian nuns outside Rome and other 'technicians' arrived to join them. All had been brought out of Germany by Lavic along similar routes. Finally the aviation experts boarded a DC4 Skymaster belonging to Perón's FAMA airline, making stopovers at Rome, Madrid, Casablanca, Dakar, Natal and Rio de Janeiro on the way to Buenos Aires. At the airport to receive them was August Siebrecht, a former Nazi spy whom Perón had befriended in the 1930s in Chile, who now formed part of the Argentine end of the rescue organization.[468]

Although Bohne had started out with Eyting's group, his euthanasia expertise was clearly less urgently required than the jet-building skills of his travelling companions. He was therefore not among the lucky few flying courtesy of Perón's airline. Instead, while the rest of the group took off from Rome, he was sent to Genoa, where he lodged with his younger sister Gisela at Via Dei Glicini 27. He already had possession of a Red Cross passport issued under his real name in Rome on 24 August 1948, barely a month after the Red Cross had awarded a passport to Priebke under the Pape alias. Like Priebke's, his application was sponsored by the Pontifical Commission of Assistance; in addition it was signed by Draganovic.[469]

Having been guided, presumably by Fuldner's organization, through the maze of Argentine paperwork necessary for a successful departure, Bohne and his sister were received at the Argentine consulate in Genoa on 7 January 1949 by diplomat Pedro Solari Capurro. The consul helped them fill out their Identification Certificate questionnaires, and proceeded to stamp visas on their passports. Strong outside influences were at work, for neither of the Bohnes could produce the mandatory Argentine landing permit or even an Immigration file number. They were granted permanent residence all the same.

Above the line 'Persons You Know in Argentina', in both cases the consul typed in: *Secretario Aeronáutico*, the Argentine air force commander-in-chief, Bartolomé de la Colina, one of the regular participants in Perón's Nazi meetings at the Casa Rosada.[470]

The formalities concluded, Bohne and his sister boarded the Italian liner *Ana C*, first class, arriving in Buenos Aires on 29 January 1949. On the ship's passenger list, Bohne declared 2484 Peña Street, fourth floor, apartment 'A', as his intended place of residence. This was the same address that the Berne police had discovered for Carlos Fuldner during their investigation of his activities in Switzerland a few months earlier. The 'coincidence' proves beyond doubt that Fuldner was involved in the rescue not only of German aeroplane 'technicians' but also of Nazis responsible for major crimes against humanity.[471]

'By chance I had made contact with an organization headed by a Catholic priest, in charge of the illegal transport to Argentina of the most diverse experts on behalf of that country's government,' Bohne himself related in 1959. 'I myself went to that country with the group of engineers sent for by the aeroplane builder, Professor Tank.'[472]

Bohne was not the only criminal connected to Aktion T4 to find refuge in Argentina. Shortly before him, on 19 November 1948, one of the earliest participants in Hitler's plan to improve the genetic makeup of Germany had arrived in Buenos Aires. Dr Hans Hefelmann followed the usual route employed by Fuldner to smuggle Nazis out of Germany. First he was taken to Austria, where the Catholic Church group Caritas International, which worked in close conjunction with the Argentine Immigration Office in these matters, took care of the paperwork for his trip. From there he continued to Genoa via the monastery route, his escape sponsored by Bishop Heinrich Wienken of Innsbruck. He arrived in Argentina, like Bohne, under his real name.

Hefelmann had been one of the main leaders of the ultra-secret Kanzlei des Führer (KdF), which acted publicly through 'The Reich Committee for the Scientific Registration of Serious Hereditary and

Genetically Based Diseases.' The committee set up a system whereby midwives were instructed to report all babies born with deformities or evidence of mental weakness and therefore considered unfit to live. Hefelmann eventually took charge of Section IIb, 'mercy killing', in Hitler's euthanasia programme, before civil resistance forced the Führer to cancel Aktion T4. 'Nazi leaders faced the prospect of either having to imprison prominent, highly admired clergymen and other protesters – a course with consequences in terms of adverse public reaction they greatly feared – or else end the programme,' Hefelmann testified during the trial against T4 medical division chief Werner Heyde in the 1960s.

Aktion T4's collapse left an opening for the SS to step into the mass killing business. 'If operation T4 had been entrusted to the SS, things would have happened differently,' Himmler boasted at the time, according to Hefelmann's testimony. 'When the Führer gives us a job, we know how to deal with it correctly, without causing pointless uproar among the people.'[473]

Like many other Nazis in Argentina, Bohne and Hefelmann returned to Germany when Perón was ousted by a military coup in 1955, fearful that they were unprotected without him. But they found that they had leapt from the frying pan into the fire: their crimes had not been forgotten at home, and they were both arraigned in the Frankfurt trials that were finally opened against the surviving T4 doctors and bureaucrats. Released on bail, Bohne took flight for Argentina again in 1963, this time employing a false passport in the name of Alfred Rudiger Kart. In Buenos Aires, he settled down to a cramped existence in a small apartment with his sister, who had become a nurse at the city's German Hospital.

But following Argentina's shameful refusal to extradite Josef Mengele in 1959 and the consequent kidnapping of Adolf Eichmann by Israel the following year, Bohne was fated to become the first Nazi criminal to be surrendered by Argentina. By the time of his arrest at his sister's apartment in 1964, he was a frail and prematurely old man in his early sixties.

Bohne's Argentine lawyer Juan Dollberg put up a peculiar fight against the extradition request, sending letters to the press denouncing international Communism and lamenting the 'dark night in history' when Argentina had broken off diplomatic relations with Hitler. In a last desperate act, he attempted to question the impartiality of one of the Supreme Court justices overseeing the extradition on the grounds that he had travelled to West Germany and 'sympathizes with the state of Israel'. Despite these startling legal tactics, on 11 November 1966 Bohne was finally bundled onto a plane bound for Germany. By all accounts he had himself become a likely candidate for Aktion T4. Half-blind, suffering from prostate cancer and a heart condition, he was declared unfit to stand trial, even though ten years later he was still living in Frankfurt on a state pension. Hefelmann benefited from the same ignominious verdict.[474]

19

JOSEF SCHWAMMBERGER

The number of landing permit applications initiated by Carlos Fuldner during his Nazi-rescue mission in Europe became so excessive that it finally embarrassed even the hardened officials at Immigration. Formally, only prospective immigrants themselves or relatives living in Argentina could present applications, and Fuldner had already amassed too many non-relatives under his signature. 'When Fuldner returned from Europe it was unsuitable for him to be handling landing permits for third parties for obvious reasons; so I suggested to him that he should find a way to solve this situation, otherwise he was putting me in a fix,' Immigration official José Bruhn related in 1949 during the secret inquest of immigration irregularities.

Fuldner decided to disguise his identity, choosing Vianord, a travel agency that had begun to apply for landing permits while he was still in Europe. Located in a shopping arcade in downtown Buenos Aires, Vianord was headed by a fellow Nazi fugitive, Swedish SS officer Hans-Caspar Krüger. To route his new applications through the travel agency, Fuldner became Carlos Brüner, adopting his mother's surname.

Fuldner often personally collected the landing permits for his applicants at the office of Immigration Commissioner Diana. 'Fuldner was an agent of the Information Bureau involved in secret official business with the knowledge of the commissioner, and in view of these facts the personnel in the commissioner's office had no inconvenience handing him the permits,' said Bruhn. During the 1949 inquest into the arrival of 'undesirable' Jews and Communists in Argentina, Fuldner himself confirmed that he used Vianord with Diana's agreement as a 'legal figure' for 'immigrants of certain characteristics' salvaged from Europe at Perón's behest.[475]

Vianord provided a complete service for its clients, from handling the paperwork at Immigration to obtaining sea and air tickets. A former German athlete from the 1936 Berlin Olympics named Grimm worked there, alongside a Danish accountant named Faber and a German female secretary named Ruthy Spielmann. In early 1951 they were joined by a young Swedish student whose family lived in Buenos Aires and who spent his summer vacations working there as an errand boy.

'There was a muted Nazi atmosphere,' recalled Ragnar Hagelin nearly five decades later. 'They kept files on everyone who had arrived and they were the ones who brought the largest number of people from Europe. Almost all of the arrivals found lodgings in the suburb of Florida, out past Vicente López. Nearly everybody who was called from Europe already had a house to stay in. They helped each other out in that respect.' Strangely for a travel agency, Vianord did not work with tourists.

Hagelin was also a singer at the Colón opera house in Buenos Aires, and one day he fell into a heated argument with his Nazi employers regarding the best language for the art. 'I said English was the language of poetry, French the language of love, Italian the tongue of angels and German the language of pigs.' Following the infelicitous remark, Olympic athlete Grimm slammed Hagelin against a wall of the agency. Not as strong but younger and nimbler, Hagelin managed to twist Grimm's arm, and the scuffle ended in a draw.

'Afterwards at the Swedish embassy I commented on the incident with a diplomat who had been a schoolmate of my father's back in Sweden,' Hagelin recalled.

'But didn't you know Vianord is a nest of Nazis?' the alarmed diplomat exclaimed.

Vianord's main business was with the steamship line owned by Perón's close friend Alberto Dodero, a businessman who accompanied Evita during her tour of Europe and who was rumoured to be the First Lady's lover. 'They used to send me cash in hand to collect boat tickets at the Dodero travel line there on the corner of Corrientes Avenue and Reconquista,' recalled Hagelin. 'I often bought aeroplane tickets for Vianord. Sometimes and with some distaste I had to go to Florida to home-deliver a ticket. That was my job. What I remember is that most of the Nazis and Fascists came out through Denmark and Sweden, and then embarked at the port of Vigo in Spain.'[476]

But can Vianord be tied to the rescue of Nazi war criminals? One small box of index cards escaped the attention of the document cleansers at Argentina's Immigration archive. Its contents prove that at least one SS officer guilty of crimes against humanity was rescued from the grip of justice by Fuldner through Vianord. Perilously jutting over the edge of a rickety shelf in the 'Fleas' section of the archive, this wooden box contains a register of politically sensitive landing permit applications. It apparently once formed part of the 'reserved' documentation kept in the private office of the Immigration commissioner, relating to applications 'initiated by personnel from the presidential Information Bureau', as Immigration official Bruhn revealed in the 1949 Diana Inquest.[477]

The information the cards hold is scanty, but they do state who presented each application and the corresponding file number. One card in particular, in favour of 'Barbara Weiss de Janko and others', shows that her entry was sponsored by Vianord, indubitably tying the agency to Perón's rescue team in Switzerland, as Swiss police records show that Weiss was Fuldner's secretary in Berne and that she had been spirited out of Austria by the former SS captain. She arrived in Buenos Aires in 1950 with 'deficient documentation', the usual situation for Fuldner's candidates.[478]

The records show that Vianord opened at least twelve Immigration files between mid-1948 and 1951, most of them collective applications for groups of individuals tied to Fuldner's rescue operation in Switzerland. The index cards show that four of these collective files were opened at Immigration in a rush after Fuldner's return from Europe, strongly suggesting that Perón's agent had arrived with a list of 'hot' Nazis requiring urgent attention. The travel agency had got off to a good start, as its first registered application, opened in mid-1948 when Fuldner was busily at work in Europe, resulted in the salvaging of one exceptionally despicable SS murderer.[479]

In 1933 Josef Schwammberger joined the Austrian Legion of the SS, the same unit Adolf Eichmann had originally enrolled in. Although he did not reach as high a position in the killing hierarchy as his erstwhile colleague, Schwammberger did prove his mettle as SS commander at three different camps in Poland, liquidating Jews at each one of them in turn.

His first post was the Rozwadow forced labour camp. Schwammberger arrived there in September 1942 brandishing a pistol and a horsewhip. The new commander received inmates personally, and demanded that they turn over all their valuables and money. Soup and bread at Schwammberger's camp arrived in a wheelbarrow which doubled as a cart on the way out to remove the bodies of those who had succumbed to typhus, dysentery or a Ukrainian guard's pistol. Although this was not a death camp in the specific sense, Jews died there by the hundred, many shot by Schwammberger's own hand.

In February 1943 Schwammberger took charge of another labour camp, marked out with barbed-wire fences from the Jewish ghetto at Przemysl. There he roamed the streets cracking his whip, randomly shooting anyone who happened to cross his path, in the company of Prinz, his black-haired German shepherd, which was trained to tear human flesh. One day he was seen in full SS uniform at the head of a group of Ukrainian guards leading a contingent of Jews. 'I heard machine guns and I understood what was going on,' recalled Przemysl survivor Arnold Suskind decades later. 'That time they killed about four hundred people.' Schwammberger himself admitted to the killings at Przemysl when the Austrian police arrested him after the war. 'I carried out executions of thirty-five individuals, shooting them in the back of the neck with a pistol from a range of about ten centimetres. If they showed any signs of life, I then shot them in the temple.' But the majority of the ghetto's population met a crueller fate. By the end of 1943 Schwammberger had dispatched the last trainload of Przemysl's Jews to Auschwitz, leaving the town 'Jew-free'.

In February 1944 Schwammberger took charge of a third Jewish community in the village of Mielec, where he was commander of a small camp providing slave labour for a Heinkel bomber factory. The Red Army was now winning the war, rapidly advancing through Polish territory and beating back the German forces. With the Russians less than a hundred miles away, Schwammberger still managed to cleanse Mielec of its centuries-old Jewish community. Only a handful of the several thousand Jews who lived there survived his command.

They managed to rid Poland of its Jews, but the Germans were less successful at winning the war. By late 1944 a mass of SS fugitives knew that surrender was not an option. The magnitude of the crimes committed by their organization made escape the only viable alternative. Schwammberger ran too, initially getting only as far as his home town of Innsbruck, where he was arrested by Austrian police on 20 July 1945. Hidden in the homes of his relatives and friends, police found eight sacks stuffed with gold, coins and jewellery, loot which he had extracted from his Jewish victims over the last three years. Schwammberger was then moved to a French camp for suspected war criminals.[480]

By early 1948 Schwammberger's situation was extremely uncomfortable. There was an extradition request from Poland hanging over him, and a prosecutor in Innsbruck ready to open proceedings against him. Perhaps because the American military authorities did not wish to hand him over to Communist judges, perhaps because Fuldner's organization had already taken him under his wing, perhaps a combination of the two, in January 1948 Schwammberger escaped France. He hid in Italy. Some accounts say he worked as a manual labourer in Florence, others erroneously state that he obtained a Red Cross passport.

The truth is that in mid-1948 Vianord applied for a landing permit in Schwammberger's real name from the Immigration Office in Buenos Aires and that on 29 February 1949, with this document in hand, he boarded the French liner *Campana* in Genoa, travelling third class. He arrived in Buenos Aires on 19 March, at 38 years of age, becoming one of the few war criminals to enter Argentina without the benefit of a Red Cross passport or an alias. He told the Argentine authorities he spoke only Italian and that he had been born in Bolsano, Italy, although he was actually born in nearby Bressanone when it was still Austrian territory before World War One. He stated his profession as 'mechanic', the same occupation declared upon arrival by fellow SS criminals Josef Mengele, Klaus Barbie and Eduard Roschmann.

Schwammberger's Immigration file 201430/48 had been opened in the name of 'H. Lechler and others', as the corresponding index card from the 'Fleas' wooden box shows. Although the file itself is among the secret Nazi documents that disappeared in 1996, matching the file numbers from the surviving passenger lists with these cards revealed that Schwammberger's number coincided with this particular collective application by Vianord. Even more incriminating is the fact that the immediately preceding landing permit applications, files 201429/48 and 201427/48, were initiated at Perón's own request by Freude's Information Bureau for two groups of Romanian fugitives. In other words, Schwammberger's landing permit was obtained by Fuldner under the cover of Vianord as part of a simultaneous presentation in favour of various other likely war criminals by the Casa Rosada itself. Over 50 years later, was the Argentine government aware enough of the fact to order the destruction of the evidence? Only the bonfire lit in 1996 prevents us from documenting further such correlations.[481]

20

JOSEF MENGELE

During his years of exile in Madrid Perón readily admitted his personal relationship with fugitive Nazi criminals to anyone who cared to ask. On the morning of 9 September 1970 he related to Argentine writer Tomás Eloy Martínez how, while he had been president in the 1950s, a German 'specialist in genetics' would visit his weekend Olivos residence, entertaining him with claims of amazing scientific discoveries. 'One day the man came to say goodbye because a Paraguayan rancher had hired him to improve his cattle,' Perón said candidly. 'They were going to pay him a fortune. He showed me photos of a stable he had around there near Tigre [a suburb of Buenos Aires] where all the cows gave birth to twins.'

The writer asked Perón if he remembered the name of the specialist.

'Who knows? He was one of those stiff-backed Bavarians, highly cultured, proud of his land. Wait a minute . . . If I'm not mistaken, he was called Gregor. That's it, Doctor Gregor.'

Never having heard the name before, Martínez filed away the tape of Perón's interview. It wasn't until 1985, when the news of Mengele's death in 1979 was revealed to the world, that he dug out the old recording and realized the full implication of Perón's words.

In the ensuing investigation into Mengele's postwar years it became evident that Perón had teased Martínez with genuine – if at the time unverifiable – information. The Red Cross would be forced to admit it had issued Mengele a passport in the name of Helmut Gregor, an alias he would continue to use in Argentina. The Auschwitz doctor had indeed been visiting Paraguay since at least 1951, a CIA document was to confirm. Perón's description of the subject also fitted the bill. Mengele came from an affluent family and was well received by the German community in Argentina. Among Perón's Nazi friends, the 'highly-cultured' doctor enjoyed a reputation as a 'brilliant man from an intellectual point of view'. And he was of course a stiff-backed SS officer who spoke with a distinctive Bavarian accent.[482]

The Perón–Gregor meetings were probably instigated by the Hitler-decorated Luftwaffe ace Hans-Ulrich Rudel, a man deeply involved in assisting fleeing Nazis. Until the moment of Mengele's death, Rudel was his secret protector in South America. Another friend of Rudel and Mengele connected to Perón was the Dutch war criminal Willem Sassen, a prominent member of the fugitive Nazi community, who was close to Adolf Eichmann as well. Sassen had started out as Rudel's chauffeur, driving a Mercedes-Benz that Perón put at Rudel's disposal. He later became himself a frequent visitor at the Casa Rosada.[483]

Other lesser-known but still important Nazis could be found at Perón's Olivos residence. For example, an SS officer was employed as a construction worker by the president. 'I was sitting on a small roof, it was about three and a half metres high, and Perón came by on a small motorcycle that I think was given to him as a gift from Italy,' remembered Herbert Habel, SS number 112171, decades later.

'Where is the architect?' asked Perón.

'The architect is not here. He left an hour ago,' replied Habel.

'But you are German,' Perón noticed. 'You are not Argentine.'

They spoke a while in German ('I must say that I understood him very well,' conceded Habel) and then in Spanish, a language that the former SS man spoke falteringly. 'I addressed him with my poor

Spanish as *Excelentísimo*. He asked me various things, where I was in the war and so on.'

'I must point out that we only entered the war pressured by the Yankees,' Perón felt obliged to apologize to the SS man.

Habel had been private secretary to August Eigruber, the wartime Gauleiter (district leader) of Linz, who was tried and executed in 1949 at Landsberg Prison for war crimes connected with the Mauthausen concentration camp. Eigruber had been involved in looting art works, some of which were never recovered, and in 1944 he tried to blow up underground galleries of treasures amassed by the Nazis in Austria. Habel himself admitted shortly before his death in 1999 to having participated in the delivery of a shipment of looted Hungarian gold in Linz. At the end of the war he had escaped from Austria to France, and then to Spain. He arrived in Argentina in 1950 under the alias Kurz Repa.

'*Excelentísimo*, I have a problem with my name. I've already given out several hundred dollars [in bribes] and nothing is working. I want to have my real name back,' Habel said to Perón.

'No problem at all. Call my secretary and tell him that I sent you and he'll take care of this matter as fast as possible.'

And so it was. Habel visited the Casa Rosada, where a certain Martínez ('he spoke perfect German') wrote out a letter of recommendation for a judge who handled citizenship applications. 'With this paper I went to the Palace of Justice to this judge. Immediately he heard my case and issued a court order. In a few minutes I'd settled it.' The former SS man was ecstatic. He wanted to know how much he owed. 'Nothing at all,' said the judge. 'If you were sent by Perón, then it costs nothing.'

Habel's proximity to Perón may not have been totally coincidental. The SS officer was connected to Franz Ruffinengo and to Reinhard Kops, two of the prime movers in Perón's Nazi rescue team. The construction firm he worked for belonged to Perón's close friend, Colonel Domingo Mercante. Habel also knew Eichmann during the time the arch-criminal worked for Carlos Fuldner's CAPRI in the early 1950s. He had even asked Eichmann how many Jews he believed had been exterminated by the Third Reich. 'I don't know how many died – half a million maximum,' Habel claimed Eichmann told him.[484]

On 17 January 1945 Mengele collected the records of his experimentation on twins, cripples and dwarfs at the Auschwitz death camp, loaded the papers and blood samples into a waiting car and began his long flight from justice. Behind him he left the countless acts of criminal cruelty that would give him a unique status among Nazi murderers. Placed in charge of the women's camp at adjoining Birkenau when he arrived at the Auschwitz complex from the Russian front in 1943, Mengele had dealt with food shortages or typhus breakouts by sending up to 4,000 women a day to their deaths.

In the camp, Mengele was known as 'the chief provider for the gas chamber and the ovens', principally because of his icy demeanour at the Auschwitz train selections, where SS doctors would examine new arrivals descending from the goods wagons and either point them straight to the gas chamber or save them for slave labour. Unlike other SS doctors who had to get drunk to carry out their inhuman assignment, Mengele was always sober, cool and cynical, always impeccable in his SS uniform. Often he would whistle operatic airs while he divided the queue of victims, pointing with his cane, right, left, death or death-in-life.

Sometimes he would run up and down the queues shouting 'Twins! Twins! Twins!' – selecting human guinea pigs for his brutal pseudo-scientific experiments. According to the German indictment prepared against him in 1981, when he was still believed to be alive, Mengele sought to attain a 'medically manipulated increase in the number of births of twins' to double the birth rate of Aryan children for Hitler. Other Mengele experiments included injecting the eyes of children with dyes to see whether he could turn them Aryan blue. After the tests, the children were sent to the gas chamber. Mengele displayed samples of eyes, from pale yellow to bright blue, on the wall. 'They were pinned up like butterflies,' said one

Auschwitz survivor. 'I thought I was dead and already living in hell.'

Shedding his SS uniform, Mengele adopted the disguise of a regular German army doctor and joined a retreating military unit. His notes he entrusted to a nurse he struck up a relationship with. As the unit fled from the advancing Soviet troops, Mengele's name began cropping up as one of the most wanted Nazi war criminals. Its earliest recorded entry in an Allied list was in April 1945. By May the United Nations War Crimes Commission wanted him for 'mass murder and other crimes'. Reports of the atrocities he had committed starting being broadcast over Allied radio.

Some time around June, his unit was arrested by US troops in the German town of Weiden. The nurse carrying his precious notes was also arrested but soon released. Although he was registered under his real name at the detention camp, the Americans failed to identify him as a wanted war criminal, or even as an SS man, simply because Mengele had refused to have his blood group tattooed on his arm or chest like other officers when he joined the SS in 1938. This didn't mean that he wasn't being hunted – on 11 June 1945 three American military policemen had shown up at the doorstep of his wife Irene in Autenreid demanding to know his whereabouts.

In September, Mengele was released by the US army in his native Bavaria. While in the prison camp, he had obtained an Allied release document made out in the name of a fellow doctor, Fritz Ulman, which he altered to read Fritz Hollmann. With it he travelled back into the Russian-occupied zone of Germany, located the nurse to whom he had entrusted his notes and specimens, and then withdrew to Munich, where he hid in the home of friends.

By October 1945 Mengele had found employment at a small farm in Mangolding, Bavaria. There he would live undisturbed as a farmhand for three years while the press published reports of his heinous crimes, and his name came up in the trials at Nuremberg. But even though Mengele was able to evade the real arm of the law, in his head a mock trial kept repeating itself over and over again. Like Pierre Daye, who sat alone in a hotel room in Madrid jotting down brilliant justifications for his collaboration with the Nazis, Mengele kept a diary, in which he became his own star witness for the defence.[485]

Some time around April 1948 Mengele began preparing his escape to Argentina. As with the other major German war criminals, his travel papers were arranged while Fuldner was in Europe rescuing wanted Nazis. (Before this, no adequate infrastructure had yet been put in place to save the biggest fish, who remained in hiding for several years after the war.) Mengele was in the hands of professionals at this point. Instead of a fudged name on a borrowed document, the Auschwitz doctor was now to be equipped with a whole new fake identity. The method employed was to pass him off as an ethnic German from the Alto Adige in northern Italy. Interestingly, Bishop Alois Hudal in Rome had taken up the case of incriminated SS officers in northern Italy with Cardinal Montini, who viewed their case with sympathy. During the postwar period Hudal maintained a voluminous correspondence with these men, arranging for many to leave for Argentina. American intelligence knew that incriminated 'Nazi Germans' were crossing the border into Italy. A 1947 report claimed they went 'via Treviso and Milan for the sole purpose of obtaining false identity documents . . . re-entering legally the British, French or American Occupation Zones'.[486]

This was precisely the method employed by Mengele and Eichmann to procure false identities for their subsequent passage to Argentina. Between April and June 1948 these two SS criminals were issued IDs by the commune of Termeno. Through Carta d'Identità No. 114, Mengele became Helmut Gregor, while Carta No. 131 turned Eichmann into Riccardo Klement. A third war criminal who ended up in Argentina, the high-ranking functionary of Goebbels' Propaganda Ministry, Erich Müller, was issued Carta d'Identità No. 111, under the alias Francesco Noelke.[487]

Under the quasi-legal aliases afforded by these IDs, Mengele, Eichmann and Müller applied for and promptly obtained Argentine landing permits within a few weeks of each other. Their applications were almost certainly routed by Fuldner's DAIE office in Genoa to the Immigration Office in Buenos Aires. This flurry of applications, including other SS officers such as Erich Priebke and Josef Schwammberger, favoured a tight pack of Nazi criminals whose Argentine papers were processed almost simultaneously in mid-1948.[488]

It's likely that Mengele paid dear for his Argentine landing permit, but money was not something his family lacked. The Günzburg area of Bavaria had been home to the Mengele agricultural machinery firm since the start of the century. His father Karl had been a Nazi party member and had even hosted a visit by Hitler to his factory in 1932. In the postwar period, despite having to endure a protracted 'denazification' process by the Allies, Karl Mengele's business prospered. Soon he was entering into ventures overseas, including Argentina, the country where his son would find sanctuary.

On 7 September 1948 the news arrived that Helmut Gregor's landing permit had been approved by Buenos Aires. Mengele disappeared from Mangolding without even saying goodbye to his employers. Returning to his home town of Günzburg, he spent the next few months hiding in the nearby forests, attempting – and failing – to convince his wife Irene to follow him to Argentina with their son Rolf.

In April 1949 Mengele set out alone, abandoning Germany. His flight through Austria to Italy was apparently arranged and paid for by his father through SS contacts in the Günzburg area. The arrangements involved clandestine border crossings, exchanged code words and forged travel documents. Mengele finally arrived at the northern Italian town of Vipiteno, the same Alto Adige locality that had sheltered Erich Priebke the year before. There he had an advance booking at the Golden Cross Inn under his Fritz Hollmann alias. A messenger from the family firm brought him money and a 'small suitcase' containing his Auschwitz notes and blood specimens, tucked tightly between small plates.

After about a month he moved on to Bolzano, where he was met by a clandestine agent identified only as 'Kurt' in the diary he kept of his journey. 'Kurt' had Croatian contacts, access to the Red Cross and the Argentine consulate, in fact, all the attributes of being connected to Perón's DAIE or to one of the Catholic priests assisting fugitive Nazis. The mysterious man had booked Mengele a passage on the *North King*, a ship due to sail for Argentina on 25 May 1949.

Mengele's first stop, on 16 May, was the office of the Red Cross in Genoa to procure a valid passport. This 'Kurt' arranged with no difficulty. Mengele was well armed with his Argentine landing permit and his Termeno ID, the same combination of misleading documents that would allow Eichmann and Müller to obtain Red Cross passports of their own a year later. The next stop the following day was the Argentine consulate for an entry visa. Mengele arrived with a forged vaccination certificate provided by a Croatian doctor. Still, the punctilious Argentine diplomats noticed that the Red Cross had mistakenly written the issue date of Gregor's passport on the line reserved for the expiration date, so that it was technically invalid. Returning with an amended document, Mengele now discovered that he still had to submit to a mandatory medical examination at the DAIE office at Via Albaro 38. The sanitary conditions the Argentine doctors worked under left even the Auschwitz doctor dumbfounded. 'They were looking for trachoma cases using the same glass rod and the same unwashed hands,' Mengele wrote in his diary. 'If one did not have a contagious disease before the examination, one most probably had it after.'

The only real hitch occurred when he tried to obtain an Italian exit visa. Unfortunately for Mengele, the Italian official usually bribed by 'Kurt' was absent on holiday. When Mengele slipped a 20,000 lira note between his documents and handed them to the Italian official on duty, instead of receiving the visa he expected, he was thrown into a gaol cell. After a few uncomfortable nights Mengele was rescued by 'Kurt', who had finally returned to the city. The Genoa police suddenly became apologetic. They asked Mengele if he was perhaps a Jew. Shaken but still in one piece, Mengele managed to board the *North King* on schedule on 25 May. 'Waves, all is waves,' the doctor mused as the Italian coastline receded from view.[489]

The *North King* docked at Buenos Aires port on 22 June 1949, after a crossing that lasted four weeks. Argentina's Immigration officials were puzzled by the medical papers and specimens Helmut Gregor was bringing into the country. 'They are biological notes,' Mengele truthfully affirmed. The port doctor was called in to examine the decidedly grim contents of the suitcase but, not understanding German, he finally waved Mengele through. Strangely, it failed to puzzle the official that a 'technical mechanic' – as Gregor figured in his passport and on the ship's passenger list – should have possession of such material. A doctor that Mengele had met once in 1939, referred to in his diary as 'Rolf Nuckert', failed to turn up to receive him. With a couple of Italians he had befriended on board, Mengele checked in at the seedy Palermo Hotel in downtown Buenos Aires. The decidedly run-down room emphasized the gloomy reception Argentina had given him.[490]

Things did not pick up when he paid a visit to a member of the millionaire Schlottmann family, the German owners of the giant Sedalana textile firm who had financed Carlos Schulz's Nazi rescue mission in Scandinavia. Mengele was offered a job as a shop-floor worker, an indignity he was not willing to accept. After sharing a windowless room for a few short weeks in a boarding house in the Vicente López suburb of Buenos Aires, his life took a turn for the better when he was invited to stay at the stylish pillared home of Gerard Malbranc, a German-Argentine suspected of wartime Nazi activities in Argentina, at 2460 Arenales Street in the Florida suburb.

Soon Mengele was being introduced to the cream of the Nazi community in Argentina. Among the first to approach him was fellow SS officer Willem Sassen. Next came Rudel, Sassen's associate and a close friend of Perón. Rudel had escaped to Argentina with the help of certain 'gentlemen' who guided him through Switzerland to Italy. He arrived in Buenos Aires on a flight from Rome on 8 June 1948 bearing a Red Cross passport made out in the name of Emilio Meier. 'We were given all the help it is possible to imagine,' Rudel wrote in his memoirs. Nominally in the pay of Argentina's National Institute of Aeronautics, the war pilot took a public role at the magazine *Der Weg*, hobnobbing with Perón and writing bestselling books relating his wartime exploits. He very quickly became a rich man, thanks to special import licences and other government contracts awarded him by Perón.[491]

In the 1970s and 1980s Rudel and Sassen were involved with a host of unsavoury South American dictators, either selling arms to or acting as advisers for Alfredo Stroessner of Paraguay, Augusto Pinochet of Chile and the 'Cocaine Generals' in Bolivia. According to one testimony, Sassen even sold arms to Argentina's General Leopoldo Galtieri, who invaded the Falkland Islands in 1982. Rudel in particular worked in the world of high finance, as a roving ambassador in South America for several German firms, including Siemens. In 1973 he acted as go-between for Perón and Stroessner in thorny negotiations for a multi-billion-dollar hydroelectric dam to be built on the border between Argentina and Paraguay. Among the bidders for the Yacyretá complex, the largest project of its kind in the world, was a consortium that included the German firm Lahmeyer. According to an Argentine police report, the company was represented in Argentina by Fuldner, who after his experience in water projects at CAPRI became a leading player in the field. Rudel was called in as a South American 'lobbyist' on Lahmeyer's behalf. After meeting with Perón in Madrid, he flew to Paraguay for a long private session with Stroessner, emerging with the Paraguayan dictator's approval for the desired contract.[492]

Even during Argentina's 1976/83 military dictatorship, Rudel still had influence. When the son of a Lahmeyer associate's friend ran the risk of being 'disappeared' by the bloody regime, Rudel was asked to use his influence to save the young man's life. 'The only chance was to get the boy out to Paraguay, and the only person I knew with contacts in Paraguay was Rudel,' Lahmeyer associate Jorge Carretoni recalled for this book. 'Rudel of course detested the Montoneros [the guerrilla group the youth belonged to] so I ran the risk he would refuse to help, but I knew his sense of honour would not allow him to betray the boy to the authorities.' To Carretoni's relief, Rudel arranged the escape at both the Argentine and Paraguayan ends.

Rudel asked Carretoni to await his arrival at Buenos Aires airport. 'If I come off the plane holding an umbrella, bring the boy to me; if I don't, leave,' were Rudel's instructions. The Luftwaffe hero appeared with an umbrella and in a matter of moments the young man was flying to Paraguay under his care. 'Rudel had even arranged for airport officials to let him through on a borrowed passport,' Carretoni recalled. 'Good photo,' the Argentine Immigration official winked at the young man.[493]

In the early 1950s, Rudel and Mengele began to realize South America's potential as a market for the Mengele firm's products. In 1953 or 1954, Mengele's father travelled to Argentina for a series of meetings with local businessmen, meetings at which he was accompanied by his 'interpreter', Helmut Gregor. A close alliance was made with Roberto Mertig, a German businessman who had made a fortune manufacturing (of all things) gas appliances. A member of the Nazi party in charge of wartime propaganda activities in Argentina, Mertig had founded his firm, Orbis, in 1942, after representing a German gas appliances manufacturer for a number of years. He was also the wartime representative of the Junkers aircraft firm. British intelligence even suspected him of attempting to manufacture two Junkers at his factory with the help of the German embassy in Buenos Aires. After the war Mertig threw himself with some enthusiasm into sending food packages to war-torn Germany and providing employment to new arrivals in Argentina. The 350 employees at Orbis included reportedly not a single Argentine in the postwar era. Employment was provided instead to deserving workers such as Mengele and Eichmann.[494]

'Mengele [Karl] told me he had liked Argentina a lot and that he wished to invest some capital in the country,' Mertig told Argentina's police in a carefully prepared statement in 1960, after Josef Mengele had escaped to Paraguay. To Mertig, the Auschwitz doctor was not a war criminal, simply a man who, in Argentina, was finally able to 'no longer feel persecuted by the Communists'. Mertig soon became both Josef Mengele's 'closest friend' and Karl Mengele's most trusted business contact in Argentina.[495]

Employed at Orbis and supported by his father, not even Perón's downfall managed to shake Mengele's confidence. In 1956 the doctor applied for and received a passport in his real name from the German embassy in Buenos Aires. Years later, the ambassador at the time, Werner Junkers, disclaimed any responsibility, stating: 'I didn't know who Mengele was.' (Historians were able to determine who Junkers was, however: a former Nazi party member, senior aide to Hitler's foreign minister Ribbentrop, and a German representative to the murderous Croatian regime from 1944 to 1945.)

In 1958 Mengele was joined in Argentina by his sister-in-law Martha, the widow of his younger brother Karl, whom Mengele would marry after being divorced by his first wife. Now he began to feel increasingly secure, buying a house at 970 Virrey Vertiz Street in the suburb of Olivos, just behind the presidential palace. Bankrolled by his father, Mengele next went into partnership with acquaintances of Mertig, setting up the Fadro-Farm pharmaceutical company. He continued to travel around South America, selling Mengele agricultural machinery and meeting with other fugitive Nazis. In February 1957 he travelled to Chile with Rudel to meet with Walter Rauff, the SS colonel who had invented the mobile gas van used for the murder of nearly 100,000 Jews, Russians and partisans in the early years of the war.

It was a blow for Mengele when in 1959 a combination of factors brought his prolonged stay in Argentina to an end. First of all, the military regime that ousted Perón, which had formerly applied a 'hands off' policy to the Nazis in Argentina, handed over government to elected officials. The sympathy of the country's rulers could therefore no longer be counted on. Meanwhile in Germany the courts had begun compiling evidence of his crimes and were working towards an extradition request, as his family in Günzburg learned from sympathetic German police officials. Mengele was also badly shaken after being arrested by the Argentine police along with a group of unlicensed doctors, on false charges of running a backstreet abortion clinic. He was able to have the charges dropped by paying the police a bribe, but his confidence in Argentina as a safe haven was completely undermined. The death of his father had also upset him badly.

Roberto Mertig had been at Karl Mengele's deathbed in Germany in 1959. 'With tears in his eyes he asked me to look after his relatives in Argentina as he feared he would never see them again,' Mertig told the Argentine police in 1960.

Mengele suddenly sold his share in Fadro-Farm, ended his marriage and moved to Paraguay. He made the right choice in leaving, for only a few months later Germany requested his extradition from Buenos Aires. When secret Israeli commandos abducted Adolf Eichmann from Argentina in 1960, Mengele's fate was sealed. From now on he would spend every remaining moment of his life looking over his shoulder. Protected till the end by Rudel, who still visited him occasionally, he lived on for almost another 20 years, descending ever lower into depression and anonymity, first in Paraguay and later in Brazil.

In 1977, Mengele's son Rolf flew from Germany to Brazil to see his father for the first time in 21 years. A product of the 1960s, Rolf questioned him at length about Auschwitz. Mengele remained unrepentant. 'He said he didn't invent Auschwitz. It already existed,' Rolf would relate after his father's death. 'His job had been to classify only those able to work and those unable to work . . . He said that he did not order and was not responsible for gassings. And he said that twins in the camp owed their lives to him.' Mengele died by drowning, while swimming at a beach called Betrioga, near Sao Paulo, on 7 February 1979.[496]

21

ADOLF EICHMANN

The most notorious Nazi to gain refuge in Argentina was Adolf Eichmann, organizer of the deportation of millions of Jews to Hitler's concentration camps. Practically the last major war criminal to arrive through Perón's Odessa-like organization, he received its full protection, under the direct care of Carlos Fuldner. Although he didn't leave for Argentina until mid-1950, Eichmann's landing permit had been applied for in 1948, while Fuldner was in Europe, less than a month after the simultaneous Priebke and Mengele applications, and only two months after Schwammberger requested entry to Argentina.

When Israeli agents kidnapped Eichmann in 1960, holding him in a secret location outside Buenos Aires, a group of young Peronists attempted to retrieve him from the hands of justice. These young men combed the streets of Buenos Aires in their motorbikes searching for clues to Eichmann's whereabouts, giving up their search only when Israel announced to the world that the arch-criminal was safely behind bars in Jerusalem.

Priebke enjoyed 50 years of freedom after Hitler's defeat, and Mengele 34, but Eichmann survived the demise of the Third Reich by a relatively brief 15 years before he was captured. His fate came as no surprise to the executor of the Holocaust, who had known even

during the war that there would be no escaping responsibility for the
unspeakable crimes he had committed.

In late August 1944, while in Budapest rounding up Hungary's Jews
for extermination, Eichmann confessed his deepest fear to the
Ausland-SD's local representative, Wilhelm Hoettl. A close collabo-
rator of Walter Schellenberg, Hoettl ran a network of Nazi agents in
Hungary, Romania and deep behind Russian lines. He and Eichmann
had first met in Vienna in 1938, when Eichmann set up his 'Central
Office for Jewish Emigration' in the usurped palace of Jewish banker
Louis von Rothschild.

A historian by vocation, who became a prime witness at Nuremberg
after the war, Hoettl later recalled how Eichmann had been badly
shaken by Romania's recent pullout from the Axis. 'Eichmann came
to see me,' Hoettl testified in 1961 for Eichmann's trial in Jerusalem.
'He was wearing battledress, i.e., not his dress uniform which he had
worn on his other visits to me. He gave an impression of being very
nervous, and this became even more marked when I told him about
the disastrous situation on the German front. Doubtless I, too, was
very dejected at the time, because I was afraid that there was nothing
that could stop the Russian advance through Hungary to my native
Austria. Eichmann then swallowed several glasses of brandy, one after
the other. As far as I remember, I set a bottle of arrack down with a
glass, so he could help himself.'

During an hour of conversation Eichmann downed four or five
brandies, enough for Hoettl to suggest he should not drive when he
left. Eichmann stood up and said: 'We shall probably never see each
other again.' Hoettl reacted with surprise. 'Then apparently he felt
obliged to explain this pessimistic attitude and indicated that he
was convinced that, with the German defeat, which was now to be
expected, he stood no chance any more. When I asked him why he
thought this, Eichmann said that, in view of his role in the programme to exterminate the Jews, he was considered by the Allies to
be a top war criminal. When he made this comment, I immediately
grasped the opportunity to say that I had always wanted to hear

reliable information about the extermination programme, and particularly about the number of Jews exterminated.'

It was this conversation that provided the conventionally accepted number of Holocaust victims, a figure first stated by Hoettl at Nuremberg. 'He said that the number of murdered Jews was a very great Reich secret, but with the situation in which he, Eichmann, found himself today, he still could tell me something about it, particularly since I was a historian. Eichmann then told me that, according to his information, some six million Jews had perished until then, four million in extermination camps and the remaining two million through shooting by the Operations Units and other causes, such as disease, etc.'[497]

Interestingly enough, two future members of Perón's Nazi rescue organization crossed paths with Eichmann in Budapest during 1944. And strangely, both these men seem to have played a kind of role in saving the lives of a small number of Hungarian Jews from among the hundreds of thousands that Eichmann rounded up for deportation to Auschwitz. 'The Croatian ambassador in Budapest, Dr Benzon,' provided 'several dozen passports' for Jews desiring to escape, Hoettl declared in 1961. Hoettl claimed he was able to convince sympathetic Hungarian officials to stamp exit visas on these passports. The Croatian ambassador providing the service was in fact Branko Benzon, the same cardiologist who would arrive in Buenos Aires two years later.

The second future Nazi-rescuer who seems to have dealt in Jewish lives in Budapest was Reinhard Kops, the Nazi spy who later, until mid-1948, served as the link between Bishop Alois Hudal and Fuldner's DAIE office in Genoa. In a rather fanciful declaration he spontaneously made before Argentine police in 1993, when he became scared of being trapped by Nazi-hunters, Kops claimed he had helped 25 Jews destined for Auschwitz to escape from Budapest by extending them false papers identifying them as members of his intelligence unit.

But since, as we have seen, Benzon became well known for turning down landing permit applications by Jews while serving as Immigration adviser to Perón, it can hardly be taken for granted that his actions in favour of Jews in Budapest were disinterested. Kops, who ran a neo-Nazi publishing enterprise from Bariloche into the 1990s, also seems an unlikely candidate for selfless conduct.[498]

Eichmann's office for 'Jewish Affairs' fed the furnaces for the industrial extermination of the Jews by arranging their registration, roundup and deportation to Hitler's concentration camps in German-occupied Europe. 'Jewish Affairs' was a division of Office IV of the Reich Security Main Office, the dreaded Gestapo headed by Heinrich Müller. The orders to local Gestapo and SD chiefs who carried out the deportations were signed at various times by SS leader Heinrich Himmler, Reich Security Main Office chief Ernst Kaltenbrunner and 'Gestapo' Müller. Eichmann also signed these orders and in some cases travelled personally to conduct the roundup operations, as he did in Austria and Hungary. In other cases, for example France and Italy, he acted through representatives. He also worked with local government officials to herd the Jews into ghettos, seize their assets and force them to accept resettlement in 'the East', which in reality meant transfer to death camps such as Auschwitz and Treblinka. From his Berlin office, Eichmann coordinated a vast array of SS units and train schedules transporting streams of humanity to certain death, a business he conducted with scrupulous dedication and bureaucratic single-mindedness.

Among his fellow SS chiefs, this kind of diligence was going out of fashion by 1945, as they were more concerned about scoring bonus points with the advancing Allies or hoarding assets in neutral countries (for example, the SS chiefs in Berlin began devising complicated Jews-for-cash deals, such as the one that SD chief Walter Schellenberg and Himmler negotiated in early 1945 with former Swiss president Jean-Marie Musy, in an almost naïve attempt to reverse the bad 'propaganda', as they termed it, that Hitler's racial policy had created).[499]

When Eichmann left Budapest on Christmas Eve 1944, having supervised the extermination of some half a million Hungarian Jews, his job description had for all practical purposes become obsolete. Against this cataclysmic backdrop, Eichmann was entrusted his final assignment; ironically enough, it involved saving Jews this time. 'Himmler told me that he intended to negotiate with Eisenhower and wished me to immediately take one hundred, two hundred, in any case all of the prominent Jews, from Theresienstadt to safety in Tyrol, so that he could use them as hostages in his negotiations.' But once in Tyrol the local Nazi boss would not even receive Eichmann, who decided to turn to Kaltenbrunner for help. 'In Alt Aussee I reported to Kaltenbrunner, but the whole matter no longer interested him.'[500]

In Austria, Eichmann again ran into Hoettl, whom he had not seen since Budapest. 'The last time I saw Eichmann was on 6 or 7 May 1945,' Hoettl recalled in 1961. Hoettl was a witness to the deep discomfort the mere mention of Eichmann's name provoked among Nazi leaders by this time. 'In the middle of the talk we were having, in which I was not mincing my words, Kaltenbrunner's adjutant came in, an SS Colonel Scheidler, and informed his chief that Eichmann had come to take his leave. Dr Kaltenbrunner made it quite clear to Scheidler that he had no intention of receiving Eichmann, and he also said to me that he considered that this man no longer stood any chance. When I left Kaltenbrunner, I met Eichmann, with some of his people, whom I did not know personally, at the so-called Donner Bridge in Alt Aussee. Eichmann complained bitterly to me about Kaltenbrunner's faithlessness.' Kaltenbrunner and his cohorts did not want 'this apocalyptic memento of their own sins' anywhere near them. 'Somehow the air became cleaner when he left,' Hoettl recalled.[501]

Eichmann was therefore dispatched to set up a resistance force in the mountains. Horia Sima, head of the deposed Romanian government, joined him. A group of SS and Hitler Youth troops rounded out Eichmann's unit. Their assignment lasted only a few days, until orders came from Himmler to cease firing on British and American soldiers. The war had ended. The once monolithic Nazi machinery had shattered into a million pieces. Accustomed to the schematic, regimented world of the SS, Eichmann felt completely lost. Realizing 'no orders or directives would come from anywhere', he fell apart. 'I lost my zest for life . . . Many others also experienced the same thing at the time, they had fought, worked, worried and feared for the Reich and now it was collapsing. The will to live was no longer there.'

Things got even worse when the former commandant of the Theresienstadt concentration camp came to inform Eichmann that he was being hunted as a war criminal, and begged him to leave lest his presence put the rest of them in danger. Eichmann bade farewell to his wife and children, leaving them a supply of poison capsules. 'If the Russians come, you must bite them; if the Americans or the British come, then you needn't.'[502]

It was only a matter of days before Eichmann was picked up by an American patrol and became one of the 3 million German prisoners in American hands. He faked his identity, becoming Otto Eckmann, and lay low at Oberdachstetten camp until 3 January 1946, when his close aide and trusted friend Dieter Wisliceny, who had worked with him in Greece, Slovakia and Hungary, testified at Nuremberg. It was Wisliceny who identified Eichmann to the world as the Nazi official in charge of 'the extermination and destruction of the Jewish race'. Wisliceny said he had last seen Eichmann in February 1945 in Berlin, when Eichmann had been contemplating suicide if Germany lost the war. 'He said he would leap laughing into the grave because the feeling that he had five million people on his conscience would be, for him, a source of extraordinary satisfaction,' Wisliceny told the court. Understandably, it was a quote that went around the world and that sealed Eichmann's fate for ever.[503]

Two days later Eichmann escaped from the American camp. He was now alone in the world. His superior Kaltenbrunner had been reduced to a broken man who could barely answer the questions put to him by his interrogators at Nuremberg. Himmler was dead, having swallowed a cyanide capsule after being arrested by British troops. Müller had vanished, never to be seen or heard from again. With the help of SS comrades, Eichmann hid in Prien in southern Germany for a while, fleeing later to Eversen, a little town near Bremen in British-occupied northern Germany, where he worked felling trees and raising chickens. During these years Nazi-hunter Simon Wiesenthal did his best to track him down, visiting Eichmann's parents and his wife in Linz. Wiesenthal needed at least a picture of the camera-shy SS officer, which he obtained by sending Romeo agents to seduce his former mistresses. But information of his exact whereabouts proved more elusive.[504]

Hiding out in Eversen, Eichmann realized how futile it had been to hope that with the passage of time his crimes would be forgotten. 'In the press, on the radio and in books my name was being constantly mentioned,' he would later recall. Around this time he seems to have come into contact with Perón's Nazi rescue team. 'I heard of the existence of some organizations which had helped others leave Germany. In early 1950 I established contact with one of these organizations.' In the spring he packed his bags and headed clandestinely for Italy with three companions, aided by the organization. They crossed the border into Austria without a hitch, but in the Austrian–Italian Alps two of the group were captured. Eichmann and his single companion now continued south. 'A Franciscan monk in Genoa extended me a passport for refugees made out in the name of Riccardo Klement together with a visa for Argentina,' he said.[505]

Eichmann's sudden departure from Germany in 1950 may have had a very simple explanation. Argentine landing permits were valid for only two years, and his application had been made in 1948. After their expiry the complicated business of renewal had to be started all over again. Eichmann's admission into Argentina was on the point of expiry. He was waiting for his crimes to be forgotten, but they hadn't been. It was time to move on.[506]

The evidence now available shows that Eichmann's passport application at the Red Cross office in Genoa on 1 June 1950 was indeed signed by a Franciscan priest. This was the same Father Edoardo Dömöter who, from his church of San Antonio in Genoa Pegli, had worked with Reinhard Kops before Kops left for Argentina. Dömöter was in turn aided in his task by Kops' boss, Bishop Hudal, who provided him with papers for fleeing Nazis. In August 1949, for example, Dömöter wrote to Hudal asking for a visa, 'it doesn't matter in whose name', for 'a German personality worthy of aid'. Hudal was only too glad to provide one. Eichmann was able to pass himself off to the Red Cross as Riccardo Klement thanks to Italian identity card No. 131, issued by the commune of Termeno in northern Italy on 2 June 1948. Other important war criminals, including Mengele, received Termeno ID cards around the same time.[507]

Although the Dömöter connection remained unknown until now, Bishop Hudal's probable contribution to Eichmann's escape was first disclosed in an article written in 1961 by Simon Wiesenthal. Hudal practically confirmed his participation in a subsequent interview. 'I'm a priest, not a policeman,' he told *Vita*, an Italian Catholic weekly. 'My mission as a Christian during those difficult years was to save anybody who could be saved and to help people without the means to leave Rome, where they would have been in danger. I can't confirm or deny whether Eichmann was among those refugees, because none of them revealed to me their past during the Third Reich and because at that time there were no photographs of them.' Hudal admitted having aided over 40 Germans who sought him out at his Santa Maria dell'Anima church. 'All of them declared they were being pursued by the Soviets as anti-Communists and that their lives were in danger.'[508]

When applying for his Red Cross passport Eichmann was able to show the landing permit issued to him under Argentine Immigration file 231489/48. He then proceeded to the Argentine consulate, where on 14 June his Red Cross passport was stamped with a 'permanent' visa and he was issued the mandatory 'identification certificate' he would need to obtain a valid ID from the police in Buenos Aires. Three days later, presumably after his medical inspection by the DAIE, Eichmann boarded the *Giovanna C* steamship for Buenos Aires. A photograph of him on deck with two companions, smiling, under a hat, and sporting a bow tie, showed him relieved to be on his way. On 14 July 1950 he disembarked at the port of Buenos Aires.

'Profession?' the Immigration clerk asked.

'Technician,' Eichmann replied.[509]

With him on the same ship apparently came SS Captain Herbert

Kuhlmann, a former commander of the legendary Hitler Youth Panzer Division. Kuhlmann had served in this unit with one of Hitler's most trusted officers, SS Brigadier Wilhelm Mohnke, a fellow Knight's Cross holder and commander of Hitler's bunker in Berlin, who accompanied the Führer up to the moment of his suicide. In Argentina, Kuhlmann became Pedro Geller, a German businessman with a shadowy past who quickly began living the life of a millionaire. Eichmann, who claimed to have paid Kuhlmann's fare over, instead found himself rapidly descending the social ladder. A deep enmity arose between the two former comrades as the gap widened. 'Imagine, Klement is really that pig Eichmann!' Kuhlmann announced everywhere.[510]

The ubiquitous Fuldner found Eichmann lodgings in Florida, the suburb where Vianord arrivals habitually ended up. On 3 August, Eichmann used the 'identification certificate' issued to him by the consulate in Genoa to apply for an Argentine identity card, presenting the mandatory photograph and having his fingerprints taken, a ceremony repeated at the Registry of Foreign Persons. On 2 October he received ID number 1,378,538 from the Buenos Aires provincial police, in the name of Riccardo Klement. The identity-transformation was now complete.[511]

Fuldner not only found lodgings and obtained Argentine IDs for Eichmann and Kuhlmann, he also gave them jobs. The two SS officers were promptly whisked off to the faraway northern province of Tucumán, where they were given cover under the umbrella of CAPRI, a company set up by Fuldner with the support of a generous state contract from Perón. The company was officially recognized by Perón's government exactly one week after Eichmann's arrival in Argentina. 'Geller and Klement joined the company in 1950,' is how Fuldner explained it to the Argentine police following Eichmann's capture a decade later. 'Geller was provisions manager and Klement led a group of workers, and as Geller proved to be very capable at his job he became a partner.'[512]

Nominally entrusted by the state utility Agua y Energía with surveying rivers for hydroelectric projects, CAPRI actually provided employment for recent SS arrivals, men with unsuitable skills who couldn't speak Spanish. Among the sizeable and affluent German community, CAPRI was referred to jokingly as the 'German Company for Recent Immigrants' (*'Compañía Alemana Para Recién Inmigrados'*), and Fuldner and its directors were known as 'The Fishermen of Capri', in reference to a popular song.[513]

CAPRI and its associated company Fuldner Bank set up head-quarters on the fifth floor of 374 Córdoba Avenue in downtown Buenos Aires, where former SS chiefs mingled with budding German-Argentine technocrats. When he was in town, Eichmann shared desk space at this office with certain youths who would in time become some of Argentina's top businessmen. Another SS criminal, Hans Fischböck, had his offices on the sixth floor of the same building.[514]

Some 300 people were on CAPRI's payroll. Among these was Siegfried Uiberreither, the notorious Gauleiter of Steiermark (Styria), in Austria. Facing murder investigations in Austria and Yugoslavia, Uiberreither arrived in Buenos Aires in 1947 after escaping from an American POW camp. At CAPRI he passed as Armin Dardieux, an alias derived from his second-in-command in Steiermark, Armin Dadieu, who facing a court investigation in Graz, also fled to Argentina in 1948. Dadieu was helped on his way by Bishop Hudal in Rome. In Argentina, he was hired by the Argentine army under the name Armin Pelkhofer.[515]

A third fugitive from Steiermark was the internationally renowned hydrologist and SS officer Armin Schoklitsch, president of the Technical University of Graz in 1941/45. Arriving in Argentina in 1949, Schoklitsch was hired by the university of Tucumán, where he was held in high esteem as a distinguished professor. Like Fuldner, he was connected to Himmler's secret service. At CAPRI he became Eichmann's direct supervisor. Despite his clouded past, his scientific credentials were impeccable and the Technical University of Graz organized an international Memorial Symposium in his honour in 1999. Other war criminals at CAPRI were Bernhard Heilig, the former Gauleiter in Brunswick, and Erwin Fleiss and Franz Sterzinger, two Austrian SS men who fled to Argentina via Rome around 1947.[516]

The upper echelon at CAPRI was a veritable Who's Who of Third Reich technocrats. Fuldner enrolled Fritz Maria Küper, the former public works inspector at Hitler's transport ministry and engineer in charge of Nuremberg port, and the Reich's expert bridge-builder, Beer. Engineers fresh off the boat such as Viktor Elleder, Heinz Ludwig Ostertag, Karl Laucher and Wilhelm Silberkuhl were also among the 'experts' taken under Fuldner's protective wing.[517]

Eichmann was a frequent visitor to the university of Tucumán, where so many fellow 'technicians' had landed. He struck up a friendship of sorts with Argentine professor José Darmanín. 'I was introduced to Klement in the professors' hall,' Darmanín recalled in 1993. 'I saw him twice a week for a couple of years. He spoke good French and our brief conversations centred on the weather and the natural beauties of Tucumán, which he admired. He wasn't employed by the university but he came to deliver his river survey reports to Professor Schoklitsch.'[518]

Another CAPRI boss was Carlos Schulz, the German-Argentine who had set up the Nazi escape route in Scandinavia. In Tucumán, the ever-resourceful Schulz handed out company IDs to the SS men and arranged for these to be signed by the city's chief of police. On 8 February 1952, Eichmann was issued a second ID, this time number 341,952, again under the Klement alias, in Tucumán.[519]

Whether CAPRI's location in a distant northern province was planned or merely coincidental, there can be little doubt that it would have received the blessing of Tucumán Bishop Agustín Barrére. As we have seen, this friend and benefactor of war criminals Pierre Daye and Charles Lesca had already played a vital role alongside Cardinal Caggiano opening up the first escape lines to South America via the Vatican in 1946.[520]

After two years in Argentina it was time for Eichmann to bring his family from Austria. In June, his wife and three children arrived in the country, having arranged the necessary paperwork through the Argentine consulate in Vienna. They travelled on the steamship *Salta* from Genoa under their real names. 'There were several gentlemen waiting at the dock,' Eichmann's son Klaus recalled in 1966. 'They were very kind to us.' The family was reunited with Eichmann at a Buenos Aires hotel and the following day set off together by rail for Tucumán.[521]

Apparently at some point Perón himself visited CAPRI. At least this was claimed by the German magazine *Bünte*, which in 1960 published a large picture of the Argentine president in the dining car of a train on its way to Tucumán, sitting next to a man purported to be Eichmann. But by July 1953 the company's fortunes began to plummet, along with most of Argentina's economy. Perón's popularity had started to diminish after the death of his wife Evita the previous year. The Eichmann family therefore packed their bags and headed for Buenos Aires, where Eichmann now obtained yet another ID from the Buenos Aires police, under a different number.[522]

Eichmann rented a house with a small garden at 4261 Chacabuco Street in the northern suburb of Olivos from an Austrian named Francisco Schmidt. Kuhlmann, despite the bad blood between them, signed as guarantor for Eichmann's rental. The Panzer commander had moved in the meantime to an expensive Swiss-style chalet at Ombú 2929, in the exclusive Palermo Chico neighbourhood, the Embassy Row of Buenos Aires. Kuhlmann now lived only a stone's throw away from the presidential residence of Juan and Eva Perón and two houses down from the Swiss ambassador, and was surely the envy of any Nazi with social ambitions in Argentina.[523]

For Eichmann the move precipitated a descent into a series of dead-end jobs and a squalid existence on the margin of the comfortable lives led by the more fortunate Nazis of Perón's court. His break with Kuhlmann now became absolute, and the former Panzer commander abandoned Argentina in 1953, apparently in search of better opportunities elsewhere. 'If there ever comes a time when I'm not with you and Kuhlmann shows up at home, give him a kick in the behind and say: Herr Kuhlmann, you are a pig!' Eichmann instructed his family. 'My father was hanged, and Kuhlmann, who betrayed him, is now a millionaire in Brazil,' Eichmann's son Klaus complained bitterly in 1966.[524]

Attempts to earn a living opening a laundry with former CAPRI workmates, setting up a textile store, or as transport manager at the Efeve sanitary appliances firm, all foundered. Eichmann then took charge of the 'Seven Palms' rabbit farm in a small town 70 kilometres from Buenos Aires, which belonged to distant relatives who had returned to Europe. The former Reich official who oversaw the transport of millions of human beings across a vast rail network the length and breadth of Europe was now reduced to tending rabbits and chickens on a tiny corner of the Pampas. His spirits slumped dramatically. According to one, perhaps fantastical, account, Eichmann took to writing science fiction, and concocted an amazing tale of a couple living in Tucumán who were visited by Martians in a flying saucer. To prevent the human race from annihilating itself in an atomic war, the Martians deliver an ultimatum and Earth surrenders. The Martians then, in a magnanimous gesture, hand over control of the planet to the pacific, fraternal Argentines.[525]

While Eichmann may certainly have been feeling low in spirits, the image projected by various writers of a solitary, unprotected outcast, avoided and scorned by his former SS comrades, is contradicted by the evidence. Not only did Eichmann escape Europe under the protective umbrella of the Vatican and Perón's rescue organization, once in Argentina he was warmly adopted by Fuldner's CAPRI, where his work was regularly overseen by an eminent fellow Austrian. Furthermore, he was aided in obtaining new Argentine papers by Schulz, a trusted aide to Domingo Mercante, the governor of Buenos Aires. While Eichmann may not have enjoyed the exalted position Mengele held within the Third Reich community, it must be remembered that Mengele came from a wealthy German family while Eichmann had no social credentials to speak of. But Eichmann's presence was well known among the postwar arrivals, who frequently sought him out, perhaps moved not so much by admiration as by morbid curiosity regarding the Holocaust.

One of Eichmann's benefactors in Argentina was Otto Skorzeny. Towards the end of the war, both men had addressed a morale-boosting conference in Berlin for some 400 police commanders, an event organized by Kaltenbrunner and attended by Müller and Goebbels. They were introduced to their audience as SS officers who had both succeeded in difficult missions. Skorzeny related his rescue of Mussolini, and Eichmann spoke of 'what was happening in the sphere of solving the Jewish Question'. Eichmann recalled during his trial in 1961 that, due to the secrecy of his activities, he consulted with Müller over whether he should report to the audience 'the number of Jews actually killed'.[526]

On 27 July 1948, Skorzeny made a typically dramatic escape from the internment camp at Darmstadt. In his cell, two days later, a letter to the chairman of the German denazification tribunal was found: 'I feel that it will be impossible for the court to uphold its freedom for a just decision and that the court must and will bow to stronger outside elements,' Skorzeny had written. 'I have only one wish: to live in honour in this Fatherland.' Little is known about Skorzeny's escape route, although some contemporary press articles pointed to Bishop Hudal and a Roman connection. He seems to have arrived in Argentina some time in early 1949. This larger-than-life figure inspired endless articles and biographies. Skorzeny himself was not averse to feeding the legend. Among other things, he was branded the 'caretaker' of Third Reich assets secreted outside Germany by Hitler's deputy Martin Bormann and entrusted to Perón. He was certainly concerned about the fate of any such treasure. While imprisoned in Germany in 1947, Skorzeny claimed to have been disturbed by Eva Perón's 'Rainbow Tour' of Europe. 'What really worried me was her purpose for travelling to Europe. I thought she might be disposing of some Nazi party money deposited in Argentina,' Skorzeny said in a 1973 interview. 'One report that I got at this time was that the only way she could be softened up was to get into bed with her when she was lonely. After being in prison for several months and not able to get near a woman, I replied that I was an ideal man to soften her up.'

The legend continues that Skorzeny did eventually seduce Evita. The presidential couple was certainly delighted to have him around and hear the wartime exploits of the scar-faced hero. Skorzeny travelled constantly between Buenos Aires and Madrid, popping up occasionally in Paris. In Spain he was well protected by the Franco dictatorship. He represented various German business interests there and was friends with fellow fugitive and war criminal Léon Degrelle, the leader of the Belgian Rexist party who corresponded constantly with Pierre Daye in Argentina. In Madrid he married the niece of former Reichsbank president Hjalmar Schacht. In 1952 he even began granting press interviews, and was seen at the Horcher restaurant in Madrid. He was definitely not a publicity-shy Nazi.[527]

Eichmann claimed that in the mid-1950s Skorzeny introduced him to Dutch war criminal Willem Sassen. 'I met Sassen, without being aware of it, when Skorzeny visited Buenos Aires. I became aware of him when his partner enquired whether I would be ready to write something down from my recollections. That was around 1956–1957. I don't remember precisely when it was. And the other occasion was some time before that,' Eichmann said in his usual confused style during his trial in 1961. It was a meeting he would live to regret.[528]

The two SS criminals actually knew each other from before. Sassen had introduced Eichmann to Mengele in 1952. Eichmann and the Auschwitz doctor met occasionally for coffee at the ABC, a German-run restaurant and coffee-house in downtown Buenos Aires. They had little in common, Sassen recalled for a Mengele documentary put together by Granada Television in 1978. 'They are two completely different kinds of people,' Sassen said. 'Moreover Mengele does dispose, could dispose of his own means, which Eichmann never had. He was a tragic figure because in reality, that [the Holocaust] was not his business. He would have liked to have been a common soldier on the front. That was his dream.'[529]

Following Skorzeny's reintroduction, Sassen and Eichmann talked themselves into an ambitious enterprise, a verbatim account by Eichmann of the 'Final Solution to the Jewish Question'. There has been much speculation in the intervening decades about Sassen's real intentions. Some have argued that the Dutchman honestly expected Eichmann to disprove the revelations from the Nuremberg trials about the Holocaust. This seems, to say the least, naïve. The real motive is more likely to have been commercial gain. Sassen was a much-sought-after publisher among members of the Nazi community in Argentina. Pierre Daye, for example, had published a book with him in 1950. Sassen and Eichmann signed a contract and agreed on royalties. According to Sassen, the book was to be published as an investigation into the Holocaust without naming the source. 'The idea was to try and keep the figure of Hitler out of the whole complex,' Eichmann said during his trial. 'The original tendency was for me, so to say, to accept responsibility for this matter. But then I said that no one would believe this if I were to say so, apart from which, I maintain that the man who gave the orders for this cannot in any way be left out.'[530]

Sassen was a conscientious interviewer and Eichmann a willing subject. Together these two men in their mid-forties spent some four or five months of 1956 and 1957 recording 67 reel-to-reel tapes. The transcript came to over 700 typewritten pages. Afterwards, Sassen handed the material to Eichmann, who scribbled extensive corrections over it, adding a further 83 handwritten pages of his own to the recorded conversations. 'Basically I was happy to be able for once to talk about the whole complex matter, and to some extent dispose of it. That was really my main motive, but I could not foresee where it would lead to,' Eichmann admitted later.[531]

One of the attendants at the sessions was Dieter Menge, a former Luftwaffe pilot who had been shot down and taken as a prisoner to Australia. Settling in Argentina after the war, Menge became successful in the scrap metal business. His home outside Buenos Aires was a regular meeting place for nostalgic fugitives, including Eichmann, Mengele and Sassen. Dutch war criminal Abraham Kipp, whose extradition to Holland was refused by Argentina in 1989, was a partner in Menge's business. The tape recorder had been brought to Argentina from the US as a novelty item by another partner, the former German soldier 'Pedro' Pobierzym, who did not share the Nazi sympathies of the Menge circle but was privy to some of its secrets.[532]

The Eichmann sessions were known to Nazi insiders in Argentina, and various other people sat in to listen. The first to do so was the director of the Dürer publishing house, Eberhard Fritsch, Sassen's partner and the original instigator of the idea. But either because he was disappointed to hear Eichmann confirm the true nature of the Holocaust or because he had other matters to attend to, Fritsch abandoned the two after only four or five sessions. A more active participant, as Eichmann recalled during his trial, was a Dr Klan, alias Lange, 'a former District Leader of the Security Service in Austria', who had attended the Berlin lecture where Skorzeny and Eichmann spoke and who now made annotations on the transcript.[533]

Perhaps the most disquieting presence was that of SS officer Rudolf Mildner, a 'close friend' of Eichmann in Argentina, stationed at Auschwitz between 1941 and 1943 and Gestapo commander in Katowice. 'I showed Mildner all over the extermination plant at Auschwitz and he was directly interested in it, since he had to send the Jews from his territory for execution at Auschwitz,' camp commander Rudolf Hoess testified at Nuremberg in 1946. After Katowice, Mildner was sent to Denmark, where he was in charge of the removal of Jews from that country. Caught by American troops in 1945, he was held under arrest during the Nuremberg trials and his affidavits were presented as evidence against Kaltenbrunner. After that his trail goes cold until, according to Nazi-hunter Simon Wiesenthal, he arrived in Argentina in 1949. During the Sassen sessions, Mildner was called in as an expert commentator, as Eichmann himself admitted during his trial in Jerusalem.[534]

But for all their hard work Eichmann and Sassen ended up empty-handed. An attempt by the Dutchman to sell the interview to a newspaper as an 'anonymous' account by a former Third Reich official collapsed when the publisher declined unless the source could be named.

It was time to find a real job again. The Orbis gas appliances manufacturer, a definitely ironic choice, became Eichmann's new employer. As we have seen, this was the company owned by Nazi party member Roberto Mertig, the 'best friend' of Mengele in Argentina. Apparently Eichmann worked as a labourer at the Orbis warehouse for about 16 months before moving on to his next employment, at the offices of the Mercedes-Benz factory in González Catán, an industrial suburb outside Buenos Aires. This was the last job he would hold in his life.[535]

Four important diplomats who were close collaborators of Eichmann also found sanctuary in Argentina. Ambassador Franz Rademacher, head of the Jewish Affairs office of the German Foreign Ministry, was one of them. Arrested briefly by the Allies in 1945, he then remained at large for seven years testifying at the postwar trials against Nazi criminals and awaiting trial himself. During the war he was involved in the execution of 1,300 Serbian Jews, and took part personally in the liquidation of the Belgrade ghetto in 1941 and the deportation of 1,500 Belgian Jews in 1942. On the voucher for his travel expenses in Belgrade, Rademacher wrote 'liquidation of the Jews' as the purpose of his trip. On 17 March 1952, after a farcical trial in Nuremberg, he was condemned to only three years and five months imprisonment. He was released on bail pending appeal, and promptly skipped to Argentina. In 1962, alarmed by Eichmann's execution, he fled to Syria. From there he was extradited to Germany in 1968 and put on trial again at Bramberg. This time he was condemned to five years, but released on bail due to bad health. Eventually he returned to Argentina.[536]

Another criminal diplomat warmly received in Argentina was Karl Klingenfuss, a subordinate of Rademacher's who had been a secretary at the German embassy in Buenos Aires in 1939/40. Klingenfuss was involved in the deportation of thousands of Jews from Italy, Croatia and Bulgaria and played a gruesome part in the sinking of the ship *Struma*, in which 677 Romanian Jews drowned when it mysteriously exploded after leaving Istanbul on its way to Palestine. In 1958, a request for his extradition from Germany sparked a minor scandal in Argentina. He had become a major figure in the powerful German business community and a trustee of the influential German-Argentine Chamber of Commerce. Faced with accusations that gathered strength following Eichmann's capture, Klingenfuss tendered his resignation. On 23 July 1961 the German business community pointedly refused to accept it. The businessmen pointed out that the German courts had finally dropped their case against the former Nazi diplomat in 1959. Perhaps the Klingenfuss-related documents presented at Eichmann's trial provide a more adequate portrait of the man who represented the German business community in Argentina: 'Draft of a letter from Klingenfuss of the Foreign Ministry to Eichmann stating that he does not object in principle to the planned deportation of Jews from occupied France, The Netherlands and Belgium to Auschwitz', 27 July 1942; 'Express letter from Klingenfuss to various Reich offices containing a report of the meeting which took place concerning the disposal of property of foreign Jews in the Reich and of Jewish property in the German sphere of influence', 1 July 1942; 'Letter of transmittal from Eichmann to Klingenfuss of minutes of a meeting on the Final Solution', 3 November 1942; and the list goes on.[537]

A third diplomat linked to Eichmann was Horst Wagner, an SS lieutenant who was the liaison between the SS and the Foreign Ministry. As with Klingenfuss, the Wagner-related material presented at the Eichmann trial is so incriminatory it practically numbs the mind. In 1948 Wagner fled to Argentina, where he lived until 1952. The following year he was arrested in Rome but the Italian authorities refused to extradite him to Germany. Investigations there continued into his crimes, which included giving orders for the execution of French General Maurice Mesny. In 1967, he was finally charged with taking part in the Holocaust, but the proceedings were suspended in 1972 when he was declared unfit to stand trial.[538]

The fourth Eichmann collaborator and Nazi diplomat with an active involvement in the Holocaust arrived in Argentina not as a postwar fugitive but as Germany's ambassador to Buenos Aires in 1964. Dr Ernst Günther Mohr, Nazi party member No. 3,500,174, was implicated in the deportation of Dutch Jews to the Mauthausen concentration camp when he was a counsellor at the German legation in occupied Holland. His role in this matter had come up during Eichmann's trial in Jerusalem long before Mohr was posted to Buenos Aires. The ambassador had joined the Nazi party in 1935 and served as one of Hitler's diplomats in China, Europe and South America. Afterwards he continued representing Germany in Venezuela, Switzerland and Buenos Aires until his retirement.[539]

Another intimate collaborator was SS Captain Erich Rajakowitsch, Eichmann's representative in Holland, who was responsible for the deportation of some 100,000 Dutch Jews. As shown in Eichmann's trial, Rajakowitsch also played a vital role in the plundering of Holland's Jews. He was, like Bishop Hudal, a native of Graz, where he had practised law; his father-in-law had been Austrian ambassador in Rome. At the end of the war he escaped to Italy with his wife and children. With them went his wife's lover, also an Eichmann liaison officer. All found refuge at a monastery provided by Hudal, who aided their escape to Argentina. Apparently preceded by his wife and children, Rajakowitsch seems to have entered Argentina for the first time on 26 February 1952 on a plane from neighbouring Chile. He travelled under the alias Erico Raja, and remained in the country until Perón's overthrow.

The former SS officer then returned to Italy under his false passport and set himself up in Milan, where he became a highly successful businessman, acquiring apartment buildings and villas in Italy, Switzerland and Mexico. By 1963, however, Rajakowitsch had run out of luck, and the Italian authorities who had been alerted to his Nazi past arrested him.

Rajakowitsch fled to Switzerland and then to Germany but finally gave himself up in Vienna, where he was put on trial. His case provoked a number of articles making him out to be one of the postwar custodians of the SS loot plundered from the Jews – a not unlikely assumption – as well as suggesting he had been the secret financier of Bishop Hudal's escape network. He was let off with a two-and-a-half-year sentence and freed in 1966, when he proceeded to sue for libel both a Spanish magazine and Simon Wiesenthal, who had tracked him down. He lost both cases.[540]

The protective bubble around Eichmann was burst not by an Israeli super-sleuth but by a blind refugee from Nazi persecution who had arrived in Argentina in 1938. Lothar Hermann had been imprisoned in Dachau concentration camp in 1935/36 for his socialist activities. Following the events of Kristallnacht, Hermann, who was half-Jewish, decided it was time to leave Germany. Some years after his arrival in Buenos Aires he lost his sight as a delayed result of the severe beatings he had received from the Gestapo at Dachau.

Hermann, his wife and their beautiful young daughter Sylvia lived in the Olivos area of Buenos Aires as non-Jewish Germans. Sylvia had become friendly with the Eichmann sons, in particular with the eldest, whom she apparently dated. Klaus Eichmann visited Sylvia's home on various occasions, and made strongly anti-Semitic remarks, including his regret that the Nazis could not complete the extermination of the Jews, and adding that his father had served in the war. Sylvia was never invited to the young man's home and was unaware that his father lived under the Klement alias, as Eichmann had insisted that his sons continue to carry the real family name.

Some time later, the Hermanns moved out to Coronel Suárez, a town 500 kilometres away from Buenos Aires, and lost contact with the Eichmanns. But in 1957 the name of Adolf Eichmann cropped up in newspaper reports of a Nazi trial in Frankfurt. It did not take long for Hermann to figure out that the man being mentioned was in all probability Klaus Eichmann's father.

Hermann dutifully sent off a letter to the Frankfurt judicial authorities alerting them to Eichmann's presence in Argentina. His letter fell into the hands of Attorney General Fritz Bauer, a brave jurist who later led the groundbreaking Auschwitz trials in 1963. Bauer sent Hermann a description of Eichmann and asked him to find out more details. The incredibly intrepid blind man and his daughter did as they were asked, travelling to Buenos Aires to try to discover Eichmann's exact address. Sylvia found the house quite quickly.

A knock at the door was answered by Klaus's mother. 'Is this the Eichmann home?' Sylvia asked. Suddenly a middle-aged man appeared at the door as well. Sylvia asked if Klaus was home. The man said he was working late. 'Are you Herr Eichmann?' Sylvia asked as innocently as she could. The man did not answer but finally conceded that he was Klaus's father. Sylvia explained that she was a friend who was looking for him, and then said goodbye. Hermann and his daughter returned home and promptly sent off a new letter to Frankfurt positively identifying, according to Bauer's description, the former chief of 'Jewish Affairs', and giving his address as 4261 Chacabuco Street in Olivos.

Bauer knew enough about the Nazi-riddled judicial system of his own country to realize that Eichmann would at once be alerted to any action against him by Germany. In September 1957, therefore, he secretly informed Israel that he had received confidential information stating that Eichmann was living in Argentina. Israel's Mossad secret service took a mild interest in Bauer's lead, sending agent Yoel Goren to Buenos Aires in January 1958. After a quick inspection of the middle-class Olivos neighbourhood he reported that it was impossible an important Nazi could be living there.

Bauer, however, was not about to give up so easily. By revealing Hermann's identity to Mossad he was able to convince the Israelis to send a second mission. Israeli agent Efraim Hofstetter now visited the Hermanns and their daughter in Coronel Suárez posing as an emissary from Fritz Bauer. Hermann complained volubly that the information he had already provided was sufficient to proceed with Eichmann's arrest. Hofstetter pleaded for patience, claiming he needed more proof, such as a copy of Eichmann's Argentine ID picture. The Mossad agent left Hermann 130 dollars to cover his expenses and gave him an address in the US to write to from now on, effectively cutting Bauer out of the loop. Afterwards the agent drove by Chacabuco Street and then returned to Israel, filing a report that went largely ignored. A blind man living ten hours by train from Buenos Aires was left with the task of proving Eichmann's identity.

It did not intimidate Hermann. From the Buenos Aires Title Deeds Office he obtained the information that the house on Chacabuco Street was owned by an Austrian named Francisco Schmidt, and for a time he became convinced that Schmidt was Eichmann's alias, and sent off more letters with this mistaken hypothesis to the new address he was given. In Israel, meanwhile, the

Mossad chiefs had lost all interest in the lead and the order was given for communication with Hermann to be gradually discontinued.

But Hermann was determined. Excited by a $10,000 reward announced in the press by Tuviah Friedman of the Haifa Documentation Centre in Israel (the reward was supposedly financed by the World Jewish Congress), he started letting more people in on his secret. In a letter to Friedman dated 17 October 1959, Hermann claimed to possess the 'name and exact details' of Eichmann's Argentine identification papers. On 29 December, growing ever more impatient, Hermann met with G. Schurman, a leader of the DAIA, Argentina's main Jewish organization. Suddenly the number of people who knew of Eichmann's whereabouts had expanded way beyond the pale of Fritz Bauer and a small group of Israeli secret agents. Now even the leaders of the Jewish community in Argentina knew where Eichmann lived. Still, nothing seemed to be happening. Fearful that his role in Eichmann's eventual capture was being minimized to cut him out of the reward, in March 1960 Hermann wrote an angry letter to Friedman. 'It seems that you attach little value to the speedy conclusion of the matter or that you have no interest at all to arrest Eichmann,' Hermann fumed.

A blind man who lived on a meagre pension in the middle of the Pampas had achieved what seemed impossible. Not only had he single-handedly located a notorious Nazi criminal, he also managed to galvanize a lethargic Mossad, which had shown decidedly little interest in pursuing the case. Israel was practically shamed into capturing Eichmann.[541]

The rest of the story is well known. A special Mossad team was assembled and sent to Buenos Aires to kidnap Eichmann, who had meanwhile slid further down the social ladder, moving from middle-class Olivos to a small house he had built for himself and his family at 6061 Garibaldi Street in the desolate outskirts of San Fernando. Seeking his extradition was ruled out from the very start, following Germany's failed attempt to extradite Mengele. Eichmann was ignominiously snatched on a dirt road on 11 May 1960 as he returned from work, and taken to a secret hiding place outside Buenos Aires.

For ten days he was kept blindfolded and handcuffed to a bed while Mossad decided how to get him out of Argentina.

The small Eichmann home in San Fernando meanwhile became a hive of activity. Eichmann's sons called in a former SS comrade of their father. 'He forced us to think clearly, suggesting three possibilities: that father had been arrested by the police for some offence, or he had been picked up for being drunk; that he had had an accident and was injured in a hospital or dead in a morgue; or that the Israelis had him,' Klaus Eichmann recalled in 1966. When two days of searching failed to produce any results, the realization sank in that 'they' had him.

In the days following the kidnapping 'a Peronist youth group' approached the Eichmanns to assist Klaus and his brother Dieter in their search. 'Sometimes up to 300 men and their motorcycles were hidden near our home.' The leader of the young Peronists proposed a drastic solution: 'Let's kidnap the Israeli ambassador, take him out of the city and torture him until your father returns home.' Then came another idea: 'Someone suggested blowing up the Israeli embassy.'[542]

Finally, on 21 May, Eichmann was disguised in the uniform of an El Al flight attendant and was bundled aboard a plane to Tel Aviv. On 23 May the Israeli prime minister announced his capture to the world: 'Eichmann is already in this country under arrest and will shortly be brought to trial,' Ben Gurion said.

In Argentina meanwhile, the Federal Police opened an investigation into the Eichmann abduction. The probe was apparently aimed at identifying his kidnappers. One single police report survives. It shows that a scrupulous investigation was made of Eichmann's workmates at Mercedes-Benz, and turned up a single Jewish employee at the company. More interestingly, when researching 'persons who might have known Eichmann during the time of the Second World War', the police discovered a Hungarian named 'Julio' Szabo, a legislator in his country from 1942 to 1944, who had joined Mercedes-Benz in 1959 and rode the bus home with Eichmann daily after work. The police also discovered that, following Ben Gurion's announcement, Eichmann's wife had vanished from view and the house on Garibaldi

Street was deserted. Another interesting fact: two men in civilian clothes had broken into the Eichmann home on 6 June and again the following day and photographed the entire premises.

Tracing Eichmann's history in Argentina, the police discovered that 'Pedro Geller' had acted as guarantor when Eichmann rented the house on Chacabuco Street, and a police delegation was sent to ring Geller's doorbell in the exclusive Palermo Chico neighbourhood. To their surprise, it was Carlos Fuldner who answered. The former SS captain was bursting with information, stating that he still headed CAPRI, engaged now in lengthy bankruptcy proceedings, and that he had known both Geller and Klement.

'Fuldner stated that until this 25 May he was unaware of the real name of Riccardo Klement, who had stopped working for CAPRI in 1953,' the suspiciously naïve police report states. 'On that day, at 10 pm, he was visited by a young man at his home, Ombú 2929, who was completely unfamiliar to him, and who, in a state of despair, said he was Klaus Eichmann, son of the alleged Riccardo Klement. This person stated that since 11 May the whereabouts of his father, Adolf Eichmann, remained unknown and that he had only recently learned that he had been kidnapped by Israeli agents and taken to Israel. Klaus furthermore stated that his brother Horst was on board the *Cap Castillo* as a merchant marine on his way to New York. The Eichmann family, aware of Horst's temperament, was concerned that, upon learning his father's fate, he would present himself voluntarily in the Arab countries for any mission against Israel.'

Straight off the cuff an extremely helpful Fuldner provided the police with the exact arrival date of Kuhlmann and Eichmann, correctly naming the *Giovanna C* as the ship they had travelled on, evidence if any was needed of his involvement in bringing them into the country. He then led the delegation to Klaus Eichmann's home at 3030 General Paz Avenue in Olivos, but Klaus slammed the door in Fuldner's face.[543]

While the Eichmann family went into hiding, Sassen realized he was sitting on a goldmine. Within a matter of days, he had sold the rights to the Eichmann transcripts to *Life* magazine, which carried a condensed version in late 1960, as well as to *Stern* magazine in Germany and to the German-language newspaper *Yediot Hadashot* in Israel. In a sinister twist, a group of men in civilian clothes reportedly turned up at Menge's home demanding the original tapes and threatened to ransack the house until they found them. Menge is said to have surrendered them without finding out if the men were Argentine police or Israeli agents. And on 9 June 1961, the transcripts handed over by Sassen to *Yediot Hadashot* were presented at Eichmann's trial in Jerusalem, and proved to be one of the most damning pieces of evidence against him. Particularly damaging were the abundant and meticulous corrections and annotations that Eichmann had added to the transcripts in his own hand. Sassen, harassed by threats and accusations of betrayal from the Nazi community in Argentina, reportedly fled to Paraguay to count his money.[544]

Argentina meanwhile railed against Eichmann's kidnapping as an infringement of national sovereignty, demanding that Israel return the war criminal to Buenos Aires. On 21 June Argentina's ambassador to the United Nations, Mario Amadeo, presented a formal protest before the Security Council in New York. He argued that although Argentina had admitted Eichmann it had also given a 'generous welcome' to many Jewish refugees who had entered the country 'fraudulently'. Amadeo apparently did not realize the contradiction in the second part of his argument. This was the same nationalist diplomat who had collaborated with Himmler's secret service during the war and who had greeted war criminal Pierre Daye upon his arrival in Buenos Aires in 1947.

Another distinguished figure who rose to Eichmann's defence was Argentine Cardinal Antonio Caggiano, the man who had helped open the Vatican escape route in 1946. 'He came to our fatherland seeking forgiveness and oblivion. It doesn't matter what his name is, Riccardo Klement or Adolf Eichmann, our obligation as Christians is to forgive him for what he's done,' Caggiano told the press.[545]

Perhaps even more grotesque than these hypocritical responses was an incident that occurred on 21 March 1961. Lothar Hermann was arrested that day at his home in Coronel Suárez, and accused of being Josef Mengele. The Buenos Aires police claimed to have been acting in response to Germany's extradition request for the Auschwitz doctor, but their action was more likely a cruel act of revenge by anti-Semitic elements in the Argentine force aware of Hermann's secret role in Eichmann's capture. A comparison of Hermann's fingerprints with those Mengele had given when he took out his Argentine ID showed, however, what the Buenos Aires police already knew – that Hermann wasn't Mengele. A distraught Hermann called a press conference at his home. He claimed that two foreign correspondents and an Argentine journalist had visited him and asked if he was linked to Mengele. Hermann said he wasn't but told them he ran an 'international information agency' and could find out where Mengele was, for a charge. The 'journalists' then threatened him. Angry words were exchanged. Hermann had called the police and somehow ended up in jail himself. 'I never had any contact with Eichmann,' a fearful Hermann lied to the press conference. 'I lost my sight in 1947 and Eichmann arrived in 1951. Also, I am Jewish, and if I had known him I would have reported it to the police.' The story merited only a few lines in the Argentine papers, but it allowed the German government to demand a copy of Mengele's fingerprints from the Argentine authorities.[546]

Eichmann was found guilty in Jerusalem and sentenced to death by hanging. The execution was carried out on 31 May 1962. His last words were: 'Long live Germany, long live Argentina, long live Austria. I shall not forget them.' The next day a young Jewish woman named Graciela Narcisa Sirota – suspected of being the daughter of the owner of the house where Eichmann was held by the Mossad in Buenos Aires – was kidnapped, tortured, and had a swastika burned into her breast. A second innocent Jewish girl named Mirta Penjerek, accused of supplying the Mossad team with food, was simply murdered.

Hermann's part in Eichmann's capture remained a closely guarded secret until 1971, when Mossad director Isser Harel revealed it to the

Israeli press. From Argentina, Hermann began to bombard Friedman with furious letters demanding his reward. Finally, in July 1972, Israeli Prime Minister Golda Meier settled the debt.[547]

Thirty years after Eichmann's execution a distant echo of that angry plan volunteered by a Peronist Youth leader to blow up the Israeli embassy reverberated under a new Peronist government. The Israeli embassy in Buenos Aires was ripped apart by a bomb that killed 29 people on 17 March 1992. The Argentine Supreme Court, which took jurisdiction over the investigation, never brought the case to trial.

CONCLUSION

'To see myself, to set the darkness echoing.'
Seamus Heaney, 'Personal Helicon'

Six years of research, interviews and digging through previously unexplored archives have gone into this book. It has been a personal hunt and it yielded more treasures than I expected at the outset. Above all, I had not thought it possible that so much incriminatory documentation would prove obtainable. The essential files in Argentina either had been destroyed or remain closely guarded. But enough survived around the edges to piece the puzzle together.

I arrived at the subject matter from an angle, having spent my formative years as a journalist in a unique position, reporting on the crimes against humanity committed by Argentina's 1976/83 dictatorship as they happened, in a country that otherwise preferred to turn its gaze from the horror. The feeling in Buenos Aires then was imaginably similar to that in Berlin in the early 1940s, living in a society that pretended to be unaware of, or even secretly condoned, the mass extermination that was taking place. By the time it was over, some 20,000 people had 'disappeared' in Argentina's death camps. With the return of democracy, the chiefs of the dictatorship were put on trial, but a series of special amnesties quickly closed the possibility of any further judicial action and the sentenced men were released. Exasperated 20 years later by the continuing lack of justice for these crimes, and for the lethal bombings of the Israeli embassy and the

AMIA Jewish centre in Buenos Aires in the 1990s, I found myself compelled to dig back into the past, to chart the long apprenticeship Argentines had in turning a blind eye to evil.

When I started I had hoped to find evidence of Nazi influence in the murderous policies of the dictatorship. But the truth that emerged was disturbingly different. In no way had the Nazis signally influenced Argentina's genocidal generals of the 1970s. The evil seed was there before they arrived. In fact, as is shown by the postwar interrogations of Walter Schellenberg, the head of Himmler's foreign secret service, Nazi chiefs had already considered Argentina's wartime military regime as being 'based upon a similar world view to ours'.

I had expected that the publication of the Spanish-language predecessor to this book, released under the title *Perón y los alemanes* in Buenos Aires in 1998, would spark an honest debate in Argentina about these questions. Concentrating on the wartime links between Perón and the Nazis, that book laid bare the meetings of special envoy Juan Carlos Goyeneche with Himmler and Ribbentrop, and Perón's links with Himmler's intelligence service, and included my early findings on Carlos Fuldner's postwar role rescuing Nazis as a special agent for Perón. Although the book quickly shot up the bestseller lists, the debate I had hoped for failed to ignite. The only measurable reaction was a letter of protest – delivered by Argentina's ambassador to the United Nations – to the editors of *Time* magazine in New York, objecting to a favourable review of my work. A senior Argentine foreign ministry official, meanwhile, suggested to me that my next book should be about the 'Argentine Raoul Wallenberg', referring to the Swedish diplomat who saved thousands of Hungarian Jews by providing them with passports to escape deportation to Auschwitz. When I answered that I was unaware of any Argentine diplomat who had displayed such heroism, he answered: 'Well, somebody must have let them in, there are so many of them!'

His odd suggestion did not puzzle me; instead it confirmed my impression that Argentine officialdom remained convinced that it was important to whitewash the country's Nazi complicity, instead of coming clean with the facts. The key to understanding such attitudes perhaps resides in Argentina's physical distance from the war. Being a country of mostly European descent, the echo of battle reverberated strongly in Argentina but nobody seriously feared that the battle itself would come to the country's shores. Not even the economy suffered. As we have seen, Argentina's rulers, who saw the country's accounts bulge during the war thanks to grain and meat sales to Britain, were secretly negotiating a postwar trade agreement with Germany, through personal conversations with leading Nazis. Seen from the balconies of the Casa Rosada, the war was a win-win situation and therefore a little unreal.

Distance wasn't the only cushioning device. Another crucial key to understanding the eagerness of Argentina's rulers to rescue postwar fugitives was the link established not with the German Nazis but with their helpers. Perón himself developed strong personal ties with French Nazi collaborators and with the Croatian Ustashi in the postwar years. They were, in fact, the first to be saved when the Argentine Catholic Church, in league with Perón and the Vatican, arranged their flight during secret talks in Rome in 1946. It wasn't until these men were safely in Argentina that Fuldner's mission began concentrating on the rescue of German and Austrian war criminals in 1948. The reason is simple: the French collaborators, the Belgian Rexists and the Croatian Ustashi shared ties of religion with the Argentines. These men reconciled Catholicism with Hitlerism, and, as we have seen, the search for such a reconciliation was a prime motive during Argentina's dalliance with Hitler. Perón and the nationalists who surrounded him had more in common with the Christus Rex party of Pierre Daye than with the godless German Nazi party.

I particularly remember a lengthy interview with Wilfred von Oven, who had been the personal secretary of Hitler's propaganda minister, Joseph Goebbels, literally until the day Goebbels drove off to join Hitler in his bunker at the end of the war. As the evening faded over the Buenos Aires suburb where he lives, I asked Oven if he had made friends among Argentina's nationalists, such as Goyeneche.

'Yes,' Oven winced.

'Why the face?' I asked.

'Well . . . they are Catholics.'

'And why is that a problem?'

'Because I am a pagan!'

Perón's racial characteristics would never have allowed him to be admitted to the Nazi party. This did not prevent him from personally receiving criminals such as Josef Mengele at his presidential weekend residence, but these German Nazis came in the wake of the larger mass of Catholic collaborators who shared a religion with Argentina's rulers.

A measure of the way Argentina continues trying to blur its wartime and postwar record was given by a government commission set up by the Argentine foreign ministry between 1997 and 1999 to probe the old Nazi links. The CEANA issued a series of reports, assembled by a team of international scholars, which failed abysmally to deal with the core issues. No investigation was made of the Nazi extortion schemes against Jews in Argentina, of the bribes charged by Argentine diplomats for visas, of Perón's connections with Himmler's secret service, of Schellenberg's intelligence-exchange agreement with Argentina. Astoundingly, no investigation was even made into Goyeneche's mid-war meetings with Himmler and Ribbentrop. My own suggestion to the commission that former Information Bureau chief Rodolfo Freude should be called to testify about the postwar rescue of Nazi criminals by his office was never acted upon. (It is worth mentioning that, with the full resources of the Argentine government behind it, the CEANA was able to identify only 180 war criminals who arrived in Argentina; the investigation for this book, conducted by one man acting alone, has identified nearly 300).[548]

I formed part of the CEANA for three days in November 1998, resigning when it became evident that there were irreconcilable differences of criteria. The only attempt from within the commission to probe Freude's and Fuldner's activities was made by Argentine researcher Beatriz Gurevich. She was not supported by the commission and eventually decided to resign as well. (All the same, some of the commission's work has been important, principally its index of the war criminals who arrived in Argentina, and the access the commission gained to the papers of Bishop Alois Hudal at his Santa Maria dell'Anima church in Rome.)

In this book I have already given some sense of the apparent destruction of essential compromising records in Argentina during recent years. We are therefore lucky that an odd series of circumstances allowed alternative records to survive. It is only chance that placed a methodical diary-keeper like Pierre Daye among the members of Perón's Nazi court. The fact that after his death in 1960 in Buenos Aires his papers were removed to his native Belgium and later donated to a public archive, far from the reach of Argentine document cleansers, has been doubly fortunate. The obsessive note-keeping of Switzerland's police chief Heinrich Rothmund, who scrupulously recorded each of his interviews with Argentina's Nazi rescuers in Berne, is nothing short of a godsend. Again, without his memos a beneficent mist would still cloud the activities of Perón's agents in Europe in 1948. We also have to thank the anti-Semitism prevalent among Argentina's diplomatic service for sparking the 1949 inquest into the admission of 'thieves . . . Communists . . . Jews' to the country, an inquest that couldn't help but trip over the Nazis working for Perón at his Immigration Office. The immigration officials who let the Jews disembark were fired, but the Nazis were spared. The transcripts of this bizarre inquest somehow magically survived, adding a third dimension to the picture of postwar Nazi rescue efforts.

The picture would not have been complete, however, had it not been for a series of American intelligence documents obtained through the Freedom of Information Act that shed light on the inception of the escape route through Madrid between 1944 and 1946, before command of the rescue effort was moved to Buenos Aires. And a series of documents obtained from the CIA describes the slow transfer of the Croatian state treasure from Zagreb to Buenos Aires by Ante Pavelic. The cautious opening up of its postwar records by the Red Cross completes the picture, confirming once and for all the role of Vatican institutions and individual prelates in issuing travel documents to criminals such as Adolf Eichmann, Erich Priebke, Klaus Barbie and Hans Fischböck. In the background, pieced together from disembarkation cards and the ragged pages of crumbling passenger lists at the Immigration Office in Buenos Aires, came the evidence of consecutive applications for landing permits for Nazi war criminals by Perón's secret agents. Now that the pieces have been assembled, the full picture is frighteningly clear.

I am wrapping up this revised edition of *The Real Odessa* in Buenos Aires, and at no time since I finally settled here in 1975, even at the height of the violence during the military dictatorship, has the outlook been so grim for this country. To the dark horrors of the recent past must now be added Argentina's sudden implosion in 2002, a social and economic collapse unprecedented in the country's history, maybe even in any country's history. The same politicians who in the 1980s signed amnesties for the murderous military embarked in the 1990s on a feeding frenzy that included bribery, money laundering and a generalized looting of public funds that has undermined public confidence. It has provoked a four-year economic depression, sent unemployment soaring to 25 per cent, forced Argentina to default on its foreign debt and plunged over half of what was a primarily middle-class nation below the poverty line. A collapse of the banking system has caused millions of Argentines to lose their life's savings and is forcing many to live in a cashless society, where barter has replaced normal commercial exchange. The behaviour of Argentina's ruling class during this time has been so perverse that one taxi driver complained, 'The problem in Argentina isn't the corruption, the problem is the outright plunder!' Unlike the time of the dictatorship, when total silence reigned, during these recent years there has been no lack of brave investigative journalists who, in excruciating detail, uncovered the criminal behaviour of Argentina's business and political class – but sadly, to no avail. No major corruption case has resulted in a prison sentence. Occasionally (as was the case with the generals) there are arrests pending trials that never occur, detentions that last only long enough for the public storm to pass, and eventually the quiet release of the politician or financier in question. To those who suffered during the military dictatorship, the scene is familiar. 'The corruption of the 1990s, like the repression of the 1970s, divides the waters,' writes journalist Héctor Timerman, son of Jacobo Timerman, the Jewish newspaper editor who was kidnapped, tortured, stripped of his citizenship and thrown out of the country by the dictatorship, after the generals desisted from their original plan of putting him on trial to prove the existence of a 'Zionist plot' against Argentina.[549]

Meanwhile, the bombings during the 1990s of the Israeli embassy and the AMIA Jewish centre remain unsolved crimes. The first attack was ten years ago and left 29 people dead. The second, the deadliest single attack against a Jewish target since the Holocaust, killed 86 and occurred in 1994. In the light of Argentina's current suffering (and the terrorist attacks against the United States of 11 September), the magnitude of those bombings in Argentina may appear reduced, their echo distant. But who can say that the lack of justice in those cases, as in so many other instances in Argentina, has not contributed to the total vanquishing of moral standards that preceded the country's latest crisis?

As for myself, after completing the first edition of this book one year ago, totally exhausted and still shocked by the accumulated evidence of Perón's connivance with the Nazis and of Argentina's secret closure of its borders to the Jews, I had hoped to leave the subject matter behind. Instead, I ended up uncovering the proof of the Vatican's eagerness to see murderous Croatian criminals escape justice that forms the Afterword in this new edition. I wonder what else remains to be uncovered. For anyone who wishes to carry on down the trail opened here, I believe there is abundant material still waiting out there to fill the remaining gaps.

Uki Goñi
Buenos Aires
2 August 2002

AFTERWORD

The concerted effort of high-ranking leaders of the Catholic Church to smuggle World War Two criminals to Argentina was proved conclusively by documentation found during the research for the British hardback version of this book. That first edition, published in January 2002, investigated the actions of individuals such as Cardinals Tisserant and Caggiano, and clergymen such as Hudal, Draganovic and Dömöter. However, the evidence linking Pope Pius XII and Monsignor Giovanni Battista Montini (the future Pope Paul VI) to the rescue of Hitler's helpers remained circumstantial; the research conducted up to that moment had failed to be rewarded with documents that proved direct Papal involvement in such matters. This led the British Catholic press to praise *The Real Odessa* for documenting the role of individual clergymen but to criticize it for assuming that the Vatican as an 'institution' had cleared the way for fleeing Nazis and for failing to provide 'evidence' of any such assumed Papal complicity.[550]

As far as Papal complicity was concerned, the charge that the British hardback edition of *The Real Odessa* walked on thin documentary ground was not without merit. This was admittedly one of the very few instances in which the book dared to elevate an assumption to the level of certainty. Fortunately, however, such evidence does

now exist. It was uncovered recently, after the completion of the first
edition of this book, through patient examination of a series of
dossiers containing documents from the immediate postwar era at
the Public Record Office in London. These demonstrate not only
how Pius XII was fully aware of the sanctuary provided to war criminals at Roman ecclesiastical institutions but also how he personally
liaised with the Nazi-smuggling operation at the Croatian
Confraternity of San Girolamo, a connection long denied by the
Vatican.[551]

The British dossiers also show that the Pope secretly pleaded with
Washington and London on behalf of notorious criminals and Nazi
collaborators. These appeals were made in writing by the Vatican
Secretariat of State, an office under the direct and personal super-
vision of Pius XII and Monsignor Montini. In at least one case,
an appeal was made in the Pope's own name.

The British documents, together with recently declassified documents from the CIA's Operational Files, throw up startling links
between Father Krunoslav Draganovic's Nazi-smuggling business and
the Vatican, as well as with the Vatican's shadowy secret service.
Simultaneously, while the Vatican liaised with the Nazi smugglers,
American intelligence began to run its own operations through
Draganovic. To the Vatican and to Allied intelligence, rescuing Nazi
collaborators and SS murderers – and not extraditing them to countries with Communist governments – formed part of a package
designed to further their shared anti-Communist agenda. This dif-
fered from the cases of Perón and Fuldner, where outright Nazi
sympathies seem to have been at work. But while this may help to
explain their activities, it can hardly justify them.[552]

The earliest written petition found in the London archives dates from
August 1945. At this time, the Vatican approached the Allies on behalf
of the thousands of Ustashi fleeing to Italy from the newly established Communist regime of Marshal Tito in Yugoslavia. Many of
these men faced extradition for their wartime collaboration with the
Nazis, others for crimes against humanity, and some of them on both

charges. But to the Vatican, they were first and foremost Catholic nationalists and die-hard anti-Communists. Oblivious to the long-term moral cost of defending such men, the Pope threw his full weight behind a secret effort to save them from the Communist courts.

The Vatican thus asked London to 'reconsider' the 'classification as prisoners of war' of a particular group of 600 Croatians being held at POW Camp 949 in Naples. This group was extended to include all possible suspected Ustasha criminals, and the Vatican asked 'that in no case they or their co-nationals in similar circumstances be turned over to the Government of Marshal Tito'. The appeal was delivered to Sir D'Arcy Osborne, the British diplomatic representative to the Holy See, soon after the end of hostilities, when the Allies were still eager to see war criminals brought to justice. The response from Osborne's superiors at the Foreign Office was predictable. The Ustashi would continue in detention as 'disarmed hostile troops pending a decision by the British and US courts', said London.[553]

The Vatican was apparently displeased with this answer. Presumably, it was also displeased with the fact that in the ensuing months some extradition requests were granted to Yugoslavia, albeit at a slow pace. On 27 March 1946, the Vatican increased the pressure. A second petition, this time in the Pope's own name, was made on behalf of the Nazi-smuggling operation run by Father Draganovic. The Vatican Secretariat of State forwarded to both London and Washington 'an urgent appeal which it has received from the Croatian Confraternity of San Girolamo at Rome on behalf of those Croatians, particularly the group at POW Camp 215, Grottaglie, Taranto, who are threatened with extradition or repatriation'. In other words, this appeal was made on behalf of Croatian Nazi collaborators and war criminals. If any doubt remained that the plea was being forwarded by Pope Pius XII himself, the document added, 'The Confraternity has appealed to His Holiness asking Him to recommend this matter.'

This second appeal sparked a flurry of communications between London and Washington, but failed, at least on the surface, to accomplish its purpose. London decided to inform the Vatican that even if the Allies did not intend to 'repatriate any subject against his or her wishes', this policy did not apply 'in the case of war criminals'. The Allies intended to extradite precisely those men whom the Pope sought to protect.[554]

During this early period before Cold War priorities emerged, a handful of British diplomats expressed dismay at the Vatican's attitude. In January 1947, Yugoslavia demanded from London the extradition of five criminals who were being lodged at the Pontifical Institute of Oriental Studies. The wanted men included some of the former ministers of General Milan Nedic, Hitler's wartime puppet ruler in Serbia, the first nation to be declared 'Judenfrei' ('Free of Jews') by the Nazis in 1942. Founded by the Vatican in 1917, the Oriental Institute was responsible for, among other things, training priests for missions inside nations that had fallen under the Soviet sphere of influence, such as Yugoslavia. Perhaps not surprisingly, one of the institute's more notorious graduates was Father Draganovic, who had studied there between 1932 and 1935 and specialized in 'Balkan affairs'. Although the Oriental Institute was located outside the walls of the Vatican City, on the historic Piazza Santa Maria Maggiore in Rome, it enjoyed the full benefits of Vatican extraterritoriality. And it was therefore an ideal hiding place for war criminals, beyond the reach of the Italian or Allied authorities.[555]

Aware of the criminal records of the men involved, London wished to grant their extradition. But Britain's representative before the Holy See was sure that the Pope would not consent. Osborne was also 'very anxious to avoid the indignation that would undoubtedly be aroused by a forced search of Vatican premises'. British officials pondered how to proceed. 'We should arrest and surrender these men if they were anywhere else in Italy than the Vatican,' fretted one British official. Finally, at the suggestion of the US State Department, London prompted Yugoslavia to request their extradition directly from the Pope. Osborne was instructed to warn Vatican officials and to impress upon them that they were being increasingly perceived around the world 'as the deliberate protectors of Hitler's and Mussolini's ex-minions'. The Foreign Office was decidedly shocked by the case: 'Though we do not for a moment wish to interfere in the Vatican's affairs . . . we should point out that the ministers of Nedic and Pavelic are not Thomas à Beckets.'[556]

In mid-January 1947, Osborne consequently hand-delivered a 'confidential' aide-mémoire to Cardinal Domenico Tardini of the Vatican Secretariat of State. (Since 1944, Pope Pius XII had gone without a fully fledged secretary of state, relying instead on his two undersecretaries, Tardini and Montini, with whom he met twice daily to micromanage foreign policy.) Osborne warned Tardini that Yugoslavia was about to present extradition requests, emphasizing that 'the British authorities entertain no doubt as to the guilt of the five men'. He also reminded Tardini of 'the undesirability of supplying material for the charge that the Vatican defends and protects the former agents and tools of Hitler and Mussolini'. Anxious to deflect Vatican responsibility, Tardini told Osborne that 'the Pope had recently issued strict orders to all ecclesiastical institutions in Rome that they were not to entertain guests, i.e. harbour refugees, without higher authority'.

This Papal injunction against aiding suspects 'without higher authority' flies in the face of present-day Vatican claims that the Pope was unaware of the Nazi rescue activities at ecclesiastical institutions such as Santa Maria dell'Anima or San Girolamo, let alone at his own Oriental Institute. It shows not only that Pius XII knew of these operations but also that the great number of criminals who continued to receive sanctuary after the order was issued could only have done so with his tacit consent. Osborne was not optimistic. If there were any more 'guests' on Vatican territory, 'I do not believe for a moment that the Pope would give the order for their surrender,' he informed London.[557]

Tellingly enough, and practically on the same day that Osborne met with Tardini, the Vatican put forward a third appeal: this time for the notorious Nazi collaborator Miroslav Spalajkovic, a Serbian diplomat who had served many years in France and was now hiding in Rome. 'The competent Allied authorities are requested to use their good offices to prevent his repatriation to Yugoslavia, where without doubt a severe sentence awaits him,' the Vatican wrote. London was astounded. 'We think that it might be as well to let the Vatican know which way the wind blows and to inform them of the present situation pointing out that he is undoubtedly guilty of collaboration with the Germans,' the Foreign Office howled. But for all its indignation, London finally relented. Instead of facing trial in Belgrade, Spalajkovic died in his beloved Paris in 1951.[558]

The moral blindness of the Catholic Church continued to vex the Foreign Office, however, and three weeks later, on 4 February 1947, Osborne again met with Tardini. The Cardinal was quick to reaffirm 'the Pope's recent strict orders against the entertainment of guests' and reassured Osborne that the five wanted men 'are no longer at the Oriental Institute'. But the meeting was overshadowed by a new and even more damaging charge that had just been laid at the Pope's door. Yugoslavia had publicly revealed that a 'great number' of war criminals were being 'helped on their way' to Argentina by San Girolamo, with the support of the Pontifical Commission of Assistance (PCA), which 'provided them with visas and financial assistance'. The PCA, Yugoslavia charged, was violating 'the decision of all the United Nations to return war criminals to the country where they committed their crime'.

The accusation was true – as Tardini surely knew. (The PCA also helped notorious SS criminals such as Erich Priebke and Gerhard Bohne to escape to Argentina.) But rather than shut down this 'ratline', the Vatican fudged the issue. Tardini claimed that the PCA 'had nothing to do with the Secretariat of State'. The Cardinal 'seemed to imply a waiver of responsibility for the commission's activities,' Osborne reported. 'I pointed out to him however that it was a Vatican organisation and the instrument of Papal charity, and that consequently responsibility for it could not be disavowed.'

Coming up once more against a brick wall, London resigned itself to the belief that 'the Vatican has not been helpful' about surrendering war criminals. The Foreign Office's intense frustration was summarized in a bitter memo: 'If Pope Pius XII wishes to assume the mantle of Gregory VII [an eleventh-century saint and one of the greatest Roman pontiffs] he can do it better than by harbouring Ustashi.'[559]

Whatever hopes these diplomats had for a Papal change of heart were roundly dashed the following month. On 26 April 1947, the Pope produced his fourth and most astonishing appeal, this time in favour of 15 Ustashi awaiting extradition at a British-controlled military prison in Rome. The new petition exceeded even the already bizarre previous attempts, somehow affirming in a single page that the men 'at present detained as war criminals in the Regina Elena Prison' had been 'at all times staunch advocates of the application of humanitarian principles'. Given the men in question and the murderous character of the regime they had served, this was a curious choice of words. The Vatican's list included thugs of the worst sort, most notably the enthusiastic Nazi collaborator General Vladimir Kren and the custodian of Pavelic's looted gold General Ante Moskov.[560]

As we have already seen, Kren was the Yugoslav Air Force officer who deserted in 1941 and revealed to Hitler's commanders the secret location of Yugoslavia's military airfields, before joining in the Nazi raids against his own country. For this, Pavelic rewarded him with the command of the Croat Air Force. When Kren was arrested in Genoa on 4 March 1947, about to board the *Philippa* to Buenos Aires with a group of other Ustasha fugitives, Draganovic's associate Monsignor Petranovic unsuccessfully pleaded with the British authorities for Kren to be allowed to continue his journey to Argentina. That appeal was now re-routed through the Vatican Secretariat of State.

General Moskov, for his part, had been a trusted confidant of Pavelic since 1933. With Pavelic's rise to power, he was named commander of the elite Poglavnik Bodyguard, one of Croatia's largest military units. After the war, the ruthless Moskov became one of the main custodians of the gold, diamonds and foreign currency plundered by Pavelic during his bloody regime. Part of this treasure had already ended up in British hands; another part had been given to Draganovic to safeguard in the Vatican.

With Pavelic in hiding, Moskov became the virtual commander

of the Ustashi, defending Pavelic's authority against those who considered the Poglavnik discredited. During 1945, he returned secretly to Croatia to promote guerrilla activity. He also ran 'his own private intelligence service', which British intelligence learned that he financed 'by helping himself to the gold and other valuables which had been brought out of Croatia'. Moskov had high connections at the Vatican. One of his close associates, Professor Vinko Nikolic, was received by Pope Pius XII in June 1946. Given such elevated contacts, the events of 23 October 1946 may have come as a shock to Moskov: he was arrested in Venice by British officers, who confiscated the 3,200 gold coins, 75 diamonds and stash of American dollars in his possession.[561]

Although the capture and extradition of Moskov and the other men on the Vatican's list was classified 'Top Secret', Draganovic's spies were fully informed of British intentions. Indeed, the Croatian priest was himself petitioning the Allies on behalf of the same Ustashi at Regina Elena. Not coincidentally, both Draganovic's and the Pope's lists were topped by Pavelic's 1944 diplomatic representative in Vichy France, Dusan Zanko, a former director of the Zagreb opera. This cultured man could presumably claim less responsibility in Ustasha crimes than coarser thugs such as Moskov and Kren. Nonetheless, he was on the Allied 'A' list of most-wanted criminals and was therefore slated for automatic extradition. In the early postwar years, Zanko had become the Croatian administrator at the British detention camp at Fermo. But covertly – as American intelligence knew from at least 1946 – he was an intermediary between Draganovic's secret service and the Vatican. Perhaps because of this, Draganovic tried to prevent Zanko's extradition by warning him of the secret British plan to transfer him from Fermo to Regina Elena.[562]

By 1947, the 2,500 Croatians at Fermo had created a miniature homeland for themselves, complete with a grammar school, a choir and a ballet. There they could count on the sympathy of the Archbishop of Fermo, although this was intermingled with the slight puzzlement of the local population. 'The Americans don't understand anything, the Italians can't do anything . . . sometimes they call us

Czechs, sometimes they call us Poles, sometimes Slavs,' recalled Zanko in bitter memoirs published in Argentina years later.

But the British camp commander sympathized with the Croatians and had promised to warn Zanko if a transfer order came so that he could escape in time. It was, however, a promise that the commander was unable to keep. One night in mid-April, the roar of British motorbikes surrounded the camp and some 20 Ustashi were carried off at gunpoint, handcuffed and bundled on to trains to Rome. Similar scenes occurred at other detention camps. 'It looked as if the most dangerous enemies of humanity were hunted,' wrote Draganovic in his appeal to Washington. 'In the middle of the night 60 trucks and jeeps with 1,000 British soldiers in full war equipment penetrated into the Bagnoli camp.'

Over 80 Ustashi captured in such raids around Italy were assembled at Regina Elena and encircled by barbed wire and armed guards. Despite the bleak view from their cell windows, some of these men still hoped to avoid extradition. 'We were sent messages telling us of the high, and most high, interventions in our favour,' Zanko wrote later. 'Pope Pius XII was sparing no effort to defend our innocence and to demand a verdict from justice. The outlook was said to be good for us, the Americans were helping, an important person was visiting and looking into some personal cases.'

This optimism was dashed on 25 April, when Moskov, Kren and five other Ustashi on the Vatican's list heard their names called out by a British officer. 'There was mortal silence as we all pressed our heads against the bars with our mouths open,' Zanko recalled. 'The officer ordered all those named to prepare themselves for departure. But to where? To liberty or . . .? It was only the next day that we learned they were being sent back to the fatherland, to death.'

Among those left behind, pessimism reigned. The commander at Fermo sent a British priest to console Zanko. 'The British people don't know what's going on here, they don't think the way these policemen do, who are at the service of misguided policies,' the blue-eyed prelate whispered. 'Be strong, God will not forsake you.'[563]

The Catholic Church set all wheels in motion to try to prevent further surrenders. On 23 April, in London, the Archbishop of Westminster, Bernard Griffin, together with the Archbishop of Canterbury, Geoffrey Fisher, met with British Prime Minister Clement Attlee. The archbishops proposed the removal of nearly 25,000 Yugoslavs from Italy to the British Zone in Germany, to reduce the risk of their extradition when control of such matters was handed back to the Italians in September 1947. Griffin travelled immediately to Rome, arriving just as Kren and Moskov were handed over. He received several Croatian delegations pleading in their favour. 'I did my best to intervene, but was too late,' the dismayed cardinal wrote later. He nonetheless took the matter up confidentially with British Foreign Secretary Ernest Bevin, expressing concern 'lest further Croats should be handed over'. Bevin's reply was itself astounding, for in it he certified that only 'traitors', not 'war criminals', were being surrendered. 'Some of them of course took part in what we would describe as war crimes, having been members of the staffs of concentration camps or extermination squads, but it is on the basis of their treason that the decision whether to surrender them or not has been taken,' Bevin reassured the cardinal.[564]

For those already on their way to Yugoslavia, there was to be no reprieve. On 27 April, Kren and five of the other Ustashi on the Vatican's list were surrendered to Tito's courts. Moskov's own handover, delayed when he attempted suicide on the train carrying him to justice, was eventually carried out three days later.[565]

In mid-June, the Foreign Office gave Osborne icy instructions to inform the Vatican of the conclusion of the extradition matter and to do so without any apologies. 'Point out to the Secretariat of State that, whatever their reputation as "staunch advocates of the application of humanitarian principles", those persons who actively supported the German invaders of Croatia and worked for the Pavelic Ustasha government were giving their support and approval to a regime which flouted humanitarian principles and which condoned atrocities unsurpassed in any period of human history.'[566]

Meanwhile, Zanko and those other Ustashi left behind at Regina Elena dreaded the worst. 'The melancholy shadow of death is floating over this sad building, and over every one of these candidates of death,' Draganovic wrote in his appeal to Washington. Huddled in his cell, his only comfort a portrait of the Virgin Mary on the wall, Zanko shared his imprisonment with Pavelic's moneyman, Ivo Heinrich, and with Ustasha Lieutenant Dragutin Dosen, who had crossed clandestinely from Austria to Italy with the Poglavnik, both dressed as Catholic priests. 'The tension rose higher each day,' Zanko recalled later. 'The Rosary was said more piously . . . Our gaze concentrated more upon the Virgin.'

Then, providentially, a cutting tool was smuggled inside a loaf of bread to one of the inmates. 'Mounted on the wings of faith, and on the shoulders of a friend', this inmate cut through the iron bars of his prison window. A young Croatian girl who visited the prisoners, Anka Rukavina, communicated the simple escape plan. On the night of 30 May, three Croatians outside the prison awaited the agreed signal from Josip Biosic, a former captain in the Poglavnik Bodyguard, who was to light a match at his cell window. The three men then climbed up the prison wall, cut through the barbed wire and inched their way below Biosic's window, attaching a strong rope to the end of a piece of twine lowered by the Ustasha captain. Biosic pulled up the 20-metre rope, tied it to one of his window's sawn-off bars and began lifting his companions to the opening, from where they slithered down to freedom.

'We gazed one last time upon the Virgin Mary,' recalled Zanko later. 'Our Mother's glance filled the whole atmosphere, as if she was taking charge of us, at this most critical moment, when our lives literally hung from the end of a rope.'

Zanko was ecstatic as he and his companions, a group of around ten men, were delivered, 'as if into the hands of angels', into the arms of their saviours. 'We hugged, we kissed and cried with emotion,' he recalled. The former diplomat ran barefoot through dew-covered fields, his shoes in his hands. 'We looked back at Regina Elena, which sailed like a dead ship towards the light of the moon . . . and simply let ourselves be invaded by waves of joy.'

By sunrise, with his shoes back on, Zanko had made his way

unhindered to the Roman Colosseum. 'We were awake like birds, light and winged with extreme excitement ... We imagined the laughter of our friends when they learned how, unarmed, we duped a whole armed-diplomatic-police-political system, which like a spider has descended on post-war Europe ... We laughed loudly at those poor English policemen in the service of Communism, and our laughter resonated down the sleepy streets of Rome.'[567]

British intelligence afterwards described this escape as 'the most spectacular achievement of the Ustashi in Italy against the British authorities'. Father Draganovic quickly sheltered Zanko and other escapees on the Pope's list. According to American intelligence, they were 'fed, clothed, housed and otherwise provided for' at San Girolamo. Zanko's group also found alternative sanctuary at the idyllically beautiful thirteenth-century monastery of San Francesco d'Assisi at Cosenza in southern Italy.[568]

The lengthy and eventful stand-off between the Vatican and London over Kren, Moskov, Zanko and the other men on the Pope's list proved, however, to be the last. For behind the scenes, and quite clearly behind the backs of some important British and American diplomats, a secret deal was agreed upon between the Vatican, London and Washington. This deal arranged that any further Ustasha war criminals would not be delivered to Tito's Yugoslavia, but instead to Perón's Argentina, where they were guaranteed a warmer welcome. John Moors Cabot, the American ambassador in Belgrade, who was out of this information loop, was livid. 'Some arrangement has been worked out with Vatican and Argentina,' he cabled Washington on 12 June 1947. 'We are conniving with Vatican and Argentina to get people to haven in latter country.'[569]

Unlike Moors Cabot, the British diplomats at the Vatican were in the know, and deeply cynical to boot. 'As regards the activities of the Catholic Clergy in maintaining Yugoslav refugees and assisting their emigration to South America, it depends on one's point of view whether one regards them as humanitarian or as politically sinister,' wrote Victor Perowne, who was previously an Argentine expert at the

South American desk of the Foreign Office. Perowne made a clear distinction between 'Black' and 'Grey' Ustashi. 'The "Blacks" have been returned to Yugoslavia, but His Majesty's Government have asked the Vatican to assist in getting the "Greys" to South America although they are certainly wanted by the Yugoslav government, because His Majesty's Government (and the US Government) do not consider them wicked enough to hand them over to certain death at the hands of the Yugoslav authorities. The latter, however, may well regard the activities of the Catholic Church in getting the "Greys" to South America as not humanitarian, but as politically sinister.'

Perowne preferred to overlook the moral implications of the secret agreement: 'There are a number of minor Fascist leaders, I believe, in sanctuary at *San Paolo fuori le Mura* [outside the walls of Saint Paul's], and it is not impossible that some Yugoslav war criminals may have taken refuge at San Girolamo, there would be nothing very unusual about that . . . It is unlikely that the Vatican approve the political, as opposed to the religious, activities of Father Draganovic & Company, so far as they can be disentangled. For this is a situation where it is almost impossible to disentangle religion from politics.'

But in London, some diplomats were still left with an unsavoury taste in their mouths. 'While we cannot condemn the charitable attitude of the Catholic Church towards sinful individuals we feel, however, that there has been much evidence to show that the Vatican has permitted the encouragement both covert, and overt, of the Ustashi,' they replied to Perowne. 'This wholly undesireable organisation has not only been collectively responsible for vile atrocities on an immense scale during the war but has ever since its inception made use of murder as a normal political weapon. There is surely all the difference between giving shelter to, let us say, dissident Slovene priests, and giving positive aid to a creature like Pavelic?'[570]

Apparently as part of the secret agreement, Britain accepted Cardinal Griffin's proposal of removing Croatian criminals from harm's way. On 9 September 1947, a combined British and American operation transplanted those still left at Regina Elena and at the Allied camps in Italy to the British Zone of Germany, where they would be protected from extradition requests placed by Yugoslavia before the new Italian government. The mop-up operation continued during October, as the British gathered left-behind criminals and sent them to safety. The Catholic Church, however, remained uneasy; Cardinal Griffin petitioned again in favour of those criminals now imprisoned in Germany. He was right to worry, for in 1948, despite all precautions, Britain handed over two more men on the Pope's list to Yugoslavia.[571]

This final handover of Croatian criminals was, however, the exception that proved the rule. In early 1947, the US State Department had already communicated to London its desire to establish 'a cut-off date, after which no further applications whatsoever for the surrender of alleged war criminals will be entertained'. Washington had already ignored nearly 600 Yugoslavian extradition requests, responding only to 'urgent individual cases as a result of constant pressure from us', as the British embassy in Washington reported. 'There is no doubt that the State Department at all levels greatly regret the past assurances which they have given to the Yugoslav government about effecting surrenders and wish to wash their hands of the whole business at the earliest possible opportunity.'[572]

Pressure for an end to extradition proceedings had come not only from the US State Department but from the American Catholic Church as well, in the figure of Francis Joseph Spellmann, the Cardinal Archbishop of New York and a long-time friend of Pius XII. Spellmann had joined the Pope and Cardinal Griffin in pleading against the surrender of Kren, Moskov and the other Ustashi at Regina Elena. He was an effective force and one whom the British respected highly. 'Yugoslav-American groups in this country are powerful and need careful handling,' the British embassy in Washington warned London. 'There are signs that they may renew pressure in Congress and with the State Department before long and we should be wise to avoid, as far as possible, bringing grist to their mill.'[573]

Until mid-1947, the British Foreign Office continued to apply pressure on the Americans to surrender Ustasha criminals, but to little avail. The US State Department had been displeased by the handover of the Regina Elena prisoners and Croatian interest groups were skilfully lobbying to prevent any further surrenders. London was increasingly finding itself in the uncomfortable position of having to justify the extradition proceedings.[574]

Britain soon found itself losing heart in the business of hunting down war criminals. By 1948, it had drafted a special directive reinforcing Foreign Secretary Bevin's criterion that only Nazi collaborators would be eligible for surrender; those guilty merely of crimes against humanity were to be let off the hook. 'The motives of those concerned, particularly of a racial, political or religious nature . . . will not be allowed to override an assessment . . . to the effect that active and wilful collaboration took place,' the directive stated.[575]

Of the 15 criminals on the Pope's list, the research for this book has been able to confirm the handover of only nine to Yugoslavia. Zanko, who escaped barefoot through the fields surrounding Regina Elena with images of the Virgin Mary and Communist British policemen swirling about him, eventually found his way to Argentina. He died in Venezuela in 1980, a respected university professor who seldom spoke of his past. The fate of the remaining five men on Pius XII's list remains uncertain. In any case, only a tiny fraction of the suspected Croatian war criminals in Italy were ever handed over for trial. When they did their final tally in May 1948, British officials found they had surrendered only some 50 men to Yugoslavia, less than 3 per cent of the 1,800 extradition requests they had received from Belgrade since the end of the war.[576]

The Nazi-smuggling operation to Argentina run by Father Draganovic from his church in Rome lies at the heart of the allegations that there was full Papal cognizance of such a network. The Croatian Confraternity of San Girolamo had a long Papal association. Indeed, in the sixteenth century, one of its principals had been Sixtus V, the first Croatian Pope, who built the present-day Church of San Girolamo. (It was also Sixtus V who excommunicated Queen Elizabeth of England.) In 1971, Paul VI finally made the Papal connection official, elevating the college to Pontifical status, when it became the Pontificio Collegio Croato di San Girolamo. This was the same standing enjoyed by other Vatican colleges, such as the Pontifical Oriental Institute. But even in the immediate postwar era, the Vatican connection was strong enough that Allied officials disagreed on San Girolamo's exact status *vis-à-vis* the Vatican. Some intelligence sources claimed San Girolamo did not enjoy Vatican extraterritoriality. But at least one American intelligence report stated quite squarely that it was indeed 'Vatican property'.

Draganovic was known to be 'under the protection of Cardinal Pietro Fumasoni-Biondi,' the Prefect of the Congregazione de Propaganda Fide, which was the Vatican's own intelligence service. (Propaganda Fide was also well known among Western diplomats as 'the Ministry of the Vatican which deals with Yugoslavia'.) Another Vatican intelligence chief closely connected to Draganovic was Cardinal Angelo dell'Acqua, reputedly Draganovic's superior in the Vatican's intelligence hierarchy and a high-ranking staff member at the Secretariat of State. Informally, among intelligence chiefs, Draganovic was known as the 'head' of the Vatican's 'Balkan desk', and Pius XII was understood to know 'everything about Father Draganovic's activities, otherwise he would never have stayed in his position', as one former British intelligence officer claimed.[577]

Indeed, as American intelligence already knew, Draganovic's work was 'well known to the Vatican Secretariat of State', which reportedly saw it in 'an unfavourable light' – although apparently not so unfavourably as to merit closing down his operation. Cardinal Fumasoni-Biondi was also aware of Draganovic's Nazi-smuggling operation and 'disapproved' of it. The Vatican intelligence chief was said to be dismayed with Bratovstina ('Brotherhood'), the 'Relief Association' set up by Draganovic at San Girolamo, which was aimed solely at providing succour for Ustasha and Nazi fugitives. (The Red Cross passport application of SS murderer Gerhard Bohne, for example, carries Draganovic's signature and a Bratovstina stamp.) This association received funding from the Vatican's PCA. As late as 1952, and in spite of Fumasoni-Biondi's 'prohibition', it still issued false identity cards to Ustasha fugitives. Washington also knew that Draganovic received 'large compensation' from Bishop Hudal for sending wanted Nazis to Argentina, and that Draganovic 'took no interest in business which did not concern Ustashi and Nazis or did not yield him a particular financial benefit'.[578]

The Vatican's official representative at San Girolamo was the Franciscan Father Dominic Mandic, who printed false identity cards for Draganovic's fugitives on Franciscan presses. Mandic was a supporter of Pavelic who only embraced the Ustasha creed after the Western Allies failed to respond to Pavelic's peace overtures in 1944. A native of Herzegovina, Mandic arrived in Rome in 1939 as the treasurer of the Franciscan Order. At San Girolamo, he managed Draganovic's accounts with the aid of Pavelic's moneyman Ivo Heinrich. As we have seen, he paid the way to Argentina for even hardened criminals such as the Jasenovac concentration camp commander Dinko Sakic.[579]

Mandic had substantial funds to manage, including donations from the Croatian community in the United States, as well as money from 'Vatican circles who had previously actively supported the [Ustasha] organisation in 1923–41'. At the same time, Mandic and Heinrich arranged 'the placing against Italian currency of the gold, jewellery and foreign exchange deposited by high-ranking Ustasha officials'. In other words, of the 'victim gold' Pavelic and his aides had brought from Croatia to Rome.[580]

Part of this gold went to finance the postwar Ustasha secret service, including its plug-ins to Allied and Vatican intelligence. Run from Rome by Pavelic's son-in-law, General Vilko Pecnikar, this service also reached across Europe, the United States and Argentina. The Vatican intelligence contact was Father Mandic, who liaised with Draganovic and Zanko. According to a highly sourced American intelligence report, the Vatican provided 'moral help', as well as practical assistance, by conveying 'a great deal of correspondence' between the fugitive Ustashi and Yugoslavia. Most importantly, the Ustasha secret service was financed from Vatican funds, 'from their means for information'. These contributions were funnelled through Father Mandic, as American intelligence learned.[581]

British intelligence had also heard that the information collected by Draganovic's service was 'passed on to the Vatican', which probably explains the grudging support from Cardinal Fumasoni-Biondi towards Draganovic's Nazi-smuggling activities. In fact, both Vatican and Allied intelligence had a vested interest in supporting Draganovic's spies. They were 'an excellent secret service, aided at times by members of the Allied services', according to one CIA document. And, until 1948, both the Vatican and the Allies cherished the hope that Draganovic's secret service could help topple Tito's Communist regime.[582]

Since 1947, American intelligence had been working with the Croatian priest to ensure the escape of 'VIP personalities' from Europe. This collaboration seems to have been kick-started by the Pope's ardent plea in favour of the Ustashi at Regina Elena. Draganovic, therefore, was now not only passing intelligence to his Vatican and Allied masters, he was also proving himself useful by smuggling Soviet defectors and former Nazis who collaborated with the US to South America.

American support of Draganovic began when special agent Paul Lyon, of the 430th Counter Intelligence Corps in Austria, was ordered 'to establish a means of disposition' for questionable CIC informants. In one of the two surviving reports on the Draganovic–CIC 'ratline', Lyon related how, in the late summer or autumn of 1947, he proceeded to Italy. There, he contacted Draganovic ('Resettlement Chief of the Vatican'), who agreed to smuggle CIC informants to Argentina at a price of 1,500 dollars per head, as long as they were 'hardworking Catholics and loyal sons of the Church'. In return, the CIC 'actively assisted' Draganovic through another American intelligence agent, Robert Bishop, who was 'chief of the eligibility office' at the International Refugee Organization in Rome. Exploiting his position, Bishop began funnelling 'documentation and IRO aid' to Draganovic's fugitives, who were otherwise singularly unfit for such consideration. Unhappily, Bishop cracked. After a few months, he started gabbling wild tales based on his real covert activities and had to be removed from service. From then on, Draganovic obtained the necessary travel papers himself.[583]

This secret cooperation was upgraded in July 1948. The CIC agreed to smuggle Draganovic's fugitives out of Germany to Austria, in return for his assistance in obtaining Argentine visas for persons of interest to the US. To fulfil this bargain, Lyon requested the reassignment of 'two detachment jeeps', apparently so they could be used for such smuggling missions. This new agreement seems to have been acted on quickly, as around the same time a group of Nazi jet-plane designers being transported to Argentina by Draganovic was indeed smuggled from Germany to Austria in US Army jeeps. As we have already seen, these Nazi scientists travelled under Croatian aliases. Among those who crossed over the border was the SS criminal and euthanasia mastermind Gerhard Bohne, one of the worst Nazi criminals to escape to Argentina, and apparently an early beneficiary of the CIC–Draganovic agreement.[584]

For his part, Draganovic notoriously kept his side of the bargain. He shipped CIC informant and SS criminal Klaus Barbie out of Genoa in 1951, at a cost of 1,400 dollars to the American taxpayer, which went straight into Draganovic's eager pocket.[585]

By 1952, however, Draganovic was on the way out. The information gathered by his secret service was now being sent principally to the 'Ustasha Central Direction in Buenos Aires', to be carried in the Croatian publications of Pavelic's government-in-exile – a far cry from the glory days when it was passed to the Vatican and Allied secret services. Similarly, the CIC–Draganovic 'ratline' died a natural death after Barbie's 'resettlement' in South America. Even so, Draganovic still managed to find clients for his 'emigration' service, charging them 25,000 Italian lire a head. But without American support it became an uphill battle, and by 1953, as the CIA heard, the Ustasha priest had 'lost face in political, civilian and ecclesiastical circles, including the Vatican Secretariat of State'.[586]

Draganovic's usefulness to the Vatican expired only a few days after the death of Pius XII, a clear pointer as to the source of his great and mysterious power since his arrival in Rome in mid-war. In October 1958, the CIA heard that the once-proud priest had been unceremoniously thrown out of his beloved San Girolamo, 'by orders from the Secretary of State of the Vatican'. This eviction was a humiliating final blow and again suggests who had been Draganovic's real master all along.[587]

No longer a pipeline to the Vatican, Draganovic was dropped by American intelligence as well, 'with prejudice, for security reasons', in early 1962. His dismissal slip reveals the priest's secret aliases ('Bloody Draganovic' and 'Dr. Fabiano'), as well as his code-name ('Dynamo'). 'Not amenable to control, too knowledgeable of unit personnel and activity; demands outrageous monetary tribute and US support of Croat organisations as partial payment for cooperation' was the conclusion of American intelligence. No longer useful to the Vatican or to the US, Draganovic decided to return to his homeland. In 1967 he crossed the border from Italy to Yugoslavia, where he made public statements praising Tito's regime. It is still a matter of conjecture whether Draganovic's defection was voluntary or whether he was kidnapped by Tito's agents. He died in Yugoslavia in July 1983.[588]

If Pius XII's secret appeals for Croatian criminals were shocking, they pale alongside his effort to seek pardons for some of the leading Nazis convicted at Nuremberg and other postwar trials. Various such pleas for hardcore Nazis were put forward by the Vatican between 1946 and 1952. Among the death sentences the Pope wished to see commuted were those of Arthur Greiser, convicted for the murder of 100,000 Jews in Poland; Otto Ohlendorf, who had murdered some 90,000 people as commander of the mobile killing squad Einsatzgruppe D; and Oswald Pohl, head of WHVA, the vast SS agency that ran the Nazi concentration camps, overseeing a slave force of 500,000 prisoners and supervising the conversion of victims' jewellery, hair and clothes to hard currency. In the last two cases, the secret appeals were to be routed privately to the American occupation authorities through Bishop Aloysius Muench, Pius XII's postwar envoy to Germany, who liaised with Montini in Rome. Aware of the disrepute that would befall the Vatican if a Papal appeal for such criminals became public but pressured by the Pope's eagerness to intervene, Muench walked a tightrope and gently counselled Montini against pressing for pardons.[589]

Montini, during this time, walked a tightrope of his own, providing Vatican support to Draganovic's Nazi-smuggling operation while keeping a safe distance from the Croatian priest. It was a hard distance to impose, given Montini's wartime personal contacts with Croatian clergymen and Ustasha leaders. Even Pavelic himself had been received by Pius XII on 17 May 1941, shortly after his installation as puppet ruler by Hitler. While the Vatican never officially recognized Pavelic's Croatia, it did keep a Papal legate in Zagreb, and Montini and Tardini continued unofficially receiving Ustasha emissaries in Rome during the war, although sometimes reproaching them for the atrocities being committed by Pavelic. These high prelates must have been hopeful that, whatever the outcome of the war, a Catholic state would survive in Croatia. The emergence of a reunited Communist Yugoslavia must therefore have been a hard blow, and these Croatian contacts were harnessed in the cause against the Communist enemy.

Montini knew Draganovic from his close association with the Croatian Bishop Aloysius Stepinac, the prelate who had set up Pavelic's audience with the Pope and sent Draganovic to Rome in 1943. He also knew Draganovic through the latter's close association with Bishop Ivan Saric, the fiercely anti-Semitic 'hangman' of Sarajevo. And it was Montini who, as head of the Vatican's Pontifical Commission of Assistance, chose Draganovic as his liaison with the Croatian prisoners of war held in Allied detention camps. In a 1988 interview, William Gowen, a CIC agent in Rome, said that he knew 'Draganovic reported regularly to Montini' in his capacity as a representative of the PCA.[590]

Furthermore, some of the priests who assisted Draganovic in smuggling Nazis freely admitted that Montini and Pius XII supported Draganovic's work, in interviews for the 1991 ground-breaking book *Unholy Trinity*, by John Loftus and Mark Aarons. The book even reproduced a picture of Montini as under-secretary of state on the terrace of San Girolamo. Draganovic 'was fully empowered by the Holy See and was in charge not only for Croatians, but for everybody', including Nazis, said Father Vilim Cecelja, who shipped fugitives from Austria to Draganovic.

Another priest, Monsignor Milan Simcic, who worked with Draganovic smuggling fugitives in Rome, claimed that 'Draganovic and Montini were together many times' discussing San Girolamo's work, adding that Draganovic sought Montini's aid in many specific cases. Montini also helped Draganovic by interceding before foreign diplomats to obtain visas for San Girolamo's fugitives. The arrangement worked both ways; in return for his favours, 'Montini got in touch with Draganovic many times, asking him to help people on his behalf.' Simcic even claimed to the authors that he possessed copies of letters from Montini to Draganovic requesting him to smuggle certain individuals.[591]

In the end, a handful of shared values, a common religion and a common enemy helped to unite the Catholic Church, Allied intelligence and fugitive Nazis and their former collaborators in setting up an escape line out of Europe for some of the worst criminals of the century. Perhaps the men who collaborated in this venture never dreamt that over 50 years later researchers would be able to piece the puzzle back together again. Perhaps they never imagined that their actions would come back to haunt the institutions they served. And perhaps, driven by the urgency of their cause, they did not care. There is a chance they thought that, failing all else, their successors would be wise enough to know there could be no shame in admitting bygone errors. It is even possible that one day soon, the Vatican and the Argentine government will realize this fact. Then maybe they will make a clean break with the past, opening their postwar secret archives so that the full truth can be told, while there are still survivors of Hitler's genocide left alive to appreciate such a gesture.

NOTES

1 *The Odessa File*, Frederick Forsyth, Viking, 1972. Organisation der ehemaligen SS-Angehörigen = Organization of Former Members of the SS.

2 'La conexión Zurich', Rogelio García Lupo, *Clarín*, 22 November 1998.

3 Despite the DNA testing, there are those who still believe that Bormann really died in Argentina in 1972 and that his bones were transported to Berlin, buried where he was last seen alive in May 1945, to be 'accidentally' dug up by a construction crew in 1973, and finally subjected to the DNA test that certified them as the real article in 1998. Thus, believers hold, the Bormann cover-up became complete.

4 Letter from Duilia Fayó de Teisaire to author's mother, October 1953. Perón's full name was Juan Domingo Perón.

5 For more on the McCarthys and the Goñis, see *Private Faces, Public Places*, Abigail McCarthy, Doubleday & Company, New York, 1972.

6 The ring was ostensibly meant to caution motorists against excessive horn use. It had been the brainchild of Oscar Ivanissevich, who, as Perón's education minister in 1949, had led a bitter campaign against 'morbid ... perverse ... infamous' abstract art. This extreme nationalist reactionary was reinstated as education minister upon Perón's return to power in the 1970s. See 'Aquel perverso arte abstracto', by Ramiro de Casasbellas, *La Nación*, 1 October 1999.

7 For a detailed account of the author's years at the *Herald*, see *Judas, el infiltrado*, Uki Goñi, Sudamericana, Buenos Aires, 1996.

8 *Prisoner Without a Name, Cell Without a Number*, Jacobo Timerman, New York, 1981.

9 *Bruce Chatwin*, Nicholas Shakespeare, The Harvill Press, London, 1999.

10 'Full Translation of Ribbentrop–Goyeneche Conversation', 7 December 1942, NARA, RG 59, Box 23. Also, *Perón y los alemanes*, Uki Goñi, Sudamericana, Buenos Aires, 1998, ch. 3.

11 For two studies of Argentina's change during the 1930s and 1940s, see *Del Estado Liberal a la Nación Católica*, Loris Zanatta, Universidad Nacional de Quilmes, Buenos Aires, 1996; and *Perón y el Mito de la Nación Católica*, Loris Zanatta, Sudamericana, Buenos Aires, 1999.

12 *Perón y los Alemanes*, Goñi, ch. 3.

13 Reinebeck affidavit, TC 21540, 4 February 1946, NARA, RG 59, Box 25. Goyeneche travelled to Europe in 1942 with two companions, the Uruguayan Juan Alberto Bove Trabal and the Argentine García Santillán. Bove Trabal returned to Uruguay in 1943, where he

was arrested for Nazi spying activities. García Santillán after the war formed part of Perón's Nazi rescue team at the Casa Rosada.

14 *Perón y los Alemanes*, Goñi, ch. 3. For Perón in Rome, *Perón 1895–1942*, Enrique Pavón Pereyra, Espiño, Buenos Aires, 1952. Letter Goyeneche to Ruiz Guiñazú-GPP, 25 January 1942.

15 Thermann interrogation, 27 September to 6 November 1945, NARA, RG 59, Box 26. Also 'top secret' cable Thermann to Ribbentrop, 5 July 1941, Documents on German Foreign Policy, D Series, vol. 13, document 73.

16 For details of these mediation approaches see 'Efforts by the Argentine Foreign Ministry to Obtain the Mediation of the Holy See to End the War', MRE, Guerra Europea, 1942, File 1, vol. IV; 'Efforts by Neutral Powers to Obtain the Concertation of a European Peace', MRE, Guerra Europea, 1939, File 163; 'Rumours Regarding a Possible Presentation of Peace Proposals by Mr. Hitler', MRE; Guerra Europea, 1941, File 329; and 'Peace Efforts With the Intervention of the Holy See', MRE, Guerra Europea, 1942, File 460. The Romanian minister referred to in Madrid was probably Radu Ghenea, a close friend of Goyeneche in Madrid and later a member of Perón's postwar Nazi rescue team in Buenos Aires.

17 For a detailed account of the operations of the Argentine embassy in Madrid, its Nazi connections and Nazi arms shipments, *Perón y los Alemanes*, Goñi, ch. 3.

18 *Perón y los Alemanes*, ch. 3. One thin dossier that escaped destruction at Argentina's Foreign Ministry records some of these Nazi arms purchases, MRE, Argentine embassy in Spain, Box 31, File 177. Sadly, this dossier was partly 'cleansed' before it was discovered by the author, various secret communications from the Argentine navy and army regarding arms purchases mentioned in its index having been torn out.

19 Knochen interrogation, 21 February 1946, NARA, RG 59, Box 24. Also, Arnold interrogation, 20 November 1946, NARA, RG 59, 862.20252/11-2246. The Argentines sought visas from Germany and France for the trip to Paris, see the series of related notes, April and May 1942, MRE, Argentine embassy in Spain, Box 26, Dossiers 143 & 145. Olivera was ambassador in Berlin from June 1939 until late 1941, transferred later to Vichy where he was the only accredited Western Hemisphere diplomat. For Olivera's pro-German stance, see Weizsäcker to Ribbentrop, 10 June 1940, DGFP, Series D, vol. 9, document 412; as well as Olivera to Buenos Aires, 5 April 1941, MRE, Guerra Europea, File 161, vol. 6. Knochen was sentenced to death by France after the war but his sentence was later commuted to 20 years. In 1962 De Gaulle returned him to Germany, where he was freed, see interview with Knochen by Lucien Steinberg, *Histoire Hors*, serie 26, Paris, 1972.

20 Coded telegrams 973 and 654, MRE, Escobar dossier. Also, telegram requesting Italian visas for Escobar and Goyeneche, 21 July 1942, MRE, Argentine embassy in Spain, 1942, Box 26, File 143. Their 'strictly private' trip to Rome was reported in the Argentine press, *La Nación*, 13 and 14 August 1942. Consul López, who was originally to accompany Goyeneche and Escobar to Rome, finally didn't go.

21 Schellenberg affidavit, TC-21364, 19 December 1945; also his interrogation, 6 February 1946, both at NARA, RG 59, Box 25.

22 United Press cable published by *El Tiempo de Bogotá*, 19 April 1943, MRE, Guerra Europea, File 1, vol. IV, p. 8.

23 Coded telegrams 1272 & 1292, from Llobet to Ruiz Guiñazú, 6 and 10 October 1942, MRE, Guerra Europea, 1942, File 1, vol. IV, pp. 5 and 6.

24 For the international repercussions, press cuttings, MRE, Guerra Europea, File 1, vol. IV, pp. 11–15.

25 NARA, RG 242, T-120, Roll 347, frames 259631–748. Paeffgen interrogation, 28 December 1945, NARA, RG 260, 390/44/33/03-05, Box 630.

26 Reinebeck affidavit, TC 21540, 4 February 1946, NARA, RG 59, Box 25.

27 For 'several hours' see Reinebeck affidavit, 24 January 1946, NARA, RG 59, Box 25.

28 'Full Translation of Ribbentrop–Goyeneche Conversation', 25 August 1945, NARA, RG 59, Box 23. For the German text, see 'Unterredung des Herrn Reichsaußenministers mit dem Argentinier Juan Carlos Goyeneche am 30. November 1942 im Gut Westfalen', ADAP, Serie E, Band IV, Nr. 264.

29 'Nationalists like Goyeneche anyhow supported the creation of the state of Israel because their Fascism was stronger than their anti-Semitism and they were with the Right against the Palestinians,' one relative of Goyeneche told the author, 29 December 1997. The former director of the Argentine National Archives said Goyeneche in the 1960s still talked about 'burning down the Jewish neighbourhoods', author's interview with Eugenio Rom, 21 November 1997. Another anonymous interview stated that Goyeneche claimed the images of the concentration camps had been faked by Metro-Goldwyn-Mayer.

30 Letter Goyeneche to Amadeo, 16 March 1943. Arnold interrogation, 20 November 1946, NARA, RG 59, 862.2052/11-2246. Blancké to Spaeth, 'Enclosing Affidavit of Hedwig Sommer', 4 March 1946, NARA, RG 84.

31 Raw transcript of Hoettl's on-camera interview for the Secrets of War television documentary, 1997, The Documedia Group.

32 Author's interview with Spitzy, 8 December 1998. For Spitzy's report, NARA, RG 242, T-175, Roll 458, frames 2975007–044. Spitzy claims that he penned the report, although it was made to look as if Hohenlohe had authored it. See also How We Squandered the Reich, Reinhard Spitzy, Michael Russell, Norwich, 1997. Also, Paeffgen interrogation, 29 December 1945, p. 28, NARA, RG 59, 250/48/30/07, Box 24.

33 For Becker, see 'The German Intelligence Services, List of German Agents Put Together by US Naval Intelligence Based on British Intelligence Reports', 10 November 1944, copy donated by John Loftus to Proyecto Testimonio in Buenos Aires. For a detailed account of Becker's activities in Argentina, Perón y los Alemanes, Goñi.

34 Reinebeck affidavit, 24 January 1946, NARA, RG 59, Box 25. For Luti, Perón y los Alemanes, Goñi, ch. 3. Also Paeffgen interrogation, 19 October 1945, NARA, RG 84.

35 Reinebeck affidavits, 24 January; 27 January; and 4 February 1946; NARA, RG 59, Box 25.

36 Magic Summary 324, 13 February 1943, NARA, RG 457.

37 Blancké to Cummings, 17 July 1945; and Blancké to Spaeth, 18 January 1946; both NARA, RG 59, Box 23. According to Blancké, records of the meetings with Ribbentrop and Hitler 'were among the Foreign Office files microfilmed and dispatched from Marburg'. Blancké seems not to have broached the Goyeneche issue during his interrogation of Ribbentrop, who proved extremely evasive regarding Argentina, Ribbentrop interrogation, 6 February 1946, NARA, RG 59, Box 25. Regarding Perón's vigilance of Blancké during the war, see Libro Azul y Blanco, Colonel Perón, Editorial Azul y Blanco, Buenos Aires, 1946, p. 39. Regarding Blancké, see Biographic Register, State Department, Washington DC; and Charles Stuart Kennedy, Foreign Affairs Oral History Program, who was posted with Blancké in Germany during the 1950s, author's interview, 2 June 1998.

38 Reinebeck affidavit, TC 21540, 4 February 1946, NARA, RG 59, Box 25. Author's interview with Sylvina Walger, who knew Goyeneche in the 1960s, 1998. Regarding the Black Forest, anonymous interview, 15 April 1999.

39 From the large group of notes Goyeneche made during his stay in Paris.

40 Letter Goyeneche to Schellenberg-GPP, 2 January 1943.

41 Schellenberg affidavit, TC-21364, 19 December 1945; also his interrogation, 6 February 1946, both at NARA, RG 59, Box 25. Letter Goyeneche to Amadeo-GPP, 16 March 1943. Arnold interrogation, 20 November 1946, enclosed with dispatch 7813, 22 November 1946, 862.20252/11-2246, NARA, RG 59.

42 Letter Goyeneche to Amadeo-GPP, 16 March 1943. Goyeneche also had fluid contact with the German embassy in Madrid, which was helping to finance various of his projects in Argentina, including the purchase with Nazi money of the influential Argentine Catholic Church mouthpiece El Pueblo, see Perón y los Alemanes, Goñi, ch. 3. Letter Jimenez Ruiz

to Dassonville-GPP, 2 November 1942. Arnold interrogation, 20 November 1946, NARA, RG 59, 862.20252/11-2246.

43 Letter Goyeneche to Amadeo-GPP, 19 July 1943.

44 Letter Goyeneche to Amadeo-GPP, 19 July 1943; Goyeneche to Mussolini, 6 April 1943.

45 Letter Mussolini to Castillo, 4 June 1943, MRE, DP, Italy 1943, Box 22.

46 Schellenberg interrogation, 6 February 1946; Schellenberg affidavit, TC 21364, 6 February 1946; and Reinebeck affidavit, TC 21540, 4 February 1946; all at NARA, RG 59, Box 25.

47 Schellenberg interrogation, 6 February 1946, NARA, RG 59, Box 23. Perón himself claimed on a number of occasions to have visited Germany although no documentary proof has been found to substantiate his claim. Italy's military intelligence suspected Perón was on an espionage mission in Europe and intercepted his correspondence, see *L'Argentina, gli Italiani, L'Italia*, Ludovico Incisa di Camerana, p. 519. Another version states that during the invasion of France, Perón awaited the arrival of German troops in Bordeaux, where he shared a hotel room for a week with Manuel Aznar, who would later be Spain's postwar ambassador to Argentina. This version was told to Argentine journalist Rogelio García Lupo by Aznar's press secretary, José Ignacio Ramos, author's interview with García Lupo, 13 October 1998.

48 For González in Germany, see the biographical details provided by González to the Argentine newspaper *La Nación*, in the *La Nación* archives, folder González. One of Perón's biographers has claimed that Perón visited González in Germany, *Perón 1895–1942*, Pavón Pereyra, 1952, p. 204.

49 See the two-part, 33-page interrogation of Schellenberg by Blancké and Collins, 6 February 1946, NARA, RG 59, Box 25.

50 *Perón y los Alemanes*, Goñi, ch. 6.

51 *Argentine Diary*, Ray Josephs, Book Find Club, New York, 1944, p. 65.

52 Becker report of meeting with Ramírez to SD Berlin, 28 June 1943, NARA, RG 242, T-120, Roll 762, frames 356225–226.

53 For a detailed account of the SD–GOU negotiations, *Perón y los Alemanes*, Goñi, ch. 6.

54 Hellmuth interrogation by the British, 28 April 1944, NARA, RG 59, Box 24. Also, Becker interrogations by Coordinación Federal, May 1945, 'Segundo Sumario', dossier 7, AGPJN, Case 793/45.

55 'Activities of Ernesto Hoppe and Osmar Hellmuth', 1944, PRO, FO 371, 37694B. This British file is 'Retained By Department' and still off limits to researchers nearly 60 years after the fact.

56 *Perón y los Alemanes*, Goñi, ch. 6.

57 Author's interview with Zaira Vélez, 6 October 1998.

58 *Perón y los Alemanes*, Goñi, ch. 8.

59 Author's interview with anonymous Hellmuth 'family friend', 28 and 30 August 1997. Hellmuth died in 1980.

60 *Perón y los Alemanes*, Goñi, ch. 7.

61 *El 45*, Felix Luna, Sudamericana, Buenos Aires, 1971, p. 55.

62 Letter Goyeneche to Amadeo-GPP, 10 March 1945. *Las Memorias del General*, Tomás Eloy Martínez, Planeta, Buenos Aires, 1996, p. 183.

63 *Así Hablaba Juan Perón*, Eugenio P. Rom, Peña Lillo Editor, Buenos Aires, 1980, pp. 107–9.

64 Wannsee Protocol, 20 January 1942, reproduced in *The Holocaust: Selected Documents in Eighteen Volumes*, vol. 11: 'The Wannsee Protocol and a 1944 Report on Auschwitz by the Office of Strategic Services', John Mendelsohn, ed., Garland, New York: 1982, pp. 18–32.

65 For a comprehensive study by the German embassy in Buenos Aires of the Jewish community in Argentina see its 27-page report 'Die Judenfrage in Argentinien', 10 January 1939, captured German Foreign Ministry records, NARA, RG 242, T-120, Roll 2679, starting frame 411930; see also frames 411925 and 411927 for Jewish population estimates

and a review of immigration policy regarding the Jews in various other South American states.

66 For a detailed and dispassionate analysis of the Army–Church symbiosis in Argentina see *Del Estado Liberal a la Nación Católica* and *Perón y el Mito de la Nación Católica*, both by Loris Zanatta.

67 *Hacía la Cristiandad*, Julio Meinvielle, Adsum, Buenos Aires, 1940.

68 *El Judío*, Julio Meinvielle, Editorial Antidoto, Buenos Aires, 1936. Not all Argentine anti-Semitism was so controlled; during the war a number of rabidly anti-Jewish newspapers financed by Berlin called for the gallows for Argentina's Jews.

69 'Die Judenfrage in Argentinien', 10 January 1939, NARA, RG 242, T-120, Roll 2679, starting frame 411930.

70 Probably the only surviving copy of Directive 11, hand-signed by Foreign Minister Cantilo, sent to Argentina's ambassador in Sweden, Ricardo Olivera, dated 12 July 1938, was found in the archives of the Argentine embassy in Stockholm in 1998 by historian Beatriz Gurevich while she formed part of CEANA, the official Argentine commission probing Argentina's role as a haven for Nazi fugitives. Gurevich's discoveries did not please CEANA, and after much acrimony she resigned from the commission.

71 Decree 8972, 28 July 1938, *Boletín Oficial*, 6 August 1938, p. 10118. For the effect and repercussion of the new restrictions, see *Argentina and the Jews*, Haim Avni, University of Alabama, 1991, ch. 5. For Solano Lima's 'ghetto' statement see Chamber of Deputies, Sessions Diary, 9/10 August 1938.

72 Letter from Consul Gavazzo Buchardo to Ruiz Guiñazú, 19 August 1942, MRE, DCA-MCT, 1942, File 240. Also instructions from the Foreign Ministry to the consulates in Asunción, Barcelona, La Paz and Santiago, 27 October 1942. See also *Argentina, la Segunda Guerra Mundial y los Refugiados Indeseables 1933–1945*, Leonardo Senkman, Grupo Editor Latinoamericano, Buenos Aires, 1991, pp. 275–8.

73 'Circular No 17', from the Foreign Ministry to Counsellor Carlos A. Leguizamón in Sweden, 22 August 1938; and 'Circular No 29', Cantilo to Miguens, 27 November 1939; both in the archives of the Argentine embassy in Stockholm. 'Circular No 29' refers to another directive on the same subject dated 25 February 1939 which remains undiscovered. Like 'Circular No 11', neither of these new orders mentions the Jews directly, referring to them instead as 'those comprised in the situations foreseen in Directive 11' or persons not considered 'adequate elements'.

74 Eugenia Sacerdote de Lustig, 21 February 1999, interviewed by the author when at age 88 she still took the bus daily to continue her work at one of Argentina's leading cancer institutes.

75 My grandfather died in 1955 in Argentina. His stories regarding Jews crossing from Bolivia were confirmed by documents I found in the basement of the Interior Ministry in Buenos Aires. See MI, 1944, File R-858, including Public Works File R-9826. See letter on the subject from the governor of Jujuy, Colonel Emilio Forcher, to the minister of the interior, Admiral Alberto Teisaire, 13 September 1944, referring to an order issued on June 26 by the Federal Police chief; also report from Ferrocarriles Argentinos to Pistarini, 6 October 1944. Pistarini had trouble controlling his right arm, most notably at a Nazi rally at the Luna Park stadium in Buenos Aires in 1937 and while buying arms in Berlin circa 1939–40 when he disobeyed an order from Labougle not to raise his arm during a gala attended by Hitler; Malena and Delia Labougle, interviewed by author, 15 April 1999.

76 Malena and Delia Labougle, interviewed by the author, 15 April 1999, both retained vivid memories of their days in Berlin with their father. Labougle's warning regarding the arrival of the Eichhorn couple in Argentina was sent from Chile, where he was transferred after Berlin. In 1997 a copy of this cable still survived in the Interior Ministry basement, on a cabinet shelf a few steps away from a giant green shredder machine, Dossier R-2, File 139.

77 FO 371/29210, 5 August 1941.

78 Marcelo Fuhrmann, 1 February 2000, interviewed by author. Fuhrmann's brother in Buenos Aires was able to obtain a landing permit for him through graft at Immigration in 1946. For Jewish arrivals, DNM, Memorias 1938-45, and Informes Estadísticos, 1938–45. See also *Argentina y los Refugiados Indeseables*, Senkman, ch. 4; and *Argentina and the Jews*, Avni, ch. 5. During 1944, the first year the Immigration Office started to keep statistics on the religion of first-class passengers, 14 first-class arrivals stated they were Jewish.

79 'Extortion Practices of the Axis Authorities', 6 February 1943, NARA, RG 59/250/34/9/3, Confidential Box 5609.

80 Kelly to Foreign Office, Letter 103, 19 April 1943, PRO, FO 371/3670.

81 XL23752, Military Intelligence Division, 12 October 1945, NARA, RG 226/190/4/19/3, Box 324. MRE, 'Legajo Personal' of Miguel Alfredo Molina.

82 Various independent diplomatic sources echoed this old charge regarding Cárcano, among them the daughters of the concurrent ambassador to Berlin, Eduardo Labougle, interviewed by the author, 15 April 1999, who said they heard it from their father and pointed out the contrast between their father's and Cárcano's attitudes in this matter.

83 There were other organizations selling Argentine visas in Europe, including one allegedly run by a certain Bishop Nafanaiz and his private secretary Lubov Aleksandrova Krilatova, at 15 rue des Capucines in Paris. The Argentine Foreign Ministry was concerned that the bishop and his assistant might be involved in infiltrating Soviet agents into Argentina, MRE, DP, Varios, 1958, Box 58, Dossier 1, p. 184.

84 Facsimile copies of a group of GOU secret documents were published in Argentina in the book *Perón y el GOU*, Robert Potash, Sudamericana, 1984.

85 Author's interview with David Hamwee, brother of the deceased 'Bob', 11 November 1997. The Hamwees came from a Jewish family in Manchester. During the 1930s they helped rescue 200 German–Jewish children who were resettled in Britain. See also 'One Man's Century', *Buenos Aires Herald*, 3 January 1999. Interview with Abel Blau, 15 July 1997.

86 War Refugee Board, Box 112 IV E20, summary based on note 14547, 21 April 1944; cited in Avni, p. 167.

87 One of the very few articles with biographical details regarding Peralta is 'Lo mejor dentro de la raza humana', by Ricardo Rodríguez Molas, *Río Negro*, 12 August 1990.

88 Héctor Ciapuscio, long-time Immigration official and head of Immigration in the early 1960s, interviewed by author, 6 June and 23 September 1997.

89 *La Acción del Pueblo Judío en la Argentina*, Santiago M. Peralta, Buenos Aires, 1943. *Argentina and the Jews*, Avni, ch. 6.

90 *Influencia del Pueblo Arabe en la Argentina*, Santiago M. Peralta, Sociedad Impresora Americana, Buenos Aires, 1946, pp. 69, 296 and 307. *La Tribuna*, 21 July 1946.

91 *Gobernantes*, 9 and 20 June 1946: also *The New York Times*, 16 June 1946.

92 Avni, pp. 180–81.

93 *Yo, Juan Domingo Perón*, Torcuato Luca de Tena, Luis Calvo & Esteban Peicovich, Sudamericana-Planeta, Buenos Aires, 1986, pp. 88–91.

94 DNM, Passenger Lists, February 1947, Number 29, note affixed to the *Campana* list. Avni, pp. 181–2. For Perón's quote regarding the Jews, *Yo, Juan Domingo Perón*, Luca de Tena *et al.*, p. 90. For the OIA and landing permits, AGN, Diana Inquest, STP, Box 547.

95 Avni, pp. 182–3.

96 Estimates of Jewish arrivals vary widely, the lowest figures corresponding to those officially documented at the Immigration Office while the highest are based on the Jewish aid and rescue groups. *Argentina and the Jews*, Avni; *Argentina, . . . y los Refugiados Indeseables*, Senkman; and Carlota Jackisch, *El Nazismo y los Refugiados Alemanes en la Argentina*, Editorial de Belgrano, Buenos Aires, 1989. The US State Department places the number of Jews reaching Argentina in 1933/45 at '25,000 to 45,000'; see 'US and Allied Wartime

and Postwar Relations and Negotiations with Argentina, Portugal, etc.', State Department, 1998.

97 Affidavit by Otto Reinebeck, head of the Latin American office at the German Foreign Ministry, 4 February 1946, NARA, RG 59, Box 25, TC-21540. For the smuggling of vital war materials, the June 1998 'Eizenstat Report', pp. 4–5.

98 *Argentina and the Jews*, Avni, ch. 5.

99 For the secret report regarding Ribbentrop's policy for the Argentine Jews, see captured German Foreign Ministry records, NARA, RG 242, T-120, Roll 4352, frame 211028; for the Greek and Dutch lists, see frames 211031 and 211034.

100 Avni, ch. 5. Irigoyen returned as Argentine ambassador to Berlin in the early 1970s.

101 For von Thadden's report on this meeting with Irigoyen, see NARA, RG 242, T-120, Roll 4352, frame 211032.

102 Avni, ch. 5.

103 Interrogation of Karl Arnold, Berlin No. 7813, 22 November 1946, NARA, RG 59, 862.20252/11-2246. Also, NARA, RG 242, T-120, Roll 2679, frame 411958. Luti to Buenos Aires, 2 September 1943, No. 379, MRE, DP, Varios, 1943, file 7. For the interception of Luti's reports by the Nazis, see *The Shadow War*, Rout & Bratzel, University Publications of America, Maryland, 1986. See also Reinebeck's affidavits of 24 January and 4 February 1946, both at NARA, RG 59, Box 25. Luti was on bad terms with his military attachés, see interrogation of SD official Theodor Paeffgen, 19 October 1945, NARA, RG 84.

104 NARA, RG 242, T-120, Roll 2679, frames 411961, 411963 and 411965, Dr Granow to Reinebeck, 12 March 1943. Avni, ch. 5.

105 NARA, RG 242, T-120, Roll 2679, frames 411969, 411971 and others.

106 For Kaltenbrunner's original order, NARA, RG 226/190/4/16/4-5, Box 178, Entry 19, XL 13164, 'Betriff: Verfolgung der Juden'. See also Eichmann's order NUE 7852 of 27 January 1944.

107 Affidavit by Otto Reinebeck, 4 February 1946, NARA, RG 59, Box 25.

108 Captured German Foreign Ministry records, NARA, RG 242, T-120, Roll 2679, frames 411974–6, and 411991. Avni, pp. 164–7, who cites Yad Vashem, 039/153, testimony of Rudolph Levy.

109 Captured German Foreign Ministry records, NARA, RG 242, T-120, Roll 2679, frames 411986–7.

110 Captured German Foreign Ministry records, NARA, RG 242, T-120, Roll 2679, frame 411972, Referat LR.v.Thadden, Berlin, 4 March 1944.

111 Captured German Foreign Ministry records, NARA, RG 242, T-120, Roll 2679, frames 411991 and 411994.

112 For a detailed account of the genesis of the Nazi ransom schemes, see 'Switzerland and the German Ransom Demands in Occupied Holland', by the Swiss Independent Commission of Experts (ICE).

113 ICE report.

114 ICE report, ch. 3.

115 ICE report, footnote 492. Of the 40,000 to be deported, 36,000 were eventually murdered at Auschwitz. Some 100,000 Jews were murdered by the Nazis in Holland during the war. ICE report, ch. 3. 'Statement of Mrs. Mathilda Reich-Visser', 13 March 1943, NARA, RG 84, Entry 3220, Box 13.

116 Frielingsdorf to Weissman, The Hague, 21 October 1942, NARA, RG 84, Entry 3220, Box 13. The note is addressed to Hernn J. Weissman. See also report by American Consul General Walter H. Sholes, 2 December 1942, including photostat copy of ransom note.

117 ICE report. Also note from British legation in Berne to American legation, 4 December 1942; and American embassy in London to Secretary of State, Number 6053, 29 October

1942; both at NARA, RG 84, Entry 3220, Box 13. As well, American embassy London to Secretary of State, 29 October 1942, NARA, RG 131, Box 357.

118 'Some Aspects of the Presentday Visa Problem', US Consul Basel, 11 December 1942, NARA, RG 84, Entry 3220, Box 13. Kuhl memorandum, 28 September 1942, NARA, RG 84, Entry 3220, Box 13.

119 Memorandum US legation Berne, 28 September 1942; Squire to Huddle, 1 December 1942; British legation to US legation in Berne, 4 December 1942; all NARA, RG 84, Entry 3220, Box 13. Also ICE report, ch. 5. A later report alleges that the final money paid in Buenos Aires for the Hirschler and Alexander ransoms was 600,000 pesos and that the money was eventually reimbursed when the relatives in Argentina decided to discontinue negotiations, see Squire to Harrison, 12 April 1943, NARA, RG 84, Entry 3220, Box 13. The ICE report lists the Hirschler and Alexander families (Cases 143 and 144) as final destination 'unknown'.

120 ICE report, ch. 5. The other two extortion cases were Bruno Hellinger and L.H. Kooperberg, Cases 142 and 145. Once in South America, Kroch forwarded to Wiederkehr a list of Jews that became known as the 'Kroch-Liste' of persons to be ransomed at 100,000 Swiss francs apiece. The Swiss report counted with oral and written testimony given by Wiederkehr himself in 1998 and 1999.

121 US embassy London to Sumner Welles, 2 November 1942, NARA, RG 131, Box 357. Also, British consulate Basel, 2 November 1942, NARA, RG 84, Entry 3220, Box 13.

122 For the Rembrandt, ICE report, Case 186. At the end of the war Miedl crossed the border into Spain with 22 paintings, including a Van Dyck. A request for his extradition by Holland was turned down by Franco, see El País, 29 November 1998. Also, ICE report, Case 386. Oppenheimer's contacts in Argentina seem to have been Max Spiess at Aguila and the Weil Hermanos firm, see British legation Berne, 12 February 1943; see also Reagan to Woods, 21 January 1943; NARA, RG 84, Entry 3220, Box 13. Also, enclosure No. 1 to Despatch 7733, 14 December 1942, NARA, RG 59/250/34//9/3, Confidential Box 5609.

123 Secret note from British consulate in Geneva, 28 November 1942, enclosed with Squire to Reagan, 8 February 1943; and 'Copies of Telegrams from Hoyman & Schuurman's', British consulate in Geneva, 28 November 1942, enclosed with Squire to Reagan, 8 February 1943; NARA, RG 84, Entry 3220, Box 13.

124 Charter, 12 May 1942, PRO, FO 115/3989. Other members of the Russian committee were Vladimir Podkin, Eugenio Fedoroff and María Zeldakova.

125 Loose sheet, titled 'Memorandum', December 1948, AGN, STP, Box 547. Also Mathus Hoyos report, 18 February 1949, AGN, STP, Box 547, Diana Inquest, pp. 12–18. The inquest identified 19 collective Immigration files initiated by Izrastzoff for groups of persons he brought to Argentina during 1947–48.

126 The Eisner–Izrastzoff connection is spelled out in FO 115/3989. Krupensky was the former wife of Eisner's partner in a pipe-manufacturing firm in Bohumin, Czechoslovakia. In Argentina she married an Italian citizen named Bordogni.

127 FBI report 'Totalitarian Activities – Argentina . . . Today', June 1943, NARA, RG 60/230/30/50/5, Special War Reports 1940-44, Entry 293B, Box 18. 'US and Allied Wartime and Post-war Relations with Argentina . . .', Department of State, June 1998. See also 'US and Allied Efforts To Recover and Restore Gold . . .', Department of State, May 1997, ch. I, section H. Hull to US embassy in Buenos Aires, 4 January 1943, 862.5151/2404, NARA, RG 59, 250/34/9/3, Box 5609.

128 MEW memo on German exit permits traffic, enclosure to dispatch from London, 17 July 1943; Circular Airgram, 24 November 1942; NARA, RG 59, Confidential Box 5609. British paper quoted in US embassy London to Secretary of State, 2 November 1942, NARA, RG 131, 230/38/26/03, Box 357.

129 British legation to US legation in Berne, 4 December 1942; and 'Some Aspects of

the Presentday Visa Problem', 11 December 1942; both NARA, RG 84, Entry 3220, Box 13.
130 'The German Exit Permits Traffic', MEW, 15 July 1943, enclosed with Air Pouch No. 10162, 17 July 1943, NARA, RG 59, LM 195, Roll 16, frames 1145-1147. 'Switzerland and the German Ransom Demands in Occupied Holland', ICE. Lord Selborne, *The New York Times* and *The London Times*, 25 November 1942.
131 'Extortion Practices of the Axis Authorities', US embassy Buenos Aires to Secretary of State, 6 February 1943, NARA, RG 59, 250/34/9/3, Confidential Box 5609.
132 British embassy to Ministry of Economic Warfare in London, 13 November 1942, Enclosure No. 1 of Dispatch 7733 from US embassy to Secretary of State, 14 December 1942, NARA, RG 59, 250/34/9/3, Confidential Box 5609.
133 See 1997 State Department report, ch. I, section B. Also 'Extortion Practices of the Axis Authorities', US embassy Buenos Aires, 6 February 1943, NARA, RG 59, Confidential Box 5609.
134 Author's interviews with Reinhard Spitzy, 8 December 1998; and with Zaira Elena Vélez, daughter of Colonel Vélez, 6 October 1998. The story is related with less detail and with the surname changed to Karlowitzer in Spitzy's book *So entkamen wir den Alliierten*, Langen Müller, Munich-Berlin, 1989. Ketelhohn had repaid Spitzy in a kind of way, by sponsoring together with Ludwig Freude the SS officer's landing permit application at Argentina's Immigration Office.
135 Hoettl testimony at Nuremberg Trials, 1945; also his testimony of June 1961 for the Eichmann trial in Jerusalem. For the wartime announcements of war crime trials and the Soviet trials in 1943, see *The Splendid Blond Beast*, Christopher Simpson, Common Courage Press, Maine, 1995.
136 Interrogation of Paeffgen, 28 December 1945, NARA, RG 269/390/44/33/03-05, Box 630. Paeffgen also mentions SS officer Scheidler as allegedly transferring funds to Switzerland for Kaltenbrunner. In the *Secrets of War* television documentary in the 1990s, Hoettl claimed he had crossed over to Switzerland to try and negotiate terms with the American OSS intelligence office in Berne.
137 *Operation Eichmann*, Zvi Aharoni & Wilhelm Dietl, Arms and Armour, London, pp. 43–5.
138 Fuldner's SS file, NARA, RG 242, BDC files, Roll 230, frames 750-832. Also two reports from the US embassy in Madrid, 3 December 1945, NARA, RG 59, Box 6746, Folder 4; and 31 July 1946, ibid., Box 6748. Also 'Hard-Core List of Germans for Repatriation from Spain', 23 May 1947, ibid., Box 6749. Regarding the Petersen–Goyeneche link, see Berlin dispatches to Petersen, 25 January and 9 February 1943, attached to Dispatch 2858 from the US embassy in Madrid, 10 September 1946, ibid., Box 6748. The American embassy had reliable informants inside the Nazi cells in Madrid; all the same it double-checked with British intelligence who confirmed that Fuldner was an SD agent. A number of files in the NARA boxes containing the Fuldner reports were removed by the CIA in 1976. See also the voluminous Argentine file regarding Fuldner's arrest on the high seas, MRE, DP, Alemania, 1935, File 16. Regarding the atmosphere at the German embassy in Madrid during the last days of the war, see *So entkamen wir den Alliierten*, Spitzy. For Fuldner's 'longtime' association with Daye, Ghenea and Serna, see Fuldner's statement of 18 August 1949, AGN, STP, Box 547, Diana Inquest, pp. 181–2. Regarding Serna and the Blue Division, see *Clarín*, 12 November 1947.
139 Interrogation of SD agent Hans Sommer, NARA, RG 242, M-1270, Roll 27, frames 884–894. Also, Madrid A-297, 8 May 1945; Secret 3019 to Montevideo with Sommer statements, 20 September 1946; and Berlin 7169 with Delfanne interrogation, 28 September 1946; all NARA, RG 59, Box 6748. Also Hoover to Neal, 27 November 1946; 'Extradition of Charles Lesca', 21 January 1947; Berlin 8029 with Sommer interrogation, 9 December 1946; US embassy 2541, 13 December 1946; and Dispatch 7199 with Mosig interrogation, 1 October 1946; all NARA, RG 59/250/38/13/6, Box 6749. Also, Berlin 7813

with interrogation of the SD chief in Spain, Karl Arnold, 22 November 1946, NARA, RG 59, 862.20252/11-2246. For Lesca's trips, DNM, Passenger Lists, August 1938, List 38; and October 1946, List 2. For Reuter ibid., February 1946, List 31. The Lescas obtained Argentine IDs (CI 2250217 and 2250215) on 2 September 1938. For Abetz, see Ribbentrop note, 3 August 1940, *Trial of the Major War Criminals*, Nuremberg, 1948, VI, 560–61. Also Levray's citizenship file, AGPJN, File 5697. Also letters Daye to Lesca, 12 October 1943, and Lesca to Daye, 8 October 1943 and 18 August 1946, ML-2570-1 and ML-2598. Also, Daye's unpublished memoirs, chapters XLIX to LIII, CEGES. Regarding General Krahmer see US embassy in Madrid, 30 January 1948, NARA, RG 84, Madrid embassy Classified General Records, Box 148. Also 'Hard-Core List of Germans for Repatriation from Spain', 23 May 1947, RG 59, 862.20252/5-2347. For Krahmer's connection to Göring's art loot, see 'Suspected Foreign Assets Held by Hermann Goering', 22 September 1945, OSS report XL 20392, NARA, RG 226, 19/4/18/6, Box 295, Entry 19. For Krahmer's listing as a war criminal, CEANA Final Report made up by articles by different researchers, Carlota Jackisch.

140 *La Razón*, 2 October 1946. *Proyecto Testimonio*, Beatriz Gurevich & Paul Warzawski, Planeta, Buenos Aires, 1998, vol. I, p. 53, and vol. II, pp. 15–16 and 55–9. For Perón's shelving of France's extradition request, MRE, DP, Francia, 1946, Box 17, File 22. Letters Lesca to Daye, Bilbao, 18 August 1946; and Buenos Aires, 9 May 1947; both ML-2598. Also, DNM, Passenger Lists, October 1946, List 2.

141 Daye's unpublished memoirs, ch. XXI. Passenger list of *Duca Degli Abruzzi*, 3 September 1925, CEMLA.

142 Daye memoirs, chs XXXVI and XXXIX. Also, *Inventaires 22, Fonds Pierre Daye*, Bernard Delcord & José Gotovitch, CEGES, Brussels, 1989.

143 Daye memoirs, ch. XLVI.

144 Daye memoirs, pp. 1136–40.

145 Daye memoirs, ch. XLIX. For the visa from Lequerica, correspondence between Daye, Lequerica and the Spanish embassy in Paris, 8 January, 18 January, 21 March, 29 March, 17 April, and 19 April 1944, ML-2570-1, and ML-2598. For his contacts with Serrano Suñer and others, invitation to meet with Serrano Suñer, 6 May 1946; and letter Aunós to Daye, 25 May 1944; both ML-2598.

146 Daye memoirs, ch. L. Ambassador Aznar was the grandfather of Spanish Prime Minister Aznar. Regarding d'Ors and Aznar standing as character witnesses for Daye, Daye's letter of 25 May 1946, ML-2598. Regarding the Marismas–Goyeneche link, author's interview with Goyeneche relative, 26 February 2000.

147 Daye memoirs, chs LI and LII.

148 Daye memoirs, ch. LIII. Regarding Daye's meeting with Paz in Madrid in 1947, Daye's letter to Paz, 15 August 1949; and Paz's reply, 19 August 1949; both ML-2598.

149 For Caggiano's European tour see *La Nación*, 12 January to 29 May 1946. For Caggiano, Catholic Action, Barrére and the 1943/46 dictatorship, see *Perón y el Mito de la Nación Católica*, Zanatta. Regarding Barrére and *Action Française*, see *L'Express*, 19 August 1993, 'La Cavale des Maudits', by Eric Conan. For the Daye–Lesca-Barrére link see letter from Daye to Barrére, 29 March 1948, CEGES, FPD, Dossier 488.

150 See instructions from Ambassador Brebbia to López, 5 February 1946, 45 CA, archive of the Argentine Embassy in Rome, Folder '1946, Consulados Argentinos, Salida, No 1 al No 211'. Regarding the SD activities of López, interrogation of the wartime SD chief in Spain, Karl Arnold, 20 November 1946, NARA, RG 59, 862.20252/11-2246. Discharged from the diplomatic service in the general clean-up that preceded Perón's assumption of office, López was later reincorporated and posted to Berne, see López's personal file, MRE. Caggiano and Barrére travelled with the priests Juan Conti and José de Anzizu.

151 For Caggiano's flu and the Pope's penicillin, see *La Nación*, 1 March and 7 April 1946.

152 For Caggiano's visits to the PCA, see letter Martin to Argentine ambassador, 13 May 1946, 377 V, archive of the Argentine embassy in Rome, Folder 'Misión Brebbia, 1946, Varios, Entradas, Mes de Mayo'. For Draganovic see *Unholy Trinity*, John Loftus and Mark Aarons, St Martin's Griffin, New York, 1998. Draganovic visited the Argentine DAIE Immigration office in Rome 'two or three times a month', according to former Argentine DAIE official Amadeo Mazzino, interviewed by author, 20 November 1998.

153 Gowen's report from Vatican City, 18 September 1946, NARA, RG 59/250/36/27, Box 4016, 761.00/9-1846. Regarding Tisserant's role at the Vatican, see *Unholy Trinity*, Loftus & Aarons.

154 Tisserant to Argentine embassy, 7 May 1946, 3115 V, archive of the Argentine embassy in Rome.

155 For Tisserant's view on Communists, see 'Vatican Pre-Election Activities', J. Graham Parsons to State Department, 16 January 1948, 865-001-2848A/VS, cited in *Hitler's Pope*, John Cornwell, Viking, New York, 1999, p. 329. For Caggiano, Grasselli and the 1976/83 dictatorship, see *Iglesia y Dictadura*, Emilio Mignone, EPN, Buenos Aires, 1986. For Grasselli's lists of the 'disappeared', author's interviews with María Adela Antokoletz, 3 June 1995; with Father Hugh O'Neill, St. Patrick's Church, Buenos Aires, 26 April 1995; and Father Fred Richards, Holy Cross Church, Buenos Aires, 13 April 1995. Caggiano as archbishop of Buenos Aires tried in particular to end Richards' human rights efforts during the second half of the 1970s. For Caggiano's Eichmann statement, see *La Razón*, 23 December 1960.

156 See instructions to Bertolotto, 15 March 1946, 126 CA; and 1 April 1946, 168 CA; both in Archives of the Argentine embassy in Rome, Folder '1946, Consulados Argentinos, Salida, No 1 al No 211'. In the case of Menou and Pincemin, Bertolotto was told that the Foreign Ministry in Buenos Aires had approved the visas on 28 March. Boucher, Menou and Pincemin are listed as war criminals in the Argentine government's CEANA Final Report 1999.

157 Notes 125 CA, 15 March 1946; 138 CA, 20 March 1946; 156 CA, 27 March 1946; 171 CA, 5 April 1946; 179 CA, 8 April 1946; and 180 CA, 9 April 1946; archive of the Argentine embassy in Rome, Folder '1946, Consulados Argentinos, Salida, No 1 al No 212'. For Lara Díaz, see note 132 CA, 18 March 1946. Italian foreign minister Alcides de Gasperi also interceded before the Argentine embassy for some of these applications.

158 *La Nación*, 1 March to 10 April 1946.

159 For Dewoitine, DNM, Passenger Lists, May 1946, List 46. Also *L'Express*, 19 August 1993, 'La Cavale des Maudits', by Eric Conan. For Daye's link to Dewoitine, see CEGES, FPD, Dossier 520. The US was alerted to Dewoitine's arrival in Buenos Aires, see NARA, RG 59, Box 6749, US embassy to secretary of state, 13 December 1946, 862.2025/12-646. Also, *Flucht vor Nürnberg?* Holger Meding, Böhlau, Köln, 1992, ch. 7.

160 DNM, Passenger Lists, October 1946, List 2. The identity of Caggiano's other 'recommendations' is not mentioned here pending confirmation of their wartime responsibilities, if any.

161 Daye's draft application for a landing permit, 18 September 1946, ML-2598.

162 Tisserant to Argentine ambassador, 7 May 1946, 3115 V, archive of Argentine embassy in Rome. In this particular case, Tisserant's request was turned down, see embassy to Tisserant, 10 May 1946, 277 V, Folder 'Misión Brebbia, 1946, Varios, del No 169 al 458'. See also memo JRX-3570, 17 June 1946, NARA, RG 226, Entry 183, Box 29.

163 NARA, RG 84, Box 148, Madrid embassy Circular Letter No. 5, 3 February 1948, Classified General Records, File 820.02. The Miss Goyeneche referred to was probably one of Goyeneche's two sisters, author's interview with Goyeneche relative, 14 August 1998.

164 Secret letter No. 144 from the Argentine ambassador at the Vatican to Foreign Minister Juan Bramuglia, 13 June 1946, released by CEANA.

165 *Yo, Juan Domingo Perón*, Luca de Tena *et al.*, pp. 85-6. The third co-author, Argentine

journalist Esteban Peicovich, had published an earlier book based on interviews with Perón, *Hola Perón*, Jorge Alvarez Editor, Buenos Aires, 1965. The story of the tapes was related to the author by Peicovich, 19 April 1997. Regarding Calvo in London, see *The Game of the Foxes*, Ladislas Farago, McKay, New York, 1971, ch. 42. Both Luca de Tena and Calvo were close friends of Perón and his business associate Jorge Antonio in Madrid. Regarding Evita and Montián in 1949, see *The Franco–Perón Alliance*, Raanan Rein, University of Pittsburgh Press, 1993, p. 189.

166 Evita's letter is reproduced in *La Enviada*, Jorge Camarasa, Planeta, Buenos Aires, 1998, pp. 45–6.

167 Ludwig Freude declaration, 13 April 1946; Nota Verbale from US embassy, 5 September 1946; Nota Verbale from British embassy, 26 September 1945; and Memorandum from US embassy, 21 December 1945; all at MRE, JVDFPE, File 50448-F-46. Interrogation of SD agent Hans Harnisch, Dispatch 11208, 31 October 1947, NARA, RG 84, Box 102. Regarding the 'stay-behind' fund, interrogation of General Wolf, October 1945, NARA, RG 59, Box 26; and its Appendix 'D', RG 84. Schellenberg testimony, 28 December 1945, NARA, RG 59, Box 25. See also *New York Times*, 8 April 1946.

168 *Juan Perón vs. Spruille Braden*, Gary Frank, University Press of America, Maryland, 1980, p. 79.

169 *Ayer Fue San Perón*, Raúl Damonte Taborda, Ediciones Gure, Buenos Aires, 1955.

170 *Juan Perón vs. Spruille Braden*, Frank, p. 79. For Freude's fear of a Communist takeover of Germany, see 'The German Intelligence Services', 10 November 1944, a list of German agents put together by US Naval Intelligence based on British Intelligence reports, photocopies of which were donated by US author John Loftus to Proyecto Testimonio in Buenos Aires.

171 *The Shadow War*, Rout & Bratzel, p. 422. Also interrogation of SD agent Hans Harnisch, Dispatch 11208, 31 October 1947, NARA, RG 84, Box 102. Also, author's interview with Oscar Contal, 13 August 1997. Harnisch said Freude was placed under custody at his home in Buenos Aires, while Contal recalled Freude retreated to his Andean holiday home in Bariloche. Regarding Perón's protection of Freude, see also the *New York Times*, 10 December 1944, 'Perón Proved Bar To Inquiry of Foe', in OSS records, NARA, RG 226/190/9/22/03, Entry 183, Box 16, File 85.

172 Presidential Decree 21284, 11 September 1945, a copy of which was found in the files of the Argentine Foreign Ministry by Proyecto Testimonio. *The Shadow War*, Rout & Bratzel, p. 422.

173 *Juan Perón vs. Spruille Braden*, Frank, p. 85.

174 *Yo, Juan Domingo Perón*, and *Eva Perón*, Alicia Dujovne Ortiz, Aguilar, Buenos Aires, 1995.

175 Interrogation of SD agent Hans Harnisch, Dispatch 11208, 31 October 1947, Enclosure No. 6, NARA, RG 84, Box 102.

176 *Eva Perón*, Dujovne Ortiz; and *The Army and Politics in Argentina 1945–1962*, Robert Potash, Stanford University Press, 1969.

177 For US charges against Ludwig Freude, US embassy Memorandum, 21 December 1945, MRE, JVDFPE, File 50448-F-46. For Freude as electoral campaign financier, interrogation of SD agent Hans Harnisch, Dispatch 11208, 31 October 1947; for the Becker link, interrogation of SD agent Josef Schroell, Dispatch 11220, 4 November 1947; both at NARA, RG 84/350/48/22/3, Box 102.

178 Secret memorandum of US embassy in Buenos Aires, 5 February 1946, NARA, RG 84, Box 84.

179 Interrogation of Koennecke by Argentine police, 10 August 1944, AGPJN, Causa 793/45, 'Segundo Sumario', Dossier 1, pp. 172–90. Also Harnisch interrogation, Dispatch 11208, 31 October 1947. Also, author's interview with secret police chief Oscar Contal, 13 August 1997.

180 Dispatch 1142, 9 November 1945, NARA, RG 59, Box 6746. Also US embassy in Madrid,

Note 1742, 7 March 1946, RG 59, Box 6747; and Dispatch 1628, 15 February 1946, NARA, RG 84, Box 84, File 820.02.

181 Interrogation of María Carmen Pera Tomkinson de Foster, 17 January 1956, AGN, CNI, Commission 47, Dossier 47-28-49-944, File 22057/56, pp. 88–9. *Técnica de una Traición*, Silvano Santander, Montevideo, 1953, p. 25.

182 See the 98-page dossier with the surviving records of the Human Potential Commission, AGN, STP, Box 547. Note in particular the minutes of 'Meeting No. 1', 12 December 1946; the 'Immigration Plan Project'; and the February 1947 Human Potential memorandum for the National Defence Council.

183 AGN, STP, Box 547, Diana Inquest, Diana statement, 13 May 1949.

184 'Hard Core List of Germans for Repatriation from Spain', 23-May-47, NARA, RG 59/250/38/13/6, Box 6749. Also, Madrid No. 1240, 3 December 1945, Subject: Alberto Horst Fuldner, 862.20252/12-345, NARA, RG 59, Box 6746. See AGN, Diana Inquest, Fuldner testimonies of 18 August and 12 September 1949, pp. 181, 182 and 340. Fuldner's company CAPRI was Eichmann's employer in Argentina, see Fuldner statement, 9 June 1960, AGN, Bormann Dossier, DAE 4550, pp. 77–9.

185 Mahieu's citizenship application, AGPJN, Dossier 19672. Regarding Mahieu's ideas see his books *Fundamentos de Biopolítica*, Centro Editor Argentino, Buenos Aires, 1968; and *Diccionario de Ciencia Política*, Books International, Buenos Aires, 1966. See also *Primera Plana*, Buenos Aires, January 1967. Also author's interview with Mahieu's close friend, former Goebbels assistant Wilfred von Oven, 26 August 1997; and with former Immigration commissioner Héctor Ciapuscio, 6 June and 23 September 1997. Regarding the 'Soap!' lectures, anonymous source, 24 November 1997. I wish to thank also Cologne University professor Holger Meding for sharing details from his personal interview with Mahieu shortly before the Frenchman died in 1990. A search among the SS records at NARA failed to turn up his name, but these records are incomplete, so Argentine reports that he belonged to the *Charlemagne* Division cannot be dismissed entirely. Regarding his faultless German, interview with Marlies Bayer, 6 January 2000, who saw Mahieu address a sonnenfest in the early 1970s. Regarding his influence over the Peronist far right as well as over Montonero leader Rodolfo Galimberti and other left-wing Peronist terrorists of the 1970s, interviews with Horacio Verbitsky, 27 January 1998; and Susana Viau, 22 February 1998. During the last years of his life Mahieu acquired a notoriety of sorts publishing books in which he claimed that the Vikings had reached South America in the pre-Columbian era. Regarding Mahieu and Menem, see 'Perón y la Conexión Nazi', *Tres Puntos*, 2 December 1999.

186 Monti's Argentine citizenship application, AGPJN, Dossier 5554. Classified Records of US embassy in Madrid, 30 January 1948, NARA, RG 84, Box 148, 820.02. Regarding Evita's first-aid stations, *So entkamen wir den Alliierten*, Spitzy, pp. 126–7. Spitzy's book includes a photographic copy of his own landing permit where Monti's sponsorship is clearly noted. Also, author's interview with Spitzy, 8 December 1998, and author's interview with journalist Pedro Olgo Ochoa, 20 April 1999. Ochoa knew both Monti and Perón and it was Perón who in conversation with Ochoa referred to Monti as a former Nazi agent. Ochoa believes Monti formed part of a core of Nazi spies recruited by Perón. For Krahmer's responsibility as a war criminal, CEANA Final Report 1999, Carlota Jackisch. The CEANA report states Krahmer arrived in Argentina in 1948 on a 'clandestine' rivercraft. US intelligence found the general arrived on an Iberia flight.

187 'Reported Arrival of Ante Pavelic in Argentina', CIA Operational Files, 16 April 1952, obtained from the CIA. Also 'Ustashi Leaders in Argentina and Austria', 20 April 1948, NARA, RG 59, 250/36/30/4, Box 6609, 860H.20235/4-2048, obtained under FOIA. Also, Benzon's citizenship application, AGPJN, Citizenship Dossier 5521. Regarding his role at Immigration, see Diana Inquest, testimony of Pablo Diana, 13 May 1949, pp. 43–50. Also, author's interview with Marcos Sinovcic, 26 August 1997.

188 'La Cavalle des Maudits', by Eric Conan, *L'Express*, 19 August 1993; also, CEANA Final Report 1999, Diana Quattrocchi-Woisson; and Guilbaud's citizenship application, AGPJN, Citizenship Dossier 8605. Regarding his role as an Information Bureau agent, José María Bruhn testimony, 29 August 1949, Diana Inquest, p. 238.

189 Letter Roover to Daye, 21 December 1945; Daye to Julio van Daele, 20 June 1947; and Daele to Daye, 10 August 1947; CEGES, FPD, Dossier 488; also Daye to Dubois, 26 June 1948, ibid., Dossier 525. Passenger Lists, DNM, July 1947, List 7. Diana testimony, 6 June 1949, Diana Inquest, p. 96. CEANA Final Report 1999, Quattrocchi-Woisson.

190 Diana Inquest, pp. 29, 356 and 359. Regarding Lagrou's collaboration with Daye and the mass migration proposal, see CEGES, FPD, Dossiers 488 and 540. CEANA Final Report 1999, Quattrocchi-Woisson. The files of Lagrou's trial are kept at the Auditorat Général in Brussels.

191 'Auswanderung von Flüchtlingen nach Argentinien, 1947/48', Handakten Bundesrat von Steiger, E4001(C)-/1, vol. 267, Swiss Federal Archives. Also, CEANA Final Report 1999, Robert Potash. And DNM, Passenger Lists, Fluviales E-F 1947, Book 137. Also, author's interview with his son Manuel Helfrich, 18 April 2000. For the arrival of Nazi agents in Argentina via KLM, Despatch 129, Hague to State, 1 March 1948, NARA, RG 319/270/11/33/03, Box 2882.

192 DNM, Passenger Lists, August 1947, List 20. Regarding his war crimes and the failed extradition request, see AGPJN, Case 26/1960; also *Proyecto Testimonio*, Gurevich & Warzawski, vol. II. Regarding his role at Immigration, author's interviews with Marcos Sinovcic, 26 August 1997; and with former Immigration official José Otero, 9 October 1998. The extradition of two other Czech war criminals, Vojtech Hora and Jan Pekar, responsible with Durcansky for the Bánská Bystrica killings, was also refused by Argentina. For Perón's appointment of Durcansky, see Presidential Decree 33531, 31 December 1949, AGN, STP, Box 547.

193 'Auswanderung von Flüchtlingen nach Argentinien, 1947/48', Handakten Bundesrat von Steiger, E4001(C)-/1, vol. 267, Swiss Federal Archives. See also Smolinski's application for Argentine citizenship, AGPJN, Dossier 4168.

194 AGN, Diana Inquest, p. 29; and Fuldner testimony, 18 August 1949, p. 181. Also, DNM, Passenger Lists, October 1947, list 24.

195 *La Nación*, 8 November 1947; also *Clarín*, 12 November 1947. Regarding de la Serna's Red Cross contacts, see letter from Serna to Daye, 23 August 1946, ML-2598.

196 Fuldner's testimony in the Diana Inquest, 18 August 1949, AGN, STP, Box 547, pp. 181–2.

197 Daye memoirs, VI, pp. 1371–4. Also, Fuldner's statement of 18 August 1949 in Diana Inquest.

198 The destruction of Perón's Nazi files in 1955 was related to German historian Holger Meding by French war criminal Jacques de Mahieu; as Meding related to the author, 19 November 1998. For Meding's written account of the destruction of these files, see *Flucht vor Nürnberg?*, ch. 6, fn. 12.

199 For Eichmann's file number see DNM, Passenger Lists, July 1950, List 24; for Mengele, ibid., June 1949, List 47; for Schwammberger, March 1949, List 52; for Priebke, November 1948, List 45. Schwammberger was included in an application for a group of Germans initiated by Vianord, a Buenos Aires travel agency through which Fuldner acted.

200 Stojadinovic's original Immigration File 87902/47 survived in the almost equally derelict archives of Argentina's Foreign Ministry; see MRE, DP, United States, 1947, Box 6, File 14.

201 Also present at the 26 October 1998 Franco interview was Ignacio Klich, coordinator of the Foreign Ministry's CEANA Commission for the Clarification of Nazi Activities in Argentina, who arranged the meeting. A record of all matters related to landing permit applications initiated by the Information Bureau at Perón's request was kept in 'Special

Copying Books' in the Commissioner's archive, according to the sworn statement by Immigration official José Bruhn, 29 August 1949, AGN, STP, Box 547, Diana Inquest, p. 237. Franco's anger at Congress was because Argentina's Archives Law forbids government departments to destroy their own files without prior approval from the Argentine National Archives.

202 The burning of the Nazi files was affirmed independently to the author by one other ranking Immigration official and confirmed by a number of lower-level employees. Franco was accused in court of verbally ordering the burning of Immigration files but was eventually cleared of the charges, see *Página/12*, 29 October 1996, and *La Nación*, 15 February 1997, although no mention of Nazi-related files was made at the time. Also around that time Franco was accused by the press and Jewish institutions of dragging his feet in providing information to the courts regarding the entry of suspected Arab terrorists who may have been involved in the 1992 Israeli embassy and 1994 AMIA Jewish community centre bombings in Buenos Aires. He claimed he lacked sufficient staff to check the arrival records; see *Página/12*, 17 August 1997. The newspaper claimed that Franco, who was security secretary at the time of the AMIA bombing, had first blamed the blast on a clash between rival Jewish groups. Some 116 people were killed in the two blasts. The AMIA bombing was the deadliest attack on a Jewish target anywhere since the Holocaust.

203 'Adiós Nonino', *Página/12*, 4 January 1999. The story was written by American journalist Joe Goldman.

204 For the period in question, unfortunately, the Immigration archives have preserved only the 'Identification Certificates' for surnames beginning with the letters A, B and C, in rusty filing cabinets in the 'Fleas' archive of the Hotel de Immigrantes.

205 An attempt to locate the records of the DAIE during the research for this book proved fruitless. Immigration also denied possessing the records of the Buenos Aires office which liaised with the DAIE in Europe. One former DAIE chief who had previously led the DAIE liaison office in Buenos Aîres recalled seeing the DAIE records at Immigration for the last time in 1958, author's interview with José Otero, 9 October 1998.

206 The main documents holding evidence of Perón's Nazi organization at work are the voluminous Diana Inquest in Buenos Aires, AGN, STP, Box 547; the Pierre Daye Fonds at CEGES and the Daye papers at the Musée de la Littérature, both in Brussels; the Handakten Bundesrat von Steiger, 'Auswanderung von Flüchtlingen nach Argentinien'; E 4001 (C), -/1, vol. 267, Swiss Federal Archives; and the Handakten Rothmund, Verkehr mit Argentinien, E 4800.1 1967/111 Bd. 70 (DNR 311), ibid. Vital data for this book regarding the escape of Nazi criminals was gleaned also from many months of work in the dilapidated 'archives' of Argentina's Immigration Office, DNM. Accessory material was found in the citizenship applications, scrupulously well preserved in this case, at the Archives of Argentina's Judicial Branch, AGPJN.

207 The file numbers are 201430/48, 211712/48, 211713/48 and 231489/48 for Schwammberger, Priebke, Mengele and Eichmann respectively. During the same two months, Immigration Landing Permit file 214878/48 was opened in favour of Belgian war criminal Georges Gilsoul, who entered Argentina on 18 December 1948 with a permanent visa. The investigation for this book was able to pinpoint some 35 other landing permit applications initiated during the same two months by Perón's presidential office, as well as by anti-Communist Croatian, Serbian, Hungarian, Bulgarian and Catholic rescue organizations, that would merit a closer inspection.

208 See the 54-page Stojadinovic file at the Argentine Foreign Ministry archives, MRE, DP, Estados Unidos, 1947, Box 6, File 14. Also, Stojadinovic's citizenship application, AGPJN, Dossier 11,358. Also, unpublished letter by Stojadinovic's daughter Ivanka Stojadinovic to *Time* magazine in response to excerpts from the author's book *Perón y los Alemanes*, carried in the Latin American issue of the magazine, 30 November 1998.

209 *Flucht von Nürnberg?*, Meding. The author based his account on interviews with Schulz

himself in 1990.

210 For proof of Piñeyro acting under direct orders from Perón as well as his membership of Freude's secret service, see letter from Argentina's ambassador to Denmark, 29 August 1947, in Piñeyro's personal file, p. 268, MRE. *Proyecto Testimonio*, Gurevich & Warzawski, vol. I., pp. 498-500.

211 *Flucht von Nürnberg?*, Meding.

212 'Detención del ciudadano argentino Carlos Schulz por falsificación de pasaporte', MRE, DAP, Dinamarca, 1947, Dossier 8.

213 The Danish Rigsarkivet national archives hold a large amount of documentation regarding Piñeyro's and Mouret's Nazi rescue mission, copies of which were kindly forwarded to the author by journalist Jakob Rubin of the *Morgenavisen Jyllands-Posten*. See also *Flucht von Nürnberg?*, Meding.

214 For Lienhardt, see interrogation of the high-ranking SD officer Theodor Paeffgen, 29 December 1945, NARA, RG 59, 250/48/30/07, Box 24, p. 19.

215 One Nazi who got left behind when the *Falken* sailed was SS Captain Arthur Gronheim, the wartime SD chief in Oslo. Recruited by Sweden after the war, he collaborated in the investigation into SD activities in Scandinavia. During 1948 Sweden asked Argentina to accept Gronheim, who arrived in Buenos Aires on the steamship *Orinoco* on 20 August 1948, see MRE, DAP, Suecia, 1948, File 9.

216 The author thanks Danish journalist Jakob Rubin of the *Morgenavisen Jyllands-Posten* for copies of the relevant Gross documents from the Danish Rigsarkivet national archives. For a detailed account of Gross and the SD's wartime activities in Argentina, see *Perón y los Alemanes*, Goñi.

217 The author thanks Hans Christian Thaysen of the Gay Holocaust web site in Denmark for drawing his attention to the Vaernet case, as well as Jakob Rubin of the *Morgenavisen Jyllands-Posten*, who during 1999 interviewed Vaernet's relatives in Argentina, for sharing his notes as well as photocopies of the Vaernet-related documents at the Danish Rigsarkivet national archives. In 1999, Argentina's Health Ministry denied possessing any records on Vaernet, but his employment record at the ministry was number 11,692; see Vaernet's citizen application, AGPJN, Dossier 3480.

218 *Flucht von Nürnberg?*, Meding. For documentary evidence of the MPE, see Dossier 21771/56, CNI, Comisión 47, AGN.

219 CEANA Final Report 1999, Robert Potash. Also, DNM, 'Fleas' archive, File 78220/46, regarding the arrival in Argentina of Polish aviation engineer Tadeusz Gordon, who was detained on board the *Buenos Aires* steamship on 31 December 1946 but subsequently released following the intervention of the Immigration 'adviser' for Polish immigration Miroslav Arciszewski and of Argentine air force C-in-C Bartolomé de la Colina. Gordon had been working for British military aviation since 1940, the file states.

220 CEANA Final Report 1999, Robert Potash. For Jeckeln's proximity to Eva Perón in Switzerland, see the 'Liste des invités suisses et Argentines' in the extensive dossier regarding her visit at the Swiss Federal Archives.

221 For Helfrich and Jeckeln, CEANA Final Report 1999, Robert Potash. For the details of his career, his alleged meeting with Perón in Germany, his escape and the barbecues with Perón in Buenos Aires, author's interview with his son Manuel Helfrich, 18 April 2000. For Perón's own claim to have ridden Hitler's autobahns, *Yo, Juan Perón*, Luca de Tena *et al.*, p. 28. Helfrich was Nazi party member 3,391,580; see NARA, RG 242, Nazi party lists. Manuel Helfrich, who flew from Switzerland with his father, remembers well the Argentine passport that remained in his family for many years. In the passenger list for the *General Alvear* ferry from Montevideo, where the KLM flight made its last stop, Herbert Helfrich is registered as carrying 'Documento de Identidad 15', see DNM, Fluviales E-F 1947, Book 137, 25 July 1947.

222 Interview with retired ambassador Guillermo Speroni, 15 November 1999. Also, anony-

mous interview, 30 June 2001.

223 'Auswanderung von Flüchtlingen nach Argentinien 1947/48', Handakten Bundesrat von Steiger, Swiss Federal Archives, E 4001 (C) -/1 vol. 267, particularly Rothmund's memo of 1 April 1948, and the memo of his meeting with Helfrich and Moss, 15 April 1948. CEANA Final Report 1999, Robert Potash. Also, author's interview with Manuel Helfrich, 18 April 2000.

224 For Fuldner's passport, Berne police report on Carlos Fuldner, 13 October 1948, Handakten Rothmund, Dossier Verkehr mit Argentinien. For his double employment and Freude's warm expression of gratitude to Llambí for assisting Fuldner, see Freude to Llambí, 6 July 1948, MRE, DP, Switzerland, 1948, File 3, p. 19.

225 For Fuldner and the DAIE in Genoa, Steiger memo, 15 April 1948, Swiss Federal Archives, E 4001 (C) -/1 vol. 267.

226 Interrogation of Schellenberg's agent in Switzerland, Hans-Wilhelm Eggen, PRO, WO 204/12814. Schellenberg, who had fingers in many pies, including a seat on the board of directors of Standard Electric in Germany and links to Unilever, was suspected of having placed assets in secret deposits in Switzerland towards the end of the war; 'External Assets of Walter Schellenberg', NARA, RG 407/270/69/23/7, Box 1044. After the war, Masson was put on trial for his presumed collaboration with the Nazis, although he was finally acquitted.

227 'Heinrich Rothmund in seinen Akten', Heinz Roschewski, in Die Schweiz und die Flüchtlinge, Haupt, Berne, 1997.

228 The Life Boat is Full, Alfred Häsler, New York, 1969, p. 323. Wenn Man Gewusst Hätte, Gaston Haas, Basel, Frankfurt, 1994, p. 125.

229 'Heinrich Rothmund in seinen Akten', Heinz Roschewski, in Die Schweiz und die Flüchtlinge, Haupt, Berne, 1997.

230 The Labyrinth, Walter Schellenberg, Harper & Brothers, New York, 1956, p. 379. The transports stopped after Hitler intercepted a French intelligence message saying they actually were for escaping Nazi leaders.

231 For the IRO's receipt of non-monetary Nazi gold, see the 'Eizenstat' reports of 1997 and 1999, published by US State Department. For the conflicting viewpoints in Argentina on the IRO, see Diana Inquest, AGN, STP, Box 547, pp. 14–18 and 19–24. In 1945–7 the IRO operated under the acronym IGCR (Intergovernmental Committee on Refugees).

232 'Zusammentstellung der am 22. Februar 1946 noch in der Schweiz anwesenden Zivilflüchtlinge nach Staatsangehörihkeit', Handakten Rothmund, Dossier Verkehr mit Argentinien, E 4800.1, 1967/111, Bd. 70 (DNR 311), Swiss Federal Archives.

233 Rothmund's memo to Steiger, 23 December 1947; and Feer's letters to Rothmund, 9 January and 20 February 1948; all in 'Auswanderung von Flüchtlingen nach Argentinien 1947/48', Handakten Bundesrat von Steiger, Swiss Federal Archives, E 4001 (C) -/1 vol. 267. Smolinski's Argentine citizenship application, AGPJN, dossier 4168. Among his other qualifications, Smolinski had provided a safe abode for Fuldner's wife and mother at a farm he owned in Buenos Aires province when they first arrived from Germany.

234 Rothmund memo, 27 January 1948, Swiss Federal Archives, E 4001 (C) -/1 vol. 267.

235 Rothmund's memos to Steiger, 19 and 20 February 1948; as well as Rothmund to Tzaut, 19 March 1948; all in 'Auswanderung von Flüchtlingen nach Argentinien 1947/48', Handakten Bundesrat von Steiger, Swiss Federal Archives, E 4001 (C) -/1 vol. 267. Regarding the 'no questions asked' Swiss attitude with departing Germans, see 'Illegal Movement of Citizens to Argentina', 1 March 1948, Enclosure No. 2, NARA, RG 319/270/11/33/3, Box 2882.

236 'Illegal Movement of German Citizens to Argentina', 1 March 1948, NARA, RG 319/270/11/33/3, Box 2882. A check of the SS and Nazi party lists in NARA, RG 242, failed to turn up the names of either Deckert or Schultz. For proof that KLM tickets were paid

for by the Argentine government, see letter from the DAIE office in Genoa, which had been wrongly charged for two KLM tickets, to the Argentine embassy in Rome, note 162 AA, 9 May 1949, archives of the Argentine embassy in Rome.

237 Rothmund memos, 18 March and 1 April 1948; letter to Zehnder, 23 March 1948; regarding Fuldner and the IRO, record of Steiger interview, 15 April 1948; all in Swiss Federal Archives, E 4001 (C) -/1 vol. 267.

238 Rothmund memo, 15 April 1948, ibid.

239 Memos 9 and 15 April 1948, ibid. For the role-playing by Helfrich and Moss, author's interview with Speroni, 15 November 1999. At least one person agreed with Rothmund; Smolinski wired the chief of police through the Swiss legation in Buenos Aires that keeping Marktgasse open was 'superfluous and dangerous considering the Allies'. Smolinski to Rothmund, 16 April 1948, Swiss Federal Archives.

240 For proof of Fuldner and Llambí responding to Freude's directives from Buenos Aires, letter Freude to Llambí, 6 July 1948, MRE, DAP, Switzerland 1948, File 3, p. 19.

241 Rothmund to Zehnder, 7 June 1948, Handakten Rothmund, Verkehr mit Argentinien, E 4800.1 1967/111, Bd. 70 (DNR311), Swiss Federal Archives.

242 Fuldner to Rothmund, 15 June 1948, Handakten Rothmund. For Rothmund's trip to Rome, see 'Schweizerisch-italienische Verhandlungen über die italienischen Arbeitskräfte in der Schweiz, Visums- und Passfragen, sowie das Statut der Schweizer in Italien vom 14. bis 22. Juni 1948 in Rom', DoDiS 2717, Swiss Federal Archives.

243 Müller report, 5 August 1948, Swiss Federal Archives.

244 *Argentina* Passenger List, 16 October 1948, DNM. *Nazi Gold*, Ian Sayer and Douglas Botting, Granada, London, 1984.

245 Berne police report on Fuldner, 13 October 1948, Dossier Verkehr mit Argentinien.

246 Feer to Tzaut, 15 November 1948; and Feer to Rothmund, same date; Handakten Rothmund, Verkehr mit Argentinien, E 4800.1 1967/111, Bd. 70 (DNR311), Swiss Federal Archives.

247 See the two separate letters on Draganovic and Fuldner, from Feer to Rothmund, both dated 17 November 1948, Handakten Rothmund, Verkehr mit Argentinien. Pomeranz also accused Fuldner of forging his official passport by inscribing the title 'Envoyé Spécial de la Présidence' on a blank passport provided by Llambí. This seems unnecessary, as Fuldner actually was an envoy of Perón.

248 Undated draft letter Rothmund to Feer, Dossier Verkehr mit Argentinien.

249 Berne police report on Fuldner, 13 October 1948; also Tzaut report on meeting with Helfrich, 29 January 1949; both in Dossier Verkehr mit Argentinien.

250 Cuttat to Rothmund, 22 March 1949, Swiss Federal Archives. For a detailed account of Cuttat's wartime activities in Buenos Aires, *Perón y los Alemanes*, Goñi.

251 'Exposé relatif à l'émigration en Argentine de réfugiés séjournant en Suisse', 2 February 1950, Handakten Rothmund, Dossier Verkehr mit Argentinien, Swiss Federal Archives. In 1955, Switzerland evened the score somewhat when it refused entry to Perón, who was seeking exile after being deposed by a military coup, Dossier Verkehr mit Argentinien, 'Perón' section.

252 Eggen interrogation, 20 February 1946, PRO, WO 204/12814. 'Le fils du général Guisan sous surveillance', *L'Hebdo*, No. 28, 10 July 1997; and the DSR TV documentary Evitas Geheimnis, Frank Garbely, 1998. Also, *Medio Siglo de Política y Diplomacia*, Benito Llambí, Corregidor, Buenos Aires, 1997.

253 Benavente Perón note of 24 March 1949, and note 503 CA, 7 June 1949, at the archives of the Argentine embassy in Rome. For Jorge, Decree 25863, 13 October 1949, AGN, STP, Box 547; and memo of meeting with Rothmund, 3 February 1950, Handakten Rothmund, Verkehr mit Argentinien, E 4800.1 1967/111 Bd. 70 (DNR311), Swiss Federal Archives. Also, author's interview with Speroni, 27 April 2000. For Walimann, see CEANA Second Report, 1998, Quattrocchi-Woisson.

254 For Dewoitine's arrival, DNM, Passenger Lists, May 1946, List 46.

255 For Daye's arrival, Iberia EC-DAQ passenger list, 21 May 1947, DNM, 'Chela' archive. See also the Argentine file containing Belgium's request for Daye's arrest, MRE, DP, Belgium, 1947, Box 14, File 9. As well, Daye memoirs, ch. LIV. For Daye's old acquaintance with Jaspar, letter Jaspar to Daye, 26 November 1935, CEGES, FPD, Dossier 17. For the joint arrival of Ruysschaert, Lecomte and Areilza, see the passenger list for the *Cabo Buena Esperanza*, DNM, May 1947, List 17. The three Croatian war criminals who came with Clayes on the *Campana* were Mirko Eterovic, Karlo Korsky and Nikolic Vinko, DNM, June 1947, List 16. In an embarrassing episode, Eterovic was discovered still alive in Argentina in 1999. He escaped abroad, returning a few months later, reassured that no extradition proceedings had been opened against him.

256 Former Immigration and DAIE official José Otero recalled that Perón and Evita attended Wednesday meetings at the Escuela Superior Peronista at the old Immigration building on San Martín Street where the rescue of Nazis in preparation for a third world war was discussed, interview with author, 9 October 1998. For the Daye quote, Daye memoirs, ch. LIV.

257 Daye memoirs, ch. LIV. Also the letters Daye to Paz, 15 August 1949, and Paz to Daye, 19 August 1949, ML 2589. In his autobiography, Paz does not mention Daye, but he does mention his visit to Spain, his private discussions with Perón regarding the Third Position, and his employment at the Beaux-Arts Museum, all of which coincide with Daye's account of their meetings, see *Memorias*, Hipólito Paz, Planeta, Buenos Aires, 1999, pp. 114, 141 and 152.

258 Daye memoirs, ch. LIV. For Daye's use of the Spanish diplomatic pouch, see correspondence between Daye and Ezequiel de Selgas, 1947–48, CEGES, FPD, Dossier 531. Selgas was the former Spanish cultural attaché in occupied Paris, see American embassy in Madrid, 5 February 1947, NARA, RG 59, 250/38/13/6, Box 6749, obtained under Freedom of Information Act, 16 June 2000. For Lagrou's mass emigration plan, see CEGES; FPD, Dossier 540. The presidential staff members on the *Stanley* list were Captain Guillermo D. Plater, Captain Antonio S. Otero and Atilio Ravanetti; also on the list were the arch-nationalist Cosme Beccar Varela, Spanish ambassador Areilza, and various fellow fugitives; see ML 2579 (1).

259 *Monte Ayala* passenger list, DNM, Passenger Lists, July 1947, List 7. Also, letter Roover to Daye, 21 December 1945; Daye to Daele, 20 June 1947; and Daele to Daye, 10 August 1947; all at CEGES, FPD, Fonds 488.

260 Daye memoirs, ch. LIV.

261 During the research for this book the author came across pitifully few American documents including direct references to the Nazi rescue activities of Carlos Fuldner and Rodolfo Freude, all of them from a group of boxes containing classified records of the State Department, Decimal Files 1945–1949 – 862.20252. Intriguingly, these five boxes (6746–6750) contained an inordinately large amount of 'pink slips' showing that about half the documents in them had been withdrawn by the producing agencies. A FOIA request for these documents resulted in the declassification of about half the documents requested, shedding a great deal of light on Perón's Nazi web. The other half has yet to be declassified. For the declassified document on Lesca's Madrid contacts, see American embassy in Madrid, 5 February 1947, NARA, RG 59, 250/38/13/6, Box 6749, declassified 16 June 2000.

262 American embassy in Madrid, 5 February 1947, NARA, RG 59, 250/38/13/6, Box 6749, declassified 16 June 2000. For the reports on Laval transferring funds to Argentina, OSS XL2888, NARA, RG 226, 190/4/13/4, Box 32, Entry 19; also American embassy in Buenos Aires to Secretary of State, No. 16827, 9 December 1944, document provided to the author by the WJC.

263 Daye memoirs, ch. LIV. For a comprehensive essay by Daye on the Third Position, 'Note remise à Guy Miermans', 16 December 1947, CEGES, FPD, Dossier 490.

264   For the Pope's approval of Hudal's proposed 'Nazi Amnesty', CEANA Final Report 1999, Sanfilippo. Hudal continued advocating an amnesty until the late 1950s, going as far as writing to President Truman in favour of former Nazi foreign minister von Neurath, whose son had settled in Argentina.

265   For a detailed account of Perón's support of Franco at the UN, *The Franco–Perón Alliance*, Rein.

266   For the ban on the celebration of the fall of Berlin, *La Razón*, 23–27 April 1945. For the attacks on students who on 2 May celebrated anyhow, see *La Verdad Sobre la Situación Argentina*, Eduardo E. Sammartino, Montevideo, 1950.

267   For a more detailed account of the icy chill between Perón and the French and Belgian diplomats, see CEANA Final Report 1999, Diana Quattrocchi-Woisson. Among the former Ustashi officers who formed part of Perón's bodyguard were Mile Ravlic, alias Milo Bogetic, and Vlad Secen. Former Croatian diplomat Branko Benzon became Perón's and Evita's personal friend. All three Croats left Argentina with Perón when he was deposed and exiled in 1955.

268   Note to Perón, 9 December 1947, CEGES, FPD, Dossier 492.

269   Daye to Serna, 25 February 1948, CEGES, FPD, Dossier 514.

270   Proposal for Ambassador Arce, 18 December 1947, CEGES, FPD, Dossier 491.

271   The endorsers of the Nazi amnesty were highly suspect themselves. Spanish ambassador Areilza was greeted with anti-Semitic chants by enthusiastic Argentine nationalists when Perón invited him to appear on the balcony of the Casa Rosada the day he presented his credentials, see *The Franco–Perón Alliance*, Rein, p. 47. Ambassador Arce, during his previous posting to China, had conducted a huge swindle of the Jews who bought Argentine visas from him at $2,000 dollars per family, see MRE, DCA-MCT, 1946, File 3263. This file contains a heart-rending number of letters from Jews who personally paid Arce to reach Argentina through China, a not uncommon route for postwar refugees and even fugitive Nazis. The number of people swindled was so vast that the Argentine government had to cancel all visas issued by Arce up to 1 September 1946, shortly before he was appointed to the United Nations, see the *Shanghai Evening Post*, 5 September 1946.

272   Daye to Serna, 25 February 1948, CEGES, FPD, Dossier 514. In this letter, Daye informed Serna that Argentine nationalist Juan Carlos Goyeneche was no longer to be kept 'up to date' on the activities of the rescue group. Serna was to be assisted in drawing up the lists in Spain by Daye's friend Count Christian du Jonchay, Clarita Stauffer and Casilda Cardenal. Stauffer, in league with the Argentine consul in Barcelona and a German businessman, aided German fugitives escaping on board the ships from Genoa that made their first stop at Barcelona, see *Flucht vor Nürnberg?*, Meding, ch. 4. For Fuldner's long-term assistance to Daye, see letter Fuldner to Daye, 26 December 1948, ML 2598.

273   Landing permit requests from Daye to Guilbaud-Degay, 31 January and 8 February 1949; CEGES, FPD, Dossier 488. For Roover's and Lagrou's roles presenting applications and Daye's link with Diana, Diana Inquest, AGN, STP, Box 547. Also regarding Daye and Diana, Daye to Lesca, 8 June 1948, Dossier 488; and the Daye–Mahieu correspondence, Dossier 552.

274   Daye to Lesca, 8 June 1948; Daye to Dewoitine, 21 February 1948; Dewoitine to Daye, 26 February 1946; also Daye to Barrére, 29 March 1948; all CEGES, FPD, Dossier 488. In the last letter Daye recommends a certain 'Dr Müller' to the Argentine bishop, apparently the alleged war criminal 'Juan Nicolás' Müller, a Belgian doctor who was interviewed by journalists of the newspaper *La Capital* of Mar del Plata in the 1990s. Dr Müller said he had been offered work by Perón's government in the northern province of Santiago del Estero, a fact mentioned in Daye's letter.

275   Passenger List of *Adelaar*, 5 November 1948, DNM. Smekens and Hollants entered Argentina under Immigration File 179095/48, while a number of almost consecutively numbered files corresponded to applications sponsored by Perón's presidential office,

and to applications for Belgian war criminal Gabriel Jooris, former Abwehr agent Reinhard Kops and SS criminal 'Francisco' Vötterl. Sassen's File 186912/48 was also squeezed tightly between applications sponsored by Perón's office, an application for Hans Hefelmann of Hitler's euthanasia programme, and other similarly distinguished company.

276 De Braekeleer citizenship application, AGPJN, File 7665. Among those who vouched for the Belgian were the war criminals Daye, Degay, Bockaert and a Peronist party official. Letters arrived from future Belgian cardinal Jozef Cardijn and from the Catholic International Union for Social Service in Brussels. De Braekeleer and Van Damme disembarkation cards, DNM, 'Chela' Archive.

277 Daye memoirs, ch. LIV. Daye does not mention the Church's ownership of SARE's headquarters, which can nonetheless be ascertained at the Argentine Ministry of Justice, Registro de la Propiedad Inmueble, Title Deed No. 18-5149.

278 For Copello's support of Franco, see Secret OSS Dispatch 'Vatican Intelligence on Argentine Attitude toward Franco', 19 December 1944, NARA, RG 226, M1642, Roll 31, Frame 358. For Copello's visits to the German Embassy, see *The Nazi Menace in Argentina*, Ronald Newton, Stanford, 1992. For the cardinal's Third Position, see *Perón y el Mito de la Nación Católica*, Zanatta, p. 46. Copello met in 1949 with Julien Dalbin of the French RTF party, which espoused Perón's Third Position, see letter Dalbin to Daye, 24 March 1949, CEGES, FPD, Dossier 493. Copello's funeral service for Pétain is recorded in Daye memoirs, ch. LIX, p. 1508.

279 SARE statutes, 29 June 1948; also undated handwritten SARE notes; all CEGES, FPD, Dossier 487. Luttor is mentioned in the La Vista American intelligence report, 'Illegal Emigration Movements In and Through Italy', 15 May 1947, NARA, RG 59, Decimal File 1945–49, Box 4080. For his arrival in Argentina see DNM, *Andrea Gritti* Passenger List, 27 April 1947, and his disembarkation card, DNM, 'Chela' archive. Luttor is also warmly mentioned in the memoirs of Hungary's wartime regent Admiral Horthy. Other SARE associates seem to have been P.D. Skúlj and Anton Kubic for Slovenia, and Protish for Bulgaria. The Haas mentioned in the SARE papers may be identical with one 'Francisco Haas' who entered Argentina through Immigration file 207206/48 initiated by President Perón's office, AGN, STP, Box 547, Diana Inquest, pp. 60 and 359.

280 SARE to its members, 11 October 1948, CEGES, FPD, Dossier 487.

281 Daye memoirs, ch. LIV.

282 The figure of well over 100 arises from the SARE file in Daye's private papers, CEGES, FPD, Dossier 488, made up mostly of copies of the correspondence between Daye and fugitives awaiting rescue in Europe. For the three Germans, see note dated 3 February 1949 in the same dossier.

283 For Lesca's death, see the remembrance placed by his wife Maria Levray in the newspaper *La Nación*, 12 January 1949.

284 Daye to Mahieu, 2 February 1949, CEGES, FPD, Dossier 552.

285 See the strongly anti-Semitic and anti-Communist Mathus–Hoyos report, 18 February 1949, AGN, STP, Box 547, Diana Inquest, pp. 12–18. Particularly incensed was the consulate chief in Warsaw, Alejandro Orfila, stating that the 'Stirleman case' and other 'undesirables' entering Argentina were 'one of the things that most pained him during his career'. During Argentina's 1976/83 dictatorship, Orfila became secretary-general of the Organization of American States in Washington.

286 See report by Carlos T. Brunel, 5 May 1949, AGN, STP, Box 547, Diana Inquest, pp. 26–8. During the war Brunel had been Argentina's consul in Prague and later Hamburg. After the war he served in both Genoa and Beirut. He eventually had to be recalled to Buenos Aires because of his immoral behaviour and his 'insulting expressions against Arabs in general', see *Proyecto Testimonio*, Gurevich & Warzawski.

287 Virasoro report, undated, AGN, STP, Box 547, Diana Inquest, pp. 19–24. For Virasoro's

criminal record, *Proyecto Testimonio*, Gurevich & Warzawski. The consulates in Europe, without counting bribes taken under the counter, raised large amounts of cash issuing visas. Virasoro in seven months alone during 1948/49 collected 270,000 dollars in consular charges for issuing around 7,000 visas.

288 Interrogation of SD agent Hans Harnisch, Enclosure No. 2 to Dispatch 11208 from American embassy in Berlin, 31 October 1947, NARA, RG 84, 350/48/22/3, Box 102.

289 Testimonies of Luis María Orliacq, Oscar Amaya, Dalmiro Amaya and Eduardo Hartkopp, 23 May 1949, AGN, STP, Box 547, Diana Inquest, pp. 32–40. Orliacq, who died in 1973, was a navy conscript who used to accompany Evita on her shopping sprees 'signing the cheques', according to his cousin Leonides Uhalt Orliacq, interviewed by author 18 November 1997. Hartkopp died in 1997 and a remembrance for his 'great and dear friend' was published by Rodolfo Freude in *La Nación*, 13 June 1997. These Information Bureau agents carried landing permit applications from the Casa Rosada to Immigration, as well as 'sealed envelopes' (presumably containing money) from Freude to various Immigration officials who smoothed out the red tape for these applications.

290 AGN, STP, Box 547, Diana Inquest, pp. 29–30.

291 Fuldner's testimony in the Diana Inquest, 12 September 1949, AGN, STP, Box 547, p. 340.

292 Magistrali testimony, 24 June 1949, pp. 136–42; Castro, 16 August 1949, pp. 174–5; Fuldner, 18 August 1949, pp. 181–2; and Mansilla, 18 August 1949, pp. 183–4; all Diana Inquest.

293 Diana testimony, 6 June 1949, pp. 95–9, Diana Inquest.

294 See conclusions by the director general of the Ethnic Institute, 27 September 1949, Diana Inquest, pp. 423–4.

295 Presidential Decree 18041, 30 July 1949, Diana Inquest, pp. 399–401. Some 1,000 landing permit files were inspected by the inquest, of which 334 were employed in the proceedings. About one third of these were collective files for associations such as Durcansky's Slovak Action Committee, the National Bulgarian Anti-Communist Committee, the Croatian Committee, Fuldner's Vianord and Perón's presidential office. The rest were mostly individual files for Jewish immigrants and these are the ones cited in the inquest's conclusions.

296 Diana Inquest, testimony of Hector Emilio Magistrali, 23 June 1949, p. 129; also p. 357. At Immigration, applications by the Peronist OIA (Argentine Israelite Organization) received preferential treatment, see Emilio Scrigna testimony, 6 September 1949, Diana Inquest, pp. 303–5.

297 Diana testimony, 6 June 1949, pp. 95–9, Diana Inquest. Also, letter Daye to Dubois, 26 June 1948, CEGES, FPD, Dossier 525. Roover was discovered by fellow war criminal Stefan Seynhaeve.

298 Daye memoirs, Tome 7, Cahiers complémentaires, ch. LX, p. 1025, 3 November 1951.

299 Daye memoirs, ch. LIV. The Argentine nationalist Juan Carlos Goyeneche was a fellow professor at the university, see letter Daye to Goyeneche, 12 January 1948, CEGES, FPD, Dossier 488; see also *Ensayos, Discursos, Artículos*, Juan Carlos Goyeneche, Dictio, Buenos Aires, 1976, p. 605. Another nationalist, Cosme Beccar Varela, was eager to help Daye regain his post, see letter Nelis to Daye, 24 July 1948, CEGES, FPD, Dossier 559.

300 See letters Daye to Paz, 15 August 1949; Paz to Daye, 19 August 1949; Daye to Paz, 13 September 1949; and Paz to La Plata University Rector Luis Irigoyen, 4 December 1950: all ML 2598.

201 See the 'Naturalization File' among Daye's private papers in Brussels, ML 2570 (1). In Buenos Aires, a careful check of the citizenship application records at the AGPJN Law Courts archive failed to produce Daye's file. See also Daye memoirs, ch. LVII.

302 'Act of Constitution of the Centre of Nationalist Forces', 21 July 1949, CEGES, FPD,

Dossier 489. For Pavelic's 'gloom', Daye memoirs, Tome 7, Cahiers complémentaires, ch. LXI, p. 1044. Father Eusebio's real name was Sigfrido Zappaterreni. The Centre was constituted at the Italian Socialist Party, 271 Pozos Street, in Buenos Aires, on 21 July 1949. A detailed mid-1949 document on the Italian Socialist Movement in Argentina is cited in *Odessa al Sur*, Jorge Camarasa, Planeta, 1995, pp. 248–50. Erich Priebke is reported to have acted as the translator at the meetings between Vittorio Mussolini and Hitler. A filmmaker by profession, Mussolini co-authored a film with Roberto Rossellini in 1938, and Luchino Visconti wrote for Mussolini's magazine *Cinema* during the Fascist era. When he died in Rome in 1997, some 60 extremists in black garb made the Fascist salute at Mussolini's funeral.

303 Daye memoirs, chs LVI and LVII. On 4 February 1952, Daye received from Brussels 75 kilos of dossiers relating mostly to wartime Rexist affairs, see Daye memoirs, Tome 7, Cahiers complémentaires, p. 1026.

304 Daye memoirs, Tome 7, Cahiere complémentaires, pp. 1044–5.

305 Daye memoirs, chs LVII.

306 Daye memoirs, chs LVII. For the coffees at La Fragata, author's interview with Rogelio García Lupo, an Argentine journalist who often saw the fugitives meeting there, 13 October 1998. According to his disembarkation card, Mosley arrived in Buenos Aires on 1 November 1950, DNM, 'Chela' archive.

307 Daye memoirs, Tome 7, Cahiers complémentaires, ch. LX, pp. 1020–21 and 1052–4.

308 Daye memoirs, Tome 7, Cahiers complémentaires, pp. 1027 and 1052.

309 Letter Perón to Daye, 28 January 1953, CEGES, FPD, Dossier 560. Daye memoirs, Tome 7, Cahiers complémentaires, ch. LX, p. 1022.

310 García Lupo, 13 October 1998. Daye memoirs, ch. LXII.

311 See interrogation of Nélida Rivas, 24 January 1956; also interrogation of Nélida Pages, 17 January 1956; both in the Archives of the Lower House of Congress, Vicepresidencia, Comisión Nacional de Investigaciones, Paquete 147-1, 1955. For Daye's comment on Perón's ouster, Daye memoirs, ch. LXIII, p. 1647.

312 See letters Daye to Goyeneche and Amadeo, both 27 September 1955; and Amadeo to Daye, 31 October 1955, ML 2598. Also Daye to Amadeo, 4 October 1955, ML 2570- (1). Ghenea to Goyeneche, 28 October 1955, GPP. Daye memoirs, ch. LXIII, p. 1647.

313 Daye memoirs, ch. LXIII, pp. 1652–61.

314 For Durcansky's promise to Göring, see Nuremberg proceedings, 4 and 5 December 1945. See also the account of Slovakia's break from Prague in *Hitler*, Alan Bullock, Odhams, 1952.

315 *The War Against The Jews, 1933–1945*, Lucy S. Davidowicz. For Durcansky's role in the extermination of the Jews and the setting up of 'protective camps', see UN War Crimes Commission, Minutes No. 74, 8 October 1946; and No. 138, 3 March 1948; both at PRO, FO 371/71335.

316 Jan Durcansky statement to Argentine judge handling failed request for his extradition, 8 July 1960, AGPJN, Case 26/1960, page 158. Also *Maria C* Passenger List, DNM, August 1947, List 20, where Jan Durcansky arrived under the slightly different alias Giovanni Dubranka.

317 Handwritten note of 22 February 1946; and War Office note of 2 May 1946; PRO, FO 371/56061.

318 For US position in favour of Durcansky's arrest see Secret Cipher Telegram 098344, 14 June 1946; for the Foreign Office's argument that he was not a war criminal see Foreign Office to War Office, 20 June 1946; for the reply to Prague see Foreign Office to Ambassador Lobkowicz, 14 June 1946; all PRO, FO 371/56061.

319 War Crimes Commission, No. 74, 18 September 1946; note from the War Crimes Commission to Czechoslovak representative, 18 October 1946; also War Crimes

Commission, No. 138, 3 March 1948; all PRO, FO 371/71335.

320 N7091/3525/12, 2 December 1946, PRO, FO 371/56061. Sidor was eventually admitted to Canada 'after the direct intervention of Pope Pius XII', Alti Rodal report, Historical Appendix to Deschenes Commission Report, Ottawa, 1985, p. 414.

321 For detailed account of Durcansky and British intelligence, see *Unholy Trinity*, Loftus & Aarons, pp. 217–23. The authors postulate that the East European anti-Communist groups sponsored by British intelligence were riddled by Communist agents posing as former Nazis. War Crimes Commission, No. 138, 3 March 1948, PRO, FO 371/71335.

322 *Maria C*, DNM, August 1947, List 20. The two Croatians who would form part of the rescue chain in Buenos Aires were Ustasha colonel Cyril Cudina and Marko Sinovcic, author's interview with Sinovcic, 26 August 1997. Also on board was the family of Ustasha criminal Ivo Rojnica, who had arrived previously under the alias Ivan Rajcinovic. On the same day the Croatian war criminal Radovan Latkovic arrived on the steamship *Santa Fe* and the Polish agent Czeslaw Smolinski arrived on a DC-4 plane at Buenos Aires airport.

323 For Jan Durcansky's wartime record see AGPJN, Case 26/1960; also *Proyecto Testimonio*, Gurevich & Warzawski, vol. II. For his role at Immigration, author's interviews with Marcos Sinovcic, 26 August 1997; and with former Immigration official José Otero, 9 October 1998.

324 Coordinación Federal report No. 234, 5 December 1947, MRE, DP, Varios, 1948, Box 58, File 1, pp. 6–18.

325 War Crimes Commission, No. 138, 3 March 1948, PRO, FO 371/71335.

326 PRO, FO 371/71335.

327 From Durcansky's CIA file, quoted in *Unholy Trinity*, Loftus & Aarons, p. 218.

328 Seven Immigration files initiated by Durcansky's Slovak Action Committee during 1948 are listed in the Diana Inquest, AGN, STP, Box 547. Another Slovak-related Immigration file was identified by the author in the archives of the Argentine embassy in Rome, note from Ambassador Gimenez to Consul Aronna, 23 October 1948. Among the many Slovak former officials and personalities who joined Durcansky, Dilong and Polakovic in Argentina were: Bor, Koloman Geraldini, Hajducek, Ferdinand Hoffmann, Jozef Hronsky, Ladislav Jankovic, Jozef Jostiak, Krchnak, the member of parliament Macek, Stanislav Meciar, Stefan Nemcok, Urban and Ernest Zatko.

329 For the switch back to their real names, see DNM, Passenger Lists, August 1947, List 20. For their Argentine citizenship, see AGPJN, Ferdinand Durcansky, Dossier 4489; and Jan Durcansky, Dossier 5489. For Jan Durcansky's extradition request, see AGPJN, Case 26/1960; also *Proyecto Testimonio*, Gurevich & Warzawski, vol. II. The extradition of two other war criminals, Vojtech Hora and Jan Pekar, was simultaneously turned down by Argentina. For Ferdinand Durcansky's move to Canada (the USA would not have him) see *Unholy Trinity*, Loftus & Aarons. For Jan Durcansky's departure, CEANA Final Report 1999, Carlota Jackisch.

330 DGFP, D, 12, minutes of Hitler–Pavelic talks, 6 June 1941.

331 *The Real Genocide in Yugoslavia*, by Srdja Trifkovic. *The Silence of Pius XII*, Carlo Falconi, Faber & Faber, London, 1970.

332 *The Real Genocide in Yugoslavia*, Srdja Trifkovic.

333 PA, Büro RAM, Kroatien, 1941–42, 442–9. IV/D/4 RSHA (Gestapo) to Himmler, 17 February 1942, cited by Trifkovic.

334 PA, Büro Staatssekretär, Jugoslawien, Bd. 4. Benzler to Ribbentrop, Belgrade, 16 February 1942, cited by Trifkovic.

335 OSS OB-6362, Report A-15489, 25 November 1943, NARA, RG 226/190/4/33/7, Entry 23, Box 30. The passports may have been supplied directly in Croatia by the Argentine diplomatic legation in Zagreb.

336 For details of Amadeo's provision of passports to the SD, see *Perón y los Alemanes*, Goñi,

ch. 7.

337 For Draganovic's extradition request, see Yugoslav note, 26 July 1947, PRO, FO 371, 67387.

338 'Consolidated Interrogation Report on Dr Krunoslav Stefano Draganovic', wartime undated; 'Draganovic, Krunoslav Stefano', 26 November 1946; 'Father Krunoslav Draganovic; Past Background and Present Activity', 12 February 1947; NARA, RG 319/631/31/54-54/1-4, Box 107, IRR Case Files. For Babic's mission, see letter to the editor of *Spremnost Hrvatski Tjednik*, Sydney, Australia, April 2000; also 'White Paper on Andrija Artukovic'; C. Michael McAdams. For Kvaternik, *The Real Genocide in Yugoslavia*, Trifkovic; also CEANA Final Report 1999. Kresimir Draganovic arrived in Argentina as a 'permanent resident' on 19 February 1948 on board the *Entre Ríos* bearing Red Cross passport 69338, he took out Argentine citizenship in 1981; see DNM, Passenger Lists, February 1948, List 33; also AGPJN, Citizenship Dossier 29165. Ivan Babic arrived in Argentina under the alias Paolo Donelli, see *Santa Fe* Passenger List, 11 August 1947, DNM.

339 For the 2,400 kilos stashed away in Bern, see *Unholy Trinity*, Loftus & Aarons, p. 132. For the two large official Croatian transfers, see 'The Fate of the Wartime Ustasha Treasury', Eizenstat Report, June 1998, US State Department The gold from these two transfers travelled to Switzerland with 25 tons of silver bought by the Swiss National Bank and was certifiably accounted for after the war. The same cannot be said however about the presumably large amount of other Croatian state and private assets Pavelic may have hidden in Swiss accounts. One US report mentions between 12 and 16 million Swiss francs that Tito's diplomats in Berne were attempting to 'unfreeze' after the war, see Houck to Bigelow, 18 July 1946, NARA, RG 226, Box 27, Entry 183.

340 Berger to Himmler, 26 August 1944, Kammerhofer to Himmler, 5 December 1944 and Pavelic to Himmler, 31 December 1944, NARA, RG 242, T-175, frames 2575473–476.

341 'Stepinac Case', pp. 19–24, NARA, RG 59, 250/48/29/6, Box 34, Entry 1073. See also 'The Fate of the Wartime Ustasha Treasury', Eizenstat Report, June 1998, US State Department.

342 'The Fate of the Wartime Ustasha Treasury', Eizenstat Report, June 1998, US State Department. *The Yugoslav Auschwitz and the Vatican*, Vladimir Dedijer, Buffalo, New York, 1992. Enclosure No. 2 to Dispatch No. 1 from American consulate in Zagreb, 26 September 1946, NARA, RG 59, 250/48/29/6, Box 34, Entry 1073.

343 'Yugoslavia: Present Whereabouts of Former Ustashi Officials', 11 October 1946, CIA Operational Files.

344 Central Intelligence Group (CIG) Intelligence Report 'Dr Ante Pavelich', 6 May 1947; 'Yugoslavia: Present Whereabouts of Former Ustashi Officials', 11 October 1946, CIA Operational Files. 'Croatian Gold Question', 2 February 1951, CIA Reference Files.

345 CIC Case No. 5650, 29 August 1947, Rome, Ante Pavelic File, NARA, RG 319, 631/31/59/04, Box 173.

346 'Croatian Gold Question', 2 February 1951, CIA Reference Files.

347 *Unholy Trinity*, Loftus & Aarons. For Pecnikar, 'Memorandum', 6 November 1946, NARA, RG 319/631/31/54-54/1–4, Box 107, IRR Case Files.

348 'Croatian Gold Question', 2 February 1951, CIA Reference Files. For Moskov, 'Surrender of Yugoslav Quislings', 15 May 1947, NARA, RG 59, 250/36/19/6, Box 3622. For Tomljenovic as a Nazi spy, *The Vatican's Holocaust*, Avro Manhattan, Ozark Books, 1986. There exists a possibility that Moskov's gold was turned over to Yugoslavia. According to one US State Department document, London wished for the 'property taken from Moskov' to be 'delivered to Yugoslavia before they ask for it', see Leghorn to Secretary of State, 15 May 1947, NARA, RG 59, 250/36/19/6, Box 3622.

349 CIC Case No. 5650, 29 August 1947, Rome, Ante Pavelic File, NARA, RG 319, 631/31/59/04, Box 173.

350 Bigelow to Glasser, 21 October 1946, RG 226, Entry 183, Box 29.
351 *Unholy Trinity*, Loftus & Aarons, pp. 132–3. The authors cite Harrington CIC memo 'Activity of Bishops Rozman and Saric', 9 March 1948, obtained under the Freedom of Information Act.
352 'Draganovic, Krunoslav Stefano', 26 November 1946; 'Father Krunoslav Draganovic, Past Background and Present Activity', 12 February 1947, NARA, RG 319, 631/31/52-54/1-4, Box 107. The six who left for Argentina were Vjekoslav Vrancic, Lovro Susic, Mile Starcevic, Dragutin Rupcic, Vilko Pecnikar and Josip Markovic. The resident war criminals and collaborators at San Girolamo received a monthly allowance of 6,000 lire, see 'Monsignor Ante Golik', 17 June 1946, NARA, RG 226, Entry 183, Box 29. When filling in their visa application forms at the Argentine consulate in Rome, some Croatians wrote in 'Via Tomacelli 132' as their last address, see Ivan Asic 'Identification Certificate', 11 March 1947, DNM, 'Fleas' Archive.
353 'Identification Certificates' filled in by the Ciklic brothers at the Argentine consulate in Paris, 25 January 1946, DNM, 'Fleas' archive. Also the passenger list for the *Cabo de Hornos*, DNM, Passenger Lists, 6 April 1946, List 14. Also, author's interview with the former head of Caritas Croata Argentina, Marko Sinovcic, 26 August 1997.
354 'Memorandum', 6 November 1946; 'Draganovic Krunoslav Stefano,' 26 November 1946, NARA, RG 319/631/31/54-54/1-4, Box 107. US intelligence reported that a Draganovic collaborator who worked at the Pontifical Commission, Ivica Elias, left for South America with a group of Croatians carrying for the most part false documents in November 1946.
355 Author's interview Sinovcic, 26 August 1997, who estimates 2,000 persons under Migrations File 72513/46 alone. The file seems to have been first extended to admit 500 extra Croatians on 17 September 1947, see Franjo Bujanovic 'Identification Certificate', DNM, 'Fleas' archive. The file's original date of 13 December 1946 is stated in various 'Identification Certificates', although Stefanic seems to have signed the original agreement with Immigration on 27 November 1946, see *Flucht vor Nürnberg?*, Meding, p. 80. Stefanic published a book, *Comunismo sin Máscaras*, in Argentina, and was followed to Argentina by his brother Urban Stefanic, also a priest, in 1950; Studia Croatica, 1997, No. 133, p. 57; and Studia Croatica, 1997, No. 134, p. 186. In the CEANA Final Report, 1999, one Blaz Stefanic is identified without further details as a Croatian war criminal. Bilobrk Identification Certificate, 19 June 1946, DNM, 'Fleas' Archive.
356 A recent Argentine government report listed a total of 49 identified Croatian war criminals who escaped to Argentina, CEANA Final Report, November 1999. The research for the present book has identified some 86 Croatian criminals. The book *Soldiers, Spies and the Rat Line*, James Milano, 1996, states that 115 Croatian criminals had arrived in Argentina by 1947 alone. The 12 identified criminals who arrived via the Caritas Croata file are Dr Josip Berkovic, 'Dinko' Bilanovic Sakic, Ivan Celan, Daniel Crljen, Ante Elez, Mirko Eterovic, Dr Ivan Korsky, Eugen Kvaternik, Radovan Latkovic, Dr Franjo Nevestic, Dr Vinko Nicolic and the German SS man Friedrich Joseph Rauch.
357 'Shipment of Ustase to South America', 16 January 1947, NARA, RG 319/631/31/54-54/1-4, Box 107. *Unholy Trinity*, Loftus & Aarons; *Odessa al Sur*, Camarasa. Hefer arrived in Buenos Aires on 2 February 1947 under his own name on the *Mary Louise* from Genoa, DNM, Passenger List. Vrancic and Starcevic probably came on the same ship under unknown aliases.
358 Author's interview with Marko Sinovcic, 26 August 1997. Caritas Croata in Buenos Aires worked out of offices provided by Father Manuel Moledo at the Ateneo de la Juventud, Riobamba 179, 3rd floor. In Rome, the Red Cross passports were taken by Father Levaiusic from San Girolamo to the Argentine consulate to be stamped, where he was attended by a 'Mr. Castelli of Trieste, Secretary of the Argentine consul in charge of visas'. See 'Organization for Clandestine Departure from Italy and Entry into Argentina of Croatian War Criminals', 16 July 1947, NARA, RG 59, 250/36/30/4, Box 6609.

359 DNM Passenger Lists, August 1947, List 20.

360 Marko Sinovcic interview, 26 August 1997.

361 Draganovic to the US ambassador in Rome, 19 May 1947, enclosure to 'Defense of Alleged Yugoslav Quislings and War Criminals in Italy', 28 May 1947, NARA, RG 59, 250/36/19/6, Box 3622.

362 Marko Sinovcic interview, 26 August 1997. At the Public Works Ministry it was a Croatian who was in charge of the 'selection of workers' and of assigning tasks to 'the new contingents of Slav origin', according to an Argentine secret police report. MRE, DP, Varios, 1948, Box 58, Dossier 1, p. 241.

363 I am grateful to the Wiesenthal Centre in Argentina for allowing me access to their voluminous Rojnica dossier, which includes a copy of File F-22659, 17 December 1947, 'Rojnica, Ivo' sent by the Yugoslav government to London, from the Yugoslav Archives in Belgrade. See also *Svjedocanstvo*, Daniel Crljen, Buenos Aires, 1984. As well, 'Prikaz Povijesti Argentine', Ivo Rojnica, Buenos Aires, 1974. See also *Maria C* Passenger List, 2 April 1947, DNM; and his disembarkation card under the alias Ivan Rajcinovic, DNM, 'Chela' Archive.

364 *La Prensa*, 15 July 1977. Rajcinovic citizenship dossier 4159, AGPJN.

365 *La Nación*, 14 May 1998; *Clarín*, 15 May 1998. In these and other press articles Rojnica has denied the wartime charges against him. *Horrors of War: Historical Reality and Philosophy*, Franjo Tudjman, New York, 1996. 'Nationalism Turns Sour in Croatia', *New York Times*, 13 November 1993. 'Presencia Diplomática de la República de Croacia en America Latina', *Studia Croatica*, 1994, No. 124, p. 35. In 1996 Rojnica was officially received by the mayor of Dubrovnik, Ivo Obuljan, see Serbian News Agency, SRNA, Republika Srpska, Review of Daily News, 8 August 1996.

366 Boston Series 693, 694 and 696, NARA, RG 226, Entry 210, Box 441.

367 Memoari Dinka Sakica, 3–17 June 1998, *Jutarnji List*. *Tucumán* Passenger List, 22 December 1947, DNM. Father Josip 'Jole' Bujanovic organized Ustasha storm units involved in the massive slaughter of Serbs up until February 1945 and was decorated by Pavelic. One Franjo Bujanovic entered Argentina under Draganovic's Caritas Croata file bearing a Red Cross passport stating his last address as the Fermo camp for Croatian prisoners in Italy, see Franjo Bujanovic 'Identification Certificate', DNM, 'Fleas' archive and *Empire Halbert* Passenger List, 29 April 1948, DNM. Josip Bujanovic later directed a choir of former Fermo internees in Buenos Aires, see *Studia Croatica*, 1997, Issue 135.

368 For a detailed account of London's procrastination over Pavelic, *Unholy Trinity*, Loftus & Aarons, ch. 4.

369 'Summary of Information', 30 January 1947, Ante Pavelic folder, IRR XE001109, NARA, RG 319, 631/31/59/04, Box 173. See also 'Memorandum for the Officer in Charge', 15 March 1947, ibid. One Ustasha war criminal, Dinko Sakic, claimed in his memoirs to have crossed from Austria to Italy with Pavelic in June 1946, stating that the Poglavnik travelled disguised as a German colonel, see Memoari Dinka Sakica, *Jutarnji List*, 3–17 June 1998.

370 Pro-Memoria, 10 May 1946, Ante Pavelic folder, IRR XE001109, NARA, RG 319, 631/31/59/04, Box 173.

371 Telegram Key to Smith, 7 January 1947; Gowen to Officer in Charge, 22 January 1947; Ante Pavelic folder, IRR XE001109, NARA, RG 319, 631/31/59/04, Box 173.

372 'Investigation Re: Whereabouts of Ante Pavelic', 18 April 1947, ibid.

373 'Pavelic, Ante', 20 June 1947; 'Summary of Information', 9 June 1947; 'Memorandum for the Officer in Charge', 15 March 1947; Ante Pavelic folder, IRR XE001109, NARA, RG 319, 631/31/59/04, Box 173.

374 For US-Anglo negotiations over Pavelic arrest, *Unholy Trinity*, Loftus & Aarons, ch. 4. For the order to go ahead with an arrest plan, Brigadier Anderson to A C/S G-2 with copies to British and US agents, 7 August 1947, Pavelic CIC file, NARA, RG 319, 631/31/59/04, Box 173.

375 'Ante Pavelic and other Ustasha Personalities', 8 August 1947, ibid. Pavelic reportedly

shared quarters with 'the famous Bulgarian terrorist Vancia Mikoiloff'.

376 Handwritten memo, 14 July 1947, Pavelic CIC file.
377 'Pavelic, Ante', 29 August 1947, Pavelic CIC file.
378 'Pavelic, Ante', 29 August 1947, Pavelic CIC file.
379 'Memorandum for the Officer in Charge', 12 September 1947, Pavelic CIC file.
380 Serna to Daye, March 1948, CEGES, FPD, Dossier 514. This was the elder Serna, father of the Serna who formed part of the group of war criminals who met with Perón at the Casa Rosada in December 1947.
381 For a detailed account of Pavelic's Krizari and their ties to the Vatican and Western intelligence see *Unholy Trinity*, Loftus & Aarons.
382 For Pavelic's Castel Gandolfo residence, 'Reported Arrival of Ante Pavelic in Argentina', 2 December 1948, CIA Operational Files. *La Repubblica*, 23, 24 and 26 September 1948.
383 DNM, Passenger Lists, May 1948, List 5; and November 1948, List 18. Argentine Citizenship application of Ana Mirjana Pavelic, Dossier 9117, AGPJN. Pal Aranyos 'Identification Certificate', DNM, 'Fleas' archive. Pavelic's eldest daughter, Visnja Pavelic, was married to Vilko Pecnikar and did not travel on the *Ugolino Vivaldi* with her mother.
384 'Reported Arrival of Ante Pavelic in Argentina', 2 December 1948, CIA Operational Files. *Terror Over Yugoslavia*, Avro Manhattan, Watts, London, 1953. *Unholy Trinity*, Loftus & Aarons. Regarding Crljen flying to meet Perón, Loftus & Aarons cite the CIC memo 'Pavelic Ante and the Legitimists in the Ustasa Movement', obtained under the US Freedom of Information Act. Crljen died in Argentina in 1995. According to his son, Crljen arrived in Argentina by ship in 1947 under the name Francisco Jurkic, author's interview with Francisco Crljen, 26 August 2000. One Francisco Jurkic did arrive on board the *Santa Fe*, a ship loaded with Croatian fugitives, see DNM Passenger List, 11 August 1947. See also 'In Memoriam Prof. Daniel Crljen', *Studia Croatica*, Buenos Aires, 1995, No. 129.
385 Author's interview with Marko Sinovcic, 26 August 1997. After the interview, Sinovcic double-checked this version with one of Pavelic's daughters and confirmed it to the author.
386 Pal Aranyos 'Identification Certificate', 12 November 1948, DNM, 'Fleas' archive. Letter ICRC to author, 24 May 2000. Initially helpful regarding the previously unreleased passport applications of Nazi war criminals Heilig and Fischböck, the Red Cross failed to respond to specific queries regarding Red Cross passport 74369, which figures in Aranyos' 'identification certificate' and the *Sestriere*'s passenger list. The Red Cross failed to respond as well to how the picture of the bearded Pavelic from his 'identification certificate', a copy of which was mailed to the ICRC, compares to the picture in their files.
387 'Reported Arrival of Ante Pavelic in Argentina', 2 December 1948, CIA Operational Files. 'Croatian Gold Question', 2 February 1951, CIA Reference Files. 'Ustashi Leaders in Argentina and Austria', 20 April 1948, RG 59, 250/36/30/4, Box 6609. 'In Memoriam Prof. Vinko Nikolic', *Studia Croatica*, Buenos Aires, 1997, No. 135.
388 'Croatian Gold Question', 2 February 1951, CIA Reference Files.
389 Draganovic to US ambassador in Rome, 19 May 1947, enclosed with 'Defense of Alleged Yugoslav Quislings and War Criminals in Italy', 28 May 1947, NARA, RG 59, 250/36/19/6, Box 3622.
390 Memoari Dinka Sakica, *Jutarnji List*, 3–17 June 1998. Also, *Vulcania* Passenger List, 31 July 1947, DNM. Among Heinrich's fellow first-class travellers were the Argentine magnate Torcuato Di Tella and the young Guido Di Tella, who would become Argentina's foreign minister during the Peronist administration of President Carlos Menem in the 1990s. Also on board was Luis Luti, the anti-Nazi Argentine wartime chargé d'affaires in Berlin.
391 'Croatian Gold Question', 2 February 1951, CIA Reference Files. 'Franjo Cvijic', 17 June 1949; 'Reported Arrival of Ante Pavelic in Argentina', 2 December 1948; CIA Operational

Files.
392 'Transfer of Croatian Gold to Argentina', 16 April 1952, CIA Reference Files. Also transferred to Pavelic from Switzerland were 5 million Swiss francs, the CIA was told.
393 Hudal to Perón, 31 August 1948, Pontificio Santa Maria dell'Anima, Hudal Papers 27, cited in CEANA Final Report 1999, Matteo Sanfilippo. Fuldner to Rothmund, 15 June 1948, Handakten Rothmund, Verkehr mit Argentinien, E 4800.1 1967/111, Bd. 70 (DNR311), Swiss Federal Archives. For Fuldner's arrival in Buenos Aires, *Argentina* Passenger List, 16 October 1948, DNM.
394 *Unholy Trinity*, Loftus & Aarons, ch. 2. A search for Hudal's name in the Nazi party and SS membership rolls at NARA proved unsuccessful. He was registered however in the Reich's Education Ministry card file with entries up to the year 1940, NARA, RG 242, Series 8202, DS/REM, Roll B1260.
395 *Die Grundlagen des Nationalsozialismus*, Alois Hudal, Günther, Leipzig, 1936. Hudal's book was proposed as evidence of anti-Semitism at Nuremberg, *Nuremberg Trial Proceedings*, vol. 14, 18 May 1946.
396 *Frieden, Krieg und 'Frieden'*, Juan Maler, Verlag Maler, Bariloche, 1987. *Flucht vor Nürnberg?*, Meding, p. 78.
397 *Flucht vor Nürnberg?*, Meding, p. 79. Minutes of NCWC meeting, 6 August 1947, HP 26, cited in CEANA Final Report 1999, Matteo Sanfilippo.
398 *Unholy Trinity*, Loftus & Aarons, ch. 2.
399 *Zwischen Deutschland und Argentinien. Fünf Jahre in Übersee, Memoiren*, Hans-Ulrich Rudel, Göttingen, 1954, vol. 3, p. 200.
400 *Römische Tagebücher*, Alois Hudal, Stocker, Graz, 1976, p. 21.
401 *Frieden, Krieg und 'Frieden'*, Maler, pp. 506–7. Declaration by Kops/Maler before the Bariloche police, 8 May 1993, cited in full in CEANA Final Report 1999, Carlota Jackisch. Kops is not listed in the SS membership rolls at NARA. He is listed however as Nazi party member No. 7,524,143, joining the party on 1 March 1940, born Hamburg, 29 September 1914, NARA, RG 242, Ortsgruppen Nazi party, MFOK L0054.
402 For Kops' use of the Mahler surname, CEANA Final Report 1999, Matteo Sanfilippo. *Frieden, Krieg und 'Frieden'*, Maler, pp. 322–3 and 326.
403 *Frieden, Krieg und 'Frieden'*, Maler, pp. 322–3.
404 'Testimonial and Character Italian Co-Operators', 19 January 1946, in Ruffinengo's Argentine citizenship application, AGPJN, Dossier 5565. Franz Ruffinengo, 16 June 1999. Interview with former DAIE official Amadeo Mazzino, 20 November 1998. *Frieden, Krieg und 'Frieden'*, p. 323. *Flucht vor Nürnberg?*, Meding.
405 *Frieden, Krieg und 'Frieden'*, Maler, pp. 327–8.
406 *Frieden, Krieg und 'Frieden'*, Maler, p. 322. Kops refers to Bayer discreetly as 'Monsignor B.' He also mentions a Father Leopold as helping the Nazis. *Into that Darkness*, Gitta Sereny, Picador, London, 1977.
407 'La Vista Report', 15 May 1947, NARA, RG 59, 250/36/29/2, 800.0128, Box 4080.
408 'La Vista Report', 15 May 1947. Spanish diplomats in Rome collaborated with Nix in providing visas under false names for his escapees, although applicants had to fill in a secret form providing their real personal data. The Villa San Francesco is today an old people's home run by the Spanish Siervas de Jesús sisters.
409 Letter PCA to Hudal, 9 April 1948, HP 27, cited in CEANA Final Report 1999, Matteo Sanfilippo. CIG report, 21 January 1947, NARA, RG 59, 840.5510/1-2447, cited in *Unholy Trinity*, Loftus & Aarons, p. 108.
410 Kops/Mahler to Hudal, undated, circa April 1948, HP 27, cited in CEANA Final Report 1999, Matteo Sanfilippo. *Unholy Trinity*, Loftus & Aarons. For Petranovic's extradition request, FO 371, 67386. For Petranovic's link to Auxilium, HP 27. Among the non-criminals assisted by Petranovic was the Hungarian-born actress Zsa Zsa Gabor.
411 *Unholy Trinity*, Loftus & Aarons, p. 107. Hefer arrived in Argentina aboard the *Marie Louise*

on 2 February 1947, DNM, Passenger Lists.

412 *Unholy Trinity*, Loftus & Aarons, pp. 108-9. Among the 23 who got away, one was positively identified by this investigation as Franjo Nevestic, see *Philippa* passenger list, DNM, Passenger Lists, 1 April 1947, List 1; and CEANA Final Report 1999, Carlota Jackisch. A second war criminal not listed by the CEANA, Captain Ante Elez, also arrived on the *Philippa* on the same date under the Caritas Croata file. Elez is mentioned in *Odessa al Sur*, Camarasa, and in 'Report on the Jasenovac Camp', Yugoslav State Commission for the Establishment of Crimes Committed by Occupiers and their Collaborators, Zagreb, 15 November 1945, Inventory No. 16261. Others supposedly on board were Ustasha secret police chief Vladimir Kretch, General Josip Tomlianovich, state police chief Radomil Vergovitch and secret police chief Georg Vrantich; American Embassy Italy No. 978, 12 June 1947, NARA, RG 59, 250/36/30/4, Box 6609; as well as *Odessa al Sur*, Camarasa.

413 Letters Dömöter to Hudal, 12 September 1948 and 28 August 1949, HP 27 and 25, cited in CEANA Final Report 1999, Matteo Sanfilippo. Eichmann/Klement Red Cross passport application, 1 June 1950, ICRC, Geneva. Kops/Mahler to Hudal, undated letter circa April 1948, HP 27.

414 José Otero, author's interview, 9 October 1998.

415 Cabot to Secretary of State, Top Secret, 12 June 1947, NARA, RG 59, 250/36/19/6, Box 3623.

416 'RPA – Mr. Martin', Top Secret, 13 June 1947, NARA, RG 59, 250/36/19/6, Box 3623. British embassy at Holy See to London, 18 November 1947, PRO, FO 371, 67402.

417 José Otero, 9 October 1998.

418 The details of Kops's escape were minutely described in his memoirs *Frieden, Krieg und 'Frieden'*, Maler, pp. 330–31. They were corroborated 13 years later when his letters to Hudal were opened to Argentine government researchers at Santa Maria dell'Anima; Kops to Hudal, 14 May 1948; 22 June 1948; 23 June 1948 and 21 July 1948; all HP 27; cited in CEANA Final Report 1999, Matteo Sanfilippo. Kops's Immigration File No. was 179124/48, see Hans Maler disembarkation card, DNM, 'Chela' Archive; and Vötterl's was 179125/48, see *Andrea C* Passenger List, 4 September 1948, DNM.

419 Rupnik and Maler disembarkation cards, DNM, 'Chela' Archive. Rupnik arrived on the *Santa Fe*, 6 January 1948.

420 *Frieden, Krieg und 'Frieden'*, Maler, p. 334.

421 *Frieden, Krieg und 'Frieden'*, Maler, p. 346. Franz Ruffinengo, 16 June 1999. For Ruffinengo's arrival, *Buenos Aires* Passenger List, 3 May 1948, DNM.

422 *Flucht vor Nürnberg?*, Meding. CEANA Final Report 1999, Matteo Sanfilippo. 'Greetings from Across the Sea', Alois Hudal, *Der Weg*, vol. III, 1949. *Römische Tagebücher*, Hudal, p. 296.

423 The Jewish refugee Marcelo Fuhrmann travelled to Argentina on the *Cabo de Hornos* in August 1948. According to Fuhrmann, shortly before the ship docked in Buenos Aires a large group of Germans and Croatians descended to their cabins and emerged disguised as Franciscan friars; interview with Fuhrmann, 31 January 2000. Fuhrmann's claim is substantiated by the ship's Passenger List, which shows an unusually large number of priests with Spanish surnames. Also on the *Cabo de Hornos* was a real Croatian priest, the bloody murderer Vlado Bilobrk, and the French war criminal Marcel Boucher, whose entry to Argentina had been smoothed by Argentine Cardinal Caggiano; *Cabo de Hornos* Passenger List, DNM.

424 Hans Sommer interrogation, 10 December 1946, p. 25, NARA, RG 59, 250/38/13/6, Box 6749, Decimal Files 862.20252. Schellenberg's special representative in Spain, Reinhard Spitzy, adds the information that Chanel paid for Schellenberg's funeral, author's interview, 8 December 1998.

425 US embassy Madrid, 'Walter Kutschmann', 17 April 1946, NARA, RG 59, 250/38/13/4-5, Box 6747. Hans Sommer interrogation, 10 December 1946, p. 25, NARA, RG 59,

250/38/13/6, Box 6749, Decimal Files 862.20252.

426 US embassy Madrid, 'Walter Kutschmann', 17 April 1946, NARA, RG 59, 250/38/13/4-5, Box 6747. Kutschmann/Olmo file, AGN, DAE 20920. *Proyecto Testimonio*, Gurevich & Warzawski. Kutschmann's arrest in Spain was requested by the US again in 1947, see 'Hard Core List of Germans for Repatriation from Spain', 23 May 1947, NARA, RG 59, 250/38/13/6, Box 6749, 862.20252/5-2347.

427 Kutschmann gave the Charcas 2345 address to Argentina's Immigration authorities upon arrival, see DNM, Passenger Lists, January 1948, List 38. See also the Kutschmann/Olmo file, AGN, DAE 20920. Kutschmann's taxi licence application was seconded as well by Baron Máximo von Merken.

428 Kutschmann/Olmo file, AGN, DAE 20920.

429 *Odessa al Sur*, Camarasa. For Hudal and Roschmann, *Flucht vor Nürnberg?*, Meding, ch. 5, fn. 53.

430 Maz Teodoro Guttermann, who sat alongside Kutschmann during his press conference and promised the 'sensational revelations', was murdered in a confusing episode near the police HQ in the Argentine city of Córdoba two months afterwards. *Odessa al Sur*, Jorge Camarasa.

431 Kutschmann was under the mistaken impression that because the journalists were from the pro-military newspaper *Tiempo Argentino*, where the sons of a fellow Nazi officer held high positions, they were on his side. Author's interview with Becquer Casaballe, the photographer who took Kutschmann's picture, 15 September 2000. As it turned out, the editors of *Tiempo Argentino* refused to run the story. The journalists therefore gave the picture to a news agency, which broadcast it to all the Argentine media.

432 *Página/12*, 19 July 1991. *La Prensa*, 11 May 1995. *Clarín*, 4 February 1996.

433 *Proyecto Testimonio*, Gurevich & Warzawski. *Odessa al Sur*, Camarasa.

434 *Perón y la Iglesia Católica*, Lila M. Caimari, Ariel, Buenos Aires, 1995, pp. 123 and 134. See various visa requests for Pratto, Jorge and Ruffinengo by the Argentine embassy in Rome, 168 AE and 169 AE, 8 July 1949; 194 AE, 16 July 1949; 196 AE, 18 July 1949; 199 AE, 19 July 1949; all archives of Argentine embassy in Rome, dossier '1949, Salidas, AE, del No 1 al No 200'. For Jorge and Ruffinengo as Perón-appointed DAIE special agents in 1949, see presidential decree 25863, 13 October 1949, AGN, STP, Box 547. Author's interviews regarding Pratto and Jorge, former DAIE officials José Otero, 9 October 1998, and Amadeo Mazzino, 30 November 1998; Horacio Carballal, 4 February 1998; retired ambassador Guillermo Speroni, 15 November 1999; nationalist Emilio Gutierrez Herrero, 29 October 1998; Franz Ruffinengo, 16 June 1999. Memo of meeting with Rothmund, 3 February 1950, Handakten Rothmund, Verkehr mit Argentinien, E 4800.1 1967/111 Bd. 70 (DNR 311), Swiss Federal Archives. See also Pratto photo file at AGN for his meeting with the Pope.

435 For Barbie, *Klaus Barbie, Butcher of Lyons*, Tom Bower, Michael Joseph, London, 1984. Barbie/Altmann passport application 18573, ICRC, Geneva. DNM, Passenger Lists, 13 April 1951, List 31. Barbie was granted permanent residency in Argentina through Immigration file 92368/51.

436 The 'Moral Reserve' stock phrase formed part of a great number of major policy speeches made by Argentina's military rulers during 1976/83. The stated policy of the dictatorship, warmly endorsed by Argentina's Catholic Church at the time, was to preserve Argentina's perceived 'Western and Christian way of life'. As a result, young people, Jews, psychologists, became prime targets for extermination. Of the death toll of at least 20,000, a mere few hundred could have been actual armed terrorists, as by the military regime's own account only some 600 people died because of terrorist action between 1960 and 1979. In September 2000, the Argentine Catholic Church publicly asked for forgiveness for its abetting of the killings during the 1976/83 regime.

437 Correspondence with Michael Butler, 3, 4, 5 August 1997 and 31 March 1999.

438 'La Vista Report', 15 May 1947, NARA, RG 59, 250/36/29/2, 800.0128, Box 4080.

439 DNM, Passenger Lists, February 1948, List 44. Also, CEANA Final Report 1999, Carlota Jackisch. Rauch travelled apparently under a Red Cross passport. In 1999 he was reportedly living in Austria. For the Reichsbank raid, *Nazi Gold*, Sayer & Botting. The Belgian who arrived on the same ship was Gérard Ruysschaert, condemned to 20 years in Belgium in 1946, travelling under the name José Ruysschaert.

440 Red Cross passport application 100980, Schramm/Fischböck, ICRC Geneva. CEANA Final Report 1999, Carlota Jackisch. Also, *Anna C* Passenger list, 2 February 1951, DNM.

441 Red Cross passport application 97583, Heilig/Richwitz, ICRC, Geneva. Richwitz to Wüstenberg, 15 December 1949; Wüstenberg to Hudal, 17 December 1949; Hudal Papers 25, cited in CEANA Final Report 1999, Matteo Sanfilippo. Heilig arrived in Buenos Aires on 17 January 1951 on board the *Buenos Aires*, DNM, Passenger Lists, January 1951, List 35. Monsignor Heinemann and Bishop Hudal both attended their flock at Santa Maria dell'Anima on Via della Pace 20 and 24, see 'La Vista Report', 15 May 1947, NARA, RG 59, 2508/36/29/2, Box 4080. For Hudal and Heinemann see also *Frieden, Krieg und 'Frieden'*, Maler, p. 322.

442 *Into that Darkness*, Sereny.

443 For Roschmann, *Flucht vor Nürnberg?*, Meding, p. 149. See letter Guth to Draganovic, 6 June 1949, HP 24, cited in CEANA Final Report 1999, Matteo Sanfilippo. For his arrival in Argentina, DNM, Passenger Lists, 8 October 1948, List 32. CEANA Final Report 1999, Carlota Jackisch. Priebke/Pape passport application 83023, 26 July 1948, ICRC, Geneva. Bohne passport application 83465, 24 August 1948, ICRC, Geneva.

444 'La Vista Report', 15 May 1947, NARA, RG 59, 250/36/29/2, 800.0128, Box 4080. The report's conclusion is corroborated by the documents found in the archives of the Argentine embassy in Rome, which show how cardinals Tisserant and Caggiano pressured Argentina's representatives to accept French war criminals.

445 Priebke's SS file, NARA, SSOK Roll 393A; Kappler testimony at the Eichmann trial in Jerusalem, 30 May 1961; *El Último Nazi*, Elena Llorente & Martino Rigacci, Sudamericana, Buenos Aires, 1998; *Oggi* magazine, May 1996.

446 Priebke interview, *Oggi* magazine, May 1996.

447 For the Priebke–Kops Mussolini rescue connection, *Il Gazzettino*, 17 May 1994. For detailed accounts of Skorzeny's rescue operation, *Skorzeny, Hitler's Commando*, Glenn B. Infield, Military Heritage Press, New York, 1981; and *Skorzeny, the Most Dangerous Man in Europe*, Charles Whiting, Combined Publishing, Pennsylvania, 1998.

448 For the deportation of Rome's Jews and the gold ransom, Kappler's written testimony in the Eichmann trial, 31 May 1961, and the Final Judgement in the same trial. *Hitler's Pope*, Cornwell. *Oggi* magazine, May 1996. *El Último Nazi*, Llorente & Rigacci. For Priebke's assurance to Pfeiffer that the Gestapo would not enter the Vatican buildings in search of Jews, see *Vatican Diplomacy and the Jews During the Holocaust*, John F. Morley, Ktay, New York, 1980.

449 Priebke's statement at 209 POW Camp, Afragola, 28 August 1946. *Primetime*, ABC, 1994. *El Último Nazi*, Llorente & Rigacci. Priebke interview, *La Nación*, 12 April 1998.

450 For claims by the Wiesenthal Centre of having found Nazi documentation regarding Priebke's alleged participation in the extermination of Jews, see *Il Giornale*, 9 May 1996. For the summons, see Priebke's SS file at NARA, SSOK Roll 393A. *Oggi* magazine, May 1996.

451 Priebke interview in *Odessa al Sur*, Camarasa.

452 *Oggi* magazine, May 1996.

453 Priebke interview by the Italian journalist Emanuela Audisio, *La Repubblica*, quoted in *Odessa al Sur*, Camarasa, p. 24. Priebke also said it was an Italian Fascist chief and friend from Brescia who arranged his escape to Argentina, see *Oggi* magazine, May 1996.

454 The file numbers appear on the passenger lists of the ships on which Priebke and Mengele

travelled to Argentina. For Priebke, see November 1948, List 45, *San Giorgio*. For Mengele, see June 1949, List 47, *North King*. Immigration opened a total of 132,458 landing permit files during 1948, with 36,000 applications arriving from Argentine consulates abroad and 95,458 presented in Buenos Aires, see Diana Inquest, AGN, STP, Box 547, p. 378. The DAIE also handled landing permit applications, author's interview with former DAIE official in Genoa, Amadeo Mazzino, 20 November 1998. Priebke's file 211712/48 included other suspected criminals; one was the Belgian Alida Dhooga, see Dictamen 2413, 29 April 1953, AGN, STP, Box 542. An almost immediately preceding file, 211669/48, was used by SS officer and former Nazi spy in Argentina Wolf Franzcok to re-enter the country illegally after being interrogated by the American authorities in Germany; see MI, 47-S-141, p. 53.

455 Priebke/Pape Red Cross application, ICRC 83023, Geneva. Priebke interview by the Italian journalist Emanuela Audisio, *La Repubblica*, quoted in *Odessa al Sur*, Camarasa, p. 24. Statements by Graham to ANSA news agency, 10 May 1994.

456 For Draganovic, author's interview with former DAIE officials Amadeo Mazzino, 20 November 1998, and Franz Ruffinengo, 16 June 1999.

457 For Priebke's arrival in Buenos Aires, DNM, Passenger Lists, November 1948, List 45. For his waiting table in Buenos Aires, Priebke interview, *La Nación*, 12 April 1998.

458 Decree 15,972, 8 July 1949, AGN, STP, Box 547.

459 For Priebke changing back to his real name, AGN, STP, Box 666, Book 4, p. 401. For Durcansky changing to his real name, ibid., p. 479. Regarding Durcansky's role at Immigration, author's interviews with former DAIE official José Otero, 9 October 1988; and with former Caritas Croata chief Marcos Sinovcic, 26 August 1997.

460 *El pintor de la Suiza Argentina*, Esteban Buch, Sudamericana, Buenos Aires, 1991.

461 Kops had been uncovered in the early 1990s, see *In Hitler's Shadow*, Svoray-Taylor, Constable, 1995. He was already running scared and on 8 May 1993 had spontaneously presented himself before the Bariloche police to declare he had actually helped save 25 Jews in Budapest in 1944, see CEANA Final Report 1999, Carlota Jackisch. *Primetime*, ABC, 1994.

462 The hugs were filmed by television news crews and caused a major scandal in Argentina.

463 For San Bonaventura and Eichmann, 'Holocaust Gold Taints the Vatican', *Sunday Telegraph*, 27 July 1997.

464 *El Último Nazi*, Llorente & Rigacci.

465 Regarding the Dortmund fiasco, Reuter news agency, 26 August 1996.

466 For the Bohne quote, *Aftermath*, Ladislas Farago, Simon and Schuster, New York, 1974, p. 346.

467 Bohne's SS file, NARA, SSOK Roll 87.

468 *Flucht vor Nürnberg?*, Meding. Meding's account of Eyting's flight is based on a 25 June 1990 interview with Eyting himself. For Draganovic and Omrcanin, see *Unholy Trinity*, Loftus & Aarons. For Fuldner's close working alliance with Draganovic, letter from Fuldner to Rothmund, 15 June 1948, Handakten Rothmund, Dossier Verkehr mit Argentinien, E 4800.1 1967/111 Bd. 70 (DNR311), Swiss Federal Archives. For Draganovic's regular contact with the DAIE, author's interviews with former DAIE officials Amadeo Mazzino, 28 November 1998, and Franz Ruffinengo, 16 June 1999. For Fuldner recruiting Nazis for the Argentine air force, Fuldner's statement of 18 August 1949, Diana Inquest, AGN, STP, Box 547.

469 Bohne passport application, 83456, ICRC, Geneva.

470 'Identification Certificate' forms filled in by Gerhard and Gisela Bohne at the Argentine consulate in Genoa, 7 January 1949, 'Fleas' archive, DNM; and the passenger list for the *Ana C*, January 1949, List 81, DNM.

471 Berne police report on Fuldner, 3 October 1948, Handakten Rothmund, Dossier Verkehr mit Argentinien, E 4800.1 1967/111 Bd. 70 (DNR311), Swiss Federal Archives. For Bohne's address in Buenos Aires, see *Ana C* passenger list, DNM, Passenger Lists, January 1949, List 81.

472 Bohne, 7 October 1959, from *Was Siet Taten, Was Sie Wurden*, Ernst Klee, Frankfurt, 1986.

473 For Hefelmann, see his testimony at the Heyde trial, 6–15 September 1960; for the role of Caritas International in his escape, his testimony in Lindburg on 18 February 1964. For Caritas and Argentina's Immigration office, see Diana Inquest, AGN, STP, Box 547, which registers the number of 18 Immigration applications by Caritas International.

474 For the antics of Bohne's defence lawyer, *Odessa al Sur*, Camarasa.

475 Diana Inquest, AGN, STP, Box 547. See sworn testimonies of Bruhn, 1 September 1949, pp. 244–6; Fuldner, 18 August 1949, p. 182; and Diana, 6 June 1949, p. 97. During 1947 Fuldner had already initiated applications in favour of former Nazi officers such as Constantin von Gromann, Immigration file 123528/47.

476 Interview with Ragnar Hagelin, 8 February 1997. The dark side of Argentine history tangled Hagelin in its web once again when his 17-year-old daughter Dagmar 'disappeared' during the 1976/83 dictatorship. The man responsible was the 'Blond Angel', Alfredo Astiz, a navy officer of the ESMA death camp where some 5,000 people were murdered. Captured by British forces during the 1982 Falklands War, Astiz was taken to London. Prime Minister Margaret Thatcher later returned him to Argentina. France eventually held an *in absentia* trial against Astiz and condemned him to life imprisonment in 1990, but he remained protected and free in Argentina. See *Judas*, Uki Goñi, Editorial Sudamericana, Buenos Aires, 1996.

477 That the records for politically sensitive cases were kept separately was stated during the 1949 Diana Inquest by José Bruhn, 29 August 1949, AGN, STP, Box 547, Diana Inquest, pp. 237–9. The cards in the box also include data regarding numerous files initiated by Perón's presidential office, the Argentine Foreign Ministry, Skoda and Catholic groups. Various officials during the author's research at the Immigration archives in 1998 confirmed the existence of separate records for sensitive cases relating to the period under study.

478 Weiss de Janko entered Argentina through Immigration file 242846/48 on 1 April 1950. For Fuldner's role in her clandestine removal from Austria to Switzerland, see Berne police report on Fuldner, 13 October 1948, Handakten Rothmund, Dossier Verkehr mit Argentinien, E 4800.1, 1967/111, Bd. 70 (DNR 311), Swiss Federal Archives. Also, Report 6661, Berne Police, 5 August 1948, Swiss Federal Archives. See also Weiss's citizenship application, AGPJN, Dossier 5577.

479 The research for this book was able to determine that Vianord made at least five collective applications during 1948, five in 1949 and two in 1950/51. Of these applications, ten are registered in the 'Fleas' box, two others are mentioned in the Diana Inquest, AGN, STP, Box 547.

480 For a detailed account of Schwammberger's wartime responsibilities, *The Last Nazi*, Aaron Freiwald & Martin Mendelsohn, W.W. Norton & Company, New York, 1994.

481 Index card 'Vianord Agenc. Viaj. Nordic. sol. perm. ingr. pais a favor de H Lechler y otros . . .', in small wooden box in DNM, 'Fleas' archive; and compare with DNM, Passenger Lists, March 1949, List 52, where the same file number is entered for Schwammberger. Regarding the preceding files, see sworn statement by Immigration Commissioner Pablo Diana, 17 May 1949, AGN, STP, Diana Inquest, p.60. Schwammberger in 1990 became one of the very few Nazis that Argentina consented to extradite. After standing trial in Germany, he was sentenced to life imprisonment in 1992.

482 *Memorias del General*, Martínez, p. 194. Tomás Eloy Martínez, correspondence with author, 5 June 1998. Regarding Mengele's trips to Paraguay, Mengele CIA file, Internal Memorandum, 18 July 1972, cited in *Mengele*, Gerald Posner & John Ware, McGraw-Hill, New York, 1986, ch. 5. The 'intellectual' side of Mengele was remarked upon in various interviews by one of his friends in Argentina, Willem Sassen, see *ibid.*, p. 102.

483 *Mengele*, Posner & Ware. Regarding Sassen as Rudel's chauffeur, author's interview with

Pedro Pobierzym, 30 April 1997, who knew both Sassen and Rudel. Sassen in a series of interviews with Argentine journalist Carlos Echeverría in 1984 claimed he was a frequent visitor at the Casa Rosada and that he knew Perón. Echeverría interviewed Sassen again for the Argentine TV programme *Edición Plus* 10 years later, when Sassen spoke openly about Mengele, author's interviews with Echeverría, 26 December 1997 and 13 January 1998.

484   'Memories of Heimat', thesis by Joshua Goltz, who interviewed Habel in Argentina, St Antony's College, Oxford, Trinity Term, 1998. Habel died on 28 July 2000, see 'Murió un oficial de las SS que vivía en El Bolsón', *Clarín*, 29 July 2000. See also 'Confesiones de un ex oficial nazi', *Clarín*, 19 July 1999. Also, author's conversations with Abel Basti, an Argentine journalist who interviewed Habel at length in Bariloche in 1999 for the local newspaper *Mañana del Sur*. Also, Habel's SS file, NARA, RG 242.

485   *Mengele*, Posner & Ware.

486   Hudal–Montini correspondence; also Hudal's correspondence with incriminated ethnic Germans from northern Italy; CEANA Final Report 1999, Matteo Sanfilippo. 'La Vista Report', 15 May 1947, NARA, RG 59, 250/36/29/2, Box 4080, p. 10.

487   Red Cross passport applications 100501, 100940, and 100958, for Mengele, Eichmann and Müller respectively, ICRC, Geneva.

488   The file numbers for Mengele, Eichmann and Müller are noted in the corresponding passenger lists at Argentina's Immigration Office. DNM, Passenger Lists; for Mengele, June 1949, List 47; Eichmann, July 1950, List 24; Müller, October 1950, List 44.

489   The account of Mengele's passage through Genoa is based on his diaries, as cited in *Mengele*, Posner & Ware. See also Mengele's Red Cross passport application, 100501, ICRC, Geneva. Trachoma examinations were standard practice at the DAIE, author's interview with former DAIE official José Otero, 9 October 1998.

490   *Mengele*, Posner & Ware. According to the authors, Mengele was held three weeks at the Genoa prison, and travelled on the *North King* on its next sailing, arriving in Buenos Aires on 26 August 1949. The DNM passenger lists however show that Gregor sailed on schedule, arriving in Buenos Aires in June. *North King* passenger list, DNM, June 1949, List 47.

491   *Zwischen Deutschland und Argentinien. Fünf Jahre in Übersee, Memoiren*, vol. 3, Rudel. *Mengele*, Posner & Ware. For Rudel's arrival, CEANA Final Report 1999, Carlota Jackisch.

492   The Yacyretá project was labelled a 'monument to corruption' by Argentine President Carlos Menem during the 1990s, when it was still undergoing construction. From an original estimate of under 3 billion dollars at the start, the final cost ballooned to some 12 billion dollars. Rudel was apparently called in to grease palms in Paraguay. Jorge Carretoni, an associate of the Lahmeyer consortium and long-time friend of Rudel, accompanied the Luftwaffe ace to see Perón in Spain and then Stroessner in Paraguay. Carretoni related Rudel's participation in his book *De Frondizi a Alfonsín*, Jorge Carretoni, Catálogos, Buenos Aires, 1998. Also, author's interview with Carretoni, 9 March 1999. For Fuldner's long-time link with Lahmeyer, see secret letter from Admiral Portillo to the Presidential Office, 22 March 1962, requesting a security check on Fuldner, AGN, Bormann Dossier, p. 92. Santiago Martinucci, an Argentine consultant representing a French bank, had already been approached by Fuldner in 1971 regarding Lahmeyer's interest in Yacyretá, author's interview with Martinucci, 19 November 1998. For Sassen and Galtieri, anonymous interview, 30 June 2001.

493   Author's interview with Carretoni, 9 March 1999. Carretoni, who declares he is not a Nazi sympathizer, affirms that despite their long friendship he was never aware that Rudel protected war criminals such as Mengele.

494   Nota Verbale on Mertig from the British embassy in Buenos Aires, 15 October 1945, No. 270, MRE, Traducciones, 'Embajada Británica 1945'. *Flucht von Nürnberg?*, Meding.

495   Undated statement by Roberto Mertig to Argentine police, Mengele file, p. 35, AGN.

496   *Mengele*, Posner & Ware.

497   Hoettl testimony at Nuremberg Trials, 1945; also his testimony of June 1961 for the

Eichmann trial in Jerusalem.

498 Hoettl testimony, June 1961. For Kops, his declaration before the Bariloche police, 8 May 1993, reproduced in CEANA Final Report 1999, Carlota Jackisch. Regarding Benzon's anti-Jewish stance in Argentina, see Diana testimony, 13 May 1949, Diana Inquest, AGN, ST, Box 547, pp. 43–50. For Kops and the neo-Nazi rings in the 1990s, see *In Hitler's Shadow*, Svoray-Taylor. The most important rescuer of Jews in Budapest was Swedish diplomat Raoul Wallenberg, who was captured by the Russians at the end of the war and apparently murdered in a Soviet camp.

499 *The Labyrinth*, Walter Schellenberg, Harper & Brothers, New York, 1956, p. 379.

500 *Operation Eichmann*, Aharoni & Dietl, pp. 43–5.

401 Hoettl testimony, June 1961. Also his comments in *Aftermath*, Farago.

502 *Operation Eichmann*, Aharoni & Dietl, pp. 43–5.

503 Wisliceny testimony at Nuremberg, 3 January 1946. Eichmann felt particularly betrayed by Wisliceny, who was so close a friend that Eichmann had named one of his sons, Dieter, after him.

504 *Operation Eichmann*, Aharoni & Dietl.

505 *The House on Garibaldi Street*, Isser Harel, Viking Press, New York, 1975. Also, *Operation Eichmann*.

506 Eichmann entered Argentina with a permanent visa granted under Immigration file 231489/48. Eichmann's file number is noted in the passenger list of the *Giovanna C*, DNM, Passenger Lists, July 1950, List 24.

507 Eichmann's Red Cross passport application, 100940, ICRC, Geneva. See also Dömöter's correspondence with Hudal, 28 August 1949, Hudal Papers, quoted in CEANA Final Report, Sanfilippo.

508 Wiesenthal's article 'Qui è rinchiuso Eichmann', *L'Europeo*, 12 March 1961; and Hudal's response, 'Eichmann giunse a Roma con passaporto Nansen', *Vita*, 30 March 1961; also the Associated Press wire reproduced in *La Nación*, 25 March 1961.

509 Eichmann's Red Cross passport application, 100940, ICRC, Geneva. For Eichmann's arrival, see passenger list for the *Giovanna C*, DNM, Passenger Lists, July 1950, List 24. This particular binder was in a very sorry condition when found by the author in Argentina's dilapidated Immigration archives, many of its pages gone and the Eichmann–Klement entry hanging on for dear life at the end of a torn page. The binder itself was thrown on a pile of similarly agonizing passenger lists. A plea with the Immigration authorities to preserve this particular binder as it contained Eichmann's entry produced only an angry snarl in response. For the detail of Eichmann's photo on deck, *Operation Eichmann*, Aharoni & Dietl.

510 Klaus Eichmann interview, *Quick*, 1966, Issue 1. For Kuhlmann-Geller's joint arrival with Eichmann, Fuldner police testimony, 9 June 1960, AGN, Martin Bormann File DAE 4550, pp. 77–9. Klaus Eichmann identified 'Panzer-Geller' with the surname Kuhlmann. Although no Geller figures on the *Giovanna C* passenger list, the Argentine police record gives the birth date of Pedro Geller as 7 April 1912, while Kuhlmann's actual birth date was 7 April 1915. In Argentina, Geller was mistakenly believed by some to have been Wilhelm Mohnke, but Mohnke was captured by the Russians and remained in captivity until 1955.

511 Fuldner police statement, 9 June 1960. *Operation Eichmann*, Aharoni & Dietl. In Argentina, where race-conscious legislation obliged all foreign names to be Hispanized, the Italian Riccardo became Ricardo, with a single 'c'.

512 Fuldner police statement, 9 June 1960. For CAPRI's recognition by the Argentine state, see Resolution 882/50; file C-63-50-Cde 1, Buenos Aires, 21 July 1950, in *Boletín de la Dirección de Agua y Energía Eléctrica*, No. 138, year IV, 18 August 1950, p. 1752, published by the Industry Ministry.

513 *Flucht vor Nürnberg?* Meding.

514 The late Argentine businessman Ricardo Zinn, who became a well-known economist during Argentina's 1976–83 military dictatorship, worked across the desk from Eichmann at CAPRI, anonymous interview by author, 3 January 1997. Fischböck's citizenship application, AGPJN, Dossier 8060. The building is now home to the private CEMA business university.

515 *Flucht vor Nürnberg?* Meding. CEANA Third Report 1998, Holger Meding.

516 CEANA Third Report 1998, Holger Meding.

517 *Flucht vor Nürnberg?*, Meding.

518 *Odessa al Sur*, Camarasa, p. 155.

519 *Flucht vor Nürnberg?*, Meding. CEANA Final Report 1999, Carlota Jackisch.

520 Daye to Barrére, 29 March 1948, CEGES, FPD, Dossier 488.

521 *Quick*, 1966, Issue I. Also, *Salta* Passenger list, 28 June 1952, DNM.

522 *Bünte* published the picture on 2 July 1960. Eichmann worked for CAPRI in Tucumán until 30 April 1953, see CEANA Final Report 1999, Carlota Jackisch.

523 Fuldner police statement, 9 June 1960. Eichmann apparently had two addresses in Olivos, Chacabuco 4261 and Chacabuco 2681, see *Operation Eichmann*, Aharoni & Dietl, p. 91, and Fuldner statement. Apparently in 1952 Eichmann subscribed to Argentina's phone company and a Ricardo Klement appeared in the Buenos Aires phone directory, see *Odessa al Sur*, Camarasa, p. 157. Interviews with Ombú street neighbours by the author.

524 Fuldner police statement, 9 June 1960. *Quick*, 1966, Issue I.

525 *Operation Eichmann*, Aharoni & Dietl. The Efeve firm was partly owned by Colonel Franz Pfeiffer, one of the men responsible for the Reichsbank evacuation at the end of the war, see *Nazi Gold*, Sayer & Botting. For the Martian novel, which a journalist in Argentina claimed to have received from Eichmann at the time of the rabbit farm, see *La Gaceta de Tucumán*, 24 December 1963.

526 Eichmann trial, Session 102, 19 July 1961.

527 'Skorzeny und Lauterbacher in Rom?' *Hannoversche Allgemeine*, 20 January 1950. *Skorzeny*, Infield. Skorzeny interview, London *Daily Express*, 7 April 1952. For the voluminous Daye–Degrelle correspondence, CEGES, FPD.

528 Eichmann trial, Session 105, 20 July 1961.

529 *The Hunt for Dr Mengele*, World in Action, Granada Television, November 1978.

530 Eichmann trial, Session 105, 20 July 1961. For Sassen as Daye's publisher, see letters Daye to Sassen, 29 January and 23 February 1950, ML 2570 (1). For Sassen's version, see *Aftermath*, Farago. Farago talked at length with Sassen about the Eichmann sessions.

531 Eichmann trial, Sessions 72 and 96. This was not Eichmann's first attempt to write a book on the subject. Already during the war he had prepared a 100-page booklet titled *The Final Solution to the Jewish Question* which was to be published by Nordland Verlag. The project was 'censored' by his Nazi chiefs. It contained 'the statistical documents for all the transports, in the sphere of the Jewish Question, the deportation of Jews, including emigration. In short, a survey of everything which took place up to the point where I wrote it,' Eichmann said during his trial. See Session 102, 19 July 1961.

532 Author's interview with Pedro Pobierzym, 30 April 1997.

533 For Fritsch and Lange, Eichmann trial, Sessions 96, 102 and 104.

534 Eichmann trial, Sessions 72, 110 and 113. For Mildner at Auschwitz, see Hoess affidavit, 5 April 1946, in *Trial of the Major War Criminals Before the International Tribunal*, Nuremberg, Doc. 3868-PS, vol. 33, 275–79. Mildner's presence in Argentina was pointed out by Nazi-hunter Simon Wiesenthal in an interview with Argentine TV journalist Magdalena Ruiz Guiñazú on 5 February 1992. In March 1992, a delegation of the German Gypsy community travelled to Argentina to seek Mildner out, receiving scant cooperation from the Argentine government, see *Página/12*, 17 March 1992.

535 For Eichmann's employment at Orbis, *Flucht vor Nürnberg?*, Meding; Meding was told the story by Mertig himself. Regarding Mengele and Mertig, see statements by Mengele's

wife and son, Argentine police report, 29 June 1960, Mengele file, AGN, DAE, p. 29. Regarding Mertig's Nazi party membership, see Verbal Note 250, from the British embassy in Buenos Aires to the Argentine Foreign Ministry, 15 October 1945, MRE, Traducciones, Embajada Británica, 1945.

536 For Rademacher's close collaboration with Eichmann, see transcripts of the Eichmann trial, among others, Sessions 43, 72, 79, 102 and 105. Also the voluminous amount of Rademacher-related documents in the trial's List of Exhibits. For his sojourn in Argentina, *Aftermath*, Farago; and *Odessa al Sur*, Camarasa.

537 *Aftermath*; also *Odessa al Sur*. The Klingenfuss affair is also mentioned in the Mengele file at AGN, DAE. Eichmann trial, List of Exhibits, items T/448, T/194, T/1024, T/191 and T/929.

538 Eichmann Trial, List of Exhibits. CEANA Third Report, November 1998, Holger Meding.

539 Mohr's Nazi party membership, NARA, RG 242, MFOK Ortsgruppenkartei, Roll P0010. Also, *Aftermath*, and *Odessa al Sur*. Eichmann trial, List of Exhibits, T/521. Eichmann also mentions Mohr in the recently released Eichmann 'Memoirs', written during his detention in Jerusalem. Ladislas Farago, who held a lengthy interview with Sassen for his book *Aftermath* and read the full transcript of the Sassen tapes, states in the book that two other Eichmann collaborators, his deputy Rolf Guenther and his aide in France, Heinz Röthke, were also mentioned as having gained refuge in Argentina.

540 *Aftermath*, Farago. For Rajakowitsch's role as Eichmann's delegate in Holland, Eichmann Trial, Sessions 4 and 13. See also the various Rajakowitsch-related documents exhibited at the trial, including exhibit T/37-194, a letter from the Dresdner Bank in Berlin concerning the role of Rajakowitsch in the disposal of seized Jewish property in the Netherlands, 4 July 1941. For his arrival in Argentina see DNM, 'Chela' Archive, Erico Raja disembarkation card, 26 February 1952. For his wife and children, DNM, Passenger Lists, *Corrientes*, 25 August 1949, and *Castel Verde*, 18 October 1950.

541 None of the main participants agree on the exact facts of the localisation of Eichmann, but the myth that he was ferreted out by Mossad agents has finally been demolished. In fact, as Hermann proved, it took only a minimum of effort to locate him. For the differing versions published so far, see *The House on Garibaldi Street*, by former Mossad chief Isser Harel, and *Operation Eichmann*, Aharoni & Dietl. For a third version of Hermann's role, see the documentary collections 'The Blind Man Who Discovered Eichmann in Argentina', and 'My Role in Operation Eichmann', by Tuviah Friedman, Haifa Documentation Centre.

542 *Quick*, 1966, Issue I.

543 Federal Police report on Eichmann's kidnapping, 9 June 1960, AGN, DAE Bormann File, pp. 77–9. The three sons of Eichmann who live in Germany were contacted during the research for this book but all preferred not to be interviewed. The fourth and eldest son who lives in Argentina proved unfindable.

544 *Life* magazine, 28 November and 5 December 1960. Eichmann trial, Session 72, 9 June 1961. Regarding Menge, author's interview with Pobierzym, 30 April 1997. For Sassen's flight and being branded a traitor, author's interview with Wilfred von Oven, 26 August 1997. Sassen reportedly netted $50,000 for the rights, although he is also reported to have later shared part of the proceeds with the Eichmann family.

545 *La Razón*, 23 December 1960.

546 *Clarín*, 25 March 1961. For the fingerprints, *Proyecto Testimonio*, Gurevich & Warzawski. See also Mengele's extradition request file at the Argentine Foreign Ministry archive, p. 52.

547 'My Role in Operation Eichmann', by Tuviah Friedman, Haifa Documentation Centre.

548 In 2002, CEANA has been revived, with a new focus on identifying Argentine diplomats who may have helped Jews escape Europe.

549 'Investigar en serio', Héctor Timerman, *Noticias*, 3 March 2001.

550 'Escape to Argentina: How Monsignors Aided the Nazis', Austen Ivereigh, *The Tablet*, 6

April 2002.

551 An earlier ground-breaking book, *Unholy Trinity*, by US author John Loftus and the Australian Mark Aarons, had received similar criticism, especially from the now-deceased official Vatican historian Father Robert Graham, who stated about Draganovic, 'It was his own operation. He's not the Vatican.' See *Unholy Trinity*, p. 89.

552 The CIA opened its files on Draganovic for the US State Department, see *US and Allied Wartime and Postwar Relations and Negotiations with Argentina, Portugal, Spain, Sweden, and Turkey on Looted Gold and German External Assets and US Concerns About the Fate of the Wartime Ustasha Treasury*, Department of State, 1998. For a detailed study of how the Vatican and Western intelligence failed to realize that their anti-Communist Nazi operations were riddled with Soviet spies, see *Unholy Trinity*, Loftus & Aarons.

553 For the Vatican's appeal, see Osborne to Foreign Office, 27 August 1945, PRO FO 371/48920 R14525. The Pope issued a similar appeal for the reclassification of Ukrainian prisoners of war at the Rimini camp, thousands of members of the murderous Galician SS Division, in 1946. In this case, the appeal was successful, and the Galician SS troops were reclassified as 'confinees', and resettled first to Great Britain and from there to Canada, Australia and elsewhere; see *Blowback*, Christopher Simpson, Weidenfeld & Nicolson, New York, 1988, p. 180.

554 Vatican appeal, 27 March 1946, PRO WO 204/1113. The Croatians at Grottaglie had meanwhile been transferred to POW Camp 209, Afragola, near Naples, the British drily noted.

555 For Draganovic's studies at the Oriental Institute, see 'Consolidated Interrogation Report on Dr. Krunoslav Stepano Draganovic', wartime undated; and 'Past Background and Activity', 12 February 1947; NARA, RG 319/631/31/54-54/1-4, Box 107, IRR Case Files. The Pontificio Istituto Orientale was first presided over by Cardinal Alfredo Ildefonso Schuster, who, as Bishop of Milan, in 1949 received Perón's Nazi-rescuing priest Father Pratto; see Pratto photo file at AGN.

556 FO 371/59423 R17521 and R17586. The five wanted men were Velmar Jankovic, former Serbian minister of agriculture Milorad Nedeljkovic, Marisav Petrovic, Milosav Vasiljevic and Ilya Vujovic.

557 Aide-mémoire, 13 January 1947, and Osborne to Foreign Office, 16 January 1947; both at FO 371/67370 R1166. Although Tardini was not known as a Nazi sympathizer, neither did he show any empathy with Hitler's victims when, on 18 December 1942, he rejected an appeal by Osborne for the Vatican to speak out against the extermination of the Jews. Tardini told Osborne at the time that 'the Pope could not take sides'; see *Hitler's Pope*, John Cornwell, Viking, New York, 1999, pp. 221 and 291. Regarding the Vatican's claim that Pius XII was unaware of the goings-on at San Girolamo, it must be pointed out that Draganovic's activities were the object of various exposés in the Italian press at the time.

558 PRO FO 371/67370 R1200.

559 PRO FO 371/67371 R1769.

560 Vatican Secretariat of State, 26 April 1947, FO 371/67376 R6058.

561 McLean to Foreign Office, 17 October 1947, enclosing 'Memorandum on the Ustasha Organisation in Italy', PRO FO 371/67398 R14409. For Moskov's capture in Venice, memo of 20 February 1947, FO 371/67371 R2394. Regarding the gold in Moskov's possession, Leghorn to Foreign Office, 3 May 1947, FO 371/67376 R5965.

562 'Memorandum on the Ustasha Organisation in Italy', PRO FO 371/67398 R14409. Draganovic to US ambassador in Italy, 19 May 1947, NARA, RG 59/250/36/19/6, Box 3622, 740.00116 EW/5-2847. For Zanko as intermediary with the Vatican, see 'The Organisation of the Ustashi Abroad', 4 November 1946, CIA Operational Files.

563 Draganovic to US ambassador in Italy, 19 May 1947, NARA, RG 59/250/36/19/6, Box 3622, 740.00116 EW/5-2847. 'Campo Fermo' and 'Un nuevo golpe', articles by Dusan Zanko, published in *Studia Croatica*, Buenos Aires, 1997 and 1998, issues 135 and 136.

564   Griffin to Bevin, 28 May; Bevin to Griffin, 18 June; and Griffin to Bevin, 25 June 1947: all at PRO FO 371/67380 R7461. Griffin may have been acting in response to an appeal from Draganovic, see *Unholy Trinity*, Loftus & Aarons, p. 117.

565   PRO FO 371/67376 R5694. The other five Ustashi on the Vatican's list handed over on 27 April were Vladimir Zidovec, Wilim Peros, Janko Vernic-Turansky, Daniel Uvanovic and Milivoj Magdic.

566   Corville to Osborne, 14 May 1947, FO 371/67376 R6058.

567   'Un nuevo golpe', Dusan Zanko, *Studia Croatica*, issue 136.

568   Apart from Zanko, from the Pope's list, Ivan Devcic and Ante Pavicic were among those 'housed' at San Girolamo after escaping Regina Elena; see memo of special agent Robert C. Mudd, 5 September 1947, Draganovic CIC file. For Cosenza, 'Memorandum on the Ustasha Organisation in Italy', PRO FO 371/67398 R14409. This memorandum states confusingly that sanctuary was given by the 'Franciscan convent' at Cosenza, but a later document places the escapees correctly during the month of July at the 'monastery of San Francesco d'Assisi'; see list of 'Leading Ustashi' in FO 371/67398 R14423.

569   Cabot to Secretary of State, Top Secret, NARA, RG 59, 250/36/19/6, Box 3623.

570   Perowne to Wallinger, 18 November 1947; and Wallinger's answer, 5 December 1947: both at PRO FO 371/67401 R15533.

571   For the transport to Germany, see Special Refugee Commission to Foreign Office, 23 October 1947, PRO FO 371/67398 R14423. Some historians have written about the transfer of former Chetniks to Germany, but the transport referred to here is of hardened Ustasha criminals and close Pavelic aides such as Dragutin Dosen; see FO 371/72563A. For the handover of Jurica Markovic and Zivan Kuvezdic, both on the Pope's list, see Cypher, 29 June 1948; for Griffin's appeal, Archbishop's House to Foreign Office, 21 May 1948: both at PRO FO 371/72563A.

572   British embassy to Foreign Office, 24 April 1947, FO 371/67376 R5696.

573   FO 371/67376 R5734.

574   British embassy in Washington to Foreign Office, 3 May 1947, PRO FO 371/67376 R5970.

575   See 'Criteria to be Applied in Considering the Cases of Yugoslav Quislings', PRO FO 371/72563A.

576   For Zanko's arrival in Argentina, CEANA Final Report, 1999. For his death in Venezuela, 'In Memoriam, Dusan Zanko', *Revista Facultad Agrononomía* (Maracay), XI (1–4). For British tally of extradition requests, see 'Confidential' note of 31 May 1948, PRO FO 371/72563A R6358. The remaining five on the Pope's list were Ivan Devcic, Marijan Dragicevic, Ignacije Dujsin, Ante Pavicic and Stephan Tomljenovic.

577   Report on Draganovic, '1945–1952', 24 July 1952, CIA Operational Files. For Propaganda Fide and Yugoslavia, Leigh-Smith to Hayter, 21 June 1946, where Fumasoni-Biondi is described as 'a rather timid old gentleman', PRO FO 371/59412 R9639. Fumasoni-Biondi, in his role as Vatican intelligence chief, had acted as intermediary for a Japanese peace offer between Emperor Hirohito and US Navy intelligence at the end of the war, see 'How We Bungled the Japanese Surrender,' by Rear Admiral Ellis M. Zacharias, *Look*, 6 June 1950. For dell'Acqua, *Unholy Trinity*, Loftus & Aarons, p. 113. Cardinal dell'Acqua was one of the custodians of the Third Secret of Fatima, finally revealed to the world in June 2000.

578   Report on Draganovic, '1945–1952', 24 July 1952, CIA Operational Files. According to this report, Draganovic also made his Nazi-smuggling services available to 'an unidentified Protestant clergyman'.

579   CIC memo, 10 October 1946, CIA Operational Files. 'Vida y obra del Prof. Dr. Dominik Mandic', M. Blazekovic, *Studia Croatica*, 1973, issues 50–51.

580   US embassy in Buenos Aires to Rome, 23 July 1947, with enclosures, NARA, RG 59/250, Box 6609. 'Memorandum on the Ustasha Organisation in Italy', PRO FO 371/67398 R14409.

581 'The Organisation of the Ustashi Abroad', 4 November 1946, CIA Operational Files. Mandic's third contact with the Ustasha secret service was Dr Andreja Jelicich, 'on service at the Vatican'. This highly compromising document's source was General Miodrag Damjanovic, the second-in-command to Chetnik leader Draza Mihailovic.

582 'Memorandum on the Ustasha Organisation in Italy', PRO FO 371/67398 R14409. 'Present Whereabouts of Former Ustasha Officials', 11 October 1946, CIA Operational Files.

583 'History of the Italian Ratlines', Paul Lyon, 10 April 1950, cited in 'Klaus Barbie and the United States Government', US Department of Justice, 1983. Also *Unholy Trinity*, Loftus & Aarons, chapter 11. See also *Soldiers, Spies and the Ratline*, James V. Milano & Patrick Brogan, Brassey's, Washington, 1995.

584 'Rat Line from Austria to South America', Paul S. Lyon, 12 July 1948, Appendix to 'Klaus Barbie and the United States Government', Department of Justice, 1983. This new agreement between CIC and Draganovic was formalized while Perón's special agent Carlos Fuldner, who organized Bohne's escape, was in Europe arranging the escape of Nazis with Draganovic's help.

585 In mid-1950, Draganovic had already applied, with the backing of the IRO, for a visa to the US; see 'Against Admitting a Former Ustasha to the USA', 11 August 1950, CIA Operational Files. Barbie was received in Bolivia by a Draganovic associate, Father Stjepan Osvald Tot, alias Rok Romac, one of the Ustasha criminals awaiting extradition at Regina Elena in 1947. See *Unholy Trinity*, Loftus & Aaron, p. 254. Also Draganovic's letter to the American embassy in Rome, 19 May 1947. Tot finally settled in Australia in 1955.

586 Report on Draganovic, '1945–1952', 24 July 1952; and Memo, 1 October 1953: both CIA Operational Files. The priest's standing with the Vatican seems to have suffered from his excessive greediness and a materialistic lifestyle that set alarm bells sounding in high circles.

587 Memos, 19 and 20 November 1958, CIA Operational Files. Pius XII died on 9 October 1958.

588 Memo, 23 January 1962, CIA Operational Files. *US and Allied Wartime and Postwar Relations and Negotiations with Argentina, Portugal, Spain, Sweden, and Turkey on Looted Gold and German External Assets and US Concerns About the Fate of the Wartime Ustasha Treasury*, Department of State, 1998. For a detailed account of Draganovic's defection to Yugoslavia and his statement to Yugoslav authorities concerning the Vatican's Nazi-smuggling activities, see *Unholy Trinity*, Loftus & Aarons.

589 See *The Catholic Church and the Holocaust*, Michael Phayer, Indiana University Press, 2000. Phayer based his account on the private diaries of Bishop Muench, stored at the Catholic University of America. See also *The Holocaust*, Leni Yahil, Oxford University Press, New York, 1991. Greiser persecuted not only Jews, but Catholics as well, leading a campaign against the Catholic Church in Poland.

590 Gowen was interviewed by Phayer for his book *The Catholic Church and the Holocaust*. Montini was also head of the Vatican Information Service, an agency ostensibly in charge of tracing refugees, missing persons and prisoners of war; see *Unholy Trinity*, Loftus & Aarons.

591 *Unholy Trinity*, Loftus & Aarons, chapter 5.

DOCUMENTARY SOURCES

Argentina:
Archivo General de la Nación (National Archives – AGN)
Banco Central (Central Bank – BCRA)
Biblioteca Nacional (National Library)
Congress – Lower House Archives
Congress – Upper House Archives
Congress – Library
Dirección Nacional de Migraciones (Immigration – DNM)
Goyeneche, Juan Carlos (Private Papers-GPP)
Ministerio del Interior (Interior Ministry – MI)
Ministerio de Relaciones Exteriores (Foreign Ministry – MRE)
Poder Judicial (Judicial Branch – AGPJN)
Wiesenthal Centre (Argentine Branch)

Belgium:
Musée de la Littérature
CEGES

Chile:
Army Archives
Foreign Ministry Archives

Denmark:
Rigsarkivet

Germany:
Auswärtiges Amt

Great Britain:
Public Records Office (PRO)

Switzerland:
Schweizerisches Bundesarchiv (BAR)
International Committee of the Red Cross (ICRC)

US:
Central Intelligence Agency (CIA)
Library of Congress
Foreign Affairs Oral History Program

US National Archives and Records Administration (NARA):
RG 59: State Department
RG 84: State Department Foreign Service Posts
RG 131: Office of Alien Property
RG 153: Office of the Judge Advocate General (Army)
RG 169: Foreign Economic Administration
RG 226: Office of Strategic Services (OSS)
RG 238: World War II War Crimes Records
RG 242: Foreign Records Seized
RG 260: US Occupation Headquarters
RG 319: Army Staff
RG 407: Adjutant General's Office
RG 457: National Security Agency

BIBLIOGRAPHY

Aharoni, Zvi & Dietl, Wilhelm, *Operation Eichmann*, Arms and Armour, London, 1996.

Amadeo, Mario, *Ayer, Hoy, Mañana*, Gure, Buenos Aires, 1956.

——— *Por Una Convivencia Internacional*, Editorial de Autores, Buenos Aires, 1954.

Antonio, Jorge, *Y Ahora Qué*, Verum et Militia, Buenos Aires, 1982.

Ara, Pedro, *Eva Perón*, Sudamericana, Buenos Aires, 1996.

Arendt, Hannah, *Eichmann in Jerusalem*, Penguin, New York, 1994.

Arredondo, Jorge Alberto, *Perón: Su Protagonismo en la Revolución de 1930*, Corregidor, Buenos Aires, 1998.

Asís, Jorge, *Lesca, El Fascista Irreductible*, Sudamericana, Buenos Aires, 2000.

Aunós, Eduardo, *Argentina, el Imperio del Sur*, La Facultad, Buenos Aires, 1944.

Avni, Haim, *Argentina and the Jews: A History of Jewish Immigration*, University of Alabama Press, 1991.

Barnes, John, *Eva Perón*, Ultramar, Madrid, 1979.

Beccar Varela, Cosme (Jr), *El Nacionalismo, Una Incognita en Constante Evolución*, TFP, Buenos Aires, 1970.

Berger, Martín, *P-2 Historia de la Logia Masónica*, El Cid Editor, Buenos Aires, 1983.

Blousson, Silvestre H., *El Caso Staudt*, Buenos Aires, 1946.

Bolasell, Rafael, Reid, Pablo & Toni, Patricia, *La Infiltración Nazi en la Patagonia*, Centro Editor de America Latina, Buenos Aires, 1992.

Borroni, Otelo & Vacca, Roberto, *La Vida de Eva Perón*, Tomo I, Editorial Galerna, Buenos Aires, 1970.

Bosca, Roberto, *La Iglesia Nacional Peronista*, Sudamericana, Buenos Aires, 1997.

Bower, Tom, *Blind Eye to Murder*, André Deutsch, London, 1981.

——— *Klaus Barbie: Butcher of Lyons*, Michael Joseph, London, 1984.

—— *Nazi Gold*, Harper Collins, New York, 1997.

—— *The Paperclip Conspiracy: The Hunt for Nazi Scientists*, Little Brown & Company, Boston, 1987.

Bowers, Claude G., *Chile Through Embassy Windows: 1939–1953*, Simon & Schuster, New York, 1958.

Braden, Spruille, *Diplomats and Demagogues: The Memoirs of Spruille Braden*, Arlington House, New York, 1971.

Bradford, Sax, *The Battle for Buenos Aires*, Harcourt Brace, New York, 1943.

Bruce, James, *Those Perplexing Argentines*, Longmans, Green, New York, 1953.

Buch, Esteban, *El Pintor de la Suiza Argentina*, Sudamericana, Buenos Aires, 1991.

Buchrucker, Cristián, *Nacionalismo y Peronismo*, Sudamericana, Buenos Aires, 1987.

Bullock, Alan, *Hitler, a Study in Tyranny*, Odhams, London, 1952.

Butler, Hubert, *Escape from the Anthill*, The Lilliput Press, Mullingar, 1986.

Caggiano, Antonio & Meinvielle, Julio, *Primera Semana de Estudios Sociales De Rosario Acerca del Comunismo*, Accion Católica, Rosario, 1938.

Caimari, Lila M., *Perón y la Iglesia Católica*, Ariel, Buenos Aires, 1995.

Camarasa, Jorge, *La Enviada*, Planeta, Buenos Aires, 1998.

—— *Odessa al Sur*, Planeta, Buenos Aires, 1995.

Cantinflas, Argentino (Juan Pérez, Jr), *Radiografías de una Dictadura*, La Vanguardia, Buenos Aires, 1946.

Carretoni, Jorge C., *De Frondizi a Alfonsín*, Catálogos, Buenos Aires, 1998.

CEANA, *First Progress Report*, MRE, Buenos Aires, 1998.

—— *Second Progress Report*, MRE, Buenos Aires, 1998.

—— *Third Progress Report*, MRE, Buenos Aires, 1998.

—— *Final Report*, MRE, Buenos Aires, 1999.

Chase, Allan, *Falange: Axis Secret Army in the Americas*, G.P. Putnam's Sons, New York, 1943.

Confalonieri, Orestes D., *Perón Contra Perón*, Editorial Antygua, Buenos Aires, 1956.

Conil Paz, Alberto & Ferrari, Gustavo, *Política Exterior Argentina, 1930–1962*, Círculo Militar, Buenos Aires, 1971.

Cornwell, John, *Hitler's Pope*, Viking, New York, 1999.

Cox, David & Nabot, Damian, *Perón, La Otra Muerte*, Agora, Buenos Aires, 1997.

Crespo, Jorge, *El Coronel*, Ayer y Hoy Ediciones, Buenos Aires, 1998.

Damonte Taborda, Raúl, *Ayer Fue San Perón*, Gure, Buenos Aires, 1955.

Darré, R. Walther, *Nordisches Blutserbe im Suddeutschen Bauerntum*, Verlag Bruckmann, München, 1938.

—— *Neuadel aus Blut und Boden*, Lehmans Verlag, 1930.

Davidowicz, Lucy, *The War Against the Jews*, Bantam, New York, 1975.

Daye, Pierre, 'Mémoires', unpublished manuscript, CEGES, Brussels.

De Dios, Horacio, *Kelly Cuenta Todo*, Gente, Buenos Aires, 1984.

De Estrada, José María, *El Legado del Nacionalismo*, Gure, Buenos Aires, 1956.

De Hoyos, Ladislas, *Barbie, La Historia Oculta*, Sudamericana-Planeta, Buenos Aires, 1985.

De Lezica, Manuel, *Recuerdos de un Nacionalista*, Astral, Buenos Aires, 1968.

Degrelle, León, *Europa Vivirá*, Editorial Avanzada, Buenos Aires, 1983.

────── *La Historia de las SS Europeas*, Editorial Avanzada, Buenos Aires, 1983.

────── *Memorias de un Fascista*, M.A.C. Ediciones, Buenos Aires, 1994.

Del Carril, Bonifacio, *Memorias Dispersas, el Coronel Perón*, Emecé, Buenos Aires, 1984.

Díaz, Claudio & Zucco, Antonio, *La Ultra Derecha Argentina*, Editorial Contrapunto, Buenos Aires, 1987.

Dujovne Ortíz, Alicia, *Eva Perón, La Biografía*, Aguilar, Buenos Aires, 1995.

Eizenstat, Stuart E., *U.S. and Allied Efforts to Recover and Restore Gold and Other Assets Stolen or Hidden by Germany During World War II*, Department of State, Washington DC, 1997.

────── *U.S. and Allied Wartime and Postwar Relations and Negotiations with Argentina, Portugal, Spain, Sweden, and Turkey on Looted Gold and German External Assets and U.S. Concerns About the Fate of the Wartime Ustasha Treasury*, Department of State, Washington DC, 1998.

Escobar, Adrián C., *Dialogo Íntimo con España*, Club de Lectores, Buenos Aires, 1950.

────── *Ideas de Gobierno y Política Activa*, Gleizer, Buenos Aires, 1938.

Estrella, Roberto, *Tortura*, Dos-Ve, Buenos Aires, 1956.

Falcoff, Mark & Dolkart, Ronald H., *Prologue to Peron: Argentina in Depression and War 1930–1943*, Berkeley, University of California, Berkley, 1975.

Farago, Ladislas, *Aftermath: Martin Bormann and the Fourth Reich*, Simon & Schuster, New York, 1974.

────── *The Game of the Foxes*, David McKay Company Inc, New York, 1971.

Farquharson, J. E., *The Plough and the Swastika*, The Landpost Press, Wayne, 1992.

Farrell, General Edelmiro J., *Mensaje y Memoria del Tercer Año de Labor*, Buenos Aires, 1946.

Fernández Alvariño, Próspero Germán, *Z-Argentina, El Crimen del Siglo*, Lex, Buenos Aires, 1973.

Fernandez Artucio, Hugo, *Nazis en el Uruguay*, Buenos Aires, 1940.

────── *The Nazi Underground in South America*, Farrar and Rinehart, New York, 1942.

Figueroa, Coronel Abelardo Martín, *Promociones Egresadas del Colegio Militar de la Nación 1873–1994*, Ejército Argentino, Buenos Aires, 1996.

Filippo, Virgilio, *Habla el Padre Filippo*, Editorial Tor, Buenos Aires, 1941.

────── *Los Judíos*, Editorial Tor, Buenos Aires, 1939.

Foppa, Tito Livio, *Servicio Exterior*, Amigos del Libro Argentino, Buenos Aires, 1958.

Forsyth Frederick, *The Odessa File*, Viking, New York, 1972.

Franceschi, Monsignor Gustavo J., *Totalitarismos: Comunismo*, Editorial Difusión, Buenos Aires, 1946.

────── *Totalitarismos: Nacionalsocialismo y Fascismo*, Editorial Difusión, Buenos Aires, 1945.

Frank, Gary, *Juan Perón vs Spruille Braden, The Story Behind the Blue Book*, University Press of America, Maryland, 1980.

────── *Struggle for Hegemony in South America*, University of Miami, Miami, 1979.

Freiwald, Aaron & Mendelsohn, Martin, *The Last Nazi: Josef Schwammberger and the Nazi Past*, W. W. Norton & Company, New York, 1994.

Galland, Adolf, *The First and the Last*, Buccaneer, New York, 1998.

Gambini, Hugo, *El 17 de Octubre*, Centro Editor de América Latina, Buenos Aires, 1971.

García Lupo, Rogelio, *Paraguay de Stroessner*, Ediciones B, Buenos Aires, 1989.

Goldhagen, Daniel Jonah, *Hitler's Willing Executioners*, Vintage Books, New York, 1996.

Goldman, Joe & Lanata, Jorge, *Cortinas de Humo*, Planeta, Buenos Aires, 1994.

Goltz, Joshua, 'Memories of Heimat' (thesis), St Antony's College, Oxford, 1998.

Goñi, Santos, 'Recuerdos de 30 años en el Servicio Exterior', unpublished manuscript, Buenos Aires, 1989.

Goñi, Uki, *Perón y los Alemanes*, Sudamericana, Buenos Aires, 1998.

González Iramaín, Héctor, *Bajo la Dictadura de Junio*, Buenos Aires, 1946.

Goyeneche, Juan Carlos, *Juan Carlos Goyeneche, Ensayos, Artículos, Discursos*, Dictio, Buenos Aires, 1976.

Gray, Ronald, *I Killed Martin Bormann*, New York, 1972.

Greenup, Ruth & Leonard, *Revolution Before Breakfast, Argentina 1941–1946*, University of North Carolina Press, Chapel Hill, 1947.

Grose, Peter, *Gentleman Spy: The Life of Allen Dulles*, Houghton Mifflin Company, New York, 1994.

Guilbaud Degay, Georges, *Frente al Comunismo*, Madrid.

Gurevich, Beatriz & Escudé, Carlos, *El Genocidio Ante la Historia y la Naturaleza Humana*, Grupo Editor Latinoamericano, Buenos Aires, 1994.

Gurevich, Beatriz & Warzawski, Paul, *Proyecto Testimonio*, Planeta, Buenos Aires, 1998.

Harel, Isser, *The House on Garibaldi Street*, Viking, New York, 1975.

Herzstein, Robert Edwin, *Waldheim, The Missing Years*, Arbor House, New York, 1988.

Hilton, Stanley E., *Hitler's Secret War in South America*, Louisiana State University Press, 1981.

Hoare, Samuel, *Ambassador on a Special Mission*, 1946.

Horowicz, Alejandro, *Los Cuatro Peronismos*, Hyspamerica, Buenos Aires, 1985.

Hudal, Alois, *Römische Tagebücher*, Stocker, Graz, 1976.

Hull, Cordell, *The Memoirs of Cordell Hull*, Macmillan, New York, 1948.

Hunt, Linda, *Secret Agenda*, St Martin's Press, New York, 1991.

Incisa di Camerara, Ludovico, *L'Argentina*, gli Italiani, l'Italia, SPAI, 1998.

Infield, Glenn B., *Skorzeny, Hitler's Commando*, Military Heritage Press, New York.

Jackisch, Carlota, *El Nazismo y los Refugiados Alemanes en la Argentina*, Editorial de Belgrano, Buenos Aires, 1989.

Jansen, Christian & Weckbecker, Arno, *Der 'Volksdeutsche Selbstschutz' in Polen 1939/40*, R. Oldenburg Verlag, München, 1992.

Jassen, Raúl, *Jorge Antonio, un Argentino Frente a la Oligarquía*, ALPE, Buenos Aires, 1961.

Josephs, Ray, *Argentine Diary*, Book Find Club, New York, 1944.

Kahn, David, *Hitler's Spies*, Macmillan, New York, 1978.

Kelly, Sir David, *The Ruling Few*, Hollis and Carter, London, 1952.

Kleinfeld, Gerald R. & Tambs, Lewis A., *Hitler's Spanish Legion*, Southern Illinois University, , 1979.

Kristenssen, Jeff, *Operacion Patagonia, Hitler Murió en la Argentina*, Lumiere, Buenos Aires, 1987.

Lagomarsino de Guardo, Lillian, *Y Ahora . . . Hablo Yo*, Sudamericana, Buenos Aires, 1996.

Lanús, Adolfo, *Campo Minado*, Buenos Aires, 1942.

Lasby, Clarence G., *Project Paperclip*, Atheneum, New York, 1971.

Laurence, Ricardo E., *Operativo Graf Spee*, published by author, Rosario, 1996.

Llambí, Benito, *Medio Siglo de Política y Diplomacia*, Corregidor, Buenos Aires, 1997.

Llorente, Elena & Rigacci, Martino, *El Último Nazi: Priebke*, Sudamericana, Buenos Aires, 1998.

Loftus, John & Aarons, Mark, *The Secret War Against the Jews*, St Martin's Griffin, New York, 1997.

—— *Unholy Trinity*, St Martin's Griffin, New York, 1998.

Lonardi, Marta, *Mi Padre y la Revolución del 55*, Ediciones Cuenca del Plata, Buenos Aires, 1980.

Lovin, Clifford R., *R. Walther Darré, Nazi Agricultural Policy, and Preparation for War*, Occasional Papers in German Studies, Alberta, 1995.

Luca de Tena, Torcuato, Calvo, Luis & Peicovich, Esteban, *Yo, Juan Domingo Perón*, Sudamericana-Planeta, Buenos Aires, 1976.

Lucero, Franklin, *El Precio de la Lealtad*, Editorial Propulsión, Buenos Aires, 1959.

Luna, Felix, *El 45*, Sudamericana, Buenos Aires, 1973.

Lutge, Wilhelm, *Deutsche in Argentinien*, D.K.B.A., Buenos Aires, 1981.

Magnet, Alejandro, *Nuestros Vecinos Justicialistas*, Editorial del Pacífico, Santiago de Chile, 1953.

Mahieu, Jacques de, *Diccionario de Ciencia Política*, Books International, Buenos Aires, 1966.

—— *Fundamentos de Biopolítica*, Centro Editor Argentino, Buenos Aires, 1968.

—— *La Naturaleza del Hombre*, Arayú, Buenos Aires, 1955.

Maler, Juan (Kops, Reinhard), *Frieden, Krieg und 'Frieden'*, published by author, Buenos Aires, 1987.

Manning, Paul, *Martin Bormann: Nazi in Exile*, Lylye Stuart Inc., New Jersey, 1981.

Mariscotti, Mario, *El Secreto Atómico de Huemul*, Sudamericana-Planeta, Buenos Aires, 1985.

Martínez, Tomás Eloy, *Las Memorias del General*, Planeta, Buenos Aires, 1996.

Meding, Holger, *Flucht vor Nürnberg?*, Böhlau, Köln, 1992.

Meinvielle, Julio, *Concepción Católica de la Política*, Cursos de Cultura Católica, Buenos Aires, 1941.

—— *El Judío*, Editorial Antidoto, Buenos Aires, 1936.

—— *El Judío en el Misterio de la Historia*, Theoría, Buenos Aires, 1959.

———— *Entre la Iglesia y el Reich*, Adsum, Buenos Aires, 1937.

———— *Los Tres Pueblos Bíblicos*, Adsum, Buenos Aires, 1937.

Mignone, Emilio, *Iglesia y Dictadura*, Pensamiento Nacional, Buenos Aires, 1986.

Milano, James. *Soldiers, Spies and the Rat Line*, Brasseys Inc, 1996.

Molinari, Aldo Luis, *Caso Duarte*, Compañía Impresora Argentina, Buenos Aires, 1958.

Morandini, Norma, *El Harén*, Sudamericana, Buenos Aires, 1998.

Navarro, Marysa, *Evita*, Planeta, Buenos Aires, 1997.

Newton, Ronald C., *The Nazi Menace in Argentina*, Leland Stanford Junior University, Stanford, 1992.

Orona, Juan V., *La Dictadura de Perón*, Buenos Aires, 1970.

———— *La Logia Militar que Derrocó a Castillo*, Buenos Aires, 1966.

Oses, Enrique P., *Medios y Fines del Nacionalismo*, Sudestada, Buenos Aires, 1968.

Page, Joseph A., *Perón, a Biography*, Random House, New York, 1983.

Pavón Pereyra, Enrique, *Diario Secreto de Perón*, Sudamericana-Planeta, Buenos Aires, 1985.

———— *Perón 1895–1942*, Editorial Espiño, Buenos Aires, 1952.

Paz, Hipólito, *Memorias*, Planeta, Buenos Aires, 1999.

Peicovich, Esteban, *Hola Perón*, Jorge Alvarez Editor, Buenos Aires, 1965.

Peralta, Santiago M., *La Talla Militar en la Argentina*, Buenos Aires, 1922.

———— *La Acción del Pueblo Judío en la Argentina*, Buenos Aires, 1943.

———— *Conceptos Sobre Inmigración*, Buenos Aires, 1946.

———— *Influencia del Pueblo Arabe en la Argentina: Apuntes Sobre Inmigración*, Sociedad Impresora Americana, Buenos Aires, 1946.

———— *Memorias de un Conscripto*, Buenos Aires, 1946.

Perón, Juan, *Apuntes de Historia Militar*, Edicions de la Reconstrucción, Buenos Aires, 1973.

———— *Doctrina Peronista*, Editorial Fidelius, Buenos Aires, 1947.

———— *Fundamentos de Doctrina Nacional Justicialista*, ESCP, Buenos Aires, 1985.

———— *La Comunidad Organizada*, Macacha Guemes Editora, Buenos Aires, 1983.

———— *Libro Azul y Blanco*, Buenos Aires, 1946.

———— *Perón por Perón, Los Más Importantes Discursos y Mensajes, 1943–1973*, Editorial Kikiyon, Buenos Aires, 1972.

Piñeiro, Elena, *La Tradición Nacionalista Ante el Peronismo*, A–Z Editora, Buenos Aires, 1997.

Poder Ejecutivo, *Libro Negro de la Segunda Tiranía* Executive Branch (the book was put together by the Executive Branch of the government that deposed Perón) Buenos Aires, 1958.

Posner, Gerald & Ware, John, *Mengele, The Complete Story*, McGraw-Hill, New York, 1986.

Potash, Robert A., *Perón y el GOU*, Sudamericana, Buenos Aires, 1984.

———— *The Army & Politics in Argentina 1928–1945*, Stanford University Press, 1969.

Rapoport, Mario, *Aliados o Neutrales*, Eudeba, Buenos Aires, 1988.

Reifchle, Hermann, *Reichsbauernführer Darré*, Berlag und Bertriebs, Berlin, 1933.

Rein, Raanan, *Peronismo, Populismo y Política*, Editorial de Belgrano, Buenos Aires, 1998.

—— *The Franco–Peron Alliance*, University of Pittsburgh Press, Pittsburgh, 1993.

Rennie, Ysabel F., T*he Argentine Republic*, Macmillan, New York, 1945.

Rodriguez, Adolfo Enrique, *Historia de la Policía Federal Argentina*, Tomo VII, *1916–1944*, Editorial Policial, Buenos Aires, 1978.

Rodriguez, Juan Carlos, *El Ministerio de Relaciones Exteriores y Culto, El Servicio Exterior de la República Argentina, Desorganización y Graves Irregularidades*, Buenos Aires, 1944.

Rodríguez Molas, Ricardo, *Historia de la Tortura y el Órden Represivo en la Argentina*, Eudeba, Buenos Aires, 1985.

—— *Historia de la Tortura y el Órden Represivo en la Argentina* (Textos Documentales), Eudeba, Buenos Aires, 1984.

Rojnica, Ivo, *Prikaz Povijesti Argentine I Doprinos Hrvata*, Vlastita Naklada, Buenos Aires, 1974.

Rom, Eugenio P., *Asi Hablaba Juan Perón*, A. Peña Lillo Editor, Buenos Aires, 1980.

Rosenstein, Perla, *El Nacionalismo de Derecha en Argentina, Bibliografía e Indización de Fuentes*, Tomo I, Alberto Kleiner, Buenos Aires, 1988.

Rouquié, Alain, *Pouvoir militaire et société politique en République Argentine*, Presses de la Fondation Nationale des Sciences Politiques, Paris, 1978.

Rout, Leslie B. Jr. & Bratzel, John F., *The Shadow War: German Espionage and United States Counterespionage in Latin America During World War II*, University Publications of America, Maryland, 1986.

Rudel, Hans-Ulrich, *Aus Krieg und Frieden: Aus den Jahren 1945 und 1952*, Plesee Verlag, Gottingen.

—— *Zwischen Deutschland und Argentinien*, Göttingen, 1954.

Ruiz Moreno, Isidoro J., *La Neutralidad Argentina en la Segunda Guerra*, Emecé, Buenos Aires, 1997.

Ruiz-Guiñazu, Enrique, *La Politica Argentina y el Futuro de America*, Libreria Huemul, Buenos Aires, 1944.

Sábato, Ernesto, *El Otro Rostro del Peronismo*, Carta Abierta a Mario Amadeo, Buenos Aires, 1956.

Salinas, Juan, *AMIA el Atentado*, Planeta, Buenos Aires, 1997.

Sammartino, Ernesto E., *La Verdad Sobre la Situación Argentina*, Montevideo, 1950.

Sánchez Salazar, Gustavo, *Barbie, Criminal Hasta el Fin*, Legasa, Buenos Aires, 1987.

Sanchís Muñoz, José R., *La Argentina y la II Guerra Mundial*, GEL, Buenos Aires, 1992.

Santander, Silvano, *El Gran Proceso*, Silva, Buenos Aires, 1961.

—— *Nazismo en Argentina*, Pueblos Unidos, Montevideo, 1945.

—— *Técnica de Una Traición*, Tricromía, Montevideo, 1953.

Sayer, Ian & Botting, Douglas, *Nazi Gold*, Granada, London, 1984.

Scenna, Miguel Ángel, *Braden y Perón*, Korrigan, Buenos Aires, 1974.

Schellenberg, Walter, *Memoiren*, Verlag für Politik und Wirtschaft, Köln, 1959.

────── *The Labyrinth*, Harper & Brothers, New York, 1956.

Schirer, William L., *Berlin Diary*, Knopff, New York, 1942.

Sebrelli, Juan José, *Eva Perón, Aventurera o Militante*, Editorial La Pléyade, Buenos Aires, 1990.

────── *Los Deseos Imaginarios del Peronismo*, Sudamericana, Buenos Aires, 1992.

Seiferheld, Alfredo M., *Nazismo y Fascismo en el Paraguay, Los Años de la Guerra 1939–1945*, Editorial Historica, Asunción, 1986.

────── *Nazismo y Fascismo en el Paraguay, Visperas de la II Guerra Mundial 1936–1939*, Editorial Historica, Asunción, 1985.

Senkman, Leonardo, *Argentina, la Segunda Guerra Mundial y los Refugiados Indeseables 1933–1945*, Grupo Editor Latinoamericano, Buenos Aires, 1991.

────── *El Antisemitismo en la Argentina*, Centro Editor de America Latina, Buenos Aires, 1989.

────── *El Legado del Autoritarismo*, Grupo Editor Latinoamericano, Buenos Aires, 1995.

────── *La Política Inmigratoria Argentina ante el Holocausto (1938–1945)*, Índice, November 1989, Buenos Aires, 1989.

Sereny, Gitta, *Into That Darkness*, Picador, London, 1977.

Silveyra de Oyuela, Eugenia, *Nacionalismo y Neo-Peronismo*, Cuadernos Republicanos, Buenos Aires, 1956.

Simmons, Walter von, *Santander Bajo la Lupa*, Editorial Alumine, Buenos Aires, 1956.

Simpson, Christopher, *Blowback*, Weidenfeld & Nicolson, New York, 1988.

────── *The Splendid Blond Beast*, Common Courage Press, Maine, 1995.

Skorzeny, Otto, *Luchamos y Perdimos*, Acervo, Buenos Aires, 1979.

Snyder, Louis, *Encyclopedia of the Third Reich*, McGraw-Hill, New York, 1976.

Sommi, Luis V., *Los Capitales Alemanes en la Argentina*, Claridad, Buenos Aires, 1945.

Spitzy, Reinhard, *How We Squandered the Reich*, Michael Russel, Norwich, 1997.

────── *So entkamen wir den Alliierten*, Langen Müller, München, 1989.

Stevenson, William, *The Bormann Brotherhood*, Harcourt Brace Jovanovich, New York, 1973.

Svoray, Taylor, *In Hitler's Shadow*, Constable & Co, , 1995.

Trevor-Roper, H.R., *The Last Days of Hitler*, Macmillan, New York, 1947.

Trifkovic, Srdja, *The Real Genocide in Yugoslavia*, Chroniclemagazine.org, 21 April 2000.

US State Department, *Blue Book on Argentina*, Greenberg, New York, 1946.

Villegas, Osiris G., *Temas Para Leer y Meditar*, Theoría, Buenos Aires, 1993.

von der Becke, Carlos, *Destrucción de Una Infamia*, Buenos Aires, 1956.

von Oven, Wilfred, *Ein 'Nazi in Argentinien*, Verlag Werner Symanek, 1993.

────── *Quién Era Goebbels*, Editorial Revisión, Buenos Aires, 1988.

West, Nigel, *Counterfeit Spies*, St Ermin's Press, London, 1998.

White, Elizabeth B., *German Influence in the Argentine Army, 1900 to 1945*, Garland Publishing, New York, 1991.

Whiting, Charles, *Skorzeny: The Most Dangerous Man in Europe*, Combined Publishing, Pennsylvania, 1998.

Yallop, David, *In God's Name*, Jonathan Cape, 1984.

Zanatta, Loris, *Del Estado Liberal a la Nación Católica*, Universidad Nacional de Quilmes, Buenos Aires, 1996.

—— *Perón y el Mito de la Nación Católica*, Sudamericana, Buenos Aires, 1999.

Ziegler, Jean, *The Swiss, the Gold and the Dead*, Harcourt Brace, New York, 1998.

INDEX